MW01400838

TIME-BASED ARCHITECTURE

time- based Archi- tec ture

Bernard Leupen
René Heijne
Jasper van Zwol
[eds.]

010 Publishers
Rotterdam 2005

CONTENTS

Introduction 9
Bernard Leupen, René Heijne and Jasper van Zwol

PART ONE: ESSAYS
Edited by Bernard Leupen and Birgit Jürgenhake

Towards time-based architecture 12
Bernard Leupen

Change and the distribution of design 22
N. John Habraken

The combination of living and working 30
Jasper van Zwol

Solids 42
Frank Bijdendijk

Has architecture lost its purpose? 52
Florian Riegler

Flex-buildings, designed to respond to change 58
René Heijne and Jacques Vink

Dynamic time – informal order. Interdisciplinary trajectories 68
Manuel Gausa

Flexibility in structures 76
Walter Spangenberg

Time-based buildings 82
Herman Hertzberger

Flexibility – Time 92
Rudy Stroink

The sustainable city is the adaptable city 98
Maccreanor

Cultural durability 110
bOb Van Reeth

Towards a non-standard mode of production 116
Patrick Beaucé and Bernard Cache, Objectile

PART TWO: PROJECTS
Edited by Jacques Vink and René Heijne
(RUIMTELAB)

Introduction 127

Fortress on The Sound 128
Bo01, Malmö, Gert Wingårdh
Cathedral for a new millennium 132
Los Angeles, José Rafael Moneo
Polyvalent houses in Vienna 136
Helmut Wimmer
Unconventional dimensions 140
Graz, Riegler Riewe Architecten
Flexible offices 144
New York, Gaetano Pesce
Estraden Houses 148
Berlin-Prenzlauer Berg, Wolfram Popp
Day and night arrangements 152
Madrid, Aranguren-Gallegos
A multifunctional entrance zone 156
Riken Yamamoto & Field Shop
Mon Oncle revisited 160
AllesWirdGut and Luigi Colani
Twenty-first century warehouse 164
Spaarndammerdijk, Amsterdam, De Architecten Cie (F. Van Dongen)
Structural facades 168
Ypenburg, Rapp+Rapp
City garden 172
Winter Palace, Aomori, Atelier Kempe Thill
Base building and fit-out 176
Next 21, Osaka, Yositika Utida and Shu-Ko-Sha arch. & urban design studio
Work building in a greenhouse 180
Crystalic, Leeuwarden, GD Architecten
Housing on IJburg 184
Lux, London, and Block 4, IJburg, Maccreanor Lavington
Billboard facade 188
INIT building, Amsterdam, Groosman Partners

Layered structure 192
INO, addition to the Insel University Hospital, Itten + Brechbühl
Living on a plug-in floor 196
Oostelijke Handelskade, Amsterdam, DKV architecten
Better and cheaper in Boliger 200
Bedre Billigere, Boliger, Denmark, Juul & Frost
Predicting the future 204
INHOLLAND University, Rotterdam, Erick van Egeraat associated architects
Neutral expression 208
De Nieuwe Veiling, Hoorn, RUIMTELAB
Developers' freedom 212
Multifunk, IJburg, Amsterdam, Ana-architecten
Elemental Chile 216
Housing, Temuco, Chile, Pasel.Künzel architects
Growth homes 220
Groeiwoningen, Almere, Architectuurstudio Herman Hertzberger
Once a factory 224
A-Factory, Amsterdam, Neutelings Riedijk Architects
A chic makeshift classroom 228
Schoolparasites, Hoogvliet, Rotterdam, ONIX, Barend Koolhaas and Christoph Seyferth
Student housing 232
Spacebox, Mart de Jong (De Vijf)
Demountable 236
Office of ABT/Damen, Delft, Hubert-Jan Henket architecten
Maximum freedom for the occupants 240
Hellmutstrasse in Zurich and Wuhr in Langenthal, ADP-architekten

Sources 246
Picture credits 248
Credits 249

INTRODUCTION

During the 20th century it became increasingly clear that architecture is by no means a timeless medium. To begin with, artists and architects like Constant, Friedman, Archigram and the Metabolists merely toyed with the notion of time. In the late 1960s, however, serious research was done into techniques that would allow buildings to adapt to meet the demands made by time. The desire for flexibility led to programmatically neutral, characterless buildings. Flexibility became synonymous with blandness and the word subsequently slipped from the architect's vocabulary.

In 2003, Bernard Leupen, Jasper van Zwol and René Heijne took the initiative to organize at the TU Delft a symposium on the influence of time on building design. This theme had figured in the Master's course in Architecture and Modernity for a while already. Key features of the symposium were flexibility and the live/work relationship. Bernard Leupen's thesis *Kader en generieke ruimte* (Frame and generic space; published in Dutch with an English summary by 010 Publishers, 2002) gave additional momentum to the research being done at the Faculty of Architecture into housing design and time.

The symposium was born on the back of major changes affecting society and the role played there by building design and development. Society is changing at such speed that buildings are faced with new demands which they should be in a position to meet. There are times when buildings change function during construction or even during the design process. For example, the currently weak office market has caused many property developers to alter ongoing projects for office buildings into housing. This usually means that the plans need redeveloping from scratch. A new approach, therefore, is to design buildings that are able to cope with such changes, in other words buildings that respond to the time factor.

Designing for the unknown, the unpredictable, is the new challenge facing architects today. 'Form follows function' is giving way to concepts like polyvalence, changeability, flexibility, disassembly and semi-permanence. The design is becoming an innovative tool for developing new spatial and physical structures that generate freedom.

Time-based Architecture divides into two parts. Part one consists of a series of essays most of which are by speakers at the symposium 'Time-based Buildings' (2004) including the symposium's organizers. Part two discusses and documents 29 projects representing a wide array of buildings that relate in some way to the time factor.

PART ONE: ESSAYS

TOWARDS TIME-BASED ARCHITECTURE
Bernard Leupen

Why this interest in time-based buildings and time-based architecture? Time has a significant influence on the design and development of buildings. The concept 'time-based' is derived from video and film art. What the ruler is for the architect, the time-base is for the video artist; it provides the basic measure for his work. Since designers of buildings – those people generally called architects – have to deal with aspects of time, the time-base could also become relevant to architects. But why has time become so important and how should we deal with time during the design process?

Before dealing with these questions, I would like to give a short historical summary. If we look at the extensive modernization that has taken place over the last 200 years we distinguish two main waves. The first, the industrial revolution, began at the end of the 18th century and was characterized by the development of heavy industries for steel and coal production and major migrations to cities brought about by the birth of the metropolis. Social disorder, caused in part by the poor living conditions of the working classes, formed part of the process.

The second wave, involving major social change, started after the Second World War. The core business of industry changed from the production of heavy materials to the production of light materials and even virtual reality; from steel and coal to the development of the chemical industry, plastics, electronics and the software industry. The same period saw an enormous increase in mass consumption, thanks to the increasing prosperity experienced by the greater part of the population.

Unlike the first wave of modernization, the second wave took place round the world. Economies in the Far East, South America and even China started to catch up with those in the western world; indeed their growth rate was often higher. In these countries the first and second waves of modernization occurred together, with all the problems that might be expected in such a violent process. Meanwhile the rate of modernization was increasing even in the western world.

You might wonder what the point is of this history lesson. What relevance does it have to time-based architecture?

The speed of modernization and the unpredictability inherent in the process makes it very difficult to establish reality for such a slow-moving medium as buildings. It often happens that programmes undergo radical change even during the design process. Consider for example the Amsterdam-Werk project (see Part Two of this book, page 164), for which the programme changed from office building to housing before one stone was laid on another. The unpredictability with which developments take place is caused by changes in the economy, in society, in the layout of the city, etc. A building that today is located on the periphery may tomorrow be at the centre of a rapid new development – and vice versa. Fifty years ago the average number of people sharing a dwelling in the Netherlands was 4.7. Today the figure is halved. This, coupled with the increasing prosperity experience by the greater part of the population, means that we need more space, more energy and more materials and consequently new ways of thinking about sustainability and density. How can we deal with all these aspects of time and uncertainty when we are designing such slow-moving objects as buildings?

Before dealing with this question, I would like to remind you of a few examples of the first time-based ideas in architectural thinking. As far back as the 1930s the Dutch architect Van den Broek designed an apartment building to be used in one way by day and in another way by night, and Mart Stam devised a scheme showing the different ways in which the rooms in a house are used by day and by night. A scheme worked out by Rem Koolhaas for a new development in Yokohama was based on the same principle. Each of these examples uses time-sharing to deal with a lack of space. Another approach was taken by Cedric Price's Potteries Thinkbelt project, which located a place of higher education on a former pottery site. Flexibility was provided by designing classrooms like railway wagons. The work done by Price in the 1960s inspired a whole range of projects involving movable buildings: indeed one of the Archigram projects involved a 'walking city'.

In the Netherlands John Habraken wrote the book *De dragers en de mensen* (translated as *Supports: An Alternative to Mass Housing*) in which he argued that support systems should be provided that would give people the freedom to build their own houses. Providing such support systems would be a task for the community: the house itself would be the result of a process he referred to as 'dwelling'. This concept was developed by Habraken for the Dutch Foundation for Architectural Research (SAR).

In principle there are three possible ways to deal with time and uncertainty:

Make buildings polyvalent.
Make buildings that are part permanent and part changeable.
Make semi-permanent buildings, e.g. 'industrial, flexible and demountable' (IFD) buildings.

■ **Polyvalent buildings**

The word 'polyvalent' has been known for years in the context of the *multi-purpose hall* or *salle polyvalente*, the kind of building that is to be found in every French village or small town, that can be used for weddings and parties, for musical and theatrical performances and as a cinema. A hall of this kind can be used for all kinds of functions without any adjustment being required to the building itself. The word was introduced to the architectural debate by Hertzberger[1], some of whose ideas on polyvalence can be seen in the Diagoon houses he designed for Delft. Here too polyvalence means that the building can be used in different ways without adjustment to the way it is built. There is however a difference: the different uses of a *salle polyvalente* take place consecutively, but a dwelling must be able to provide space for all the different activities which it is capable of accommodating to take place at the same time. Polyvalence in the context of housing relates primarily to the interchangeability of activities between different rooms.

The consequence of this difference is that polyvalence imposes different requirements on the spatial organization for housing than it does for commercial and industrial buildings. Whereas in a hall polyvalence can be achieved by the use of the proper dimensions and ratios and by the provision of special service areas such as dressing rooms or a foyer, for housing the degree of polyvalence depends primarily on the relationships between the various rooms, i.e. on the spatial composition. The spatial system of a house can be expressed by a topological diagram, a graph. A spatial system in which different rooms can only be accessed through another room, for example the living room, is less capable of being adapted to suit different living patterns. The contrast here is with dwellings in which the spatial system allows every room to be reached from a central point or by a number of different routes.

▌ Diagoon houses

Herman Hertzberger's Diagoon houses in Delft (1967-1971) demonstrate what he saw as implied by polyvalence. The polyvalence he achieved derived mainly from the spatial organization of the dwelling (see fig. 1). The spatial system he designed was able to suit a variety of different living patterns. Each dwelling consisted of a number of more or less identically shaped rooms, displaced half a floor relative to one another and displaced horizontally relative to one another along the depth of the building. The rooms were partly separated from one another by a vertical pair of closed elements, one containing the staircase, the other the service areas, including the kitchen. A void between these two dominant vertical elements made it possible to appreciate the split-level. Because all the rooms had more or less the same dimensions and were positioned differently relative to the shaft containing the service areas, their functions were not predetermined.

Graz Strassgang

A more recent project in which polyvalence plays a part is the Strassgang housing project in Graz, by the Austrian architects Riegler and Riewe (see Part Two, page 140). The fact that the proportions of the rooms did not immediately suggest any of the accepted categories of living space, invited the occupant to use the house in an original way, unique to himself. The architects described the arrangement as follows: 'Our intention when we designed this project was to have a room that would be too large to be an entrance and too small to be a living room or bedroom, with a service area in the middle of the apartment, leaving the occupier free to choose how to use the series of rooms lying behind the facade'.[2]

The floor plans that resulted from this approach are more reminiscent of excavations of Greek or Roman antiquities than an accepted floor plan for a modern dwelling (see fig. 2). But perhaps the secret of polyvalent housing is to be found in these archetypal characteristics. The composition of a floor plan that makes a house possible to live in is not based on modern analyses but on a blueprint that has proved its value for thousands of years.

Buildings that are part permanent, part changeable

This is the most comprehensive category, occupying the entire space between the two extremes represented by polyvalent buildings on the one hand and IFD buildings on the other. Two different, partly overlapping, concepts can be grouped within this category. The best known is the *support concept*, which developed in the 1970s into the *carcass concept*. These concepts have been set in a broader context in the book *Kader en generieke ruimte* (Frame and generic space).[3] This was the origin of what I have termed the *frame concept*.

The support concept

At the end of the 1950s the Dutch architect N.J. Habraken, perhaps inspired by Le Corbusier and the Metabolists, wrote the book *De dragers en de mensen*[4] in which he described how he thought the problems of mass housing might be solved, based on ideas he had developed about support and infill. Government should be responsible for providing major structures, 'supports' in his terminology, on or in which occupiers could construct their own homes. Habraken provided the following outline description of a support: 'The support consists of a concrete construction (fig. 3) of superimposed floors winding its way through the town. A strip on one side is left free to serve as a gallery connecting regularly spaced free-standing staircases and lift shafts. Between two such floors is an open space, recently occupied by a dwelling, now demolished, bounded vertically by load bearing floors and horizontally by blind dwelling walls'.[5]

The further development of the support concept became increasingly concerned with levels of decision-making. An extension of this thinking is to be found in the declared aims of the *werkgroep Open Bouwen Ontwikkelings Model* (Open Building Development Model working party)[6]:

1 To restructure the entire building market (in particular in public housing and commercial and industrial buildings) with the aim of opening up the interaction between supply and demand.

2 To bring about a new arrangement and reorientation of decision-making. A point needing particular attention is who decides what on what level.

3 To introduce modular coordination.[7]

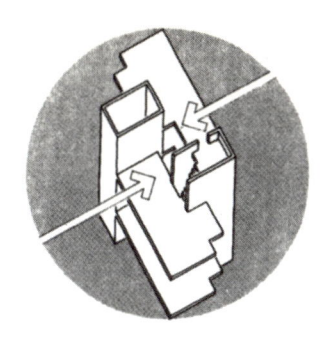

1 – Diagoon houses, basic principles

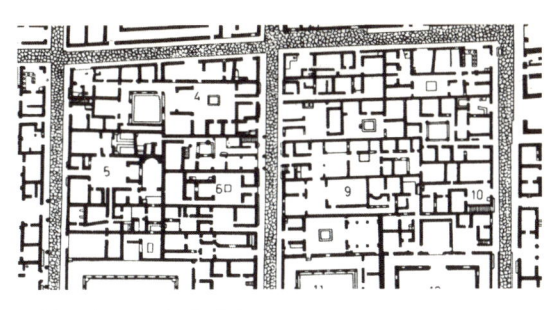

2 – Herculaneum, detail of plan

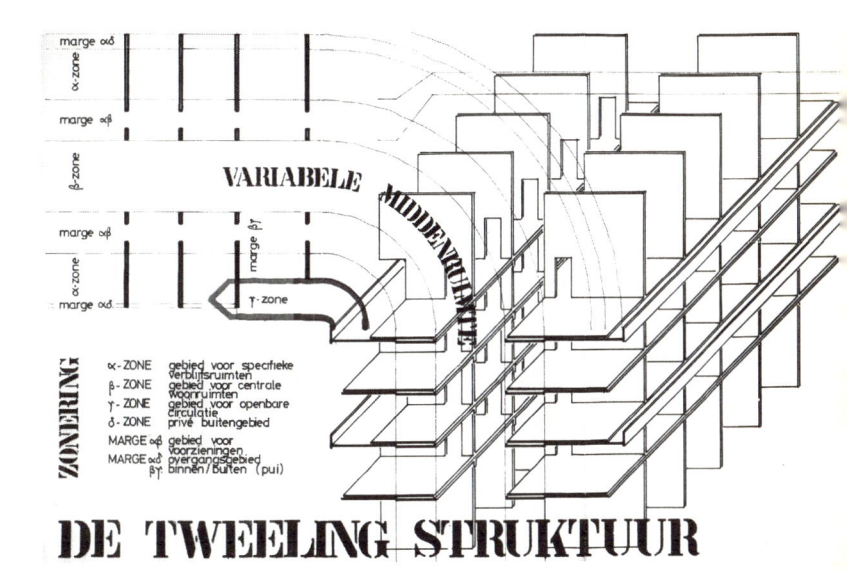

3 – Support system based on principles established by SAR (Stichting Architecten Research – Foundation for Architectural Research)

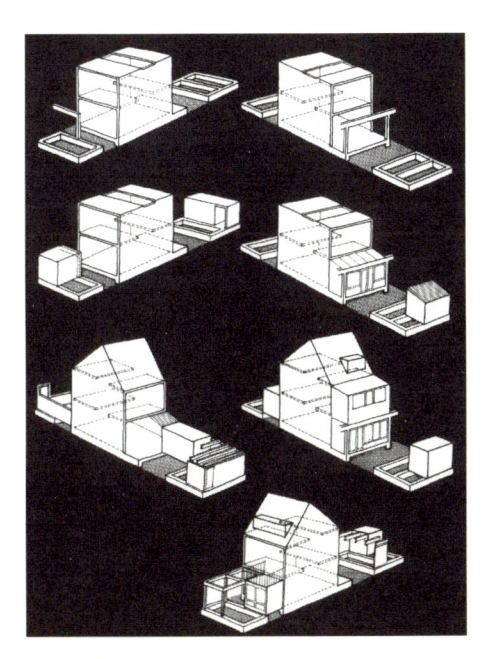

4 – Basic principles of the carcass house

5 – Domus Demain

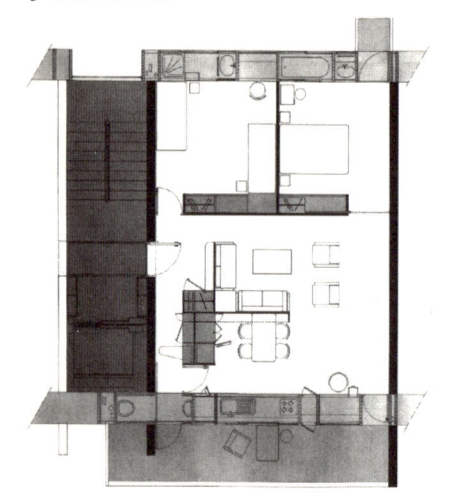

6 – Domus Demain, floor plan

7 – XX office, interior

8 – Emotive House

The carcass concept

The powerful association between the support concept and high rise led to a new concept when in the 1960s the term *carcass* (Dutch: casco) came into use. The use of the term was never based on thorough research or an unambiguous vision. It has never been defined with any precision and so not surprisingly has been applied to a wide range of solutions. It may perhaps be most closely related to the idea of a cocoon, in which a living organism changes from one state to another. In this sense the carcass unites the principle of security and enclosure with the modern wish for adjustability and flexibility.[8]

The term carcass is often used to refer to a basic dwelling, an empty space with no divisions or fittings; in fact 'base building' is the generally used term these days.[9] The essence of this concept is often a support structure containing separate compartments providing the insulation required between different dwellings. The two carcass projects discussed below clearly show that the word carcass is capable of a wide range of meanings.

In 1970 Habraken's ideas inspired the Dutch architect Sjirk Haaksma to develop the carcass dwelling (see fig. 4). The support construction for the project, a two-storey-high tunnel-shaped structure, had an open zone in the middle of each floor which could be used to house vertical elements such as access structures and ducting. If the void was not required the opening could be finished with a wood floor. The tunnel structure guaranteed the compartmentalization required for housing. The carcass provided facilities for rebuilding within the limits imposed by the tunnel but also for extension to the rear and upwards by means of light structures. An extra piece of foundation was provided to enable the building to be extended into the garden.

Integrated frame of skin and servant elements

The French architect Yves Lion takes an original line on the problem of pipes and cables. In his Domus Demain project of 1984, the servant elements are taken up in the facade zone (see fig. 5). The rooms for ablutions, the island kitchen unit, the toilet and the service ducts are integrated in this zone.[10] The architect describes it as an 'active layer'.

'Our approach is to bring the technical functions out to the façade and express them through an "active layer" which will serve technical equipment; this vertical band will be considered as the light and services supplier for a more inert and passive zone. This division corresponds to the separation of responsibilities between the heavy, approximate, structural work and the mechanically precise, light, industrial finishing work.'[11]

The question is whether the facade has here taken over the role of the services or vice versa. Neither of these is true – facade and services are integrated. Here the facade has become the intermediary[12] between inside and outside in the widest sense of the word. This regulates not just the insulation, ventilation and daylight penetration but also the supply and discharge of clean and dirty water, information and energy. The facade zone is entirely unhitched from that part of the scenery (the space-defining elements) that determines the internal subdivision of the spaces. At the same time the facade zone seems also to be part of the scenery (see fig. 6). In the same way that every layer can have its own secondary supporting structure, some layers can have their own scenery. This holds particularly for the access and the servant elements. The servant rooms, after all, can have their own spatial divisions, as is clearly the case with Domus Demain. There too we can identify what is described in *Kader en generieke ruimte*[13] as 'the fractalizing of layers'. To separate main issues from side issues, however, the subdivision of the servant space in the facade zone should be treated as part of the layer of servant elements.

The sanitary facade zone serves the zone of living quarters beyond it, entirely freed as this is from all servant elements, service shafts, etc. and therefore freely subdivisible. Just as the facade zone and scenery are said to be uncoupled, so too are the facade zone and the concrete loadbearing structure including the stairs and lift shafts.

The frame concept

In the thesis *Kader en generieke ruimte* (Frame and generic space) the author developed a concept for the changeability of dwellings based on permanent elements. These permanent elements were termed the *frame*. The assumption underlying the frame concept is that the average life of a building is 100 years. During this period the way the building is used will change radically and repeatedly. Often the attempts made to solve this problem make use of ingenious flexible structures that can easily be changed. The keyword here is flexibility. But the emphasis in the development of the frame concept is not on what can be changed but on what can be permanent and lasting. By determining what can be permanent now, i.e. the nature of the frame, opportunities can be created to deal with future unpredictability.

A building can be divided into a number of layers, and in principle each layer or combination of layers can be seen as the frame, as a permanent part of the building. In this view each layer or combination of layers can generate freedom for other layers, and so for other parts of the building. The most obvious example is the liberating effect of providing loadbearing columns, making loadbearing walls unnecessary: the columns liberate the walls, because a wall that is not loadbearing can be placed anywhere. According to this principle, the permanent part of a building can be thought of as the frame which creates freedom and enables various adjustments to be made without requiring such adjustments to be precisely determined in advance. The frame is not just the permanent part of the building: it also embodies the building's most important architectural and cultural values, which means that the building can react to changes in the requirements imposed on it over time without damaging its essential character.

In principle a frame can be defined for each distinct layer or combination of layers. Two examples are given below. The first example concerns flats in which the frame consists of a combination of support structure, access arrangements and service elements. The second example, less obvious, concerns a building whose frame is provided by the skin or elevations.

Elemental Chile

Pasel and Künzl's Elemental Chile project, the outcome of a competition for housing in Chile, is a good example of the frame concept (see Part Two, page 216). The idea was that occupiers would acquire a plot of land which would be divided from its neighbours by a boundary wall. A zone running parallel to this boundary wall would contain stairs leading to an upper floor and a number of service areas, adjoining an empty 'free' zone which the occupiers could fill to suit their individual needs. Where the zone containing access points and service areas had a presence on the street, it would also act as a visual frame, giving structure to the constantly changing individual infills.

Cristalic

The second example in this category is the Cristalic building in Leeuwarden (NL) designed by the architect Gunnar Daan (see Part Two, page 180). The building consists of a gigantic glass roof sheltering several buildings. The roof itself is an independent construction comprising the frame which uses an ingenious ventilation system to produce a constant internal climate. The roof shelters one large building and a number of small ones. The large building was designed as an office building, the small buildings contain a restaurant, a crèche and suchlike. The uniformly mild interior climate provided by the huge roof makes it possible to erect buildings of various sizes by relatively simple means. The simplicity of the smaller buildings makes them easily adjustable to suit changing circumstances. The building can be seen as a realization of the Climatroffice designed by Foster and Buckminster Fuller.[14] Their design, which was of course basically dome-shaped, also involved an independent roof construction creating a climate-controlled interior as a shelter for autonomous buildings.

▪ Semi-permanent buildings

Although an IFD building need not be completely demountable – buildings are also referred to as IFD when, for example, only the finish is industrially fabricated and demountable – in the following a building will only be referred to as IFD when it is indeed completely demountable.

▪ XX office

An excellent example of this approach is the XX office, designed by Jouke Post (see fig. 7). The XX office concept is described in the following terms: 'On average, office buildings last no longer than 20 years before requiring large-scale rebuilding or even demolition. By then the interior will often have been frequently subjected to complete renovation, necessitated by internal removals and changes in user requirements. Although the technical quality may be sufficient to allow the building to remain standing, companies would rather have a new property. The old property will after all already have been written off. The result is miserable looking office parks and an enormous amount of rubbish created by repeated building and demolition.

'The XX office came about as an experiment prompted by a totally different concern, in this case with sustainable building. The technical life of the building was set to match its 20-year economic life, hence the name XX. After 20 years the building can simply be dismantled and its building materials reused, recycled or dumped without damage to the environment. The use of demountable connections ensures that this can be done quickly and easily.'[15]

This description clearly shows the fundamental difference between the frame concept and the IFD concept. The frame concept assumes that a building will have a permanent part which will last at least 100 years. Post on the other hand assumed a life of 20 years for the entire building.

Finally I would like to look at one more exceptional project. In one sense it falls into the category 'industrial, flexible and demountable buildings' though it can also be seen as a modern variant of Johannes van den Broek's day-and-night dwelling discussed at the beginning of this piece. But in contrast to Van den Broek, what we have here is not a minimum dwelling designed to solve social problems but comfort created by applying the most modern technology.

▪ Emotive house

The Emotive house, designed by Kas Oosterhuis, is experimental and highly futuristic. Oosterhuis is currently working on prototypes with students from Delft University of Technology. Oosterhuis describes this house (see fig. 8) in the following terms: 'A house with a character of its own, sometimes unyielding, sometimes flexible, at one time sexy, at another unpredictable, stiff and unfeeling. This is the Emotive House, a house in which everyday reality is complemented by virtual reality. The central feature of this far-reaching experiment is the emotional relationship between the house, its occupiers and the elements. The Emotive House is a single, large, elongated and highly mobile space, with at both ends a relatively inflexible space containing a kitchen unit and sanitary facilities located in front of a window that is sometimes real and sometimes virtual. The construction of the house is completely industrial and demountable, showing home automation in a new light. Both the construction of the house and the furnishing are programmable. Sensors record the users' movements and changes in the weather and translate them into particular actions. Thus not only the appearance of the room can change, but also the information content of the virtual windows and other displays. The permanent structure can consist of solid wooden beams and metal coffers filled with clear glass or steel ventilation units. The variable structure consists of oblong inflatable rooms placed between them. The construction is held in shape by a spatial system of hydraulic cylinders and the outer surface is clad with photoelectric cells. The Emotive House was first subjected to a number of years' intensive testing as a living and working laboratory. The intention is that it will subsequently become a studio in which artists or architects will work and live'.

The preceding review has covered a number of concepts and possible ways of allowing buildings to react to changes brought about by the passage of time. The primary intention of the review was to explore the wide field of time-based architecture, a field that extends from polyvalent buildings to completely demountable buildings, from solid, permanent, stable constructions to mobile buildings that might even be capable of reacting to our thoughts. Although this last is undoubtedly an interesting technical task, for the present my preference is for buildings that can accept many different programmes and many different types of use with the fewest possible special constructions or technical interventions, if any.

My preference is for sustainable polyvalent buildings in cases where any form of intervention in the built environment (and certainly the complete demolition and replacement of buildings) would place a major burden on the environment as a whole. If buildings have a short life it can be assumed that much of the built environment will always look like a building site, which not only represents a burden on the environment but also an assault on our collective memory, our collective recollections. We need to deal carefully with the dissociative processes brought along by the current second wave of modernization. But technological development is unstoppable. In time particular parts or layers of a house will be even more permeated by the latest technology as they are today, acquiring a structure related to the Emotive House and so becoming increasingly remote from architecture in its original sense. But at the same time it is these layers that will make architecture time-based.

I would like to end with two statements which apply to every type of approach to time-based buildings and emphasize the necessity for new concepts for time-based building.

A building is not longer a single object, a single whole, a single entity. In future a building will have to be seen as a combination of systems, each system with its own design process, production process and lifetime. Some of these systems will be foreign to the field of architecture, but time-based architecture would be impossible without them.

There are many ways in which buildings can react to changing requirements. It is clear, however, that buildings which are totally lacking in the capacity to react will not be granted a long life but will quickly be demolished, a process which is itself no more than another kind of adjustment to changed circumstances.

1 Hertzberger, H. 1962. 'Flexibility and polyvalency'. *Forum* 3, pp. 115-118.
2 See F. Riegler's paper, 'Has architecture lost its use?' on pp. 52-57 of this book.
3 Leupen, B. 2002. *Kader en generieke ruimte*. Rotterdam: 010 Publishers.
4 Habraken, N. J. 1961. *De dragers en de mensen*. Amsterdam: Scheltema & Holkema. Translated as *Supports; An Alternative to Mass Housing*, UK: The Architectural Press, 1972/ Urban International Press, 1999.
5 Ibid., p. 84.
6 Werkgroep_OBOM 1985. Open Bouwen: Stichting Open Bouwen.
7 Ibid., p. 5.
8 Heynen, H. 1999. *Architectuur en kritiek van de moderniteit*. Nijmegen: SUN. Translated as *Architecture and Modernity: A Critique*, Cambridge (Mass.): The MIT Press, 2000.
9 The term 'base building' came from American office buildings with empty floors which could be filled in with 'fit-outs'.
10 A connection with climate facades (e.g. in Herzog & de Meuron's SUVA project in Basle) immediately springs to mind. In climate facades, the facade acts as a building service. In winter the facade absorbs passive solar energy and in summer it provides cooling ventilation. In this respect, the climate facade can be conceived of as integrating skin and servant elements.
11 Lion, Y. en F. Leclercq (1987). 'Domus Demain, la bande active.' *L'Architecture d'Aujourd'hui* 252: 16-18. p. 10.
12 Nouvel uses the term 'interface', among other things in connection with the facade of the IMA in Paris.
13 Leupen, B., 2002. *Kader en generieke ruimte*. Rotterdam: 010 Publishers, p. 146.
14 Chaslin, F., F. Hervet, et al. 1987. Norman Foster, *Beispielhaften Bauten eines spätmodernen Architekten*. Stuttgart: DVA, 1987, p. 16.
15 www.xxarchitecten.nl

CHANGE AND THE DISTRIBUTION OF DESIGN
N. John Habraken

■ A two-level environment

In January 1699 Jules Hardouin Mansart, Superintendent of Buildings and 'Premier Architecte' to Louis-le-Grand, King of France, put his signature to the design for what we now know as the Place Vendome. (fig. 1) His design included a monumental facade wall of exquisite proportions in the neo-classical manner. The square, including the facade wall, was subsequently built by the city of Paris at the king's request. But no buildings were behind the facade. The land behind was for sale. In the next decade noblemen, bankers, tax farmers and other prominent and wealthy citizens who served the king in various administrative and financial functions built their houses there with their own architects. These buildings kept changing and adapting over time. But the facade as Mansart built it is still what we see today.

Mansart's scheme was a remarkable interpretation of what we may call a 'two-level organization', by which we mean that one designer provides the spatial framework within which other designers subsequently can do their own thing. We have here an instance of time-based building in a very straightforward way. Mansart built what was to perform for a long time and to serve many. He thereby provided a context for what might change more frequently and serve individual clients. In general, such a distinction of levels of intervention separates what is relatively permanent from what is relatively changeable. But the way Mansart applied this principle challenged conventional notions. The facade of a building is normally seen as the expression of that particular building. Here it became part of the level of urban design. We are more familiar with a level distinction in which the facade of a building is part of the lower level of architectural design. When, for instance, H.P. Berlage designed the new extension of Amsterdam in the first half of the 19th century, he designed public spaces such as boulevards, streets and squares. He also determined the height of the buildings along these spaces, but architects designed them and produced the facades that made those spaces become real.

■ Another example

The Place Vendome was not a unique intervention. Earlier in the 17th century Henry IV initiated the building of the Place Royale (today Place des Vosges). (fig. 2) Citizens could buy lots around it on the condition that the facades of their houses would be built according to a preconceived design including an arcade on the ground floor. The Place des Vosges is larger than the Place Vendome and makes a more domestic space with its trees and flower beds and its more home-grown architecture. But the square's facade wall is clearly the result of a unified design, although in practice it was built one lot at a time. Although both squares have uniform facades all around, the distribution of ownership is different. In case of the Place Vendome, the facades were actually part of the urban infrastructure, like the pavement of the square, or the statue at its centre. But in Henry IV's Place des Vosges the facades were owned and erected by the private citizens. Taken as examples of two-level thinking, the difference is significant, however. In the case of the Place Vendome designers only decided on their own level of control behind the already erected facade. In that of the Place de Vosges, the higher level designer put down rules to constrain lower level design. He basically told the lower level designer: 'Do whatever you want, but make sure you do the facade my way.' The latter case is more complicated, but also more flexible because laying down rules for lower level design can be done in many different ways. The set-back rule, for instance, telling architects to keep houses at a certain distance from the street, belongs to that mode of interaction. By the same token an urban designer may impose a building height restriction, or stipulate that facades be done in the same material, or that certain patterns should be followed for the sake of a consistent and well conceived public space. This way of working makes the urban designer reach across the level distinction to constrain lower level design. It introduces a certain coherence in the lower level where normally variety is the inevitable result of different designers doing their own thing.

■ A natural phenomenon

In history such coherence in variety came about in a less formal manner. The 17th-century facades along the canals of Amsterdam are all the same kind but no two are alike. That did not happen because a higher level designer had laid down rules, but because the house as a type was familiar to both inhabitants and builders. Coherence resulted from the culture at work. Yet the level distinction was very clear. Each house could change, or be replaced, without disturbing the higher level urban organization.[1]
Distribution of design responsibility along different levels of intervention comes naturally with complex form making. We may shift the boundaries a bit, but life itself imposes the level distinction. When ignored, it will re-establish itself in the course of time. The famous 'Crescents' in 18th-century Bath by father and son Wood, were originally designed as identical houses behind a common monumental facade. But since home ownership was dispersed, individual houses changed in the course of time: expansions were made and interior spaces were altered. But the facades remained unaltered by common consent. The result, eventually, was similar to the Place Vendome distinction: variation behind an urban screen. Eventually similar projects with unified facades came about in English domestic architecture. Most of them were built for speculation. Variations in a house plan might be made already when the house was sold before building started, but otherwise would surely come later on.

■ The disappearance of levels

In Amsterdam, Berlage was the last to heed the level distinction in urban design. Cornelis van Eesteren's internationally renowned post-war extension of the city was not structured by urban space. Following CIAM ideology, he arranged building volumes within free flowing space. Urban space was no longer structuring lower level design. As a result, urban designer and architect both used the same medium, and it was no longer clear where urban design stopped and architecture began. This confusion still plagues the profession.

The disappearance of levels of intervention was not restricted to the distinction between urban design and architecture. It also took place within the building itself. Modernist architectural ideology claimed top-down design control. The masters of the avant-garde such as Le Corbusier, Mies van der Rohe and also Frank Lloyd Wright taught us by example that full vertical control, including even the design of furniture, was necessary to achieve good architecture. They lived in a time of fundamental change in which all design conventions and building habits were rendered obsolete. In such uncertainty it is understandable that those responsible for large projects insist on full vertical control.

However, the upheavals of modernity only reinforced an attitude that already prevailed in the time when architects only did special buildings like churches, palaces and grand houses. It goes back to Palladio whose marvellous villas we tend to understand as firmly controlled by a single hand. In that sense, Le Corbusier's Unité d'Habitation, fully controlled too, and conceived as standing in a park, is very Palladian. We have been educated in a tradition that was ignorant of the uses of levels in urban form. Mass housing in which inhabitants cannot influence the layout of their dwelling is part of that ignorance. Our present interest in time-based building seeks a remedy to the rigidity and uniformity that comes from excessive vertical control.

Learning from the past

As I have shown, level distinctions in complex environments may be achieved in different ways. Those we have noted so far, the Place Vendome, the Place des Vosges, Berlage's Amsterdam extension, the Amsterdam canals, are architectural expressions of a primarily territorial level distinction. Yet a hierarchy of levels may result from technical conditions as well. In climates where protection from cold, wind or rain is important the first act of building usually was to create a large envelope later to be subdivided. Medieval European architecture was based on a single large volume, defined by stone walls and a timber roof, erected as quickly as possible to provide sheltered space within which further subdivision could take place in a more protected environment. The English custom to refer to large buildings as 'Hall' still comes from that practice. So does the 'grange', or barn, used in medieval French agriculture: a timber frame held up a large roof that extended outward to low but heavy stone walls. This model was followed in buildings for a wide variety of purposes as we could learn from the 9th-century St. Gall manuscript plan of a monastery.[2] This way of building produced a large volume of interior space which was subsequently subdivided in response to practical needs. The same custom could still be witnessed a few generations ago in the New England tradition of 'barn-raising' where the agricultural barn's timber structure was prefabricated by the local carpenter to be erected in a single day with the help of many neighbours in a kind of festive ritual. In China, about a decade ago, I saw a house just built in a country village. After materials had been amassed over a period of time, a solid brick masonry shell, some six by ten metres in surface area and two storeys high with a symmetrical facade, had been built in a few weekends with the help of neighbours. Inside, the roof was supported by two timber posts and the entire space was temporarily partitioned by a few bamboo screens just two metres high. The subdivision within the house had yet to be done in more solid materials as soon as resources would allow. (fig. 3) Similar examples are found in many other vernacular architectures.

Once technically feasible, internal adaptability can achieve its own architectural expression. Most vernacular residential architecture has a dominant space in relation to which smaller-scale change can take place. The houses of Pompeii, preserved by volcanic ashes for almost two millennia, show us for instance that each house had an atrium: this large space with an inward sloping roof open in the centre to let rainwater fall in a basin on the floor, was where guests were received and business was done. It was formed by two-storey-high walls behind which rooms were located. The ground floor rooms were open to the atrium and those on the upper floor had light coming in from above the atrium roof. Pompeii's excavations show us irregular distributions of these surrounding spaces suggesting change and adaptation over time. In fact, we sometimes find that rooms have been turned around from one house to the neighbouring house. The upper floors under a timber roof must have been even easier to subdivide. There is also evidence that these spaces could form suites for relatives within the extended family or could be rented out as separate apartments. We see the atrium function the way a public space functions in a city: allowing change and adaptation behind surrounding walls. In this way atria were stable islands in the dense Pompeiian field, around which second-order design decisions were made over time. (fig. 4) These were buildings without an exterior. The spatial sequence from street to atrium, with a possible extension to a second courtyard behind, identified the house; actual boundaries with neighbouring houses behind the surrounding rooms remained visible if the street front was occupied with shops and workplaces.

The Venetian Gothic palace is another example. It had on its main floor a large hall running from canal front to backyard, with open facades so that air could move through the house. On both sides of that central space were rows of rooms whose arrangement

1 – Place Vendome, Paris. Different houses behind the uniform facade

2 – Place des Vosges, Paris. Different interventions but identical facades

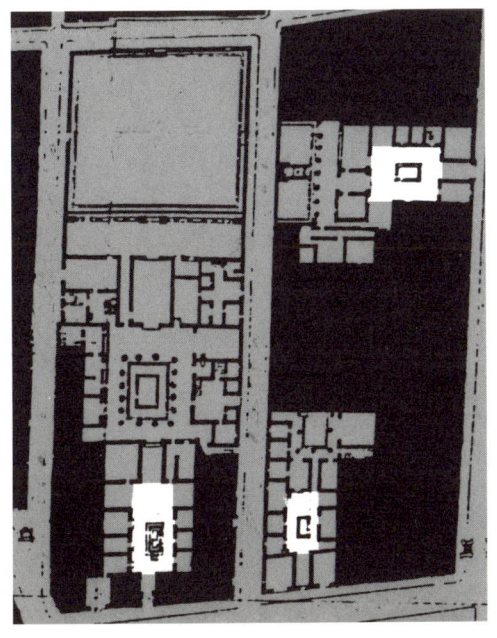

3 – Near Xi-an, China. Farmhouse shell just built

4 – Pompeii, atria in houses of different size (drawn over detail of Overbeck's Plan der Stadt Pompeii, 1866)

5 – Venice, central hall on main floor of Gothic houses (drawn over detail from Moretto, *L'edilizia Gotica Veneziana*, Venice: Filippi, 1978)

6 – Left Bank, Paris, courtyard

7 – Tunis Medina, courtyards and dead-end streets (drawn over a base map by the Association Sauvegarde de la Medina, Tunis)

8 – Molenvliet project, Papendrecht, Frans van der Werf

allowed not only different uses but also changes in size and decoration. Here again we find a two-level spatial organization securing permanence of the major space while allowing adaptation to second-order preferences of inhabitation. (fig. 5)

From these two examples of major spaces in vernacular houses, it is only one step away from the courtyard house. The open courtyard too, is the 'public' space within the residential unit around which rooms are ranged like houses around a square. The Mediterranean courtyard house is also found in a variety of interpretations along the North African coastline and all the way eastward across the Arabian peninsula; and it travelled westward from Spain to Latin America. Indeed, its influence extends as far north as Paris, where gates give access from the street to courtyards surrounded by apartments. India and China have their own traditions of courtyard dominated urban fabric in many variations going back thousands of years. The Medina of historic Tunis may serve as a case in point for many others. The rooms around the courtyards show a clear typology by themselves: they have a niche in the back wall facing the double courtyard door and two other niches to each side. This pattern is executed in endless variations of size and shape: even in a single house no two such rooms may be the same.

These few examples may show how vernacular architecture usually provides a dominant space that is stable relative to second-order variety and change in response to day-to-day uses.

■ **New ways of time-based building**
As a counterpoint to these many historical examples we may note how large contemporary buildings tend to change their skin. The high-rise office building in The Hague, for instance, for which Michael Graves designed a new envelope is in many ways the opposite of Mansart's Place Vendome. Here the building, to prolong its life, sheds its skin when the urban environment changes. The curtain wall facade almost acquires autonomy; it may be part of the building but it may also help shape the urban fabric.

We are beginning to understand how the large contemporary building will, eventually, establish its own hierarchy of changeable subsystems. The very size and permanence of such extensive frameworks make their facade a relatively short-term garb. At the same time, interior flexibility must respond to a large and varied population. Through their sheer bulk the high-rise and other large projects have de facto become three-dimensional extensions of the urban fabric. Inside, public space becomes increasingly important as a permanent framework around which day-to-day use, whether residential, commercial or administrative, may settle. Seen in this way, we become aware of the latent architectural potential of such new environments without historical precedent.

■ **A debilitating heritage**
Modernist ideology did not recognize architecture in relation to levels, neither upward in urban design nor downward in interior organization. Indeed, the Modernist environment, for all its novelty, can be understood to a large extent as the reduction of complex urban fabric to a coarse single-level product. Hence its inability to make large things without imposing uniform repetition on inhabitation. In this respect the avant-garde movement was a regressive movement. It is truly ironic that our time, which calls itself dynamic and full of change and individuality, has produced an architecture more rigid in its articulation and less capable of dealing with the dimension of time than any period before in human history. We still suffer the consequences of a functionalist tradition. We proudly rejected the Modernists' dogma of 'form follows function', but still expect each project we engage in to respond to a 'programme' listing in some detail expected functions to be taken care of. A time-based architecture must assume functions to be largely unpredictable except in the most general of terms. Where architecture cannot follow

function anymore it must take over by itself to establish a context for change and variety by inhabitation. This new initiative will lead to an articulation of levels of form-making. But that also implies distribution of design responsibility and we have not yet abandoned the Modernist opinion that such distribution is a dilution of the architect's role. The dilemma renders academia clueless. Change and the distribution of design tasks are not yet subjects for architectural theory, nor do they feature in school curricula.

■ A new architecture?

But practice already knows better and real life runs ahead of theory and teaching. Commercial office buildings offer empty floors for lease, to be filled in by specialized fit-out contractors executing designs by specialized fit-out designers. Shopping malls leave retail space open for leaseholders to employ their own designers.

Residential architecture slowly follows suit. In the Netherlands the work of Frans van der Werf, for some 30 years already, has been the most extensive and the most advanced so far. His Molenvliet project in Papendrecht (fig. 8), done in 1974, was the first project ever to explore the architectural and urbanist potential of a distinction between a 'base building' designed by the architect and the subsequent 'fit-out' done by the user. Frans van der Werf developed an 'urban tissue' in which public courtyards giving entry to the dwellings alternate with garden courtyards to be cultivated by the users. Within this fabric, users chose the location and size of their units and designed their own floor plans. Van der Werf's most recent project in Zevenaar follows the same basic principles and received a prize for durable building. An international network for Open Building meets yearly at different places throughout the world and in several other countries, most notably Japan and Finland, similar open residential projects have been executed.[3]

It is now clear that in commercial architecture, workplace architecture and residential architecture distinctions between levels serve the need for change and adaptation by day-to-day inhabitation. The dynamics of time-based building are already a fact of life and come naturally to the built environment, but as long as that reality is not fully embraced by the architectural profession as inspiring and challenging, a truly new time-based architecture will not take wing.

---

1 Actually, there were at least two types along the three major canals of Amsterdam. The type with a gabled facade similar to what had already been done in the medieval core of the city, and the broader facade with a cornice which was introduced in the 17th century.

2 See Walter Horn & Ernest Born, *The Plan for St. Gall*, in three volumes, California Press, 1979. One-volume brief version by Lorna Price, U. California Press, 1982.

3 See also Kendall and Teicher, *Residential Open Building*, London: Spon, 1998, which gives an overview of more than a hundred projects executed by that time.

THE COMBINATION OF LIVING AND WORKING

Jasper van Zwol

In the 19th century, the Industrial Revolution ushered in an age when dwelling and the place of work became separate entities. Before then, living and working were often enacted within a small geographical area with a limited need for mobility. In the farming sector living and working are by their very nature closely linked; this holds equally for the artisans' workshops in the towns prior to the Industrial Revolution. Industrialization made it possible to concentrate production processes. The growth of industry brought about an increase in the demand for homes in the towns, so that large residential areas sprang up around the town centres. The need for mobility attendant on this development was satisfied by the arrival of steam-driven trains (in the Netherlands in 1839) and the invention of the automobile with a petroleum-driven engine (1885). A new infrastructure of roads and railways was laid out.

In 19th-century Europe the towns underwent an explosive growth. London's population swelled from 900,000 souls in 1800 to 6 million in 1900. Berlin had 419,000 inhabitants in 1850 and 2 million in 1900. With these rapid urban expansions came a rash of jerry-building which meant appalling living conditions for many. Some factory owners, out of a sense of idealism, had centres for dwelling and training built near the work premises. In 1846, Jean-Baptiste Godin had a 'Familistère' built in the grounds of his factory for stoves and heaters in the French town of Guisse. He had been inspired in this by the ideas of Charles Fourier (1772-1837) who in 1829 had published plans for a *phalanstère* to house an ideal community. Already before the Industrial Revolution Claude-Nicolas Ledoux (1736-1806) had designed the 'ideal city' of Chaux around his salt works at Arc-et-Senans (France); it was built in part between 1774 and 1794. The inhabitants of this ideal city, which was graced with a neoclassical architecture, were to live and work in accordance with the philosophy of Jean-Jacques Rousseau (1712-1778). Its form, a circle with the director's house at its centre, was also a symbolic means of retaining control over the inhabitants.

As the 20th century dawned, garden suburbs arose on the outskirts of many towns. These gave even greater emphasis to the division between living and working than in the 19th-century districts, where small businesses and workshops were still part of the street scene. The distinction between the functions of dwelling, work, transportation and recreation was at its greatest in the large expansion schemes of before and after the Second World War. Those years were coloured by an unshakeable faith in mobility, which was increasing hand over fist. This course was to alter around midway through the 1970s, when the need arose for greater variety among the homes on offer and for smaller industrial areas on the city's outskirts. People were becoming aware of the negative impact of a burgeoning mobility on the residential environment and on the environment in general. They rediscovered the dynamism of a city where many functions co-exist in time and space, and the attractions of living in a 'compact city'. The Team X group of architects elevated 'social relations', numbers and configurations of dwellings to principal themes. This is turn led to more complex structures for mass housing. Parts of the city – the former industrial and dock areas, old railway zones, elements of existing residential districts earmarked for reconstruction – were transformed into attractive locations for building.

The services or 'tertiary' sector has made stronger headway than the primary (agriculture) and secondary (industry). We are now living in an age when it has become easier to combine dwelling with work, in a particular relationship with the home. Production processes are getting cleaner and the means of communication are developing at a furious rate. This is making it progressively easier to work at home. The rise of modes of living and dwelling other than in the traditional family unit (single-person households, households with divided duties) and the space required for small startup businesses in the services sector, lend relevance to thinking about combinations of dwelling and work. The current stock of housing and office buildings, but also planning mechanisms such as land use plans, cannot adequately respond to today's changing demands. We need to develop new dwelling types that are able to accommodate changes of programme, also where space and use requirements are as yet unknown. Planning mechanisms like the land use plan should create more room for building for non-specific ends.[1]

An example of a dwelling type with a high accommodation capacity (the potential to accept changes) is the old Amsterdam canal house. These houses are able to keep accepting changes of function because of their oversized loadbearing structure and floor areas. In the 17th century, they were large dwellinghouses with reception areas and rooms for the domestic staff. In the 20th century these were converted into offices and recently many were converted again into apartment buildings.

Such changes of function are not discernible on the outside. The form is defined architecturally, it is the function that can change. If a cultural durability also obtains, this building type can be termed a 'solid', a fixed form with changing content and lasting quality. Functionalism in architecture has cut away many overlapping areas by making the required programme 'to measure'.

The need and necessity to economize on production these days places limits on the potentials of changeability in the future. Walls separating dwellings largely coincide with the loadbearing structure, where soundproofing requirements are achieved through sheer mass. A building with a frame as loadbearing structure and flexible party walls is more able to accept future changes. This reduces the risk of premature demolition if the demand for other programmes and spatial needs should arise.

With the present plummeting demand market for office buildings, resulting in many vacant properties, we need to develop plans that will enable some future exchange between residential and commercial or office functions. This vacancy has reached a historic level; at present the major towns in the Netherlands have some five million square metres of unoccupied office space, while there is a shortage of 160,000 homes. At least a million of those square metres can be expected to stay vacant, according to the association of Dutch property developers. There is a real threat of 'ghost towns' of empty office buildings springing up around the major cities.[2] Despite this forecast, office building activities are continuing at full tilt, as these were planned during a period of high returns. The upshot is that a number of plans for office buildings have had to be redeveloped for housing. Squats in office premises are on the rise. A number of unoccupied office buildings, some of which were only recently completed, are being primed to accept student accommodation or studio houses for artists. Many shops in old districts are being converted into housing.

These days we are witnessing a mounting interest in the life of buildings once they have been designed and delivered. The part played by the user is being reassessed. What will be possible in the coming 50 or 100 years, and which elements need introducing back at the design stage to allow for change? Extra floor-to-floor height, services zoned in carefully positioned shafts and floor systems, multiple access systems, facades and a loadbearing structure suited to the different programmes – these are the relevant issues today's design processes should be picking up on. This would give time-resistant buildings. It would make thinking about the life history of a building part of the actual process of designing. 'A building is not something you finish, a building is something you start'.³

To sum up: we need to develop strategies that respond to the following four aspects which are becoming increasingly important these days:
• *Changing lifestyles and the instability these bring to the way dwellings are organized.*⁴
The current construction flow, with its constant repetition of the three-room dwelling type for the nuclear family unit, will in the long run offer few opportunities for other living arrangements and lifestyles with their various combinations of living and working.
• *The unstable and rapidly changing demand market for office buildings.*
This gives rise to the need for buildings without a specific programme, that could contain homes as well as offices, depending on the demand, whether or not in flexible combinations. This way, long-term vacancy or demolition can be avoided.
• *The increasing tendency towards monofunctionality among new residential districts, business parks and industrial estates resulting from a rigid separation among functions based on a non-flexible zoning plan.*
Industrial estates and business parks without a mix that includes housing fail to contribute either to a secure living environment or to a dynamic cityscape. Zoning plans should be able to respond more quickly to changing circumstances.
• *The increase in mobility and the problems this has for commuter traffic.*
Stimulating homeworking potentially reduces the number of traffic jams during the rush hour.

These developments call for buildings and new dwelling types that facilitate all possible combinations of living and working. Before being able to describe plans, we need to define the different combinations of living and working. We can distinguish four possible relationships between the two, ranging from fully integrated to entirely separate.

1 *Two-in-one.*
Living and working are integrated.
2 *Together but separate.*
Living and working take place in parallel.
3 *Shared premises.*
Living and working take place in the same building.
4 *Separate premises.*
Living and working take place at entirely different locations.

1 In the two-in-one variant living and working are part of the same process, confined as they are to a single residential unit. There is no clear distinction between the two; there are no official working hours. The work activities take place in the living quarters or in a separate workspace. Examples include one-man business operations, student rooms, in-house workrooms for homeworkers and studios for artists.

2 Living and working together but separately is the traditional form. The two are kept apart for practical reasons. Examples include farms, companies with a live-in unit, shops with residences above, homes with a room for a private practice, canal houses with work premises in the rear section and the garage of drive-in houses. In these combinations there is a particular relationship between the private aspect and the spaces of a more public nature.

3 Living and working on the same premises can be spatially fixed, for instance homes above shops or offices, or it can spatially flexible and more a question of timesharing as functions change.

4 For most people, working away from home is the most common of the four. People are themselves flexible and regularly change the places where they live and work. The zoning plan stipulates a distinction between living and working based on the aspects of noise, odour and other work-related nuisances.

In practice, we often encounter hybrid forms and changing combinations of the integrated live/work variant and working away from home. As important as the the degree of interlacement of living and working, is the extent to which the work part of the house is exposed to the public; a room for deliberating with clients, for example, or a workspace for the staff. How the live/work unit is accessed determines whether working and domestic circulation in a housing block are kept separate or not. Often a slight oversize in the access leaves room to make the necessary distinction but also enables programmatic flexibility.

I would now like to examine in some depth a number of plans for live/work buildings related to the aforementioned strategies for combinations of living and working. Our concern here is with the following categories:
• buildings for living and working without a specific programme;
• live/work buildings that pick up on changing lifestyles;
• live/work areas with mixes of functions.

Buildings for living and working without a specific programme
Solids
The term solids, introduced by the Amsterdam architectural office 'De Architecten Cie', is taken to denote a building type of fixed form, lacking a specific programme but with a cultural durability (see also Frank Bijdendijk's paper on Solids on pp. 42-51). Multifunctional and flexible, it puts the notion of 'form follows function' in question. It harbours the potential to accommodate programmes of every kind, from housing to offices, in various live/work combinations of the first three types: integrated, in parallel and sharing premises. It permits some future exchange between programmes for living and working should there be a change in the demand. The form stays the same; different functions may be accommodated within a certain bandwidth. 'De Architecten Cie' designed a solid as a competition entry for Het Sluishuis, a housing block at the entry to the new residential district of IJburg in Amsterdam. It proposes the use of loadbearing facades with a system of shafts and vertical circulation cores, so that a variety of programmes can be accommodated (fig. 1).[5]

Waterstad Noord, Amsterdam
Waterstad Noord, a project located along the north banks of the IJ Inlet in Amsterdam, is one of the plans in a key transformation area of that city's former industrial estates and docks. When redeveloped, the area will present a dynamic axis of urban work, urban dwelling and urban leisure. It therefore looks ahead to forthcoming changes and mixes of function. A subarea has been given contextual form by the firm of Rapp+Rapp (fig. 2). It is primed to accept changeable combinations of living and working of types 1, 2 and 4: integrated, in parallel and at separate locations. 'Flatted factories' have been proposed; these are generic buildings with an air of architectural distinction. Constructed using loadbearing facades and generous floor-to-floor heights, such flatted factories can accommodate the widest range of internal subdivisions. With a uniform block depth, the width of the units can vary.

At present, the layout of perimeter blocks containing courtyards for parking rules out the possibility of housing as a result of the national noise abatement act (Geluidshinderwet). It is expected that this act will eventually be revised and made less rigid. Consequently, the urban plan and the proposed building type (perimeter blocks) have a neutral configuration with an eye to the possible future inclusion of housing. All blocks are 30 metres high and begin with a 6-metre-tall lower floor corresponding to two parking levels in the courtyard. Above this are six 4-metre-high levels of which the top two are each set back 2.5 metres, generating roof terraces and improving the light level in the street profile. The block depth is set at a minimum of 14 metres. Leisure functions occupy strategic positions throughout the plan.

Amsterdam-Werk

Across the IJ Inlet on the south bank is the proposed site for Amsterdam-Werk, a scheme designed by De Architecten Cie (Frits van Dongen) and Het Oosten development corporation (Frank Bijdendijk). With the air of a latter-day warehouse, Amsterdam-Werk has great potential in terms of accommodation and great flexibility in terms of programming. Four scenarios have been worked up:
• just housing;
• living and working at home (live/work units);
• living and working in the same building;
• just businesses and offices.

The conditions built-in to facilitate the four scenarios are:
• loadbearing facades;
• a wide range of possible access types: corridor access (single- or double-height) and gallery access;
• a grid of 7.2 m and module of 1.2 m to enable many wall-to-wall connections;
• the services take an integrated form whether for housing or offices; different requirements obtain for housing and offices: dwellings mainly need heating whereas cooling is more important for offices;
• floor heating is adjustable for individual floor areas 3.9 metres wide;
• floors are dimensioned to take up the greater loads of business premises and offices.

(See also the description on p. 164 in the 'Projects' section of this book.)

Live/work buildings that pick up on changing lifestyles

Shinonome Canal Court

Five kilometres south-west of the centre of Tokyo in the Koto-ku district is Shinonome Canal Court, a large-scale building scheme of over 2000 dwellings in combination with shops, offices and parking facilities realized on a site in the Tokyo waterfront area. This land in Tokyo Bay was reclaimed during the past few decades to create building sites to meet the overtaxed demand market. The scheme consists of six large blocks around a court, with for each block a team of architects, including Riken Yamamoto and Toyo Ito. The diversity on offer is extremely wide, from one-room apartments of 43 m² to family dwellings of 132 m². Shinonome propagates a new style of dwelling in Tokyo in which Small Office/Home Offices (SOHOS) are to feature prominently. SOHOS are residential units that can be used for an office, a studio or a showroom. The blocks consist of 14 levels of housing atop a ground-floor 'plinth' of facilities. In Yamamoto's design the larger dwellings come complete with an 'F-room' (foyer-room), directly accessed from the eccentrically placed corridors. These F-rooms can do duty as workspace (fig. 5). The walls between them and the corridor are partially of glass. The corridors receive abundant daylight, as double-height voids have been hewn in the block on each level but at different places; these are the communal terraces. These spaces constitute an 'oversize' in the block's communal spaces and may be used flexibly in the future. All in all, Shinonome represents a new urban housing form that integrates dwelling and working and enables other modes of living in the future.

(See also the description in the 'Projects' section, p. 156)

Student plan 'Living and Working in Waterstad Noord', Amsterdam

Erasmus exchange students at Delft University, developing a block from Rapp+Rapp's aforementioned plan Waterstad Noord in Amsterdam, created a housing block with a wealth of possibilities as to adaptability, mixes of function and differentiation into types of space. It can accept many types of dwelling and many modes of living among their occupants. The suggested design strategy is a perimeter block involving a welter of different block depths, floor-

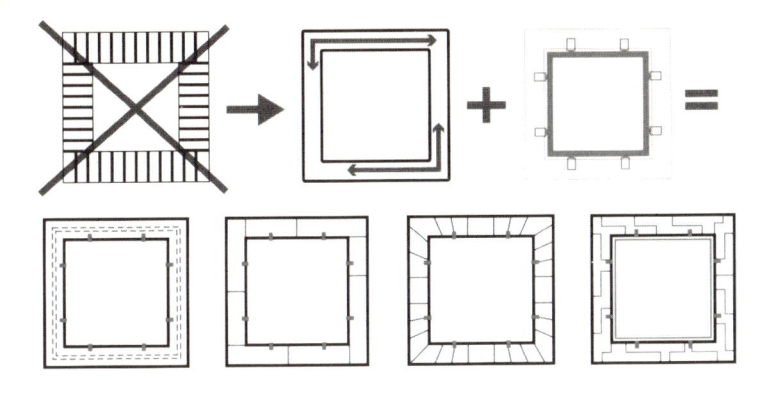

1 – De Architecten Cie, 'Het Sluishuis', IJburg, Amsterdam, 2003

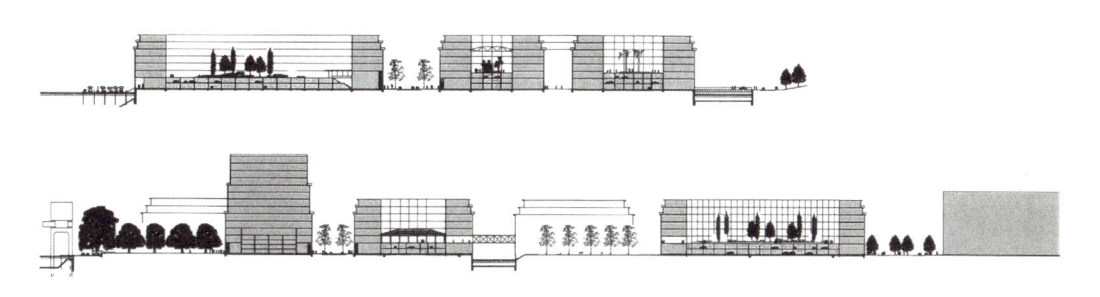

2 and 3 – Rapp+Rapp, Waterstad Noord, 2002. Plan and section

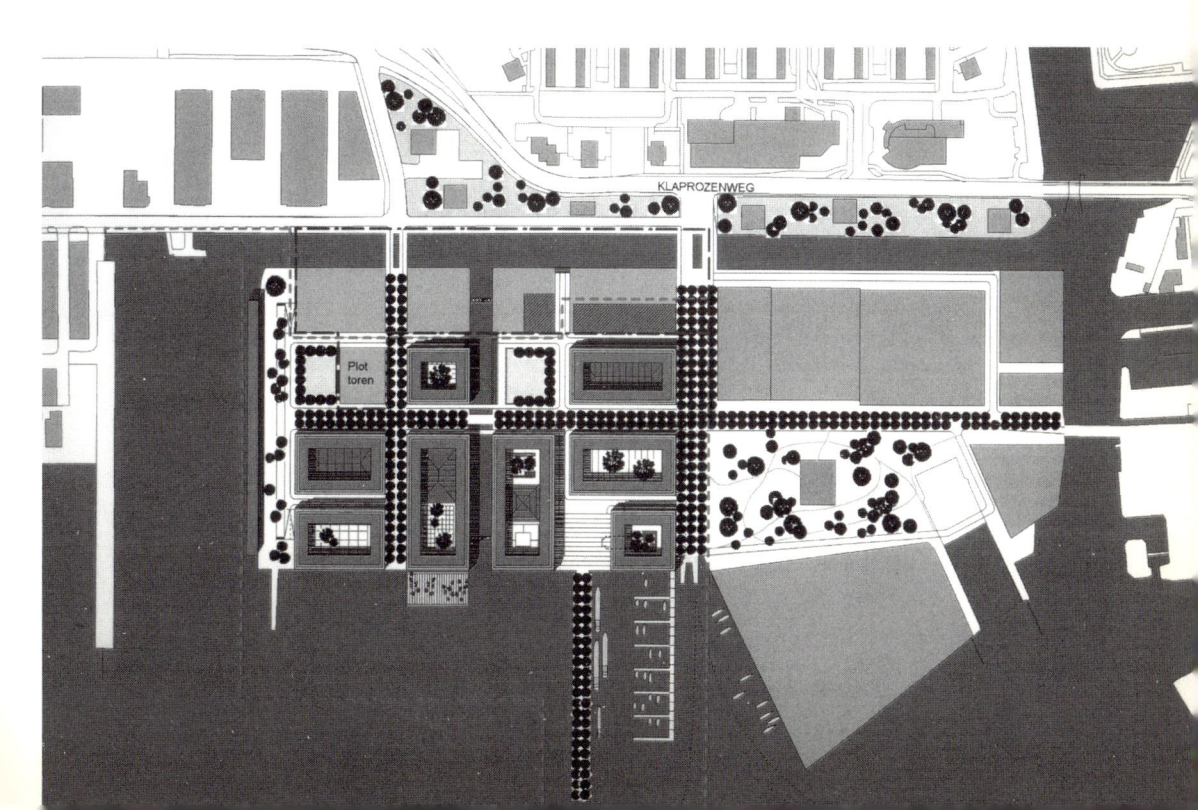

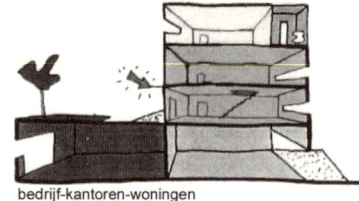

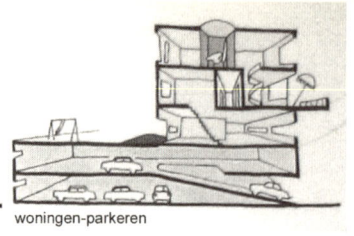

4 – De Architecten Cie, Amsterdam-Werk, scenarios, 2002

5 – Riken Yamamoto, Shinonome Canal Court, Tokyo, 2000-04. Plan

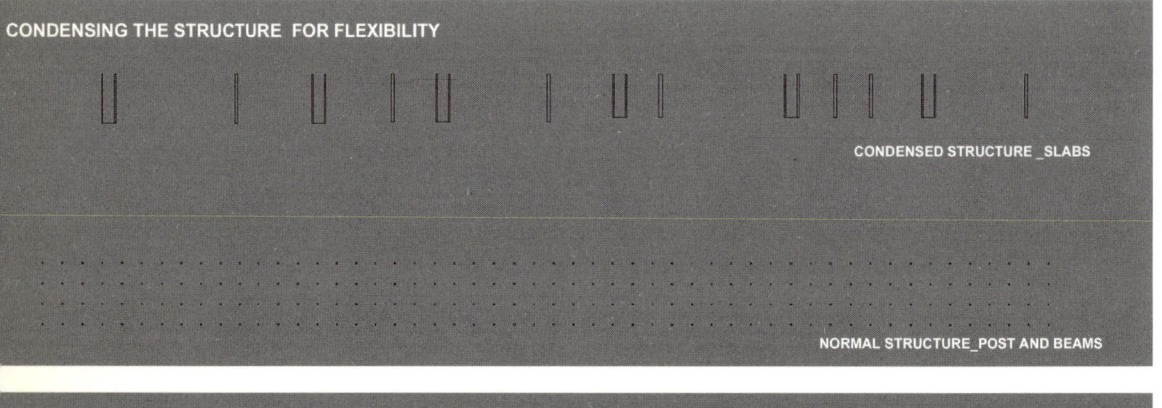

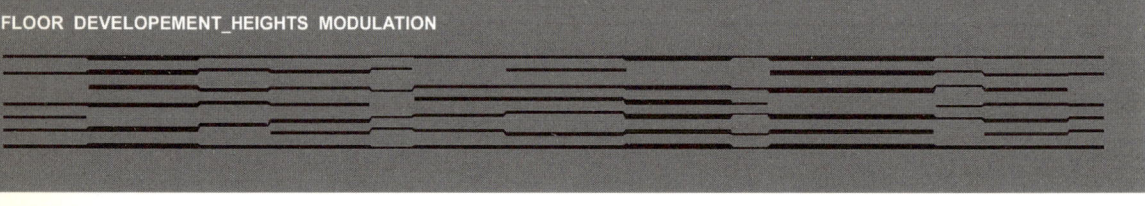

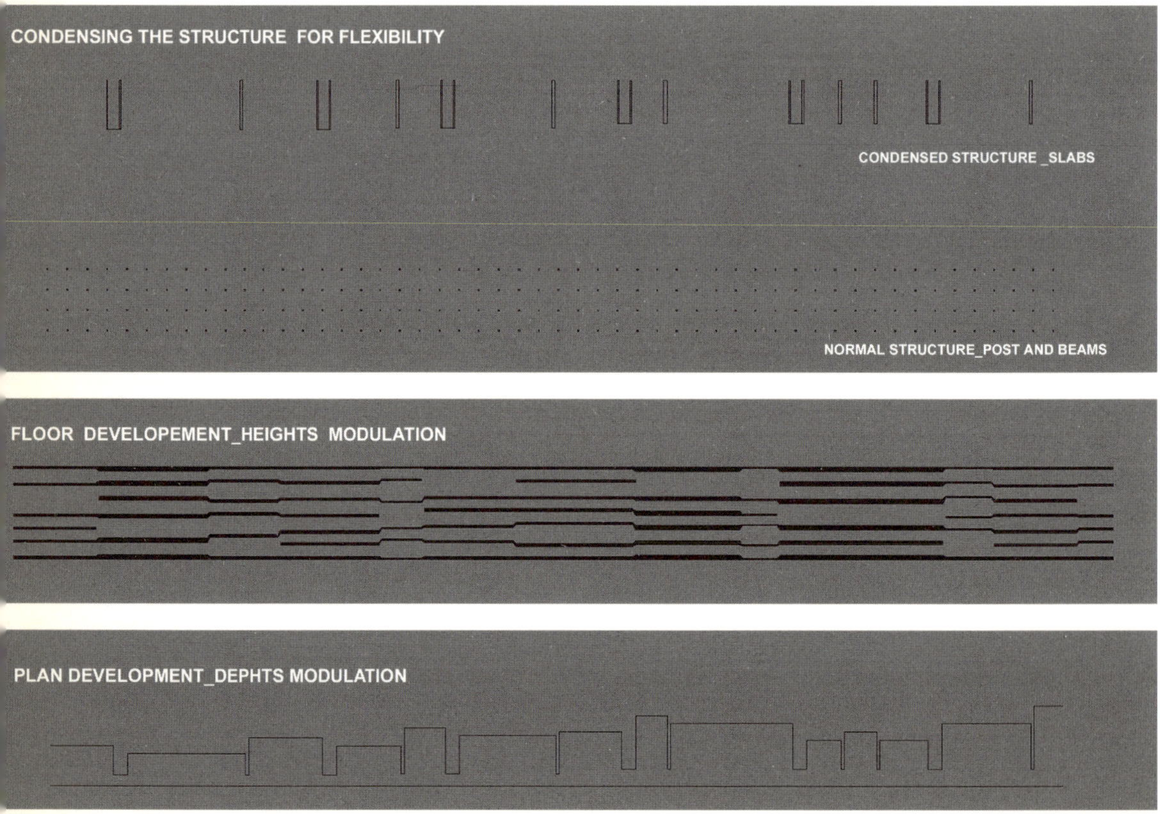

CONDENSING THE STRUCTURE FOR FLEXIBILITY

CONDENSED STRUCTURE _SLABS

NORMAL STRUCTURE_POST AND BEAMS

FLOOR DEVELOPEMENT_HEIGHTS MODULATION

PLAN DEVELOPMENT_DEPHTS MODULATION

6 – Pestellini, Pagliaro and Fricout (TU Delft), Waterstad Noord, 2002. Diagram

7 – Pestellini, Pagliaro and Fricout (TU Delft), Waterstad Noord, 2002. Elevation

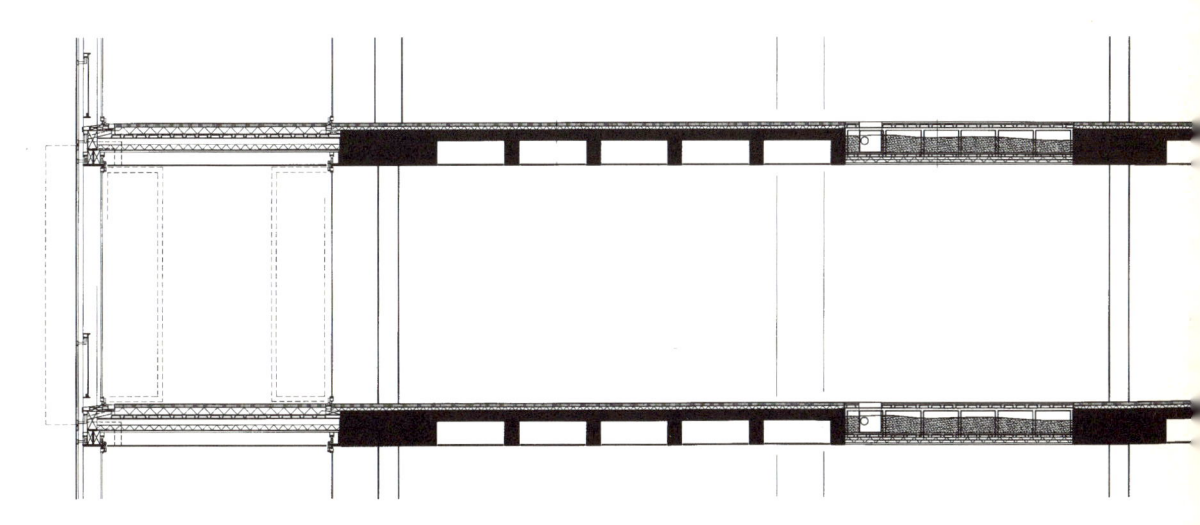

8 – Colly (TU Delft), Katendrecht, Rotterdam, 2002. Floor systems

9 – Diener & Diener, housing, Ypenburg (subarea 6), 1999-2003

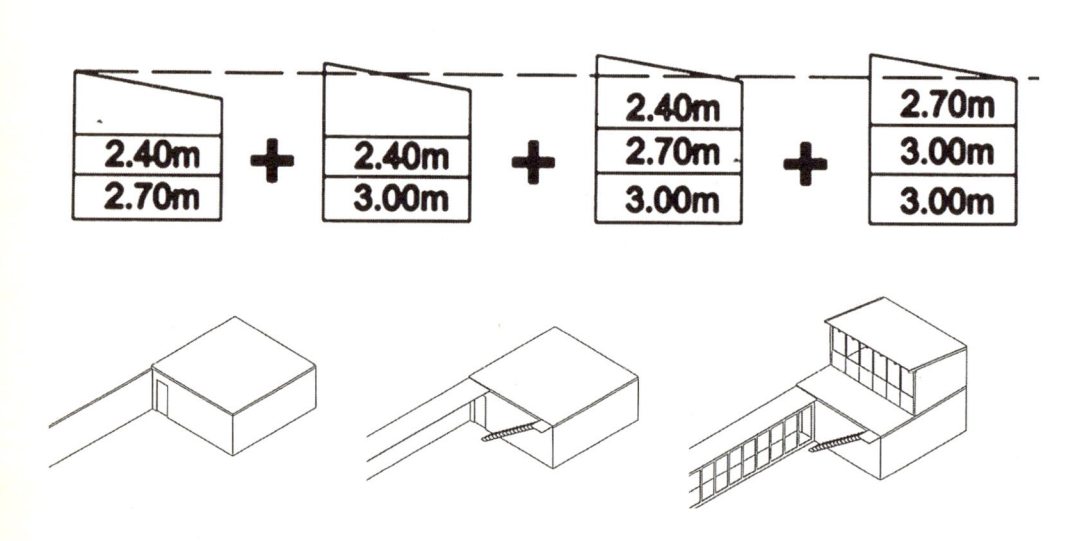

10 – West 8, Ypenburg (subarea 6), 1999-2003. Ceiling height and garden houses

to-floor heights and spans (fig. 6). Not everything has been made flexible and interchangeable; the range of flexibility is curbed by particularizing the spans and floor-to-floor heights: call it a zoned flexibility. This deliberate restriction makes this scheme a lot less neutral than in Rapp+Rapp's masterplan. The parts with a less generous floor-to-floor height are preferably to contain housing. Much more is possible in the taller parts; dwellings with a mezzanine level, larger office units or spaces containing communal facilities. The greatest span is 20 metres. This zone can accommodate larger offices and communal spaces; the smaller spans are for dwellings and studios. The tall steel joists have space for cables and services. The block also includes spaces for theatrical performances, sports facilities, outdoor refreshment areas and for unforeseen functions as in Yamamoto's project in Tokyo (Shinonome Canal Court). Units are accessed from a gallery along the rim of the central courtyard. The elevation expresses the dynamic programme by means of concrete strips along the floors that trace the changes in level indoors. In this case flexibility fails to produce a neutral look (fig. 7).

■ Student plan 'Living and Working in Katendrecht', Rotterdam

Another final-year project, a plan to redevelop an old dock area in Katendrecht south of the river in Rotterdam, constructs a modern 'warehouse' with a block depth of 75 metres. It deploys the loadbearing structure, floor system and zoning of cable runs as design tools to realize many different types of dwelling. The loadbearing structure consists of a concrete skeleton. Floors are composed of floor units with steel joists whose bottom flange is cast into a concrete panel. This leaves room for ducting. Removable floor slabs in the middle and at the edges enable the loadbearing structure to be broken open vertically, should new demands be made on the space in the future (fig. 8).

■ Live/work areas with mixes of functions
Subarea 6, Ypenburg

A drop in density in the new residential areas being developed in the urban periphery is leaving less room for functions other than dwelling. The shop on the corner or in the housing block is disappearing and there is less and less available surface area per contingent of dwellings for facilities such as shops and schools. In the recently completed 'Subarea 6' in Ypenburg (West 8, 1999-2003) in the vicinity of The Hague, ingredients are enlisted to combat the monotonous image of repetition but the functions themselves remain limited to mainly housing and the occasional school. In the overall plan for Ypenburg with its rather more than 15,000 units, there is room for only one centre of amenities and offices. In Subarea 6 an attempt has been made to go some way to alleviating the monofunctional condition. But it proves to be little more than variations on form. The rows of housing consist of a necklace of constantly differing dwelling types; two to four units of the same type and then the link up with another type. Residents can choose from a great many different dwelling types. The ceiling height of the ground floor is higher than is customary. In theory other functions than dwelling could occupy the taller spaces. In a single case a dwelling is combined with an art lending library, an example of living and working in parallel (figs. 9-10). The garden shed has the potential to grow into a garden house or studio – and indeed some such studios have been developed.

■ Research

Our changing society makes it necessary to look for a broader perspective on dwelling. In 1998 the conclusion reached in one study by a major Dutch property developer into the need for live/work homes was that the greatest demand for these came from the least affluent in society such as artists and fledgling entrepreneurs. This was why the development of live/work units has remained a niche market, even today. The unpredictability of the demand market and the problem of unoccupied offices forced a number of developers and architectural practices to do research into 'solids' without a fixed programme as a form of time-based building.

Homeworking is on the increase, according to a study done by Ernst & Young among people working in ICT. This brings a decrease in the need for mobility as well as in the problems caused by tailbacks and long travel times due to the drop in commuter traffic. The conclusions are as follows:
• four out of ten interviewees work at home for an average of 15 hours a week; homeworking is especially prevalent in small businesses and within the services sector;
• the principal reasons for homeworking are to be able to work quietly and efficiently and not have to spend time travelling or in traffic jams;
• the number of homeworkers is expected to swell considerably in the coming year, particularly among large companies.[6]

Universities are doing research by design into buildings that facilitate the integration of living and working, hitched to a form of flexibility, polyvalency or a separation of base building and fit-out. In this research by design, the tools required for designing this type of building are being crafted. Studies done into the typology of plans, elevations, loadbearing structures and modes of access can help us to define the conditions buildings with mixed and exchangeable functions are to meet.

■ Conclusions
In the projects described above, an accommodation capacity has been built-in as a form of durability, a capacity that can meet the change in demand under changing circumstances that are impossible to predict. Given the instability of the programme, the principle of 'form follows function' can no longer be regarded as a general stepping-off point for a design. No tailor-made affair then, with close-fitting spaces for specific functions, but sustainable buildings capable of accommodating change. The present housing stock leans too heavily on three-room houses for nuclear family units. These are not equipped for changing ways of living and dwelling. Programmatic flexibility with an interchangeability between functions of living and working are, together with cultural durability, key to a a building's useful life. Design strategies differ. At times neutrality is maintained, at others the loadbearing structure, the services and the cable run are deployed to enable changes in the short and long term. An important design strategy for conditioning mixes of function and interchangeability of living and working is to provide more than one access system. A degree of oversize in the dwellings creates potential workspaces. This enables new dwelling concepts with room for the unexpected, the unpredictable. This is the way to face the 21st century.

1 F. Heddema, 'Interview met Frank Bijdendijk van Het Oosten. Bestemmingloos bouwen is nodig', *Binnenstad 185*, VVAB (De Vereniging Vrienden van de Amsterdamse Binnenstad), November 2000.
2 'Kantoorparken worden spooksteden', *de Volkskrant*, 16 December 2004.
3 Stuart Brand, *How Buildings Learn: What Happens After They're Built*, New York: Viking Penguin, 1994.
4 A. Reijndorp et al. (eds), *Leefstijlen. Wonen in de 21ste eeuw*, Rotterdam: NAi Uitgevers, 1997.
5 M. Milanovic and I. Deong, *Het Sluishuis. Landmark in het water bij IJburg*, 2002. Bussum: Thoth, 2002.
6 Ernst & Young, ICT *Barometer* no. 11, 2004.

SOLIDS
Frank Bijdendijk

▊ Introduction

A Solid is a sustainable building; sustainable in the economic, functional, technical and emotional senses of the word. In my opinion this is achieved through two qualities: *accommodation capacity* (accommodation in the sense of being able to adapt) and *preciousness* (the emotional value).[1] A Solid, then, is a precious building that is constantly accommodating new uses. These uses are located inside the building. It is precious on the exterior and in the shared spaces such as entrances. This is the way a Solid responds to the question of how to deal with the time factor in buildings.

Accommodation capacity is targeted at individual values. By this is meant the building's ability to give every successive user per floor the freedom to adapt their part of the Solid to their particular use – that is, arrange and equip it to their own requirements. A system of Solids should in turn possess the qualities of accommodation capacity and preciousness at city block level. Accommodation capacity at this scale is achieved by placing in juxtaposition buildings that may in time be individually replaced without damaging the whole.

Preciousness is targeted at collective values. It's about a building's identity: the degree to which people can relate to that building, become fond of it, feel attached to it, want to see it preserved. These people are not just the ones who make regular use of the building but everyone else too, such as visitors and those passing through the surrounding public space.

To achieve accommodation capacity and preciousness means making targeted additional investments in qualities of the 'base building' over and above the customary standard. These extra investments can be justified if they yield additional returns in the long term.

This essay seeks to make clear why and how these qualities lead to economic, functional, technical and emotional sustainability, what the underlying philosophy is, and what role the time factor plays in all this.

▊ The philosophy

The dawning of the 1990s brought with it an increased concern with preserving our living environment. The concept of 'sustainability' made its entrance. This concept is related to long-term recycling processes that occur in nature. (Sustainability is rendered in Dutch as *duurzaamheid*, a word that can also be said to mean immutability, or enduring through time.) The front ranks of designers applied themselves eagerly to this sustainability and looked for constructions and methods of building that would tax the environment as little as possible. Economy held the key: economy in the use of energy, space and water, and a handling of materials that would have a minimum effect on the environment. This last-named aspect ushered in discourses on the use of tropical hardwood, on whether aluminium – from extraction to reuse – would be less environmentally damaging than steel and whether demolition waste might not be recyclable. In 1996 the first National Package for Sustainable Building saw the light of day. This sustainable building 'checklist' gave concrete and practical tips to builders regarding measures that would lead to the conditions described above. However, the building construction industry saw this list as something of an obligation that would only bring extra expenses. So sustainable became synonymous with cost-raising. And to this day there is little call in the market for this kind of sustainability.

In 1997 I published a booklet entitled *Duurzaamheid loont* (sustainability pays)[2], whose subtitle translates as 'How building soberly and objectively keeps poor people poor' (see fig. 1). In it I argued that the train of thought that produced the dictum 'build soberly and objectively' in public housing led in the longer term to waste and so to unnecessary impact on the environment. This way of thinking can be briefly explained as follows. The rationalism that had made its entrance during the Renaissance – Descartes' 'Cogito, ergo sum', Newton's law of cause and effect – led in the 19th century to unprecedented successes in science and technique. Progressive thinking was born. This was the firm belief that an analytical approach could solve problems and improve the condition of humanity; analysis as the division of a large seemingly opaque issue into smaller, more manageable sub-issues. And the view of mankind changed with it. Instead of being a part of nature and subordinate to it, there was now the image of man as nature's ruler. The Industrial Revolution of the 19th century took this a stage further, bringing with it the shift to the large scale and the emergence of major industries. Individuals were immersed in the masses. This painted a picture of 'everyone is equal' and enabled totalitarian ideas about the state to take hold. People became stereotyped: 'we all have the same needs'. In the Netherlands the notion of a 'makable society' stemmed from this way of thinking.

The success of progressive thinking and the analytical approach had not left the design world unaffected in the early years of the 20th century. Many architects felt that architecture at that time had outstayed its welcome, relying as it did on antiquated forms (classicism, eclecticism), and was badly in need of fresh inspiration and a new lease of life. Thus, in the 1920s, modernism in architecture was born, otherwise known as progressive architecture or 'functionalism'. This took as its premise the fact that a building, structure or space primarily fulfilled a function. A road was for vehicular traffic, a cycleway for bicycles, a dining room for eating, and so forth. By meticulously analysing a function it was possible to determine with great accuracy the form (the dimensions) the function in question was to receive. 'Form Follows Function'[3] was the watchword. Adding up the functions in a building gave you the form and dimensions of that building. The same held for infrastructure and urban planning. A city or building was regarded as an assemblage of functions. Now that form was to serve function alone, all superfluous forms – those with no function, such as ornamentation[4] – could be left out. The upshot was an architectural style couched in the language of restraint. Moreover, the building had to express its function outwardly. 'Outside is inside'. This gave modernism its own vocabulary which inspired many architects, certainly in the years preceding the Second World War. But legislators were inspired by this too. If people have uniform needs, they reasoned, we can accurately predict beforehand which functions a building must fulfil. For each function we can precisely determine the space needed for it. A living room is 4 x 4 metres, because here a father, a mother and two children sit at a table with a lamp above it. A child's bedroom is 7.2 m² because a bed, a cupboard, a small table and a chair have to fit into it. This way of thinking has produced sober, objective public housing. On first sight, this seems a sympathetic goal, as no-one can complain about restraint and fitness for purpose. However, the way it was applied has led to mind-numbing repetition, alienation and to buildings with no future value. It is for good reason that the Bijlmermeer residential district, delivered in 1968, was already being demolished in 1998; for good reason that many post-war districts are due for major restructuring. It has transpired that thinking analytically, and solving sub-problems, does not automatically lead to the best overall solution. It has transpired too that conventionalizing needs and therefore doing others' thinking for them (the makable society, 'I know what's good for you') fails to produce satisfying solutions for the people it concerns. In this sense 'functionalism' has had its day.

That takes care of the subtitle of my booklet.
Now for the title.

My argument is that sustainability in the building construction industry should extend further than just economizing on energy, water, materials and space. In the booklet three models for buildings are compared in terms of environmental impact and economic sustainability. These models are the log cabin, the pyramid and the social housing unit. The first is illustrative of a building that perishes, being built of branches, leaves and mud. In today's terms this is a demountable building. The second represents a building that lasts for ever, which is what the Pharaohs intended for their pyramids. In the booklet I showed that in the long run the 'pyramid' model is economically superior to the other two. This is because pyramids require less upkeep and never need altering. We shall return to that last-named aspect, as it is precisely here that the break with functionalism occurs. (Let us leave aside the log cabin for brevity's sake.) The initial investment in the 'pyramid' is admittedly much higher than in the sober and objective building, but far fewer costs are incurred during use. Another thing: during its history the pyramid increases in value far more than the sober and objective building. Here too we can discern a major break with the way of thinking until now. Functionalism, hitched as it is to conventionalized needs, gives a maximum of economy; the new approach on the other hand additionally leads to a maximum of value (read quality), to forms and dimensions that no longer need to express one function to the exclusion of all others.
The pyramid lasts longer, costs less and grows more strongly in value. This, then, explains the title: Sustainability pays.

What must a building achieve to last for ever? What properties, what qualities must it have? To be able to answer these questions, we must first bring our view of humanity up to date by rooting it in the reality of today. This reality can be described as follows.
Not all people are equal, far from it. In fact no two people are equal. We live in an individualized society. This has to do with our increased economic independence (prosperity), the increased availability of information, increased knowledge and increased emancipation. Obviously these aspects are related. There is no single stereotype we can apply here. There are no longer rigidly defined classes, no hard and fast life patterns, no fixed properties that can be attributed to gender, age group or income group. Not just that, our needs are constantly changing; they change during a lifetime and with the passage of time in general. This last-named factor is the result of social and technological developments. Someone aged 30 today has other expectations and needs than someone aged 30 a decade ago. These will be different again ten years from now. Ideas about homes and dwelling today are a lot different from those ten years ago, 20 years ago, 30 years ago... The living room then with the table in the middle is now crammed with electronic gadgets. What used to be the nursery is now where the dog lives or the skiing equipment is kept. Working and living environments are getting to look more and more like each other. Private life and work are no longer as strictly separated as they were. Change is the only constant factor. And that change is becoming more rapid all the time. It is also becoming more unpredictable. What has functionalism to offer us today, based as it was on fixed functions requiring fixed dimensions and forms? What use is market research to us now, leading as it does to a stereotyped representation of reality and just one moment in time? Some researchers seek solace in lifestyles, but even these will prove to be transitory. What are we to build if we don't know what purpose it is to serve? Building means investing for the long term. So what *does* provide us with a firm basis?

If unpredictable change is the only constant factor, it is there that we must look for certainties. We must build for changeability, for constantly changing use. Nor should we try to predict this use. After all, who would have thought 100 years ago that churches would be used today as sports halls, schools as housing, factories as museums, houses as mosques?

1 – Cover of *Duurzaamheid loont*

2 – Buildings on Place Stanislas in Nancy. From top to bottom: offices, hotel, museum and opera house

3 – Bijlmermeer residential district, Amsterdam, built to CIAM principles

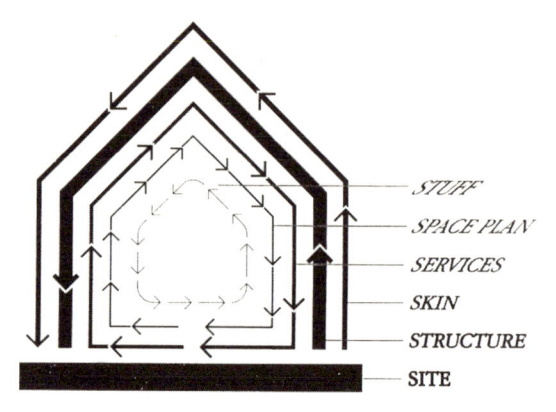

5, 6 and 7 – An excellent example of an area that has proved to possess the future values described in this essay is SoHo in Manhattan. Generous floor-to-floor heights in section, good communication between inside and outside on the ground floor, a freely subdivisible plan with large spans and columns and a thoughtful material form and detailing (in this case cast iron)

4 – Different layers in buildings respond at different speeds to varying use, depending on their nature. This produces a hierarchy among these layers. This hierarchy is a key design premise that takes account of the time factor

5 – Residential loft

6 – Overlap between inside and outside

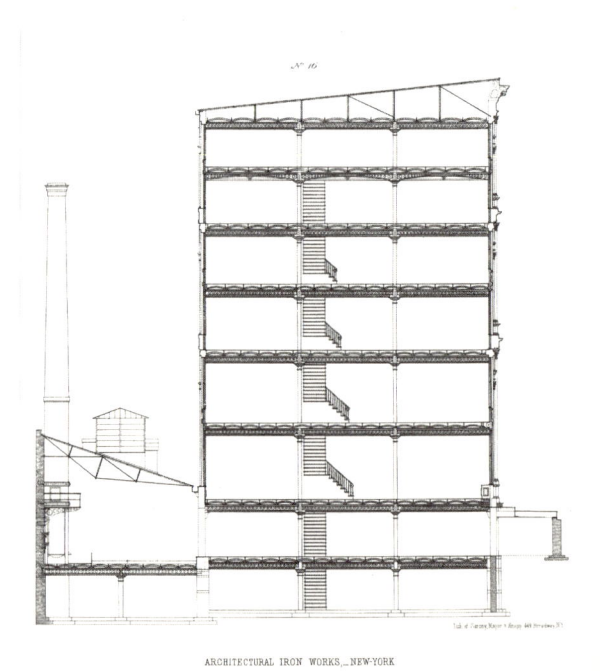

7 – Cross-section of a typical cast iron building

Function evidently has little inclination to follow form.

At the famous Place Stanislas in Nancy (dating from 1752) can be seen four buildings that are utterly identical from the outside. Inside, however, they could not be more different. Building number one contains a restaurant on the ground floor with offices above, number two contains a theatre, three a museum and four a hotel. Everyone is bowled over by these buildings (see fig. 2). But not one of the four is in any way an expression of what goes on inside. Evidently this is not a prerequisite for a building to possess value.

Truly valuable buildings are constantly changing function. Take the centre of Amsterdam, and more specifically its canal houses, which have changed function countless times during their existence though with no apparent effect on their outward appearance. Amsterdam has been a live/work city for 350 years where both dwelling and working are continually changing character and location, while the outward appearance, the facades and entrances, remains the same. Changes of function are normal, the city is alive, it has a metabolism. Functions that remain the same over time are abnormal and will be come across less and less. So let us abandon this notion of functionalism where the form has to fit the function like a kind of clingfilm. Let us not try to devise a form that fits any one function perfectly, as there is no way we can predict what that function's successor will be.

To what extent is changing use within fixed forms applicable to people today? As I see it, to every extent. There is one need we do share today, in my opinion, regardless of income, social status, age group or lifestyle. And that need is to be able to choose how we live or work, how we use and equip our living or working space – in short, freedom of choice. Buildings that offer freedom of choice have true future value for that very reason. And this brings us to our concept of *accommodation capacity*. Accommodation capacity makes technical and legal demands on a building. Legal here means freedom in allocating space. So instead of land use plans which give legal certainty by fixing functions, we need *changing use plans*. These will offer legal certainty too, not through fixing but through meticulous decision-making procedures regarding changes of function. Technically, freedom of function requires a space, its surface area and height to be such as to be freely subdivisible at all times. This is why vertical loads can better be transmitted to the ground along columns rather than piers. Columns are less coercive. Freedom of function requires a wide range of possible connections for services; it also requires accessibility. This last-named is particularly important in a urban setting, where functions are often stacked simply because there is not enough room to place them side by side. In sum, then, we are providing the changeability, the multifunctionality and the freedom of choice users are going to need for as long as there are buildings.

But in observing the reality of cities and buildings with value (with a long past, and a long future) I have been struck by something else, namely, that the outward appearance, the facade, the exterior scarcely changes at all. Isn't this in contradiction to the foregoing? This would indeed be the case in a mindset where – externally – form has to follow function, where 'outside is inside'. The mindset so enthusiastically embraced by so many architects since the 1920s; the mindset that created the La Sarraz Declaration of CIAM, the *machines à habiter*, the *unités d'habitation*, the *villes radieuses*, Bijlmermeer (see fig. 3), the post-war residential areas, post-war office districts, post-war industrial estates; the monofunctional areas with their monofunctional buildings – one look, one price – whose function is as clear as day. In this mindset an unchanging 'base building' would indeed clash with a changing use. But this is not the case in the mindset of most normal people. I at least have never met anyone who objected to the fact that a canal house switched function for the umpteenth time from living to working or vice versa. Quite the opposite, in fact.

There are strong signs that a great many people in our individualized and changeable world actually need fixed points, means of identification, something to hold on to, something *precious*. Nature (the beach, the woods) and the urban environment lend themselves well to this need. For they share the quality of having been around longer than a human life and are larger than a person. So preciousness fits into a human society in which change is the order of the day. This makes it a quality with future value. And that making precious buildings with a great accommodation capacity is a real option, is borne out by the best parts of our existing cities. In earlier times we could manage that very well – probably even without being aware of the fact. Why shouldn't we be able to do that today? For buildings with these qualities, buildings that take account of the time factor, we use the term Solids.

■ The investment strategy

Solids are buildings that everlastingly yield a profit because they everlastingly fulfil a function and are everlastingly attractive. Solids are buildings that make a distinction between the base building (the loadbearing structure, access and exterior) and the fit-out (whatever is needed for a particular use). Solids admit to two types of investor: the one that invests in the base building, and the user who determines and pays for the fit-out. The greatest investment by far is in the base building. This investment is particularly high when measured against standards customary at present, and for two reasons. The first is that the base building must possess accommodation capacity and must be precious, and this brings additional costs. The second is that in the 'compact city' and in our increasingly complex surroundings, extra money is required for the elaborate structures resulting from these conditions.

In view of the size of the investment, then, it is in the investor's interests that operating costs for maintenance and transformation are low and the lifespan is extremely long. It is in the user's interests that the internal organization and equipment can be altered very easily and therefore cheaply. The fact is, this fit-out has a brief lifespan and therefore a short depreciation period. So the fit-out in fact is not an investment at all, more a commodity expenditure outlay of several years' benefit.

What are the investor's prospects today for investing in the base building? This investment is geared to generating accommodation capacity and preciousness. Perhaps that investor should settle for a comparatively low return to start with. This can of course be acceptable if this return is higher than normal in the long term. This means that costs during use must be low and that the base building must increase in value. Tentative calculations have shown that it is realistic to assume this to be possible. Precisely because the initial investment is higher (between 20 and 30 per cent) and targeted at preciousness and accommodation capacity, it is not just the maintenance costs that will be lower (10-15%) but most of all the transformation costs (60-70%). Because of this the direct yield alone will be between 20 and 25 per cent higher after, say, 100 years. But there is an additional factor: time can also bring about capital growth. Every private home-owner and every institutional investor in the Netherlands periodically records a rise in value of their property. This is because the value of existing real restate in the longer term on average parallels if not exceeds the rising prices of new property. But the value of precious buildings and precious places rises even faster! Everyone knows that a square metre of living space can yield utterly different prices in different contexts. Under normal market conditions an old building kept in good working order – providing the site is right – has more value than a new one! For Solids, then, the time factor brings about additional yield whether directly (through development) or indirectly (through capital growth) in the long term.

Now that the investment strategy is targeted at obtaining future value we can identify two types of optimization: cost optimization *and* value optimization. The functionalist conceptual model, which proceeded from conventionalized needs, in fact focused solely on cost optimization. And we have given it our best during the past 50 years. This is only logical. If you are geared to short-term sales and know what the client wants, the only thing you still have to do is see to it that the product in question is made as cheaply as possible. In the marketplace, the product and the selling price are generally fixed and the only aspect to vary is the cost price. We can see that this has been the prevailing train of thought during the past half-century just by looking at the quality of what we have built: sober and objective, and downright shabby at times.

Value-based optimization is much more difficult, as how do you equate capital with value? How much should accommodation capacity cost? How much should the thoughtful handling of materials and detailing cost? What does it yield? This optimization aspect is an ideal subject for design research.

A second scale is that of the system of Solids. Here accommodation capacity is achieved through site layout and by building Solids side by side. And in such a way that small-scale individual Solids can be replaced without the character and the ambience of the whole suffering as a result – just like the Amsterdam canal houses. We can narrow down the issue of optimization to two subjects: plot size and serial production. Would it be a good idea to repeat certain building components? Should we resort to off-the-shelf elements, a construction kit, or do we make everything in situ? This too is a subject for design research.

And at system level we also have to take account of users who may need more or less space in the future. In the latter case they can make space for new users. In the former, they may want to rent additional floor space. How do we attach that to the floor area already in use? Should we assume that there will be internal cuts, or will it be done along the outside? In that case, shouldn't we provide an external walkway sheltered against the elements, an arcade? Yet another subject for design research.

The third scale is that of the area, the location. In time the quality of the setting is key to determining the capital growth. At which sites do we invest in Solids and which do we avoid? How do we influence the quality of the environment both during the project's development and later when in use? This is one of the most important issues facing investors.

Preciousness and accommodation capacity pursued further

Of the two future qualities *accommodation capacity* is the easiest to objectify. Preciousness is a much more subjective concept. Accommodation capacity is reasonably easy to programme. This cannot be said of preciousness. Countermanding this, however, is the fact that once in place, preciousness is far easier to assess. Everyone can do that as we all have a heart. But you have to be a professional to judge the achieved accommodation capacity. Each of these qualities requires its own course of action, but both are of crucial importance.

We shall start with the easiest of the two. In the preceding paragraphs we have seen how accommodation capacity can be achieved. Let us recapitulate. It begins with the separation between base building and fit-out. The base building is to last for ever and has to be able to accommodate all kinds of temporary fit-outs. How those fit-outs evolve over time is not our concern here.

It is conceivable that if this mode of construction were to become more common practice, the manufacturers of interior fittings would turn to fit-outs and have all kinds of interesting new solutions to offer. But where exactly is the dividing line between everlasting and temporary? What are the permanent facilities? What physical components are clients bringing with them? Clearly the finishes of floors and ceilings are temporary – fit-out elements in other words. But is the complete facade everlasting or is part of it temporary? Does the base building contain the services on a permanent basis or do all services (heat, energy, water, air, alarms) get fed into a meter cupboard or a central point and laid out by the user/client? At all events, what does belong to the base building is the unchangeable (everlasting) part of the facade. But does the facade also have a changeable part? And lastly, what about the outdoor spaces upstairs? Are these fully internal or external? Are they changeable or fixed?

Whatever the case, my philosophy includes the following design determinants for the base building.

• Proportionally generous floor-to-floor height leaving room for raised floors and/or suspended ceilings in the future (ground floor communicating with the street, c. 4.5-5.0 m, upper storeys c. 3.3-3.6 m gross height).
• Proportionally few fixed vertical structural components, so preferably columns as supporting structure. The 'everlasting' part of the facade may also be loadbearing.
• Large spans, few obstacles, large open floor areas.
• Proportionally high load-bearing capacity.
• Proportionally generous vertical access for people, piping, ducts and cables.

In short, freedom in internal subdivision and oversize on a number of points.

In this way accommodation capacity leads to technical, functional and economic sustainability. But also emotional sustainability! For nothing is so attractive for users as being able to decide for themselves how they will use the rented surface area, how they will divide up their space, as well as the quality level and the costs involved. Real freedom of choice at all times is of enormous value.

With *preciousness* we arrive on much more difficult terrain, as the core of this concept is emotion. It concerns the degree to which people (and not just those using the building!) can become attached to the building in their environment, can identify with it, can come to love it! It is this emotional value that makes it a precarious subject.

Let us try to approach the concept of preciousness as openly as we can, and see it as the result of a love of buildings by a wide audience. A love that comes from an inner need, a love that satisfies and delights. Let us not treat the research done by market researchers, trend watchers and other specialists into the elements that bring preciousness, as an excuse not to engage in it ourselves. Let us try to develop an empathy for the subject. After all, empathy is a unique human quality possessed by no other mammal. Creative empathy is the key – that and a sincere concern for what people find attractive and compelling.

How do we get at it, that last-named quality? It would definitely help to find out how people react to what has already been built. Many modernist designers prefer not to do that, fearing that they will be considered reactionary and therefore not progressive. I can see nothing wrong with such research myself. After all, most things have been built already. What gets added every year is but a fraction of what exists. And we already know what people find attractive or ugly about a great many cities, districts, neighbourhoods and buildings. It is not difficult at all to assess the preciousness of the existing. Assessing the consequences of this for the new and yet-to-be-built is another matter. Yet this is where one of the very greatest tasks of the designing architect lies. With what visual form do you appeal to people's emotions?
I myself have a number of suggestions in this respect,

based on my observations and my attempts to empathize with the subject. I think they may be of help.

• Consider the building in its context, the way it slots into its setting. The setting is uppermost, the building comes next. Buildings are daughters of the city.
• See to it that the building can communicate with its setting and doesn't turn away from it.
• Provide the most inviting and attractively designed (shared) entrance, tall and broad.
• Provide thoughtful detail, choosing materials that weather well and age gracefully. Materials which, rather than perish with age, indeed become more attractive (surely the worn stone steps leading up to an Amsterdam canal house are much to be preferred to new ones?).
• Show how things hang together in a way that everyone can understand. No hidden constructional solutions, no granite panels hung on hooks you can't see. Such contrivances fail to project a feeling of permanence, no matter how permanent the material granite may be.
• Ornaments are embellishments to the base building, belonging to every era and every country. Theirs is a special claim to preciousness.

Make a precious base building with an open mind, with empathy and great creative endeavour – that, to my mind, is the pre-eminent brief today.
(figs 5-7)

Solids and Vitruvius: the design challenge

It was more than 2000 years ago that Vitruvius described how Romans ought to build. Strength, beauty and usefulness – these, translated freely, are what he regarded as the most important qualities of good architecture. Our Solids are strong, beautiful and of lasting use. In that sense they fully satisfy the classical Vitruvian triumvirate. This use, however, is not singular and based on a known requirement, as in functionalism, but is constant, eternal and based on an unknown requirement. This presents us today with a great design challenge. What does a beautiful (read precious) building look like, one that has been made to satisfy the lasting needs of people who wish to dwell and/or work there? Time as a design brief! Form now takes on another meaning than the one it had in functionalism. It is no longer the expression of a function. That standard no longer applies. But what is to take its place? How are decisions on form justified in buildings with future value and of lasting use?

1 The Dutch terms I use for these two concepts are, respectively, *accommodatievermogen* and *dierbaarheid*.
2 Frank Bijdendijk, *Duurzaamheid loont*, Haarlem: Architext, 1997.
3 From 'The Tall Office Building Artistically Considered', an essay by the Chicago School architect Louis Sullivan, 1896: 'form ever follows function, and this is the law'. By this Sullivan means the function a structural component serves in a building, not the use function which the 20th-century modernists took this 'law' to mean.
4 From Adolf Loos, *Ornament und Verbrechen*, 1908. 'Jeder ornament ist ein verbrechen'. According to Loos, style and form were not relevant to buildings in daily use such as dwelling-houses, shops and the like. The modern metropolis could not be represented by 'deceitful and symbolic' ornamentation as it was all about the shaping of space.

HAS ARCHITECTURE LOST ITS USE?
Florian Riegler

Has architecture lost its use? One might get the impression that it is at least subject to much greater demands than it can meet. When assuming that today hardly any buildings are constructed that are dedicated to *one* purpose only, one might be inclined to think that a logistic phenomenon is to be solved – resulting in maximum flexibility. The facts are as follows: Functional changes come about more rapidly – periods of dedication are shorter – and so greater flexibility is required at all levels, both by the user per se and by the entire lifestyle, and consequently by buildings too. When it is a matter of regarding flexibility as a logistic subject only in order to improve a location, more flexibility as a minor difference in a sea of equal projects may become a decisive marketing edge.
This is a fact that must not be neglected. However, it is probably not the commercial approach alone that causes us to reflect about our new responsibilities.

Where do the new requirements come from?

I should like to state: because we have learnt to handle new types of lifestyle and workstyle. We enjoy thinking about the use of things as a process. Something that cannot be foreseen – that things happen that we cannot imagine, not even based on the boldest scenarios.
We hate to live in patterns.
Whilst doing our work, we therefore constantly examine the extent to which architecture and town planning can still be an expression of our social conception of ourselves.
So many things are produced that bypass life.
- All this traditional town planning: where architectural decisions are only based on space as a morphological criterium, bereft of any realistic social background.
- This includes eternally static residential building concepts, based on petty bourgeois family patterns.
- But even the superimposed scientific character of town planning theory fails to yield a suitable planning tool.
- Or this whole 'author architecture' disaster, blossoming in the most bizarre fashion; I'm referring to those autistic loners rooted exclusively in the phenomenon of the extraordinary, thus providing completely incompatible projects. (See fig. 1)

Today we are dealing again with the subject of newly interpreted flexibility or the extent to which buildings can be ambivalent, which also implies that contradictions are included per se – up to the question of whether a building can be polyvalent, e.g. have more than one effectivity.
In Austria, flexibility and polyvalence will no doubt have a different meaning than in the Netherlands or in Switzerland, for instance, or in third-world countries. Is this a result of a fanciful lifestyle or a necessity?
What subjects are we dealing with that are urgent? Is accommodation for migrants a subject in Europe? Living as a transitory solution?
Or are we rather busying ourselves by launching new lifestyle products on the market, as we can assume with certainty that users will quickly abandon their accommodation and look for an adapted new one?

Who or what is flexible in this case, residents or accommodation? People are arranging their own lives. They do not need street space in front of their accommodation, a coffee bar around the corner – they are meeting in shopping malls and for that they may drive to the next part of town.
They need no park in front of their house – for doing their type of sports. They have long ago found and adopted a disused warehouse or a similar facility out of town.
And they do not rely on their children's school being around the corner, as they are selecting their schools

1 – Kunsthaus Graz. Photo: Riegler Riewe

2 – Europan 1, floor plan

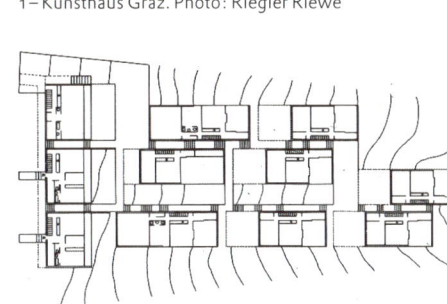

3 – Casa Nostra, residential properties

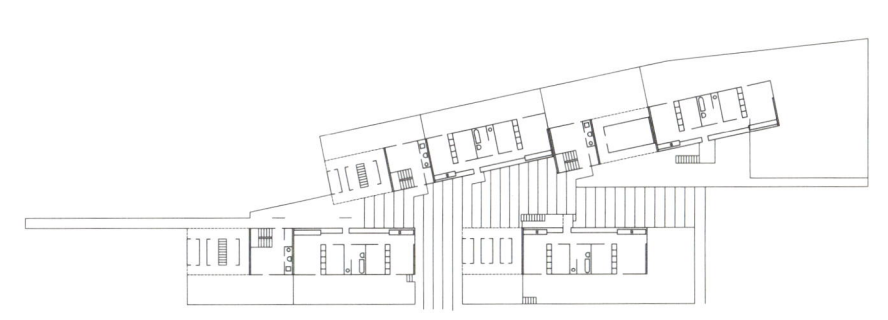

4 – Mautern, residential development

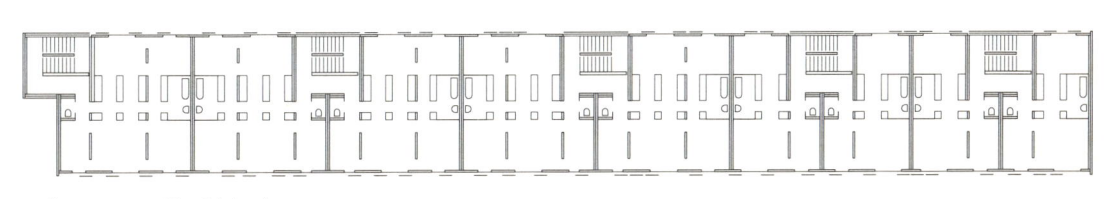

5 – Strassgang, residential development

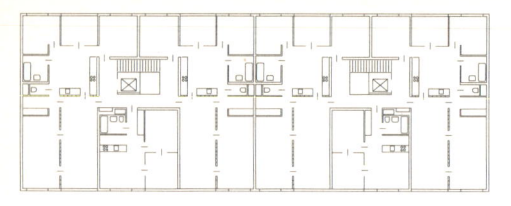

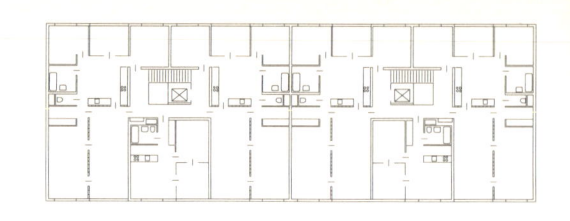

6 – Wienerberg City, Vienna, residential development

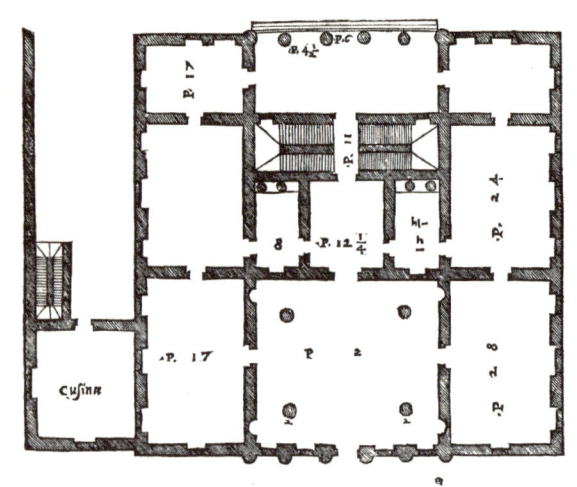

7 – Palazzo Antonini, a Palladian villa (1570) *L'architettura di Andrea Palladio*, secondo libro, p. 5

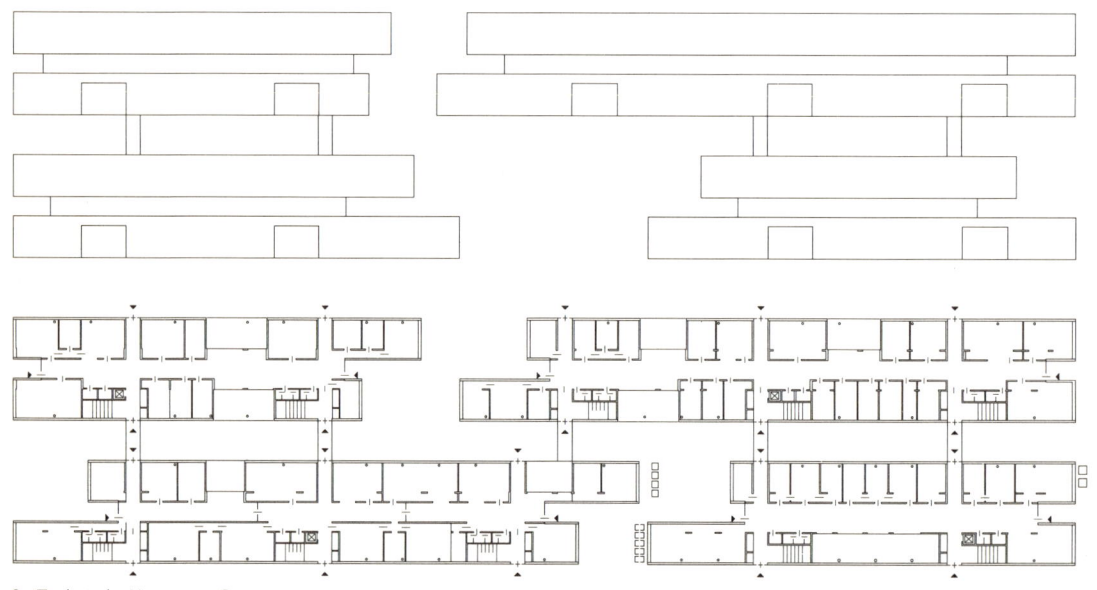

8 – Technische Universität Graz

54

by completely different criteria anyhow, e.g. what languages are offered, school fees, etc.
Today's city dwellers have a will of their own and certainly do not want to be led by the nose by town planners.
Last but not least they have accepted being personally and individually prepared to make decisions for anything – and to be capable of it.

■ **And how about planning our towns?**
No sooner has the character of an area or a region been discovered than we set to adapting and harmonizing it.
At the same time we produce more and more specific and specialized buildings.
In fact, we are more or less developing new typologies of dwelling and living, giving way to new lifestyles within a conventional family network or as a substitute for it.
For instance, we are developing new concepts for communal living, for young and old, e.g. specific target groups.
One particular example is long-term therapeutic accommodation for substance abusers funded by the national health system.
In addition, we wrap specific school programmes in appropriate space concepts.
The more we, the planners, are adapting to it, the question increasingly arises of whether these new typologies will still be useful for any other purpose.

■ **Where are the spaces that are interpretable and not specified?**
The following examples will give you an impression:

▌ Europan 1
By lateral positioning of an infrastructural block, including a 17 m deep base in the centre, innumerable variations for use may be generated (according to a report by the jury covering 40 variations). (See fig. 2)

▌ Casa Nostra residential properties
In this case, too, the principle of a sanitary installations block, attached centrally and laterally, has been applied and combined with two living spaces of absolutely identical dimensions on the ground and first floors.
This suggests uses that depend on the season: in summer preferably on the ground floor and in winter on the first floor. (See fig. 3)

▌ Mautern residential development
A passage 2 m wide, including a shelf in front of a window, connects the kitchen to a living room, each positioned at the opposite ends of the apartment.
A passage, which is too wide to just be a passage and too narrow to be a living space, challenging its users to use it according to their very personal tastes. (See fig. 4)

▌ Strassgang, Graz (Austria) residential development
The starting point of the concept was a small room of approx. 8 m² at the entrance, suitable for combining with another room.
As a consequence, the use of this small space unit determines the entire apartment. (See fig. 5)

▌ Wienerberg City, Vienna, residential development
In this case, a deep loggia forming an open connection to the staircase, is sited in front of the living room.
An option for a still unknown user taking possession. (See fig. 6)

▌ Plan of Palazzo Antonini, a Palladian villa
Additive space units arranged in succession and radially, a great challenge to the user.
Did the introduction of a passage in the plan really offer benefits alone? (See fig. 7)

If we do not manage these, we fall victim to a new error, although we have only just admitted to an old one, e.g. the error of the 1970s, where we assumed that flexibility would be feasible by pushing walls etc about – although it had never been assumed in this manner.

I claim the following to be true:

The perspectives remain open, irrespective of newly created qualities. Uses of buildings are only adapted slowly, irrespective of sophisticated conditioning, sensitive dimensioning and other cleverly set incentives for changes and in small areas only.

In general, major changes are dictated by efficiency. In this case, the rule is: flexibility is demanded of the user. He will have to vacate and change his apartment, his job or whatever else.

In regions where land prices are high, demolition will very soon be on the agenda, where development could provide additional arguments for a general increase in value, e.g. in the sense of gentrification. Or should it be regarded as incorrect to define the term of polyvalence by use alone?

In the town planning sense, for instance, a railway station must be regarded as a space intervention. Is it to be evaluated by volume?

Should it be regarded as an atmospheric intervention – a specific location in town?

Does it stand as a symbol for travel, a monument or landmark?

Or is it to be regarded as a mere system of passages and spaces for boarding or changing trains as another form of mobility? Without weighting entrances and exits, a uniform network of movement patterns, a matrix for eternally static functions?

Innsbruck station is changing consciously in both directions. In this sense, Innsbruck is polyvalent. Innsbruck station is in the town centre, on a rectangular square, a traffic square – the course of events in front of the station is always the same. A space of passage, like the station itself – where people remain anonymous. Even after redesign, the square and the station remain a sort of non-location, by offering a widespread system of travel when coming in from the town. As in any other station, passengers on arrival are guided into town through passages underneath the station platforms.

Access in either direction is feasible on two levels – from the underground parking deck and from the square, without any weighting, and via two tunnels, each connected uniformly to the platforms at the end of the hall, with a hierarchic order only being suggested.

Consequently, the station, being part of the city's infrastructure, can be understood as a structured network of traffic connections.

Due to increased action in the square and inside the building, it remains defined as a location, but due to major alterations is the opposite of the traditional image of a railway station.

The TU Graz (Technical University) project may be perceived as a system of axes and paths, identical room sections and room sequences – but also as a three-storey building in a heterogeneous peripheral suburban location. (See fig. 8)

What becomes of it and how it is presented will be very much dependent on the user.

Within the context of its surrounding, contours are clearly defined, thus generating the effect of a global system like a monolithic building, although it is organized like an open campus, becoming an interface in its environment.

The project is a continuous system of paths (a grid structure) and open spaces inside and outside. A changeable matrix of spaces is our reaction to the actual requirements of individual faculties. During the design phase, it was, of course, continuously modified. Buildings comprise two blocks each with a void between them. Offices are located in areas facing south. Seminar rooms, libraries and students' work rooms are facing north. The length of the building is defined by an establishment located on the top floor.

Establishments below it extend over the specified length and are provided with a recessed volume, ac-

cording to the programme, forming an orthogonal space structure with the central tract.
In this context, I would like to quote a description by Eva Meyer-Herrmann of a project by Carl Andre:

'... so indefinite are the manifold options of imagination to remain in one landscape.
'You may go from here to there, visit a locality in order to perceive it, add or omit other locations. Or simply skip a location.
'But these options are never a cause for randomness. Once a decision has been made, the location becomes the centre point, allowing you to find your bearings from there and shortly after, the whole situation may have completely changed again.'[1]

Which does not mean that individual components are exchangeable – they are accurately fixed, precisely defined. Components have no compositional centre of gravity – a structure without a hierarchy.

Lastly, there is a project that demonstrates beautifully how little is needed in order to mobilize the latent polyvalence of a space. A project where we had to make do without any architectural means, as they were not needed. But where social relevance was achieved, at least temporarily.

Brief: an invitation to design an intervention on the Placa des Angels in Barcelona, directly facing the Museum for Contemporary Art (Museum d'Art Contemporani) in the medieval part of town (Raval), part of a project of four museums designed by four different architects:
MOMA, New York
Wexner Center, Columbus, Ohio
MOMA, San Francisco
Museum d'Art Contemporani, Barcelona

- the Placa des Angels has never been a square
- it only resulted after construction of the museum by the partial demolition and
- widening of the street – none of the adjoining properties has been made for the square (no design continuity, no size ratios, and no social structure)

Our proposal: an outline, a broken line, placed on all building facades at a continuous level, surrounds the open space. The line generates a request to read different buildings and their social importance and to include them in the square.
In addition to the intervention by W. Maas, there is an additional use for sports. The size of the sports areas discloses and allows us to perceive the space dimension – although the social aspect of the intervention is more important. An ensemble of different facets is manifested as a space and urban unit, a 'public space', where spontaneous use and interpretations are feasible, very much like those situations used by Bas Princen – a well-known figure in the Netherlands – as the contents of his work.
Situations defined by confident towns, which are not predefined.
Perhaps in the future, our towns will be judged and assessed by the presence of such options.

1 Eva Meyer-Hermann (ed.), *Carl Andre, Sculptor 1996*, Stuttgart: Oktagon Verlag, 1996 (German issue), p. 13.

FLEX-BUILDINGS, DESIGNED TO RESPOND TO CHANGE

René Heijne and Jacques Vink

Through our studies into flexibility and our work as architects we developed a number of design insights which are summarized below headed by a relevant key term. It should be stressed that these are not hard-and-fast conclusions but more in the region of statements and reminders for those involved with flexible buildings.

Many of these design insights we found studying the Groothandelsgebouw in Rotterdam. A city in itself, this building has fascinated us since the day we started studying architecture. Cars driving in via ramps over several floors, a building with roof terraces, a supermarket and a cinema. It reminded us of worlds yet to come. But most of all we like the Groothandelsgebouw because it is one of the most successful flexible buildings we know. It inspired us with the design of our own flexible buildings or 'flex-buildings' as we started to call them.

■ Our definition of flexibility[1]

Flex-buildings are buildings which are literally designed to respond to change. A flex-building must be able to accept different fit-outs and its users must be able to easily adapt their surroundings. Flexibility in a building is its capacity to undergo modifications and accept changes of function with limited structural interventions. More than 40% of the activities housed in a flex-building can continue to function during modification. Because changes do not mean a large-scale renovation, flex-buildings are sustainable.

■ Why is flexibility important?

Our living and working environment is subject to increasingly frequent change. Unlike in the past, buildings will easily change a few times within a single lifetime. The cycle of building and demolishing has become visible for everyone, as is the influence of fashion on buildings. Functions merge and the role of the car is getting more and more important. These trends demand new forms of living/working spaces and buildings which deal with changes of function in a flexible way.

■ Groothandelsgebouw, Rotterdam

The Groothandelsgebouw in Rotterdam is an interesting example of a flex-building (see fig. 1). It is a constant source of inspiration for many architects in the Netherlands. Due to the bombing of Rotterdam in the Second World War most of the merchants and traders lost their commercial spaces. After the bombing, but before the end of the war, they had already decided to work together to create one big new building for trade and commerce in the new city centre of Rotterdam. This 120,000 m² building is the enduring symbol of Rotterdam's resurrection. It was designed by Maaskant and Van Tijen and opened its doors in 1953.[2]

The commercial spaces are organized around three courts. On the lower levels lorries can deliver goods. The roads are stacked on three levels with a total length of 1.5 km; 40% of all the commercial spaces are directly accessible by car and lorry. Five vertical circulation cores and a double horizontal corridor system provide guaranteed accessibility to all levels. Oversized corridors were easily accessible by fork-lift truck; fork-lift trucks were considered by Maaskant to be a revolution on the scale of the conveyor belt. The flexible nature of the building's spatial organization had specific consequences for its design: behind every window in the Groothandelsgebouw one could expect a workshop, or a warehouse, or a showroom, or an office to be realized. The window would have to be suitable for all these different spaces, as the use of different window types was unrealizable. Not only its size but also its constant state of change and its clearly defined image makes this building unique within the modern architecture of the Netherlands. At the moment the building is undergoing a major renovation while the majority of its companies continue to function.

Design insights
Cycles

Buildings aren't just buildings. They can be divided up into seven system-based layers, as illustrated in the diagram on p. 61. Each of these has its own lifespan, all the way from centuries down to a couple of years.

Diagram

To realize a flex-building one has to bear these internal dynamics in mind. Flexibility can be greatly reduced when the different layers are combined. Take installations that are embedded deep in the structure of the building; in order to change these, the building would have to be gutted. In the high-tech Centre Pompidou in Paris designed by Piano and Rogers in 1977 the installations are all placed on the outside in order to create the most flexible spaces possible. In any case the installations can be reached very easily. In our view one layer is to be added to the diagrams as proposed by Francis Duffy[3] and Stewart Brand.[4] The circulation system within a building is crucial to the future possibilities.[5]

Timelines

The thicknesses of the lines within the diagram are an indication of the time the system-based layers are meant to last. The structure in many buildings is long-lasting and therefore indicated by a fat line. The furniture is indicated by a thin line because it's just there for the time it's needed. However for each building the configuration of lines differs. In movable buildings for example, the location, normally permanent and therefore very fat, will be indicated as a very thin line. The thicker lines together form the frame and the thinner lines are what is called the generic part of the building.

Integration

It can be advantageous financially to integrate and combine layers in a building – such as the construction and the frontage in a load-bearing facade. This can be extremely impracticable however where flexibility is concerned. Necessary changes can lead to the building being demolished prematurely.

Drive-in

Access as mentioned in the diagram (see fig. 2) does not only apply to accessibility on foot, but also to accessibility by car. The usability of higher floors in a building will increase when cars have access to those higher areas. It enables the establishment of functions that would otherwise be restricted to the ground floor.

Prisma 1, Bleiswijk (mixed-use building)

Prisma 1 is not only an example of intensive land use but also an illustration of the importance of the circulation system within a building. In boomtown Zoetermeer near The Hague, at the intersection of the A12 motorway from The Hague to Utrecht and the high speed railway line to Paris, a new industrial estate has been planned. Large infrastructure dominates this site. The main topic is intensive land use. In ordinary industrial areas in the Netherlands the ratio between site (lot) and brief is about 0.5. In this new industrial estate the value known as FSI, 'Floor Space Index', should be no less than 1.0.

Another important aspect is that the future building stands on Zoetermeerselaan, an avenue which will have a public quality and will be car orientated. Since the programme was not clearly defined but a large number of parking spaces had to be built, we proposed a building which could contain a variety of programmes. The drive-in helix would make all of these programmes accessible for cars. The shifted section would reveal the stacking of programmatic form on the side to Zoetermeerselaan. (See fig. 3) This may sound complicated but actually the plans are very simple, also due to the limited budget. A structural grid of 14.4 metres allows for many programmes to be incorporated. The architecture is inspired by the motorway and drive-in culture – that is why we used lamp-posts, railings, billboards, metal cladding. The big logo 'PRISMA 1' is orientated towards Zoetermeer, marking the entrance to the industrial estate and functioning as a billboard pointed towards the motorway. (See fig. 4)

■ **Friction vacancy**
In mixed-use commercial buildings renters come and go. Each removal brings a certain friction with it. In the Groothandelsgebouw for example, three to five per cent of the office spaces are usually vacant. Easily adaptable interiors can reduce friction vacancy, but it will always be there. Vacancy is something you have to plan.

■ **Nodes**
The developments at nodes in the personal transport network are dynamic and difficult to predict. Flex-buildings are able to take up these changes. The Groothandelsgebouw, sitting next to the central railway station in Rotterdam, was able to absorb the many changes this area has undergone.

■ **Shrinkage**
Building flexibly is not just about growing but also about getting smaller.

▌ Master plan for the university campus in Wyong, Sydney, Australia

This master plan for a university campus in Wyong, Australia anticipates shrinkage. The internet enables education to reach the most inaccessible areas. For the moment a relatively large complex is still required but in the future the university will be able to manage with far fewer buildings.

The university consists of two types of buildings:
• lightweight structures that can easily be moved and serve to house some 2500 students;
• heavier and thus more durable working buildings situated in the centre of the site.

We combined these with the public facilities (conference centre, library, theatre). If in the future the university disappears, these buildings can be integrated in the communities of Warnerville and Wyong. The originally virgin wetland area is left behind with a minimum footprint. (See fig. 5)

■ **Dilemma**
Buildings should be able to change quickly to keep abreast of the city's growth. At the same time there is an urgent need for buildings that act as enduring landmarks in the city. Flex-buildings have an answer to this dilemma. They don't have to be demolished to keep up with changing demands.

■ **Cultural durability**
Cultural durability[6] is the public resistance against demolition. Cultural durability can make a flex-building in good working order a major success, but it can also obstruct change, say if there is resistance to demolishing a poorly functioning building.

■ **Spontaneous**
Sometimes buildings are flexible without this being calculated beforehand. Many warehouses are able to accommodate different kinds of uses through the sturdiness of their architecture.

▌ Scouting club, Reeuwijk near Gouda

Farms and stables have also proved suitable for many

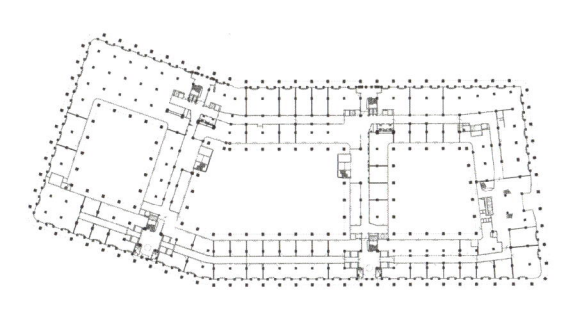

1 – Typical floor plan: three courts and five vertical cores – the Groothandelsgebouw in 1953

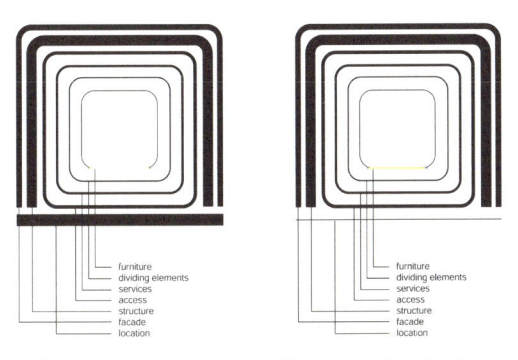

2 – Diagram showing system-based layers including circulation diagram of a movable building

3 – Shifted building section, drive-in helix

4 – Drive-in!, balcony overlooking Zoetermeerselaan

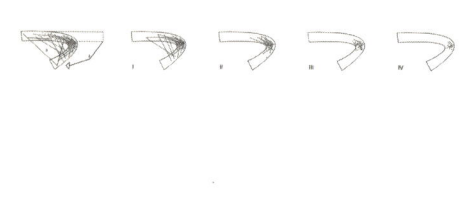

5 – Shrinking in time; lightweight and durable buildings in the wetlands

6 – Matrix as a design tool, facade facing square

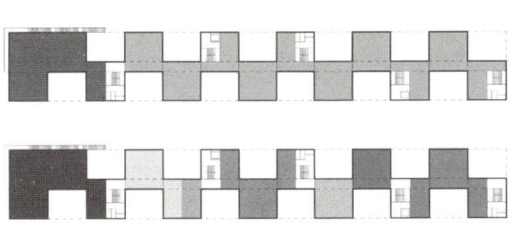

7 – Oversized circulation allows different plan layouts

8 – Closed shutters in street facade during daytime, transparent at night

63

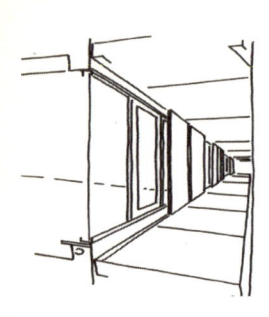

9 – Diagram of a double facade; detail of double facade

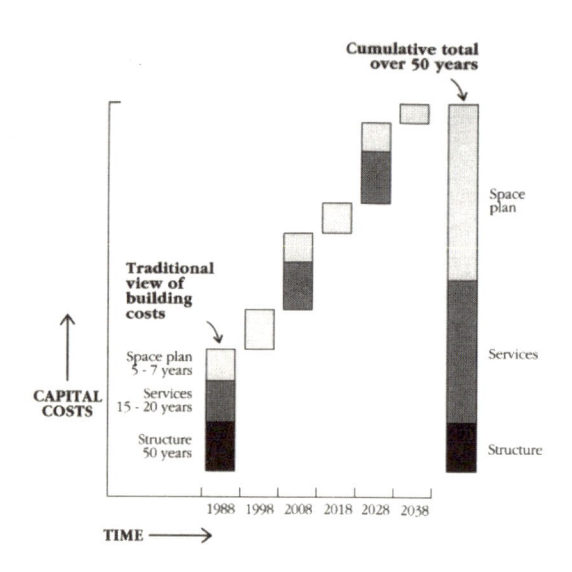

10 – Diagram showing costs in time.[7]

64

kinds of use. The modern modular construction used for the agricultural industry seems to have saved the day for a scouting club (Cornelis de Houtmangroep) in Reeuwijk near Gouda. Although it didn't have enough money for a new clubhouse, it did have enough enthusiastic and practically-minded members. So the club commissioned a construction company to erect an inexpensive and roomy stable that its members could fill in themselves.

■ Designing
Many architects (certainly Dutch ones) have been trained along functionalist lines. Functional design assumes buildings with a clearly described brief. In flexible buildings however both the future use and its users are largely unknown.

■ An observation
Building regulations are not geared to buildings developed without a pre-established programme. Thinking in terms of function begins with the land use plan. Land use plans in the Netherlands define the functions of future buildings. Flex-buildings, without predetermined functions, don't fit in.

■ Time horizon
A time horizon is the span of time assumed in a design brief: 20 years means making other decisions than when the horizon is 200 years. It's not just about what a design should do but also for how long.

Ice-chapel
There are specialized architects and engineers who are exclusively concerned with ice and snow constructions. For example the Finnish architect Kino Kuismanen and engineer Seppo Makinen are the founders of 'Snowhow Ltd.'. They strive to make designs of snow and ice that make optimal use of the special qualities of this short-lived building material.

Even in the cold north of Sweden ice has a limited life span. Every year in Jukkajarvi a hotel, a chapel and exhibition spaces will melt away in the sun.

■ Bandwidth
A flex-building need not necessarily be able to take up every possible function. 'Functional bandwidth' is a current term: which functions are involved? You don't always need flexibility.

Student housing, Wageningen
Define the bandwidth of the brief together with your client; which uses can be expected and which uses are unlikely to be expected? Matrices can help! You can use this tool to accommodate the process of defining the bandwidth. It shows the client the potential new functions (bandwidth) combined with the technical demands (floor loads, sound insulation, daylight requirements etc). From the matrix the client can choose the degree of flexibility and investment. (See fig. 6)

Facade: just like the Groothandelsgebouw we have tried to create with simple means an interesting image: single glazing at the external spaces and staircase and double in front of the rooms, so that a box-within-a-box appears. This student accommodation in Wageningen was designed to be able to change in the future. Not everything is possible however. The construction is such as to accept hybrid forms of dwelling and working. But you can't park on the roof! The structure includes reserved space, and once again 'oversize gets the prize'!

■ Not everything
The flex-building concept suggests an opposite pole: a building made to measure. Not all functions are suitable for inclusion in a flex-building. A printing works for instance, with enormous floor loads, is better off with a building made to measure.

▪ Oversize

By deliberately incorporating excessive space and construction a building has the necessary leeway to accommodate future developments. A building's flexibility is enhanced by overmeasure in structure as well as space.

> North West Building (mixed-use building, 1998), architect Tjeerd de Jong

Lorries and container ships were models for this building in the North-West industrial estate in Rotterdam. Not only for their formal qualities, but because the building should function literally as a collection point for lorries. The lower level contains various provisions such as a large transport café/restaurant, a bank, a post office and shops.

By oversizing the vertical circulation different layouts of a floor plan are possible, with one or several clients per floor. The offices in the upper level can be filled and linked in different ways. (See fig. 7)

▪ Architectural expression

The facade design figures prominently in designing flexible buildings. It makes special demands on the design's presentation during the design process, as the building can assume different appearances over time. Avoid anonymity; design a building with a facade that gives the building a clear identity.

> Twin houses, Amsterdam

In the evening when the lights go on inside, the facades of these twin houses on Borneo-eiland in Amsterdam become transparent. During the day, the position of the hatches makes for a changing image. The cladding of the facade with Robinia hardwood also changes in time: yellowish when applied, silver when the patina process has finished. (See fig. 8)

▪ Compartments

For large buildings erected in stages it is handy to work with compartments. Parts that are finished combine as one large complex. They can always be recast as individuals at a later date.

> De Nieuwe Veiling, Hoorn (mixed-use building, see also Part Two of this book, p. 208)

For large buildings erected in stages it is handy to work with compartments. Parts that are finished combine as one large complex. They can always be recast as individuals at a later date.

In Hoorn, a small town on IJsselmeer 50 kilometres north of Amsterdam, we had to deal with this problem. For the municipality we designed a service building on four different lots in an old industrial estate in decline, one owned by the municipality, the other three by private companies. Since it was unclear when and where these lots could be built we had to phase the design in different compartments. The column grid was defined by the need to park in or under the building.

▪ Double facade

The double facade is a promising concept that allows for expressive and/or open facades in flexible buildings. It can also help to reduce a building's energy consumption.

> De Nieuwe Veiling, Hoorn (mixed-use building, see p. 208)

This mixed-use building in Hoorn sports a double facade. This renders the activities inside the building visible in the exterior. The facade works as a display window in which each of the companies can present itself. (See fig. 9)

▪ Active management

Flex-buildings require active management. Besides the day-to-day business of upkeep and repair, there needs to be a policy for the building's fit-out. This includes deciding which users and uses are desirable and in which proportions, and fixing the requirements for user representation in the facade.

De Nieuwe Veiling, Hoorn (mixed-use building)

Lots of different sorts of people work in and visit large buildings: white collar workers/businessmen and blue collar workers can be separated. The building management can stimulate companies to stick together; synergy can emerge. In a flex-building different functions can profit from their proximity, for instance they can share the garage, the reception area or the canteen. Energy management and waste processing are also synchronized. The plants in the garden centre flourish with the excess heat from the offices. Furthermore building advertisement zones were anticipated in the facades.

Costs

A flexible building is no more expensive than a conventional building. It depends on how you look at it. Calculations where savings on future renovations are compared to the higher starting costs, show us that a flex-building will in the long term easily earn this initial investment back.

During a period of 50 years the installations of a building will be modified twice on average. The interior will change on average five times. The structure will remain unchanged. If we add up all the costs we find that the original investment in the structure is low. (See fig. 10)

Conclusion

It takes more than building technology to successfully realize flex-buildings. Aspects of use and management are at least as important. Besides, it requires designers who are willing to let go of their design. For the result is not a completed 'architectural' product but a continually changing object.

About RUIMTELAB

The RUIMTELAB architectural practice is a laboratory for flexibility where the architects René Heijne and Jacques Vink liaise with a network of experts. Our stepping-off point is that you can only achieve ground-breaking projects through a combination of research and design. RUIMTELAB has carried out studies commissioned by the Dutch government into buildings that can be easily modified: flex-buildings. We research in order to bring the design to a higher level. Our aim is to share knowledge of research and construction with other designers. So our research is clearly different from academic research.

At the time of going to press, RUIMTELAB is working on designs for soon-to-be-built flexible buildings.

1 Heijne H.P., Vink J.A. (2001). *Flexgebouwen*. Rotterdam, RGD.
2 Provoost M. (2003). *Hugh Maaskant*. Rotterdam, 010 Publishers.
3 Duffy, F. (1997). *The New Office*. London, Coran Octopus.
4 Brand, S. (1994). *How Buildings Learn: What Happens After They're Built*. New York, Viking Penguin.
5 Leupen, B. (2002). *Kader en generieke ruimte*. Rotterdam, 010 Publishers.
6 Bekaert, G. (2000). *A.W.G. bOb Van Reeth architects*, Ghent, Ludion. See also p. 110-115 in this book.
7 Duffy, F., Henney A. (1989). *The Changing City*. London, Bullstrode.

DYNAMIC TIME, INFORMAL ORDER, INTERDISCIPLINARY TRAJECTORIES
SPACE-TIME-INFORMATION AND NEW ARCHITECTURE
Manuel Gausa

For a long time we have been defending a reading of the production of current architecture based not only on disciplinary reference, professional practice or the mere succession of events, but on a 'transversal' view of the contemporary scene[1], making it possible to relate the definition and organization of the habitat and the environment (ultimate essence of architecture) to the proper interpretation – scientific, social, philosophical and artistic – of space, time and its associates.

This approximation is not especially new. It relates to similar attempts aimed at connecting the ('local') critical diffusion of the facts – the technical or artistic creation – with a proper ('global') cultural understanding of reality.

'Knowing the nature of things in order to act upon them'[2]

This is a 'holistic' vocation that traverses the recent history of critique, from Veyne to Virilio; from Kübler to Jencks. Yet perhaps it has been the paradigmatic *Space, Time and Architecture*, written by Sigfried Giedion in 1941, which has best reflected in its time the will for interaction within architecture, art and science. When Giedion published his book in 1943[3], it had been only 36 years since Albert Einstein proclaimed his famous Theory of Relativity that was to exert so much influence on our understanding of the universe. On its own the term 'space-time' used by Giedion assumed voluntary scientific resonances that implicitly suggested the correlation between the new aesthetic experimentations and the new scientific theories about relativity.[4] These theories had done away with the Aristotelian (and with it, the Newtonian) conception of time as essential, metaphysical – separated from space – to end up with new ones definitely involving both concepts: from then on, the measurement of time depended on the position of the observer in space and therefore on the relative movement.[5]

The compact idea of a continuum universe, hierarchical and absolute, was substituted for the fragmented idea of discontinuous experiences in 'relative positions' that had left their mark on a great part of the modern movement and our later tradition and interpretation of space.

With great skill, Ignasi de Solà-Morales notes[6] the comfortable analogy between Einsteinian space-time and the analytical cubism or 'post-cubism' of l'Esprit Nouveau where 'more traditional terms such as order, geometry and composition, recaptured the roll of tools facilitating the understanding of the new architecture', which the first analysts of modern architecture had already put forth. This led to the substitution of the classical 'absolute' order – continuous, homogeneous, compact and determinist – for a new one, more relative and discontinuous but not less convinced of the strict (rational) control of form and results.[7] The Einsteinian vision of the universe essentially underlay this vision of 'determinist' control. Einstein himself had never accepted a universe governed by chaos or chance – 'God does not play dice' – but rather a universe ordered by generalizing rules that imply the predictability of the results.[8] We could say, though, that the modern concept of space – that is, the relativist attitude towards space – meant the transition of the hierarchical idea of *composition* to the more free idea of *position*, but the latter still continued to underpin itself in the stable and coherent definition of some prefigured results based on the strength of vertical vectors (volumes) and their precise (exact) organization on the horizontal plan. The horizontal and vertical planes as elementary ('rationalist') Cartesian geometries had to transform themselves into the basic mechanisms of a fragmented spatial conception, but still related to strict prefiguring definitions.

Giedion himself wrote: 'Volumes are those that engender space. Today architects should constantly confront the task of arranging volumes in diverse heights in reciprocal correspondence. The new history starts with the optical revolution that abolished the hierarchical perspective with only one point of view. Today we are able to perceive the energy of volumes freely situated in space and without any relation to perspective …'[9]

■ Dynamic systems – <in> properties

We are still using the remains of this modern conception of architecture – positional, Euclidean and linear – in the same way that we use ancient scientific laws such as gravity and even relativity, still 'functional' to a great extent, though hardly operative when measured against the complexity of phenomena that we now know define our surroundings.

As put forward by mathematician Peter Saunders, physicists themselves do not believe anymore in that eternal universe, solid and exact, which yielded so much support to the determinist paradigm. Today, he continues, a dynamic universe has been suggested in its place, where space and time depend, indeed, of the observer and where the majority of all properties only exist in an uncertain way, hardly predeterminable.[10]

The Newtonian paradigm, and a large share of the Einsteinian one, now faces the challenge of a 'squirmy' universe in which the majority of the processes, including those of more apparent stability, are extraordinarily undisciplined and end up displaying non-linear behaviour, a product of its own interactive and dynamic character. In such processes, the (global) position in space should combine with the impact of the (local) information that every 'particular' situation (or moment) contributes to the whole. This information affects the whole considerably, continually modifying its trajectories. The global system varies when varying – and accumulating – the received local information. The study of the dynamic systems, related to chaos theory and quantum mechanics, has shown a progressive development in the last 50 years thanks to the recent technological capacity to simulate (and calculate) by computational methods trajectories of uncertain and complex geometry[11]; it has also unveiled the evidence of the 'uncertainty principle' which governs our universe, representing another step towards an understanding of it beyond the theory of relativity.[12] Although there is not yet a whole theory on this matter, we know today, as Stephen Hawking notes 'the principle of uncertainty – related to the interactivity and the dynamic character of quantum information – has already profoundly affected our contemporary view of the world, and in spite of the fact that more than fifty years after their exposition, these theories still have not been totally appreciated by philosophers and creators, its setting out has meant in any case, the end of the determinist dream that was introduced in the 18th century, the Age of Reason, by Laplace and Newton, subsequently evolving until Einstein.'

Quantum mechanics and the chaos theory introduce an 'inevitable element of randomness in science'; indeed, they do not suggest precise and invariable (unique) results but announce only possible 'protocols': systems and combinations of results, as well as the probability of their generation, depending on tactical processed information.[13]

Here we could say that classical space and modern 'space-time' was followed by an 'informational (interactive) space-time' causing more instability and indetermination in our understanding of the universe but, at the same time, allowing the permanent introduction of the influence of information (diversified and abstract, individual and global, contradictory and combinable), as well as its undisciplined effects upon the dynamic manifestation of processes.

Our universe, our cities, our behaviour, even our time, respond largely to dynamic, non-linear processes.[14] However, architecture continues relying on models based on rigid, pre-established, implicitly unchangeable and permanent structures: pure, strict and indisputable.

In some of his recent writings Cecil Balmond has noted on more than one occasion the situation of separation and disharmony between new science and 'old' architecture. How to relate architecture – as defined on the basis of fixed forms and static structures – to the current investigations on dynamic systems? he asks. How to achieve a translation from the new science to a new architecture? Due to the Cartesian tradition we divide a priori space into compartments according to strict vertical and horizontal lines. Our projects reinvent the topography of rigid skeletons, right angles and of an order understood as rigorous delineation.

But in the irregular rhythms and in the diversity we see around us, he continues, reality is more unpredictable and rich in situations. Chaos manifests itself as a succession of diverse orders, rather different from that traditional idea we call 'order'. Is this a new order that is neither 'informal' nor forcibly random and arbitrary, based on a 'series' of certitudes, as well as changing and surreptitious information? Informally there are no established rules or fixed patterns suitable for indiscriminate copying, but only a rhythm of inferred relations and interconnections among events.'[15]

Our challenge nowadays as architects is to produce new mechanisms of action, responding to the stimuli of a global 'new' order in a constant state of excitation. An order sensitive to the dynamic (interactive) processes that define our understanding of the contemporary universe – and of time. Indeed, complex processes, defined by what we shall here call the <in> factor associated with: a high degree of information, the **in**certidumbre (uncertainty) principle; **in**determinateness, **in**stability and **in**coherence; **in**frastructural property; **in**manencia (immanence), **in**termittence and **in**teractivity; vocation for **in**completeness; **in**finitude; and above all, as Balmond himself notes, a tendency towards the '**in**formality' directly associated with its apparent '**in**discipline'.

Routine and disciplinal convention favours indeed the use of repetitive laws – continuous and foreseeable – like traditional forms of action. These tend to refer to linear processes, based on stable trajectories, fixed and balanced **(com)**positions.

Their trajectories show indeed multiple fluctuating and/or combinatory movements – 'latent states', diverse and possible – which yield to precarious situations of equilibrium. They are movements which generally speaking, although they tend to seek support in generic schemes that show a greater or lesser degree of prediction and recurrence ('certitude isles'), trace surprisingly 'spontaneous' and by definition increasingly free trajectories: 'while the linear systems have almost always only one point of equilibrium, the non-linear systems have more than one state of equilibrium which includes bifurcation points, as well as transmissions from a stable trajectory towards another one, causing great changes at brief intervals'.[16] These speak of a topology of tracing, based on the movement and interaction of the particles – on the strength of individual information – that includes its own (positive) alteration of the initial schemes and therefore a higher versatility with regard to what is contingent, the 'exterior'.

The traditional idea of order that marked the classical interpretation of space (based on the idea of composition as a hierarchical relation, but also as a cohesive, closed figuration, predictable among the parts)[17], had been impugned by the modern ideology, expounding an alternative 'new order' associated with a relativistic interpretation of space and time (based on the spatial position as a freer connection, but not less strict for this reason – measurable – among the objects). Position as organization but also as an inalterable, sharpening principle (in tune with the proper 'ideological' – dogmatic – moment of modern time-space).

The contemporary change of paradigms, and the new idea of time associated with it, brings about a new unprejudiced and 'informal' order based on dispositions, open to diversity and individuality. Disposi-

Beach

Tornado 1

Tornado 2

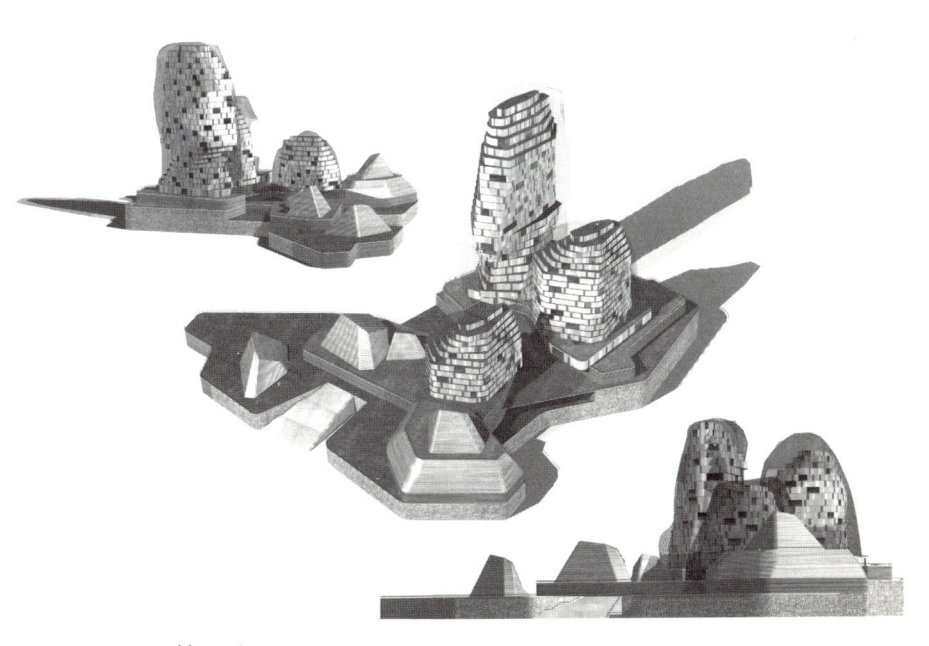

71 Mountains

Swimming pool

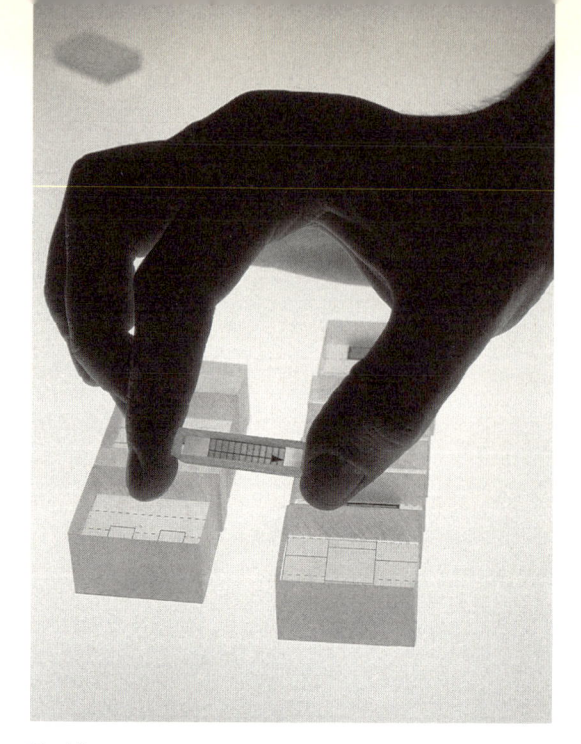

The Mhouse

Housing in Ceuta

72

tions as combinations but also as tactical decisions, produced from a processed reading, deliberate and flexible, of variable information able to bring about multiple and heterogeneous events.
Decisions rather than design.
Criteria rather than figuration.
Operative, but at the same time infrastructural criteria more than figured (or prefigured) answers.
Versatile systems rather than spotless compositions.
During this century we have seen the transition from the classical notion of time and space: continuous, solid, absolute, static, exact and regulated but also eternal, symbolic, metaphysical and ritual (based on the 'harmonic' aesthetics of evocation) to a modern 'space-time': discontinuous, fractured, relative, precise but also rigid, inalterable and mechanical (as derived from the functional and machinist rigour, severe, technical, typological, precise).
The contemporary 'space/time' nevertheless presents itself as a progressively unprejudiced landscape, mutable and – as it has been said – informal; subject to the strength of the individual and the contingent, of the heterogeneous as much as the diverse but also of the infrastructural. A 'space-time' of interconnected and interactive messages possessing a new dimensional vector in information. A 'space-time-information', combinatory, 'open' and differential; probable rather than regulated, precise or exact; tactile and digital rather than evocative (ritual) or mechanical; opportunist rather than symbolic or dogmatic; mutable rather than eternal or positioned.

If the concept of modern space in its time meant the transition from the idea of composition, as regulation (of the position), as co-relation, the concept of contemporary space means, today, the transition from the idea of position to the idea of disposition – as a tactical decision, but also as a possible combination of information. From a predictable vision of the universe we first evolved to a measurable one; today we have arrived at a differential one.

From the acceptance of that odd situation of cohabitation, made of pacts and cross-breedings, today we are able to understand the culture of the contemporary project. Departing from a willingness for intervention, based on the acceptance of a hybrid contract (rather than on the imposition of a new – unique – totalizing order), with its own starting conditions that require us to apply selective criteria instead of pre-established models: flexible (dis)positions, able to process received information and 'mutate' with it. This is a hybrid, fluctuant and elastic situation that translates a new 'unforeseeable' order, defined from the premise of complex geometries of variable topology and freer and 'extroverted' forms.

■ **Spirals, curls, shining lights. Triptych of time**
We shall consider various approaches of this contemporary interpretation of space and time – in connection with the new understanding of the dynamic systems favoured by the new technologies – highlighting some potential in connection with the proper implicit notions of order, structure, geometry and growth, as well as with other more ambiguous notions, such as the past and the present – memory and history – or perception, occupation and appropriation. Approaches to be realized by means of some fundamental trajectories – spirals and rhizomes, intertwinements, curls, jumps or sparkles, enabling us to link the events with, just as in their own dynamic systems, a 'condensing generic movement' around certain recurrent diagrams or figures: 'odd attractors' of an habitually fractional geometry, allowing us to talk about an 'undetermined pseudo determinism'[18], associated with the <in> properties of that new 'space-time-information'.
By doing so, we shall stimulate the investigation of new approaches to the project: organizational systems, flexible and able to generate 'relational' structures that are more open, but also able to articulate the appearance of spaces of contradiction and incoherence.

Paradoxes

Unusual utterances as possible protocols associated with the local system but suddenly generating 'rebellious dynamics' in the meta-superior system – globally – thus **distorting its convention** when articulating apparent combinations (or absurd ones). Intrusive movements that destabilize the 'dynamics of routine' through proposing unexpected trajectories, combinations, etc.

We have written once[19] about the transgressive will of the contemporary project and its capacity for **putting forward and resolving new paradoxes in the system** through the proposition of 'alternative' solutions destined to knock down the orthodox codes (and secular ones) of the discipline by merging disparate concepts (up and down, exterior and interior, inside and outside, background and figure, private and public, etc) in new hybrid unions. These are *possible protocols* that are put forward at the same time '**in** the system and **outside** it' – 'they serve it and they destabilize it'[20] – while laying at the bottom of the 'undisciplined' definition itself of the dynamic systems, alluding to the flexible character of the form and order associated with them, as much as to its own (and implicit) possibility for transgression and alteration.

Paradoxes, operatives

1 'To be oneself and several others at the same time: to be case and class'.

The matter would be to access the **un**finished definition and the '**in**frastructural' character of the dynamic systems through the analysis of combinatory mechanisms, destined to bring about processes of spatial organization in which the final form manifests itself as the precise snapshot of an interrupted development (a form in a 'state of latency' – on 'standby' – able to be associated with incompleteness and infinitude, properties emblematic of all open systems). Mechanisms constructed through basic evolvable geometries (armatures, matrixes, tornados, rhizomatous meshes), capable, nevertheless, of embracing surreptitious information, and mutating along with them. Evolutive diagrams manifested through 'immanent structures' – although flexible when varying the scale and mutable in their development – accessible from the mathematical theory of fractals in which also globalism and fragment respond to open parameters such as 'clambering' and self similitude. The relationship with genetics as 'basic information' would be interesting and capable of provoking complex interactions, starting from elementary initial guidelines: 'configurations' of variable development from which serialization, interaction and internal displacement – or untwisting – permit a growth and a virtual mutation of form in combinatory 'spirals' proper of an 'open' time and definitely incomplete.

2 'The efficacious past is the transferred now'

Finally we shall look at that undisciplined – and apparently incoherent – characteristic of the dynamic systems applied to the ambiguous relations that can develop between memory and action: 'now' and 'then', history and actuality, past and present, no more as solid categories, stagnant, but as open and manageable coordinates, compressible or expandable in new unexpected combinations. Beyond a linear – static – reading of the events, I would defend a possible 'tactical' reading – free of prejudice – made of jumps, leaps, setbacks and twistings: a naughty and contemptuous game of associations and displacements in which the past always 're-encounters' the present and the present moves back to the past. The ancient behaviourist direction – chronological, hierarchical, purist and dogmatic – of the historiographic orthodox readings gives way to an operative view – tactical and activist – where dialogue does not imply reverence or respect for the past, but complicity between 'cultural echoes', like elements of tuned information, suddenly detecting each other and intertwining.

Trajectories in motion – not stagnant compartments – that allow strange associations between 'now' and 'then', no longer as 'anticipation' and 'actuality' but as search sequences, in resonance, in which even certain images of the past – why not? – could be seen as images of the present, abducted 'backwards'; witnesses of a 'remembered' action transported by the curls of a space-time of curved dimensions. History as a linear – and disciplined – trajectory of events giving way to a 'landscape of offers and possibilities' with changeable angles, unexpected tumbles and interpretations free of prejudice. Expressions of an entropy of a non-linear order that would imply a discontinuous idea of progress, based on thrown and caught folds, curls, tangles of 'messages': signals – light pulses – whose trip intersects our interests and reveals information until 'now' hidden and suddenly visible. For that reason, instead of talking about remembering, one should talk about reappearance, not of anticipation but of re-encounter.

1 'Helicoid' for some.
2 Guallart, Vincent, 'Vivienda en el l'mite e la ciudad' (Living on the limits of the city), in *Quaderns* no. 211.
3 Giedion, Sigfried, *Space Time and Architecture*, Harvard University Press, Cambridge, 1941.
4 Solà-Morales, Ignasi, 'La construcción de la historia de la arquitectura' (The construction of the history of architecture), in *Quaderns*, 181/182, April-Sept. 1989, pp. 192-207.
5 'Both Aristotle and Newton believed in absolute time. That is, they believed that one could unambiguously measure the interval of time between two events, and that this time would be the same whoever measured it, provided they used a good clock. Time was completely separate from and independent of space. That is what most people would take to be the commonsense view. However, we have had to change our ideas about space and time. Although our apparently commonsense notions work well when dealing with things like apples, or planets that travel comparatively slowly, they don't work at all for things moving at or near the speed of light.' Hawking, Stephen W., *A Brief History of Time*, Bantam Books, New York, 1988/1996.
6 Solà-Morales, Ignasi, op. cit.
7 'The concept of relativity, which came into being at the turn of the century in art and science simultaneously, implies that the coherence of things lies not in their subordination to a central, dominant principle but in their reciprocal relations. It states that reality has no inherent hierarchical structure, governed by a fixed centre. It repudiates an absolute frame of reference within which all things and events are relative, considering all frames of reference to be relative instead. But far from being a chaos of unrelated fragments this polycentric reality has a complex coherence in which things, though autonomous, are linked through purely reciprocal relations; a coherence in which these relations are as important as the things themselves.' Strauven, Francis, *Aldo van Eyck's Orphanage: A Modern Monument*, NAi Publishers, 1996.
8 'The whole history of science has been the gradual realization that events do not happen in an arbitrary manner, but that they reflect a certain underlying order, which may or may not be divinely inspired'. Hawking, Stephen W., op. cit.
9 Giedion, Sigfried, op. cit.
10 See Saunders, Peter, 'Nonlinearity: What is it and why it matters', in Di Cristina, Giuseppa (ed.), *Architecture and Science*, Wiley Academy, London, 2001.
11 'The so called linear systems behave in a very simple way: they are never chaotic, their trajectories are always foreseeable and their movements regular; up till the invention of the computer, around 1950, they were the only ones whose trajectories and movements could be studied. Science developed a natural interest in them and during four centuries we have seen the evolution of a universe of linear models from physics to economy. However, thanks to the development of informatics, numeric simulation has allowed us to reveal very different characteristics of the non-linear systems. Mathematical analysis has confirmed that. The theory of chaos has originated from that relationship between computerized instrument and mathematical analysis: the computer reveals to the mathematician phenomena to be studied and the mathematician demonstrates the limits of the computer…' Ekeland, Ivar, *Le Chaos*, Flammarion, Paris 1995.
12 Hawking, Stephen W., op. cit.
13 Ekeland, Ivar, op. cit.
14 Saunders, Peter, op. cit.
15 See Balmond, Cecil, 'New Structure and the Informal', in *Architectural Design*, vol. 67, 9-10, 1997, pp. 88-96.
16 See Saunders, Peter, op. cit.
17 'The conventions of classical architecture dictate not only the proportions of individual elements but also the relationship between individual elements. Parts form ensembles which in turn form larger wholes. Precise rules of axiality, symmetry or formal sequence govern the organisation of the whole. Classical architecture displays a wide variation on these rules, but the principle of hierarchical distribution of parts to whole is constant. Individual elements are maintained in hierarchical order by extensive geometric relationships to preserve overall unity.' Allen, Stan, 'Distributions, Combinations, Fields', in BAU, no. 014, 1997.
18 'The Chaos Theory has contributed by putting forward a pseudo-determinist model that leaves room for chance, as well as for the unpredictable, and the aleatory. The system is confined to more or less stable trajectories – odd attractors – but its movement escapes us. Its time T – 'characteristic' – also puts a limit to the capacity for prevention.' Ekeland, Ivar, op. cit.
19 Gausa, Manuel, *Arquitectura reactiva* no. 219, 1997.
20 The notion curl itself entails the notion of infinite growth; 'in spiral', an expression characteristic of all evolvable and open processes; yet it also implies the ambiguous notion of 'intertwining'. The curl is a Tangled Hierarchy, capable of causing the surprising conversion on itself (as in the celebrated Klein's Bottle) of several hierarchical levels – read here, for example, 'territory', 'city', 'landscape', 'building', etc. – violating its own initial hierarchical principle. In that way a surprising and disconcerting phenomenon arises, inciting 'propositions to end up talking about other superior propositions that in turn refer to the initial ones'. See Hofstadter, Douglas R., *Gödel, Escher, Bach: An Eternal Gold Braid*, Penguin Books, London, 1979.

FLEXIBILITY IN STRUCTURES
Walter Spangenberg

▪ Introduction
The time factor is a major influence on advances being made in building construction today. Blindly continuing to develop buildings that can satisfy one function only has, in a number of cases, proved to be an untenable strategy.
This contribution gives a picture of how such aspects as flexibility can influence the way a building is constructed. At the same time, it enters into ways of addressing 'flexible buildings'.

▪ Standards
In the Netherlands our Building Decree has a tight hold on the reins, and in the European context a similar situation obtains. So our standards leave little room for the 'flexible' approach. We are obliged to determine a building's purpose beforehand, and many requirements are hitched to that purpose. The next thing needed is a period of reference, a lifespan. This is usually either short (about 15 years) or long (about 50). All told, it is hardly a framework given to propagating flexible buildings.

▪ Flexibility
There are many other terms related to the subject of flexibility, such as durability, sustainability, adaptability, demountability. All describe a longer useful life through flexibility of application or design in a building or its structure.
When talking about flexibility in buildings, it helps to give a more exact definition of the word flexibility. It has also proved important to engage in dialogue with clients about what *they* understand flexibility to entail.
Possible forms of flexibility and their relationship to the construction are:

- flexibility in latitude: the capacity to make recesses or cuts in a structure;
- flexibility in subdivision: the capacity to variably organize the interior;
- flexibility in load: the structure has a greater capacity and the possibility of taking up greater loads locally or across larger surface areas;
- flexibility in services: the capacity to modify a building service at a later date;
- flexibility in expansion: the capacity to add square metres to the building later, say by adding an extra level or sealing off a void. Generally speaking, the best option is *alongside* the building, without having to invest in foundations and the like;
- flexibility in function: more than one function is possible.

By incorporating the flexibility aspect at the design stage, it is possible to limit or entirely rule out investments beforehand to achieve a measure of flexibility.

▪ Examples
It is for good reason that old warehouses or sturdy skeletons with generous storey heights prove ideal structures to inhabit, with many possible variations in time.
Below are some examples that specifically indicate what degree of flexibility was key to the design process and what its consequences were for the construction.

Terminal West, Schiphol (see fig. 1)
- c. 80,000 m²
- architect: Benthem Crouwel Naco
- principal flexibility in construction: the capacity to insert a variety of luggage systems, the 'throbbing heart' of every airport, and also to make a very large number of cuts in the floor.
- consequences for the construction: exhaustive research produced a module of 8.4 x 12.6 metres. Also, a floor system that allows c. 20% of the floor to be perforated. A unique control protocol was set up for

1 – Terminal West Schiphol: extreme degree of elasticity of the floors. Photo: ABT bv, consulting engineers, Delft

2 – INHOLLAND (Ichthus) Hogeschool Rotterdam: a school that can also be used as an office. Photo: ABT bv, consulting engineers, Delft

3 – Clubhouse, Schietbaan Amersfoort. Photo: ABT bv, consulting engineers, Delft

4 – IFD building for ABT-Damen, Delft,
Photo: ABT bv, consulting engineers, Delft

6 – Montevideo Tower (rendering by Mecanoo). Photo: ABT bv, consulting engineers, Delft

5 – IFD building for ABT-Damen: demountable connection. Photo: ABT bv, consulting engineers, Delft

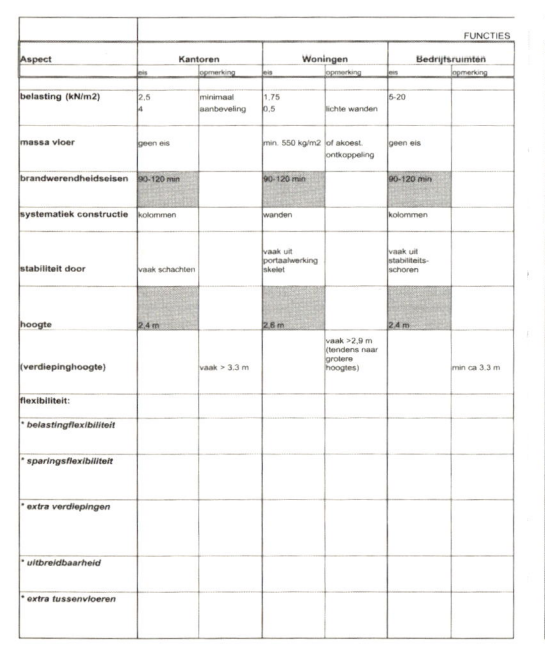

7 – Matrix method. Source: ABT bv, consulting engineers, Delft

this project, whereby all future cuts would be judged by ABT, registered and kept up digitally in a file.

| INHOLLAND (Ichthus) University of Professional Education, Rotterdam (see fig. 2)
• c. 20,000 m²
• architect: Erick van Egeraat associated architects
• desired flexibility of construction: a school able to be used or reused as an office. Also, flexibility in subdividing the space and a great measure of freedom for future building services.
• consequences for the construction: we at ABT chose flat floors with integrated floor beams and channel sections. These combine as a floor plane that can be freely subdivided using lightweight partitions. It also makes it easy to run ducting under the floor.
The design took into account the fact that parts of the building were to be let separately.

| Clubhouse for shooting range, Amersfoort (see fig. 3)
• architect: Jaco de Visser
• desired flexibility: no diagonals in the space serving as a clubhouse, whose roof juts far into space.
• consequences for the construction: the cantilever is resolved using a massive vierendeel girder.

| Delftech Park office complex for ABT-Damen, Delft (see figs 4, 5)
c. 2000 m²
• architect: Hubert-Jan Henket
• desired flexibility: freely subdivisible spaces, industrial, flexible and demountable building, the possibility of sealing off the ground floor and adding an extra level.
• consequences for the construction: we chose a system of integrated steel and concrete beams and columns in a fixed grid. Floor slabs consist of specially developed reinforced concrete panels with T-section.

| Montevideo, Rotterdam (see fig. 6)
• c. 45,000 m²
• architect: Mecanoo architects (Francine Houben)
• desired flexibility: the need for more open spaces low down in the building and freely subdivisible unit plans in the tower.
• constructional concept: we divided the tower into three zones. Each has its own stabilizing system and floor system, in the lowest zone heavily buttressed steel columns and a concrete floor, above that an interstitial zone created using a sliding form with a rigid structure of walls and floors. The uppermost zone is constructed as a tube building with a steel frame. Its floors have an entirely open structure devoid of barriers. In this zone buyers can be very precise in stipulating their homes using lightweight partitions for this purpose.

■ **Course of action/strategy**

Structures can be approached in different ways. For flexible construction in general it is best to integrate disciplines as little as possible. For example, services should not be cast into the structure.
Another avenue often taken for flexible buildings is the philosophy applied to industrial, flexible and demountable (IFD) buildings.
Here the primary supporting structure functions as the component able to survive many modifications. The secondary structure is the skin. The tertiary structure consists of the finish and the fit-out kit.

One way of analysing the consequences of different functions for the structure or for other disciplines is to use a matrix method.
This method (see fig. 7) works as follows:
• the various functions are indicated on the horizontal axis;
• their characteristics are given on the vertical axis, for example changeable floor load or storey height;
• the table can then be filled in;
• the highest requirement in the table should obtain

for all functions if the space is to be flexible;
- in general it has proved practical to cluster spaces sharing certain characteristics.

■ Stacking of functions

Stacking functions is one of the tasks most often come across. A currently popular brief is that of parking facilities below with a 'plinth' of ground-floor functions (often retail) above that and offices or housing on top.
All three zones have their own characteristics.
The structures can be variously approached (see figs 8a, 8b, 8c):
- sketch a: a deep beam on columns;
- sketch b: structure in the facade only;
- sketch c: columns in a continuous structure.

■ Recommendations

Begin with a thorough analysis:
- is it necessary for the entire building or the entire structure to be flexible with regard to the various desired functions?
- can we identify a particular type of flexibility (for example, in subdivision or in load)?
- is the situation such that a number of functions can be stacked?
- the future management situation is important when considering changes of function: are there to be private buyers or will the entire building be managed by one user?

This can point the way towards a solution:
- if there are different functions it is recommended that the matrix method be used;
- more than one structural possibility should be examined, particularly where different functions are stacked;
- it is recommended that initial investments be limited;
- however, making inventive use of the construction can enable an extremely high degree of flexibility with limited investments.

Lastly, some statements about the construction:
- great spans lead to free floor plans. But also to thicker floor systems and a limited flexibility as regards cuts in the floor and in the loads of a facade on the floor edges.
- constructionally the aim should be to design a continuous structure without bridging elements. Though it is still worth considering bridging elements in light of other aspects (lettability, versatility).
- if bridging elements are applied, then structural systems that transfer forces by means of tension and compression are more economical than bending structures (a thick slab, for instance).
- if the design includes a measure of flexibility, it is important to convey this information to the client or user in a 'flexibility protocol'.
- in structural terms it is simpler to achieve greater loads with smaller spans. Floors subject to extremely heavy loads can best be situated on the ground plane.
- greater spans are easier to achieve when there is no floor in use above the space.

■ Future

It is expected that the flexibility aspect will become a standard consideration when designing buildings. Exactly what that flexibility will entail is a matter for the designers and the client.
Time will tell whether there is a market for physically changing buildings, that is, buildings whose structures allow for a variable volume.

deep beam

columns

sketch a

structural facades

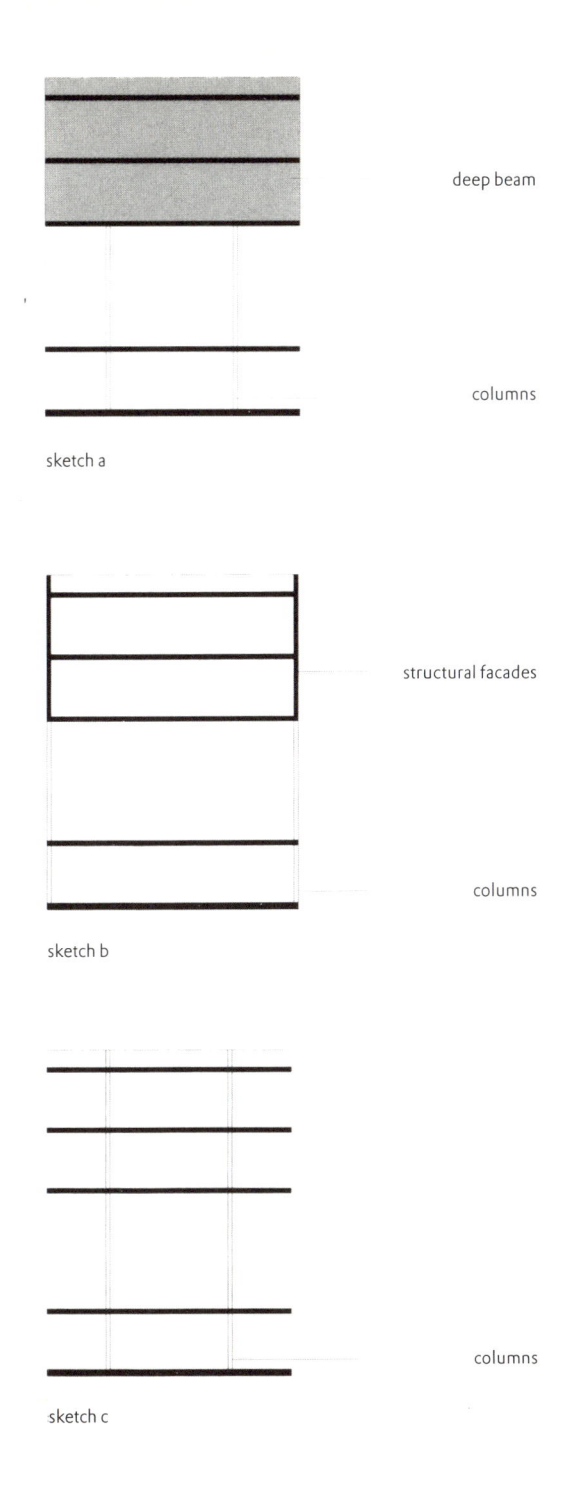

columns

sketch b

columns

sketch c

8 – Stacking of functions.
Source: ABT bv, consulting, engineers Delft

81

TIME-BASED BUILDINGS
Herman Hertzberger

These two photos just happened to be lying on my desk in 1962 (fig.1). Seeing them together like that had this effect on me, you could say it changed my life. Both photographs are of amphitheatres. One is of the theatre at Arles in France, the other of the theatre in Lucca, Italy. As we know, an amphitheatre for the Romans was something of a standard building. You could make it on the production line, so to speak. You could trot out a slew of them, exactly the same building with exactly the same dimensions and forms. It was at that moment that I saw that a particular form can be something entirely different in other circumstances. This started me off on the idea of 'polyvalency'. It is a word I introduced into architectural discourse, although the French use the word *polyvalent* for something like 'multipurpose'. Actually the word multipurpose is fine, except that it is too broad. What I mean is that multipurpose gives an idea of flexibility. But the word flexibility is inappropriate. Flexibility produces neutral containers in which you can do what you want. It was that very neutrality that needled me, because that leads to neutral architecture. An architecture of boxes, containers you can use in different ways. For me the idea of 'polyvalency' is that you can make forms that are in themselves lucid and permanent, but can change in the sense that you can interpret them differently.
I promoted the idea of different interpretations perhaps too much in relation to different individuals who interpret the same form differently. This is of course the case with houses, where it concerns individuals, but it no longer holds for buildings where larger groups gather temporarily. The idea of different interpretations, however, can of course also be seen in relation to time. What I am trying to say is that being aware of the temporal dimension in architecture means being aware of the interpretational dimension in architecture, and of the fact that what you make should be able to be interpreted differently in the course of time. In fact this means that you should not interpret the programme (the brief) too precisely. These days briefs are drawn up most meticulously by agencies specializing in doing just this. The architect is put under the greatest pressure to stick closely to the precisely worded requirements of the brief. This almost automatically produces buildings with an all too specific quality. I'm not saying 'fuck the programme', just that each project must be suited to the brief – *and* to so much more. So you have to be aware that the programme is only a temporary thing that may even have lost its validity by the time the project is in place. It is this notion I would like to talk about. Those same structures of the amphitheatres are now being used in another way. Time has made those structures another thing altogether. But the object is still an oval, a profoundly expressive form. Not neutral, but very expressive. I am not saying that everything you make should be hugely expressive but neither am I saying that neutrality alone gets you to your goal, as then one would have to live with exclusively neutral objects.
At this moment we are in the process of designing schools. Schools need classrooms – or not, for perhaps the entire educational system will have changed in two years' time and classrooms will no longer be needed. The same goes for schools we have already built. At the time of designing those schools a classroom had to be 57 m². Later this became 42 m². So I was then asked to turn two classrooms into three. But this would have ruined the entire building. Luckily we are now back to the original requirement of 57 m². In a number of new schools they have abandoned classrooms altogether. And because schools don't know how many pupils they will have in ten years' time, they are now asking us to design schools that can be transformed into housing. A bay width of about seven metres is suitable for both a classroom and a home. So it is possible in principle, but it does cast an entirely new light on designing for schools. A photograph of a baseball stadium in Osaka, where

1 – Amphitheatres in Arles and Lucca

2 – Stadium in Osaka, Japan

3 – Hakka community, China

4 – Apollo Schools, Amsterdam 1983

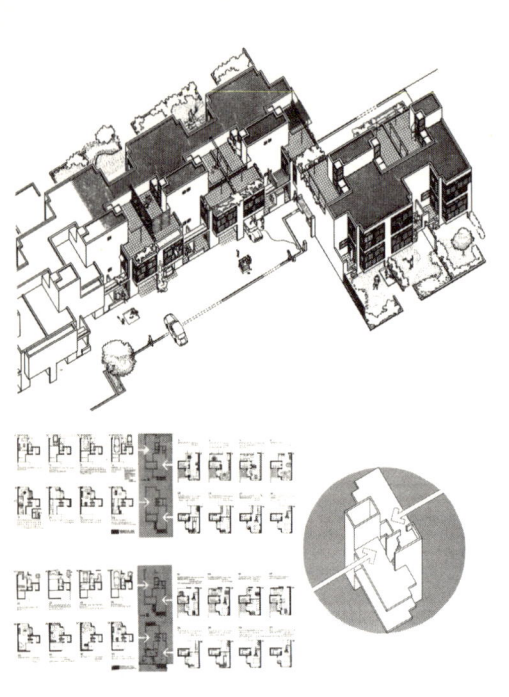

5a, b – Experimental houses: Diagoon, Delft

6, 7 – Experimental houses: Diagoon, Delft

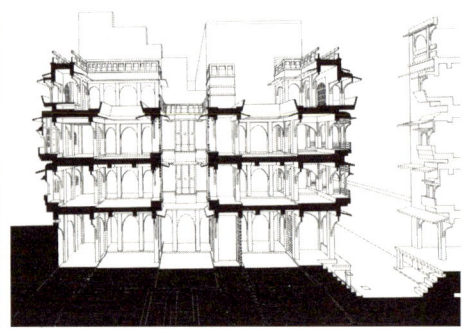

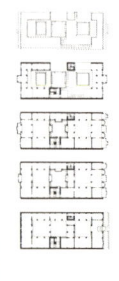

8 – Havelis, Jaisalmer, India

9 – Temple on Bali

84

baseball is no longer played, shows the stadium being used for housing exhibitions (fig. 2). There was also some kind of pop music centre in the stadium. The next shot however shows only cars. And that is the reality of our profession in this day and age. Living in the Netherlands, you are constantly fighting for your square metres of space and are forever occupied with flexibility, polyvalency or, a term I prefer, 'interpretable architecture'. This is easy when you have enough square metres – take the warehouses in the old docks that were built to hold heavy goods and are now transformed into houses, schools, offices and so on. Over-dimensioning in an upward direction is extremely important here. My architectural office is domiciled in a former school where the ceiling is so high that we have added mezzanines in places. Only the legislation has now changed to the extent that the clear height between floors must be no less than 2.4 metres. 2.4 metres + 2.4 metres + construction is an awful lot and so intermediate floors are now almost always out of the question. Change, then, is subject to change or, better still, changeability is subject to change.

I encountered similar forms in China (fig. 3). They are 'living units', one of which is filled with what seems to be an entire town and the other used as communal working space. And again, these rings of houses are not neutral but have a distinctive form. Some years before my discovery of the ovals, I came across another example. This was the great flight of steps leading up to the library of Columbia University in New York. These steps are used as tiers of seating where people observe and converse. However, the architect made the stair to give the library an additional touch of grandness; to upgrade it with these time-honoured means into a key building. It transpires that some architectural forms, given the right expression, have the capacity to change function entirely. Instead of acting as an introduction to a building, they can change into an element that militates against that building, that turns its back on it. From the school building of 1983 (fig. 4)

I have learnt that a stair like this is extremely important for spontaneous activities and for, let's say, an element of theatre. It is the main theme of this school – a stair as a place where parents, children and teachers converge without it being an official assembly hall or auditorium. Hall and auditorium are too specific. Whenever a space is too specific, it forfeits the possibility of being interpreted for different occasions and programmes. Assembly halls and auditoria are often a little too specific, in the sense that you may have to get the key from the caretaker who in turn might have to make such preparations as turning on the heating several hours before use.

I am always looking for forms or designs suited to more than one application, forms with great 'competence'. Competence in the sense of a potential possibility, a potentiality. I try to embed this competence in the architecture; to charge the architecture's batteries, so to speak. 'Competence' is pitted against 'performance'. Competence and performance signify structure and infill.

The Diagoon housing in Delft, designed in 1964-65, rallies against the unbending programme for houses, against the idea of so many square metres for this and so many for that. The premise of a brief is based on the idea that we think we know how people live. This goes back to the 1960s. We would be better to proceed from individual options.

My mistake was perhaps that I was beginning to place too much emphasis on the idea of individual interpretation when this also applies to time. I could have told the whole story then in terms of time and that is what I'm going to do now. What you see in the designs of the houses in Delft (fig. 5a) is nothing less than an exercise in how to interpret and therefore flesh out the same building in 100 different ways (fig. 5b). All at once there's a garden house standing on the roof and this makes demands on the architect's attitude, particularly towards aesthetics (fig. 6). We architects are too intent on finding a perfect form, perfect in the way we want it, but when thinking along these lines you have to let go of the idea that we are the only ones to decide what the final outcome is to be. It's like city planning. There you can decide where a street is to be, but you don't decide what it will eventually look like. After 50 years it will have changed completely. Every corner will have been transformed, from house to shop or vice versa. The only thing you can hope for is that they respect your street in planning terms. You are allowed that hope. And it is this thinking that is commensurate with what I am looking for in architecture. In the Delft housing we chose to make the frames black so as to force a contrast with what we expected the residents to make of their homes – not in black, I assumed. However, the residents were so respectful towards the architect – much more than I had anticipated – to the extent even of using black (fig. 7). And then you get the ambiguity of whether the architect was responsible for the design or not. There is an example from Jaisalmer in India. Here you have buildings, originally palaces, that are now occupied as dwelling-houses. Each such building has an 'open-ended' plan. Its occupants live there like nomads. They inhabit different parts of the building with respect to the movement of sun and light. They move from place to place depending on what they want of light and air. So it is an open skeleton within which there is room for change (fig. 8). Another example with similar implications is the structure-like building in Fatehpur Sikri close to New Delhi. The beautiful thing about this building is the open skeleton in which curtains sometimes hang to mark off places. But you might easily imagine them being filled in with structural glazing. These are constructions treated as structures and not determined by the programme. Let us try to make buildings that are expressive because of the construction and not the programme. Because of conditions. I try to create conditions in my designs for all kinds of inducements.

The most famous example is Le Corbusier's 'Plan Obus' for Algiers. This consists of large concrete floor slabs on which everyone could build their own house. Here you see modern houses like the ones Le Corbusier himself would design, but also Islamic house types, Florentine types and standard housing too. The most important form-defining element was the motorway running through the building from end to end. It was something of a visionary image. And even though it underestimates the baggage a motorway brings with it, the great idea is the structure that can be filled in with so many smaller interventions.

Another example is the use of temples on the island of Bali (fig. 9). It is only when a temple is being used for a celebration that it is a holy place. That holy status vanishes when the celebration is over. And then it belongs to everyone. Children can play there and a lot more besides. When there is a celebration the space is transformed completely (fig. 10). The building changes in time. For us a church is a church at all times, even when not in use. The point is that the structure is open-ended and therefore freed for different uses and different meanings.

The famous Rockefeller Center in New York is itself a centre within a city centre (fig. 11). In winter, there is an ice skating rink around which thousands of people assemble and in summer it is one mass of outdoor seating for the surrounding restaurants. And once again in time, here from season to season, its characteristics change, save for the expressive form with its walls, flags and whatnot, into something utterly different. It is this type of construction, whether building or structure, that shows us how we should design. And so when you see students designing magnificent forms for a specific aim, you wonder how long that building is going to work. The most telling example for that matter is Lingotto, the old Fiat works in Turin. It is over half a kilometre long. The production hall, which was designed without an architect, is little more than a tedious repetition of the same elements. This factory has since been transformed into a small city. What was origi-

10 – Transformation of Bali temple

11 – Rockefeller Plaza, New York

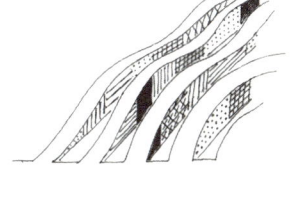

12 – Model of 'Gebaute Landschaft', Freising

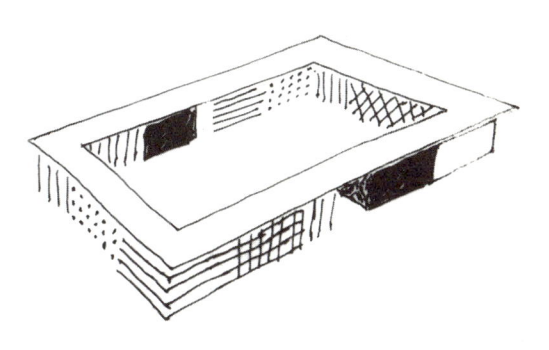

13 – Housing complex, Düren

14 – Paradijssel housing project, Capelle aan den IJssel

15 – Growth homes, Almere

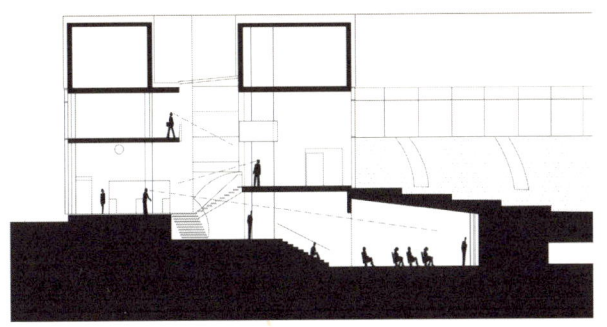

16 – CODA building, Apeldoorn

17 – CODA building, Apeldoorn

18 – CODA building, Apeldoorn

89

nally a factory now includes a congress centre, a hotel, a school, a commercial centre and an auditorium. All these functions now have a place in the former factory. Renzo Piano has only added what was necessary in a modern building. Of course this building's dimensions are capacious in the extreme and would never do in the Netherlands, where everything is done to the nearest millimetre to ward off all forms of what is considered to be waste. This makes it very difficult to design in any other way than for a specific purpose.

In a science park you see many different architects each with their own design that is to distinguish them from the others. I don't think you can create a meaningful city this way. This was an attempt to impart unity with a built form whose roof makes for continuity in the surrounding landscape rather than intruding upon it. It is accessible to people and blends into its setting. You could see it as something of an interpretation of Le Corbusier's Plan Obus (fig. 12). For a housing project in Germany, where the setting consisted of an immense sea of freestanding houses, we opted for a larger form able to accommodate the different dwelling types required in the brief. Here the large form is, as it were, the competence and the diversity of infill material the performance (fig. 13). Our idea for the competition for Malmö University library consisted of a folded plane that could envelop everything like a gigantic taco. Once again, it is somewhere between architecture and urban design, with the folded plane acting as an expressive holder (19a, 19b). Beneath the great jutting roof there unfurls an urban place, much like the ice rink of the Rockefeller Center. The cantilever can be walled in with a giant canvas curtain, creating an enclosed piazza where all the university's formal meetings and informal encounters could take place. Everything that needs to happen, can happen in this 'envelope'.
In Capelle aan den IJssel, in the north-east of Rotterdam, we realized a housing project with roof terraces looking out over the river dyke (fig. 14). These roof terraces have been designed with an architectural enclosure – that is, the matrix of the open terraces can be filled in by the residents with, say, an extra room. Whenever you design buildings, and housing in particular, you have to find themes that allow them to be interpreted by, and adapted to, those who use them.

In Almere each house admits to a built unit and a do-as-you-please intermediary space. The built portion contains everything you need (fig. 15). The empty space is there for individual interpretation. In diagram form it gives you a determined zone and an interpretable zone executed as a glass nursery house with all the challenges that entails. If I look now at what people have added to it, I must admit to feeling somewhat disappointed. I am a child of the 1960s. In those days there was lots of energy for adding things everywhere, but since then people have become lazy and the economic situation too comfortable besides. Yet I am convinced that if you were to return after a year a lot would have changed.

We are being seduced more and more by the idea of simple, container-like masses with little architectural expression and much contextual precision. The CODA building in Apeldoorn shapes the streets around it and the courtyard within it (fig. 17). Here the construction creates the basis for a more timeless building – transparent, so that you can look through it. From the street you can look both in and over the main exhibition room, half tucked below the ground plane. The brief called for an auditorium seating 100 that could be opened up with two large sliding doors. Outside the auditorium, you can still follow what is happening inside from the added stairs (fig. 16). This, then, is flexibility, in the sense that you can make a space considerably larger or smaller. The undulating courtyard is clad with the rubber granules used for the surfaces in children's playgrounds. This is now a perfect place for outdoor performances. The existing building on site can be used as a projection screen for film showings and the courtyard can do duty as an auditorium on summer evenings (fig. 18).

So it's all about the architect being disposed to designing not for just one condition but always for so much more. Perhaps this covers the words polyvalency, competence and performance. You have to be constantly aware of the fact that everything you make should be open to new interpretations as time goes by.

FLEXIBILITY – TIME
Rudy Stroink

In order for you to understand the roots of my company, TCN Property Projects, I have to explain my admiration for American real estate. Anybody who visits an office building, shopping centre or apartment complex in the United States will have noticed the quality of the maintenance and the general good looks of the buildings. I am not referring to the architecture, which by the way is not bad either; I am referring mostly to the quality of the management of real estate after completion. This is in stark contract with the management of Dutch real estate. A case in point being the architectural faculty which I attended during my study 30 years ago. After I saw it again today I can assure you not a lot of money has been invested in the building since my graduation. It looks very used and the layout is exactly the same as it was 30 years ago.

In general terms it is hard to explain to American real estate professionals how passive and poor our general building management in the Netherlands is. Our focus seems to be the construction of buildings, the process of getting from demands and specifications to realizing real estate. As soon as the building is complete, we seem to lose interest or are not willing to reserve enough funds to maintain our buildings and adapt them to the changes of use that undoubtedly will happen over time.

■ **American real estate**
So why do American buildings look so good? First it was explained to me as a cultural thing, Americans being more service oriented and focused on presentation. But this of course flies into the face of the consensus that American society has a strong tendency to spoil resources at a higher rate than other societies. The explanation is more directly linked to differences in the development process of the American real estate market, and most importantly the specific role of the various players in this process.

First let me explain the main stages of the real estate development process, the process that leads to the commercial production of buildings.
The main stages are:

■ The entitlement stage
Usually the work of local government. Here the usage and function of a site are set based on a politically accepted zoning plan (in the Netherlands 'bestemmingsplan'). This leads to a general plan which sets the boundaries for the actual production of real estate.

■ The pre-development stage
From the site limitations and functional programme of the zoning plan the developer develops a business plan including a concept, a budget, marketing plan, financing plan, etc. in order to shape the conditions to create and finance the real estate.

■ The development stage
Building permits are being obtained and the production of building plans and the actual construction process takes place.

■ The investment stage
Here the production of real estate is completed and the building becomes an asset that needs to be managed. Usually a period of three months is necessary after completion of a building to stabilize the use. Sometimes it takes three years to achieve a stabilized asset, especially with management sensitive projects like shopping centres and hotels.

Stage A is typically government controlled, stages B and C are the responsibility of a developer. Stage D is controlled by a third party, the real estate investor (usually).

In the Dutch real estate industry there is a general practice to make a clear distinction in responsibilities between stages A and B and between stages C and D. Crossover responsibilities between stages are not common practice and in general terms limited through complicated regulations and practices. Our fiscal rules are also based on a clear cut between stages C and D. In other words, the responsibilities of the developer end when a building is completed and sold to an investor. And since the real estate industry in the Netherlands (and in Northern European countries in general) is very rich in investors it is these that dictate it.

For the investor the building is first of all a financial product. He prefers a steady, undisturbed cash flow and not too much hassle. Since the developer is selling the building to the investor, the investor's demands and requirements are key to the decisions the developer takes in the development stages. It is a balancing act between the public demands of the local government and the very specific and most of all risk-averse attitude of the investor.

This typical Dutch development process automatically raises the question 'and what about the actual users of the real estate?', the tenants in the office buildings or shopping centres and the occupiers of houses.
Well in the end the conclusion is that they play a limited role in the process. They are reduced to a prototype user of the building, no specific knowledge of their demands is put into the development process. This is mostly so in commercial buildings. (See the A-Factory in Part Two of this book, page 224.)

In the USA this works differently. The most important difference is the relationship between the developer and the user of the building. The value of the building is created by the stability of its use. It is not sold on completion, but usually two to three years later. The stabilization process is an integral part of the development process; it is only after stabilization that a building can be sold. This means that much more attention is spent on creating real estate with a high appreciation of the user, who will reward this with a stable income stream.

Also at the front end, the role of the government is different in the US. In Europe the post-war urban development tradition dictates not only a controlling but also an active development role for local government. In the USA not the development role but the controlling role is emphasized. This means that the developers' role encroaches into the public area, where developers take it upon themselves for instance to develop master plans or are willing to accept public tasks like developing the public infrastructure. Such a role would still be unthinkable in Dutch practice.

This practice causes US developers to define their role differently and to be much more sensitive to the quality and management of the buildings after completion. This also creates a different relationship between developer and architect. The architect in Holland plays an important role in the overall process and steers the developer towards generic, politically correct buildings. In the USA the developer claims a more central role, making sure the building meets the needs of his specific clients. This is also reflected in the fact that in the Netherlands a building is 'owned' by the architect (this building is by Van den Broek & Bakema) and in the USA by the developer (the Trump Building).

▪ Time-based buildings
What is the relevance of all this to the title of this paper, which is about time?

Well, time is everything in the development process. I am aware that architectural students are trained to deal with a limited and well-defined time frame concerning the production of buildings. A process from first design to completed construction drawings takes maybe six months to a year and the construction process maybe 18 months. For a developer however the time frame of a project is closer to five years. In a world that is in constant movement, in which demands change rapidly, in which the preferred demand of a tenant is flexibility, five years is a very long time.

If a programme is too fixed from the start and unable to change over time, there is a greater possibility that the building when constructed will no longer fit the demands of the specific user. More importantly, when the building is completed we know for sure that it will have to change over time to fit the demands of a ever changing pool of users.

So the development time of a building is too long for 'form follows function' – a more correct statement would be 'form dictates function' and this would be unacceptable.
Since the most important goal of a developer is the control of risks, inflexibility is your worst enemy and nothing is so inflexible as the production of buildings.

■ TCN Method
Based on my American experience TCN developed a different approach to real estate development. So here it is; seven easy steps to become a new-generation real estate developer, less depended on time. (See fig. 2)

■ Step 1
Understand the developments that effect real estate
Develop know-how into the underlying processes that determine the demands for real estate now and in the future.
We have set up our own independent market research office called TCN Concepts which works as a consultancy for cities and real estate owners throughout Europe. It is being paid to analyse the logic behind the major changes in real estate demands, define the opportunities and gather information to develop new ideas and concepts. We also research major challenges in the quality of the real estate over time and define necessary interventions. We made ourselves independent from the specific demands of local governments as expressed in their zoning plan and/or master plans. We concentrate on ascertaining which economic processes are relevant.

■ Step 2
The product
Develop a real estate product based on step 1. Precisely define the product and its conditions for successful deployment in the market. We recently developed and are currently working with five products: @work, Retail, B2B, New Urban and Health Parks. A product is not a design nor a specific programme, it is a concept for a new real estate product based on the assumption of a broad demand in the market.

■ Step 3
Find the location for your product based on its specific characteristics
It is important to understand after step 3 that this approach is fundamentally changing the relationship between local government and the developers. Until recently, the government controlled the planning of real estate. At the beginning of the real estate production, opportunities were based entirely on a political demand. The real estate developers responded to that. The product approach requires a much more proactive attitude by the real estate industry. So we go out and visit cities where we feel our products have a potential.

■ Step 4
Analyse choices and define the context
Ultimately the product has to land on a specific location within a specific urban structure. This is where

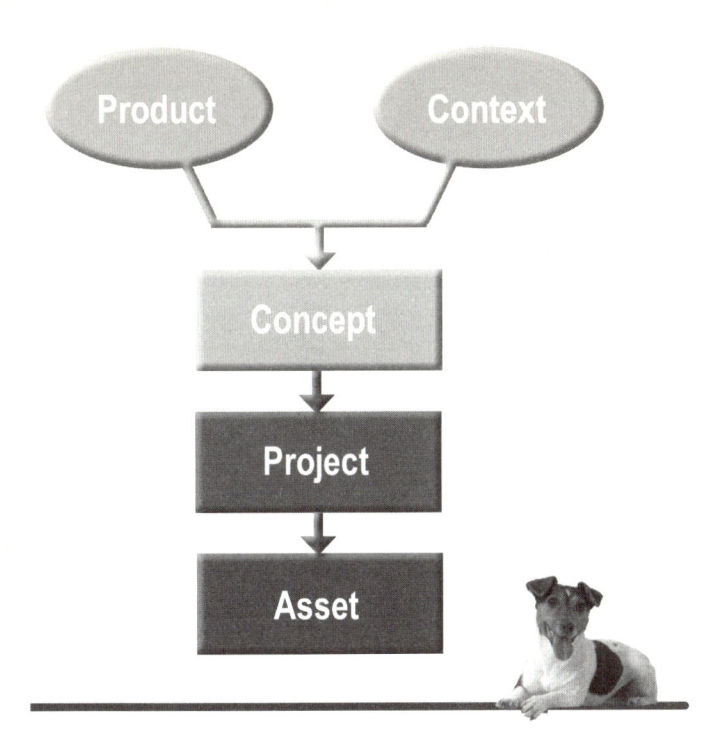

1 – TCN Method.

2 – American real estate.
Photo: Rudy Stroink

For all photos of the A-Factory see Part Two of this book, pp. 224-227

the cooperation between local government and real estate developers becomes productive. Products will have to be adapted to fulfil the requirements of the specific location. You have to understand the physical layout, the social structure, the political requirements, the economical structure of the area and most of all the relationship with other functions around the location.

The key to success is a correct understanding of the characteristics of the context; most of our analysing techniques were developed during my study here at the university.

Up to this point no relation with a user is functional in the process. We analyse general demands but they are not yet specific.

Until now the developer has not really been working with a building programme, nor with a specific design. I am sorry to inform you that the role of the architect up to here is limited. However, working from step 1 to step 4 has created the circumstances to develop the specific project. With this approach the developer knows that the location and the product at least fulfil the minimum requirements of a realistic demand for the project, and more importantly in a context that makes it possible to successfully complete the development process.

Understanding the context of a possible location also means one is comfortable with the conditions for the success of the real estate in the future after development.

Step 5
Select locations and start the design process
Here the urban designer and architect are hired to develop the specific project. It is also at this time that we like to meet and contract future users (owners and tenants) of the project. When developing the specific building, user requirements and specifications and their demands for the quality and functionality of the building drive the design process.

Step 6
Construction
We like short construction processes. That is why we redevelop real estate more than construct new buildings. Permit processes are shorter, construction take usually less time and the neighbourhood is much more grateful for your intervention. Since we try to develop context sensitive buildings we have found that buildings generally are easier to adapt to new users than one might think. The fit of a building for a specific demand not only lies with the appearance and functionality but also with the management after completion. Proper servicing by users can eliminate a lot (but not all) of the restrictions an existing building might have.

Step 7
After construction comes stabilization of the real estate to fit the needs of the users
Most of our effort is invested in the stabilization period which can last up to five years in order to create the right conditions for a financially healthy asset. Understanding all aspects of this would require a separate article and would be more than I can burden the reader with at this point.

So what have we achieved with all of this? A development process that is less dependant on time and has a more direct relation with the market in general and the qualities of a specific location. The execution of the development depends largely on the skills of the project manager governing the process and his relationship with the main players. The real estate process is so complex that the chance of failure is always present. The biggest enemy is time; slowing down processes creates disasters, changes in concepts and unhappy customers. In following our method we have produced real estate that is less time-sensitive and because it is based on a general market understanding it will be easier to adapt to the certain and mostly predictable changes in its use. Most importantly, the concentration on long-term management and the direct relationship with the users are in my view the only way to protect the value of buildings. Buildings should be built for ever and not just to fulfil today's demands. I hope to have explained to you that this will require a changed relationship between public agencies, market and architects.

THE SUSTAINABLE CITY IS THE ADAPTABLE CITY
Maccreanor

Sustainability has been discussed everywhere since the Rio Declaration of 1992. The most widely known definition of 'sustainable development' comes from the Brundtland Commission, which defines sustainable development as 'development that meets the needs of the present without compromising the ability of future generations to meet their own needs.' (See fig. 1)

The meteoric rise of the concept is due in part to the fact that it can be easily hi-jacked for other means. In the public discussion there are endless definitions of the term which has in fact become something of a catchphrase, used by every politician, urban planner, regeneration advisor and ecologically minded civil servant alike. Overused, the word is beginning to lose its dictionary meaning: to maintain, to be able to continue or last for a long time.

In this paper there is no attempt to further define the term but rather, by looking only at one aspect, adaptability, to give form to a part of the concept. The paper will look principally at the following questions: Why do some buildings stay and others get demolished? Can there be criteria developed for buildings to last longer? In considering these questions, the term 'sustainable development' is assumed to encompass more than environmental science or business development to include human development through the medium of the urban environment.

The permanence of buildings was until more recent times one of the main obsessions of the architectural world. Today permanence, often unfortunately associated with immutability, is a term that does not often occur in the architectural discourse.

Certain historical buildings, such as the Amsterdam canal houses or the London Georgian town houses, are well known for their ability to adjust their use to new demands and requirements. We are all familiar with the idea that those buildings changed from large single-family houses to apartments, offices, workshops, hotels, clubs, art galleries etc. with an astounding ease.

More recently, industrial warehouse buildings dating from the late 19th and early 20th centuries have also found new uses. The apparent robust identity and enduring presence of an urban context allowed those buildings to cope with future needs and changing conditions. (See fig. 2)

The ability of a building to cope with changing uses is becoming increasingly important. The working environment of today is not as predictable as it was 20 years ago. Significant changes in the way we work suggest an increased interest in urban settings. More and more companies prefer an urban environment with a diverse character over the more anonymous and exclusive edge of city business parks. Within the inner city environment they find an attractive combination of something new, and something known: a post-industrial form of socialization, yet one that responds to our memories. It is well recognized that those who carry on the activities of both working and living in the same place do more fully inhabit that place and consequently feel more involved and caring towards it.

There have been many studies carried out internationally to support this. People have more control of the timing, the context, the tools and the place of work. Work is becoming more varied and creative. Many straightforward procedures are being automated or exported to economies where they can be carried out more cheaply. The words that previously described how businesses used space such as 'distribution', 'manufacturing', 'office', 'shop', 'showroom' etc. are inadequate and out of date. These classifications come from an era of certainty, of zoning and of fixed expectations. Today many businesses can be

1 – Why do some buildings stay and others get demolished?

2 – Will you be the next user?

3 – The working environment is not as predictable as it was 20 years ago

99

4 – Long life through loose fit

5 – The Lux building by Maccreanor Lavington architects, London 1987; the building has already seen many changes in the first seven years of its life, tenants come and go yet the building professes an enduring quality

6 – The Park Flats, Rotterdam

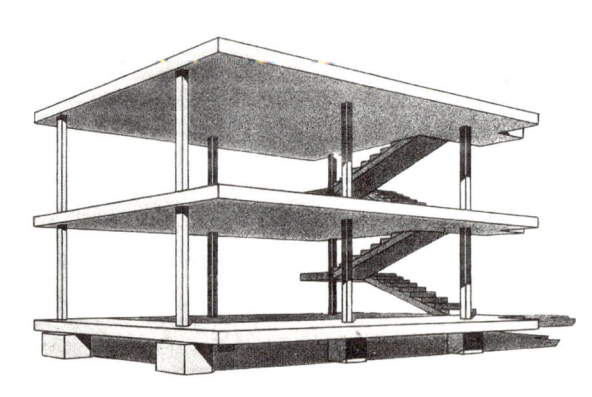

Diagram 1 – Dom-ino System

7 – The F-Buurt, Amsterdam Zuidoost, Bijlmermeer

categorized under more than one title and a few may even be able to use all of the names mentioned above. (See fig. 3)

There is a need to find ways to accommodate ever-changing organizations that have to respond to an increasingly unstable and unpredictable business environment.

This asks for a less traditional perception of space as well as of use. If we want to reach entrepreneurs in craft, trade and culture, we need to offer them contemporary working conditions with a high diversity of functions and services. As work becomes more creativity-based and displays more diversity, it is necessary to create an environment capable of reacting to changes in use.

Extending the useful life of a building is the essence of adaptability. The adaptable building is both trans-functional and multifunctional and must allow the possibility of changing use – living into working, working into leisure – or be a container of several uses simultaneously. It is the adaptability of these buildings that creates a vibrant urban structure: ever changing and lively, with different parts of the city developing different characters and generating new forms of urban contact and sociability.

Adaptability is a different way of viewing flexibility that is not primarily concerned with a designed flexibility based on the collapse of the traditional layout. Designed flexibility has for a long time been a subject of interest for architects. In 1923 Le Corbusier published *Vers une architecture* which included ideas on mass-produced and flexible housing based on the Dom-ino system that he developed in 1914. This text is still perhaps the single most influential architectural manifesto of early modern times. The Dom-ino system (see diagram 1) proposed an open plan with ribbon windows that provided endless flexibility in the arrangement of the interiors. In the years to follow, this resulted in many buildings with open changeable planning around fixed service cores. This greater spatial indeterminacy was thought to allow greater changes in use and occupancy.

Our experience now shows that the potential of this flexibility was rarely used to its full extent. A lack of technical expertise with new materials often resulted in building facades that did not last and failed to meet ever-increasing energy requirements. Buildings that were designed to be flexible in their internal arrangements had minimum floor to ceiling heights and therefore could not accommodate raised floors and suspended ceilings, or they had deep plans appropriate for open plan secretarial staff but inappropriate for secular offices. Problems arose even when the same use was proposed and it was often more cost-efficient to build new accommodation rather than to renovate or rearrange the existing.

One conclusion is that the buildings that have proven to be the most adaptable were those not originally conceived to be flexible, and that in most cases a designed flexibility has failed to live up to the promise.

Generators of adaptability:
What are criteria in order for buildings to stay?

■ Over-dimensioning

Adaptable buildings achieve long life through a loose fit ideal. The over-dimensioning of ceiling heights, circulation space and mechanical services and going beyond the present energy requirements can encourage the prospect of future adaptability. The increasing demands of cost efficiency no longer permit this generosity. Over-dimensioning therefore implies a change in the now common practise of strictly defining a building programme. A design based on volume rather than area should be proposed. (See fig. 4)

■ Neutral facades

Neutrality proposes facades that have no symbolic indication of a particular use yet are capable of strongly suggesting activity. Neutrality should not be confused with standardization and repetitive dullness. Neutral architecture doesn't rely on the big gesture but rather seeks for a building to fit quietly into its surroundings almost as if the simple fact of being there is enough. This implies a conscious decision against frivolous decoration, drama and extravagance. (See fig. 5)

Context

The adaptable building, capable of coping with changing use and changing conditions, is primarily concerned with the quality of urbanism. The building functions as a part of the city backdrop; the urban setting being more important than the image of the building as an exclusive object. 'The relatively inconspicuous built edifice is born from an attitude that understands it as just another element in a broader context, even to the extent of allowing it to both exist as an independent, coherent statement while also sharing the formal and spatial sensibilities of its neighbours and predecessors, however banal these may be.'[1] Contextualism should not, however, be confused with a simplistic interpretation that implies reproduction in the name of local vernacular. It is the idea of a context that can allow for an emphasis on particular characteristics that are part of our collective memory and at the same time different and unknown.

Ordinariness

A proposed contextual approach is closely intertwined with a fascination for the ordinary and everyday. Ordinary architecture is storytelling about the roots and conditions of the landscape, and conversely each landscape generates its own specific anonymity. The power of the ordinary is that when you look long enough, almost everything begins to display its own particular 'specialness'. Finding the 'specialness' in the ordinary, will increase any potential for adaptability. By using the potential for inventiveness within the language of the ordinary a building can become timeless and therefore genuinely 'up to date'.

Address

The adaptable building has an address. Address asks for a clear distinction to be made between private and public, avoiding the confusion of semi-public or semi-private space. The facade can act as a strict boundary between internal and external activities with the entrance directly related to the urban space. The building therefore becomes street conscious and recognizes the importance of the street as a public space. The emphasis is on vertical rather than horizontal circulation, eluding forced meeting spaces and inviting communal activities to take place within the realm of the street. On an urban level, the notion of address can be further extended by the creation of clearly defined streets, squares and borders.

Timelessness

Ordinary buildings, designed for living or working, don't require a revolutionary concept, but rather accept the slow pace at which ordinary activities evolve. Such architecture should attempt neither nostalgic repetition nor extravagant invention, but must use a language that talks about a shared experience, a shared memory and an 'ordinariness'. A form cannot immediately be traced, but can provoke the thought 'this I have seen before'. An expression of this quiet understanding makes the building independent of fashion. It doesn't wear, it lasts. It is this enduring presence that invites a powerful engagement with the building, an endearing quality that seduces people into adapting themselves to it.

Timelessness promises the return of a reality that was itself an abstract ideal. Timelessness and nostalgia are therefore inevitably connected. In these terms nostalgia is a difficult word to link to architecture, signalling a negative retreat from the present and implying a meaningless adoption of seemingly 'complete' images from past architectures. The emotive power of nostalgia lies not in the desire to physically reinvent something lost, but in the way idealized and fragmentary images of the past are sometimes summoned unexpectedly into the context of a very different present. It is the simultaneous and contradictory awareness of past and present which is of importance.

▪ Materials and detail

The material quality of the building is essential for establishing the desired sense of timelessness and robust identity. To meet these ambitions, materials should allow the building to weather beautifully and grow old gracefully. A sense of detail implies a cared for building. An accepted architectural view is to consider detail as an obsolete irrelevancy that distracts from the overall concept. On the contrary, it is the cared for, finely detailed building that manages to retain its value.

▪ Irrationality

Buildings are rendered more approachable by any apparent incorrectness, lack of precision or irrational intervention. Historically, this happened either through the imperfections and nuances of individual craftsmen or because adjustments were made as a result of imprecise building information. This is not a plea to bring back craftsmanship or out of date working methods, but a realization that the appearance of incorrectness has to be found within the rationality of the programme, construction and context. In an article on La Tourette (Le Corbusier, 1960), Hans Soeten outlines the exceptions to consistently applied design principles that give La Tourette a special quality. 'The rationality of the building is disturbed at those places where the ordering principles, structural clarity, functional use of space and architectural image, conflict with each other. What is illogical in plan appears natural in practice and results from one principle becoming dominant.' This confusion in an otherwise harmonious meeting of structure, use and architecture can be viewed as a conscious decision to place the requirements of context and spatial awareness above the desire to create a perfect object. Such deviations allow a sense of rawness to be retained in the midst of rigidly controlled environments, a personalization that in turn creates a recognizable identity. (See diagram 2)

A disparity arises in the columns of the library. Here, two wings meet, exposing a structural seam. A round column in this space is in fact constructed of two semicircular sections, one of which supports an edge beam that in similar situations elsewhere in the building is carried by a square column 22.5 cm thick. The other semicircular section supports the principal structure, which elsewhere utilizes a column 40 cm in diameter. The load on the column is thus increased while its section is reduced by half. Whereas everywhere else the intention of juxtaposing blocks to form the U-shape is clearly visible and used architectonically, on this occasion it is rejected.

▪ The city of adaptable buildings

The city of adaptable buildings is not a city of zoning. Zoning leaves parts of the city empty for long periods. Empty business districts in the evening and empty housing estates during the day. Zoning generates traffic, the morning and evening rush hour. Zoning is inflexible and thus unsustainable.

The city of adaptable buildings is a city in which the achievement of commercial objectives is accelerated; properly used and professionally managed adaptable buildings can be instrumental in driving forward change rather than only keeping up with tendencies. The city of adaptable buildings is a city of live/work in the broadest sense. It is a more fully inhabited place.

The city of adaptable buildings reduces the need for wholesale refurbishment or demolition and conse-

8 – Groothandelsgebouw, Rotterdam

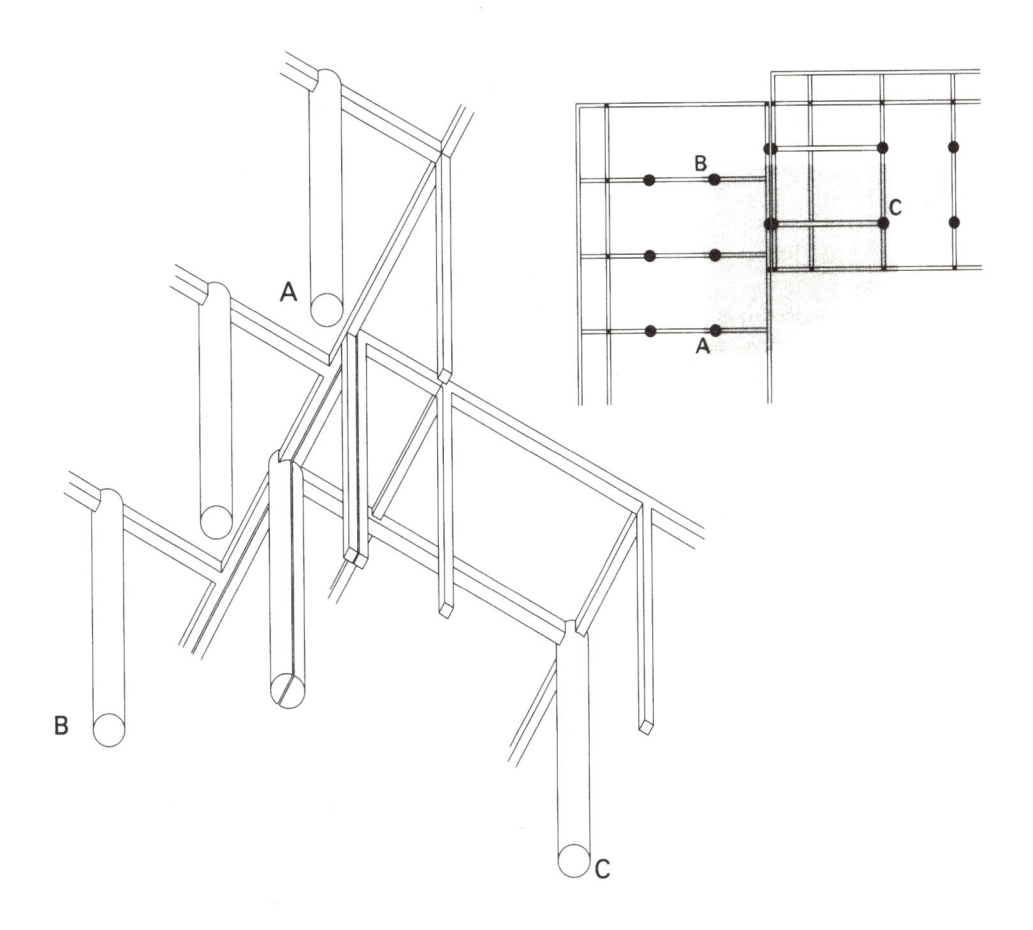

Diagram 2 – Le Corbusier; Convent of La Tourette in Eveux, France, 1956-1960. Detail of the third level. Axonometric seen from below

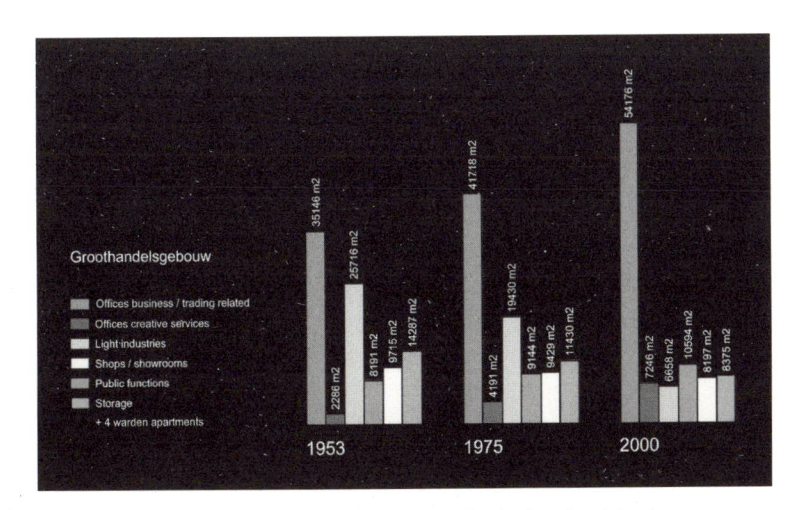

Diagram 3 – Changes in occupants over a 50-year period in the Groothandelsgebouw

1953 1975

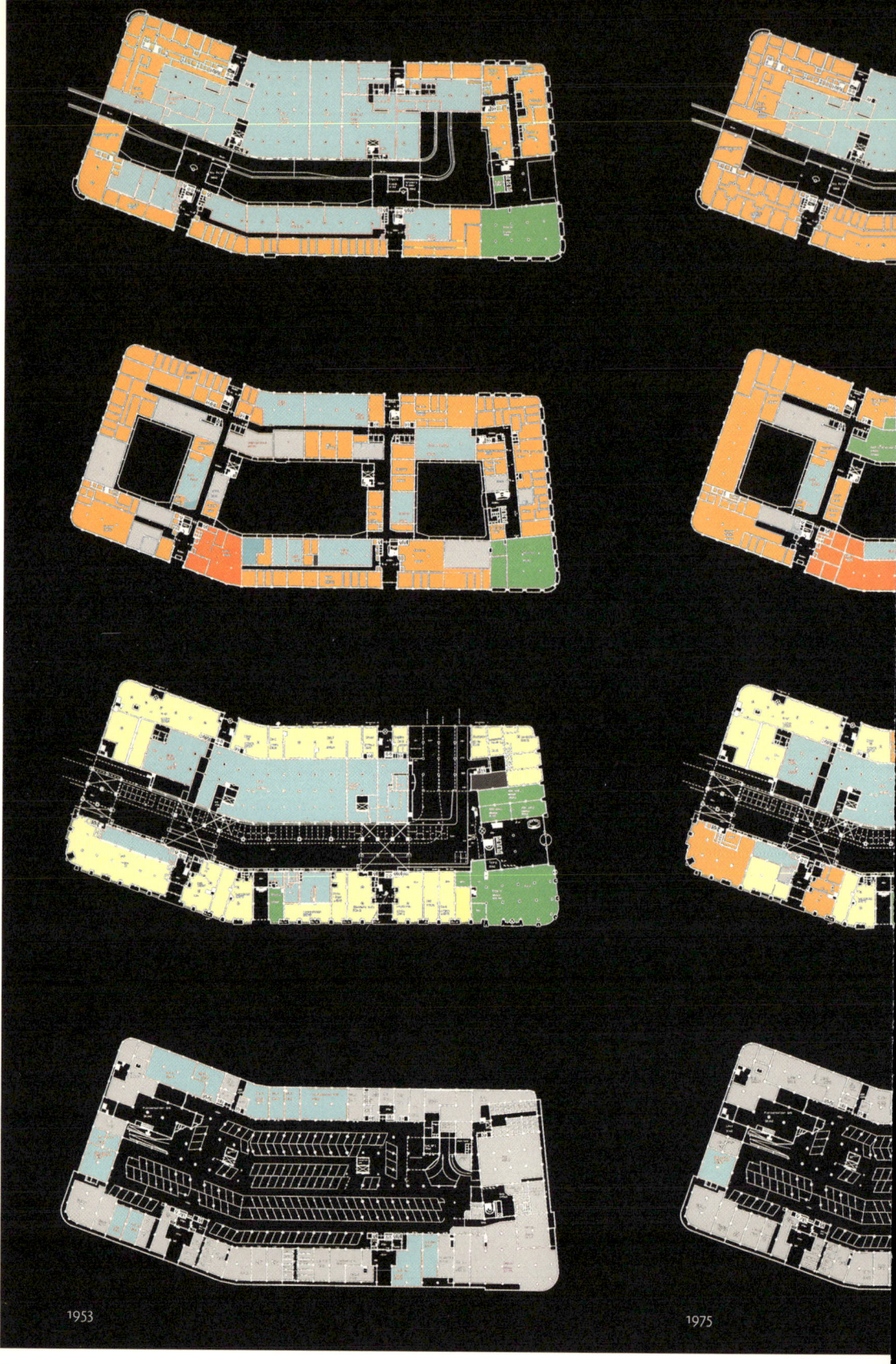

Diagram 3 – Changes in occupants over a 50-year period in the Groothandelsgebouw

2000

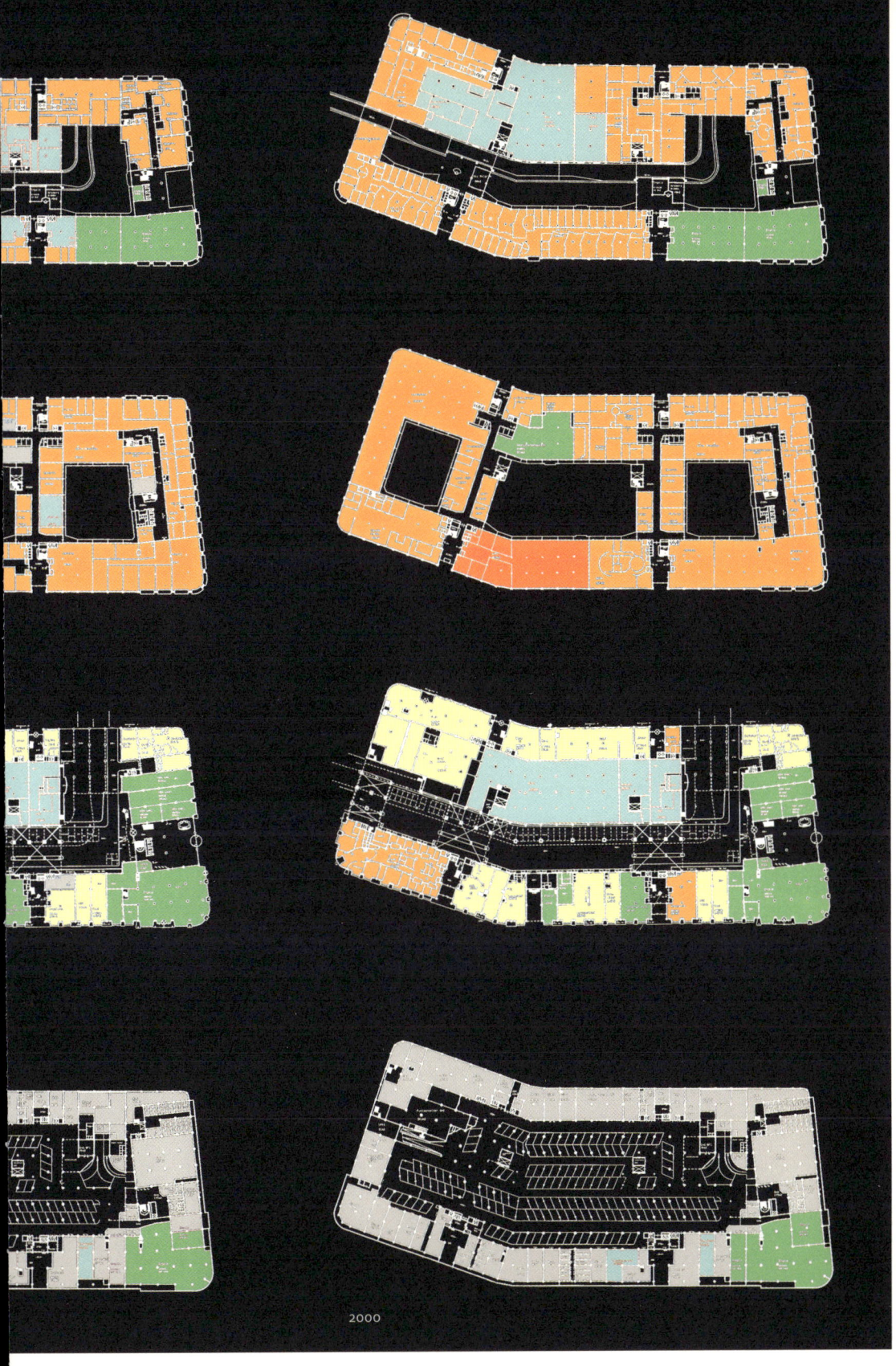

quently is one of the simplest means to achieve a reduction in the environmental impact of any project by placing more value on the embedded energy component.

The city of adaptable buildings can be a growing city or a shrinking city or a city with a stable population. Adaptability is needed in order to answer the contemporary demands that come from uncertainty, conflicting interests, unpredictability, diversity, changing demography and changing lifestyles.

The building that cannot adapt: Park Flats Rotterdam (See fig. 6)

Built in the 1950s, this building is typical for the period. Apartments for sale in this building, which is in a highly desirable location on the edge of a city centre park, are valued below the market rate. The reason is due to the extremely small bathrooms, three sqm, and kitchens, five sqm. The building has low ceilings with services in the concrete slab, therefore it is impossible to move them or alter them without affecting apartments below. In order for the building to meet present-day space standards the building has to be emptied and all the apartments renovated at one time, an apartment by apartment approach to renovation is not possible. The building is in multiple tenure and therefore locked in a downward spiral in value compared to surrounding property. Buildings similar to this one are being demolished at an ever increasing rate.

The neighbourhood that cannot adapt: F-Buurt, Amsterdam Zuidoost, Bijlmermeer (See fig. 7)

The Bijlmermeer is a district in southeast Amsterdam developed between 1965 and 1973 as an area of long honeycomb-structured, high-rise buildings with a total of 9000 apartments. The urban plan and architecture were based on the ideas that came out of CIAM and characterized by separation of uses and a narrow definition of how people would use the buildings and places. The subsequent building programme was particular to time and place but soon obsolete. By 1990, 17 years after the completion of the last phases, the problems had already reached a crisis point and demolition of a part or the whole was being discussed.

Similar to the Park Flats building in Rotterdam, the architecture brief was defined too closely; alterations that were desired by the occupants to suit changing living expectations could not be met and wholesale renovation, which was possible due to single tenure of the buildings, was as expensive as redevelopment. Added to the inadaptable building structure was an urban conception that positively discouraged other uses. The area was never changing or lively and different parts did not develop different characters nor generate new forms of urban contact and sociability.

This estate is not unique; many such neighbourhoods are undergoing the same fate. Large tracts of cities are being redeveloped; communities are being uprooted and displaced in an attempt to 'get it right this time'.

The adaptable building: Groothandelsgebouw, Rotterdam (See fig. 8; see diagram 3)

The studies, made at three points in time – 1953, 1975 and 2000 – show a marked change in the general types of business and more importantly show that the building is 'adaptable', it has accommodated new users and new programmes.

The Groothandelsgebouw was designed in 1953. It has a rentable floor area of 120,000 sqm; it is 220 m long, 85 m wide and 43 m high. It has 11 floors. It has 5 public entrances, 30 lifts, 1.5 km of internal roads and 5 km of corridors. It employs 190 people to run, clean, secure and organize. Initially built to provide accommodation for businesses involved in the rebuilding of the city, it first appeared as an iconic object standing in a wilderness. Since then it has become an anchor for business, generating other activities in and around the station, and is established as one of the landmark buildings of the city. The building is primarily for working, although four apartments exist on the upper level originally designed for the caretaker staff that would look after the building as well as some specific leisure functions, the cinema and ballroom for example. It has had a very low void percentage of 4-5% since it opened – a reflection of just how well the building has coped with the changing demands of business. At present the building is undergoing renovation that will shift the business profile further towards creative, finance, banking and legal activities and bring an end to the light industrial, showroom, distribution and office trading related uses. The fact that this shift in use is possible is remarkable; most working buildings from this period are demolished and the sites redeveloped.

1 Wilfried Wang, *From Normality to Abstraction*, catalogue of the exhibition 'From City to Detail, the work of architects Diener & Diener'.

CULTURAL DURABILITY
bOb Van Reeth

What is architecture? In my view, architecture is the search for architecture. Search methods vary, and lead to various types of interesting architecture. Not everything built is architecture. The most important prerequisite for architecture is the context: the site and the time. These are the first and the most difficult conditions. To ascertain what is right in its context, in its place, is to determine which projects are just in time.

In the last century, preoccupied with planning the future, the single most important insight designers made was the recognition of environmental consequences, the acknowledgement of the extraordinary effects on the environment brought about by planning cities and erecting buildings.

Acknowledgement of this fact led to the conclusion that the high costs involved are untenable and that we must all look for ways to bring about change. Since all problems are so-called limitations, the new environmental awareness generated new sources of creative, urban and architectural energy in designers. It seems to me that sustainable urban development, sustainable architecture and cultural durability, are the important challenges for design in the next few years.

Architecture is probably the search for architecture. An environmental conscience makes that search even more complex, and therefore more interesting. Design is becoming an increasingly fascinating activity because it involves more and more varied challenges. The test for designers is to produce innovative, efficient, total, just-in-time concepts. In other words, sustainable concepts for sustainable urban development and durable architecture.

All this is possible. In fact, all this is a practical necessity, essential for the future. The environmental requirements and the demand for sustainability should be seen as unique opportunities and should be used for new scientific architectural research. They are incentives for developing new design strategies. They can and will lead to re-sourced concepts in urban development and architecture.

The discourse on architecture based on pure formulae and aesthetic issues, as it is still put forth far too often in today's education, in welfare commissions, in heritage agencies, and even in architectural criticism, can perhaps move towards a debate more focused on content, a debate more focused on the reasons for and the foundations of sustainable urban development, durable architecture, durable buildings and sites, and on the criteria for assessing these concepts. Perhaps educators in architecture should forget for a while that architecture is an art.

Being as sparing as possible with energy means not using it. Reducing pollution as far as possible simply means not producing any waste. The most ecological house is the house that is never built. This should be our starting point.

Our most valuable resource, that which is most dear to the environment, is the countryside. It is quite simple to halt consumption of this resource: it is merely a matter of not building on it any more. This is essential and easy to achieve.

Population growth and changes in our standards of living must be tackled by consolidating municipalities and cities, by using space in many different ways, sustainably.

In other words, by making the best possible use of occupied urban zones. This strategy makes use of existing infrastructure and the rhythm of urban life, while emphasizing the character of the city.

All educators, all investors and developers, all policies must encourage projects which, to give an example, produce energy instead of consuming it. Such projects already exist and have been carried out, and have not necessarily involved so-called high-tech schemes; they are not necessarily those fully recoverable buildings which can be dismantled down to the last nut and bolt. Such buildings are usually twice as expensive and deliberately temporary. They are

1 – Averbode, plan

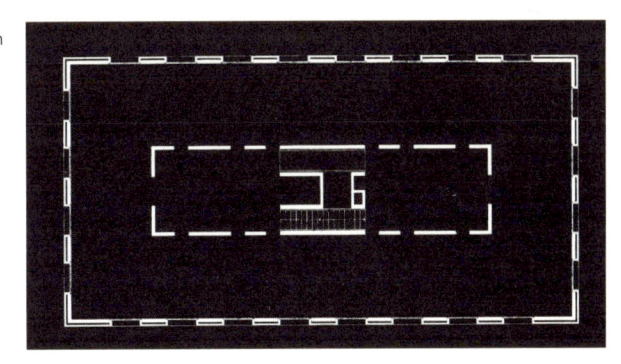

2 – Averbode, aerial photo

3 – Godfried warehouse, Godefriduskaai, Antwerp

4, 5 – IMALSO ventilation building, Oude Leeuwenrui, Antwerp

6, 7 – Tour & Taxis, Brussels

8 – Unalit warehouse, Antwerp

9 – Lombardia, Antwerp

10 – Nieuw Amerika housing project, Amsterdam

not durable because they have no future. Sustainable buildings do not have to look like showrooms of new technology, full of solar panels and photovoltaic cells. Ecological awareness can be visible in a modest way and put into practice in total concepts in a direct way. Invisible and mute are not synonymous with inconsistency or a lack of character. Silence is often an expression of an intellectual and intuitive capacity and progressive insight.

Architectural durability is not primarily a matter of material choices and ecological energy. It is a concept, which must constantly be reinvented and studied on the basis of growing knowledge and insight, always within the particular conditions of each specific project. Architectural research = Research into design.

A sustainable architectural concept is not possible without quality-related terms such as permanence, inflexibility, durability, multifaceted and (not a contradiction) changeability.

Clients must invest and commission, architects must design buildings which will last a long time, 400 years for example. Durability endures. Urban time is a very long time.

Urban development and architecture consists of several layers:
the site, the place, the footprint;
the loadbearing structure + the skin.
This is the durable structure, intended to last a long time. In addition, there are the various installations, the layout, and finally the finishing. These are more temporary.

Each of these layers has its own pace, and its own cycle.

The place, the location, lacks mobility and in a way it disassociates itself from time: it is, so to speak, eternal. The urban fabric of our cities is at best unchanged. To occupy a site is the decision and responsibility of the client. I believe that we should design the loadbearing structure and also the skin of the buildings so that it need not be necessary to demolish them for the next 400 years. Demolition is not sustainable and certainly not durable.

It is clear that skin and construction are one and the same, they enhance each other, are synchronized. The skin of a building is not a separate design set apart from the concrete and the construction; it is part of the total integral concept. The skin is not the exact translation of the structure and most certainly not the expression of so-called 'programme function'. The skin doesn't talk about anything other than architecture; can buildings talk anyway? The core of the building, as an intelligent ruin, is the key to sustainable buildings. History has verified this.

In my view, we must emphasize the contrast between the transient and the long-term and between the impermanent and the permanent, particularly from the point of view of construction. Obviously this is an integral aspect of the stability and strength of the structure selected and the materials used.

Culturally durable projects presuppose an approach to the design process, the design method, that differs from the so-called 'functional programme of requirements' method, which is still the basis of architecture, both in education and in practice.

In the year 2000, the architect Kees Christiaanse wrote in *Archis*: 'Fuck the programme'. Well, 'Architects should design intelligent ruins', is what I've been saying for more than 30 years now.

In future, architects must design buildings for polyvalent use, keeping the programme of requirements for present use in mind as an alibi.

Buildings with an option for modification, which accommodate a wide variety of possible functions, must be designed with a view to a wide variety of possible scenarios. Buildings designed for a myriad of possibilities will be, as it were, broken open by time in order to serve new tasks. We as a generation occupy the city like squatters. We constantly adapt the original function of buildings. We design buildings in which to live; we do not design methods of living. We create the temples, the inhabitants create the passion.

Architecture is still too often caught up in outlining a programme of requirements, organizing how to live, even creating homes. What we should create is what will be left over after the building has been lived in, what can make events happen, whether or not they actually come to pass.

Sustainable buildings are designed for unpredictable events. Durable buildings are made to change. A building is not complete upon completion, at that point a durable building just starts to live, it merely begins its career as a construction.

An edifice must be built for change.

Assessing a structure's ability to change helps determine a project's spatial quality. In turn, this architectural quality can induce the likelihood of diverse applications and add special significance.

This order is authentic. This order focuses more on being open to possibility than on carrying out a programme of requirements (requirements which are often out of date even before construction is finished anyway). This authentic order helps qualify a building as architecture even before it is used: the structure is prepared for permanent change. It is a project with a memory of what is yet to occur.

This is cultural durability: something which does not change but nevertheless summarizes the passing of time.

New concepts sometimes give rise to resistance, loathing and even rejection. Perhaps this will result in buildings which do not, in the first instance, have a place in the mental landscape of many people, and are found to be ugly. 'Finding something' is part of looking for something. And looking for something is the relative autonomy of our profession.

Many buildings, including government buildings now considered beautiful, are constructions which relate to architecture in the way that a clinically dead patient compares to a top sportsman. Buildings divinely dead. Buildings in which not a single window opens, where the word 'climate' is confused with a constant temperature of 22° C. These buildings are like messages received too late. Durability has nothing to do with beauty; it is about integrity and generosity. Durability is a basic characteristic of architecture. The fundamental structure of a building, the carcass, the skeleton, the frame, consists of the load-bearing structure and the skin. This primary construction should be able to last for many hundreds of years.

Therefore it must be strong and immutable.

In order to last, for the sake of continuity, change must be a built-in quality. Change upholds the unchanging. Evolution reveals a curious permanence, and this is sustainability. It is absolutely essential that the concept be clear and distinct. Make no mistake, because what has been laid down determines what the building will become.

Contemporary architecture is not special; it is ordinary. The search for architecture results in simplicity, in concentrated complexity.

Integral concepts are not simple, but they are straightforward. Design must attempt to achieve the mundane, even though some interpret this as a provocation in the discourse on aesthetics.

If you believe some current training and recent architectural journals, design is either a sort of hyperventilation with artistic freedom, or it is the incorporation of architecture with historical context into a superficial, urbane cosmetic.

In Europe today, there is an avant-garde of environmentally aware designers who use their energy, talent, intuition and courage to confirm their work in the environment, the contemporary context.

Durability involves added value, achieved by the factor of time. If durability results in buildings of which we need not be ashamed in the next 50 years, then, as history has already shown us, these same structures will be loved for the following 350 years, and will be cherished as monuments. The more easily adaptable a project is, the longer it will last, and the greater the chance that users and inhabitants will become attached to the building and to the environment.

Cultural sustainability in a project also means honouring the culture which has created the particular site. In the first instance, this concerns not the building itself but its context, the specific gravity of a place in urban development, and our own time. All architecture has a collective value because of its relation to a place and a time.

For the owner and/or user, a building has a particular value. A building determines a public space and makes room in a public space and acquires a collective value in a public space. The longer a building lasts, the more it becomes part of the identity of the city and of the community. In time, buildings acquire a collective urban value. History has passed on to us many districts and buildings which keep the city or the district going, regardless of their dimensions. Durable architecture is also concerned with the intellectual and emotional needs of inhabitants and users.

Town and country planners, urban developers and architects must above all invest in these non-tangible requirements. Great precision, intelligence and intuition is expected from designers to respond to these practical desires.

We must transcend our profession.

We must produce generous designs.

Architecture must give you what you could not demand yourself, but expected anyway.

Our cities and buildings must contain within them what Vittorio Lampugnani calls 'the perspective of improvement', therefore transcending the social, economic and technological situation which created them. This truly cultural dimension of architecture is reflected precisely in that 'perspective of change', in this critical generosity.

Research:

Investors, developers, clients and above all, politicians, must give designers the chance to design, elaborate and build comprehensive, generous projects.

Policies for urban development, architecture, public spaces and buildings, must not dictate how things should be done, but ask for research into design, both in training and in practice. Policies should stimulate, encourage and value this search. Policies should create and make room for culturally durable, sustainable spaces, for constant research into design; both in education and in day-to-day practice.

Architecture must participate in improving the future.

This is a matter of cultural durability.

It is a long-term process.

Architecture is the search for architecture, and if searching means searching for happiness, searching for architecture is searching for a moving experience.

TOWARDS A NON-STANDARD MODE OF PRODUCTION
Patrick Beaucé and Bernard Cache, Objectile

This text, which on the face of it seems to have no connection with Time-based Architecture, has been included as the editors feel that Time-based Architecture can necessitate a new relationship between design and production. The ideas it advances about geometry and about developing products using a new generation of software for CAD can bring us to new insights that may relate to the way different layers in a building, each with their own dynamics and time span, can cultivate their own geometry. (eds)

'This text is the thorough version of the manifesto written by Objectile on the occasion of the "Non-Standard Architecture" exhibition at the Centre Pompidou in Paris (December 1st 2003 – March 1st 2004). Objectile explains how new software techniques enable the creation of sophisticated invariants that allow for ever wider variations. These invariants by variation were already a preoccupation in some texts like Plato's *The Sophist*. Even more than time-based, this approach to new technologies in architecture is deeply rooted in the past.'

Under what conditions can a term like 'non-standard architecture' have meaning? Perhaps it's easier to begin by answering in a negative way. If, indeed, a non-standard architecture consists of generating more or less soft surfaces which will then be called a building by transferring them onto a battery of production software in order to create very expensive kinds of sculpture which no longer have any relationship with the historical and social sedimentation that makes up a city, then we are only perpetuating the Romantic myth of the artist-architect.

Over and above any polemical intention, this negative exordium must serve us for making a list of a series of criteria to which we would wish to try to positively respond, so as not to allow what is really in play within the possibility of a non-standard architecture at the present time, to escape us. It is a question of form, city and productivity.

Let's begin by form, since why deny it? this is where the 'fascination' lies. And sure enough an extraordinary feeling of power consumes any architect to whom the modellers of CAO[1] give the means to generate surfaces that he or she generally cannot design with a ruler and compasses. In that respect we may consider three different cases. The feeling of all-powerfulness may come in the first instance from such highly ergonomic modellers as Rhino, which provide the means to readily design surfaces sufficiently complex for us that we can no longer even be certain of their spatial coherence. The man in the street still has no idea of this, but delineating the control points of a Nurbs surface in order to generate a fluid surface is now within the range of any user after an apprenticeship of just half an hour, and that's how it should be. That on the other hand it may then be a question of controlling these surfaces, of modifying them by intervening on their coordinates, of giving them a thickness and of fabricating them – that's a whole new ball game; namely, to shift the problems onto someone else while multiplying the budget. Whence the adage, repeated time and again by lucid architects like Alejandro Zaera-Polo: nothing gets built that isn't transposable onto Autocad.

Second case: the use of complex generators such as simulators of particle movements that we find on imagery software programs like Maya, Softimage and others. Software programs that are not criticizable in themselves, but which were never intended for fabricating concrete objects, and which therefore hardly concern themselves with assuring, for example, that the four corners of a flat board are coplanar. In the first instance, the fascination grows out of the simplicity of an extremely transparent interface; in the second this feeling comes, on the contrary, from the fact of us having available motors so complex that we no longer control the generation drive, and that the result gets to us as if covered with a mantle of innocence, so to speak: that of randomness or of accident. In the event, this chaos is entirely determinist, but as we don't understand the algorithmic determinants, the forms are stamped with a sort of aura conferred by their alleged aleatoriness.

Lastly, there's a third and finally much more honest instance which consists of dispensing with the computer black box and simply twisting sheets of paper, like a time-honoured sculpture sketch, a process that has the advantage of creating developable surfaces, namely of nil curvature, which boils down to saying that these surface are intrinsically Euclidean.[2] The paper model will then have to be digitalized in order to transfer it onto a software program that regularizes its surfaces, before turning over the files to virtuoso outfits in architectural *prêt à porter* like Permasteelisa.[3]

In these three strategies the 'non-standard' amounts to saying 'original' or 'complex', but in all these instances we remain stuck in a Fine-Arts state of mind which seeks to turn the architectural project into a work of individual creation. And from this point of view non-standard architecture is inscribed within a tradition of the unicum cutting across all sorts of output: artisanal, artistic, industrial or digital. The alternative viewpoint is the series: the object as a particular instance on a continuum. Yet even here things need to be clarified. Because today we know, through the magic of the workings of morphing, that anything can be transformed into something else. In seeking to avoid Charybdis and the unicum, we quickly fall into the Scylla of transformations lacking proper consistency that guarantee an artificial continuity between forms that are unrelated to each other.

Morphè, indeed. What is a shape? What must two objects have in common for one to be able to say that they have the same shape? The answer lies in a basic concept of architectural theory, but also in the modern axiomatics of geometry as formulated by Hilbert in *Grundlage der Geometrie*.[4] Two objects have the same shape when, independently of their size, their elements form between them the same angles, and above all abide by the same proportions. The word is slipshod – the preoccupation with shape is nourished by a theory of proportions that it is essential to understand if we want to avoid the dangers which have all too often beset the course of architectural thinking from neo-Pythagorean acoustics to the Modulor of Le Corbusier. In fact the philosophy that poses the problem most clearly, and this in relation to architecture, is Plato's *The Sophist*.

What's involved here? Plato is preoccupied with these people, the Sophists, who profess all things and their contrary, and who give lessons in overturning all arguments in order to defend theses that are totally opposed to them. In short, the Sophists are image-makers who practise morphing by means of rhetoric. As is his wont, Socrates dialogues and arrives at an examination of two major positions. On the one hand, it isn't difficult to reject the notion of Heraclitus, for whom everything is in movement. Because if everything was change, and change alone, how could we even give a name to the things we speak of? The possibility of the logos presupposes that the invariant exists. On the other hand, however, the position of Parmenides seems hardly more tenable, for he wants Being to be One and that only the One is. This second thesis is all the more difficult to sustain if we keep to Parmenides' famous dichotomy, according to which 'one must be absolutely or not be at all.' For, then, how do we address the Sophist's discourses, discourses that at once 'are' and yet are 'false'? In *The Sophist* Plato comes to recognize that we live in a world which is an intertwining of being and non-being. The Greek word is extremely precise: *sumplokè* means 'intertwining' in contexts that extend from the intermingling of bodies in lovemaking or combat to the combinations of letters in the forming of words. A world of images and simulacra is involved. The visible world is a copy of Ideas, which are the only entities that escape immanence and corruption. But all these copies are worthless since they don't necessarily have the same relationship to their model. There again, Plato is very precise and refers to the visual arts and to architecture. On the one hand we have good copies that respect the proportions of the model, and on the other we have simulacra: shadows and reflections which do not do justice to proportion. In Latin proportion was called 'ratio' and in Greek, 'logos'. We are at the very foundation of rationality and of discourse. For Plato every physical thing is manifestly corrupted by the *becoming*. So much so that no physical model can equal the Idea. The perfect relationship in Plato is the one which will convert identity into an ideal proportion: the isometric relationship of sameness, the ratio of 1:1.

There it is, we have everything necessary for constructing a philosophy of the image that was certainly not foreseeable in Plato's time, but which nevertheless creates the technical specifications of it. Ideas, those abstract events, are so many invariants that escape corruption. In the first rank we find identity, the relationship of sameness which enables the thing to be superposed upon the image, or rest upon movement. The same goes for those perfect forms, the circle or the sphere, which remain identical to themselves in the movement of rotation around their centre. In rotating invariants the same measurements are preserved. And next we have those somewhat degraded copies that reproduce the model while altering its dimensions. These copies remain good, however, to the degree in which the painter, sculptor or architect has respected the correct proportions of the model. These artists will have produced a number of 'similitudes' which preserve both angles and proportions. The ratio is invariant through homothety (similarity), this being the leitmotif of Greek philosophy after Thales. The shadow of the pyramid varies according to the hour, day and season, but the relationship of the pyramid to its shadow remains identical to the relationship between the gnomon planted in the ground and its own shadow – these relationships are variable invariants, intertwinings of being and non-being. Plato also keeps back his criticisms for attacking those sculptors who alter the proportions of statues placed on temple acroteria in order to correct their optical deformations. And sure enough the apparent angle of the different superposed parts changes very quickly when statues are seen from below, in perspective. We enter, here, into the realm of optical corrections adopted by Vitruvius and repeatedly relayed since then by different writers of treatises on architecture. But let's be ultra careful here. Plato doesn't question the raison d'être of these deformations. In that respect he adopts an attitude very different to that of a Perrault, who as a good Cartesian will categorically reject the idea that our senses may be deceived. A circle will always be perceived as a circle, even though its apparent profile is an ellipse when seen sideways on. The devil take those people who, like Caramuel de Lobkowitz, intend to deform the real section of the columns in St Peter's Square so as to take account of their perspectival deformation. Cartesian rationalism remains wholly within this rejection of the hypothesis of the evil genius. Here, there is total incompatibility between Descartes and Desargues, both of who wrote their fundamental texts in 1638. And in point of fact we would have to take the time to look closely at whether there wasn't just as wide a gap between the two great projectivists, Desargues and Pascal, the latter totally commanding the thought of the former, but in a sense that leads to a mystique of the infinite[5], unlike a Desargues, who treats the vanishing point as an ordinary point. This 'hic et nunc' of French rationalist philosophy between 1638 and 1640 is not dependent on any Zeitgeist: we are in the presence of highly divergent lines at the core of so-called 'classical' thinking.

But let us return to Plato, who himself recognizes the validity of optical corrections. He doesn't deny

1 – Library, front view

2 – Library, front view 2

3 – Library, slant view

119

4 – Library, slant view 2

5 – Library, detail

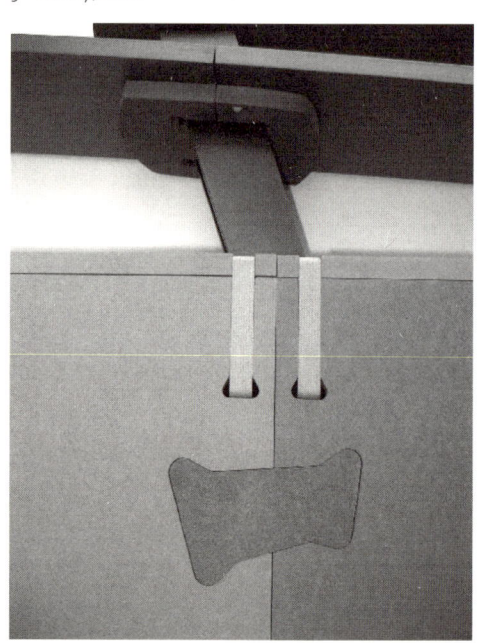

6 – Library, detail 2

7 – Library, detail 3

artists their reasons for minimizing the importance of the model – what he objects to is the result. A statue placed atop a column has to be distorted, yet this copy with altered proportions is the very prototype of the simulacra discredited by Plato. This is because, in comparison with the mathematics of his time, Plato lacks the means to cogitate Ideas that, due to projective deformation, remain invariants. In order to see something other than corruption in this, it would have been necessary for Plato to have projective invariants available to him, and in particular the relationship of relationships, that second-degree logos Spanish mathematicians rightly call *razón doble*, which expresses the number of that which is conserved in projective deformations. We observe, as well, how the discourse of science proceeds. The primitive invariant is the relationship of identity, an isometric relationship of sameness. Next we come to that second variable invariant which articulates Greek rationality and of which we do not take our leave until 1638, at least as far as its translation to geometrical space goes: the homothetic relationship. Desargues makes his entrance here, followed closely by Pascal, the two of them creating the first geometrical projective invariants, alignment and intersection, prior to the invention of the numerical bi-ratio. Following Desargues only a dozen years or so will be necessary before Euler produces, in 1736, the first topological invariants, which are preserved through surface deformations of any kind, insofar as their continuity is respected. Euler's famous formula, which established the invariability of the sum of the number of vertices and faces reduced by the number of edges for any polyhedron, constitutes the first topological invariant, based on which an area of investigation opened up which is far from being exhausted, since, for example, the theory of invariants characterizing knots remains a very active subject of research within contemporary mathematics. But it is in 1872 that it will be given to Félix Klein[6], better known for his bottle, to grasp this movement of geometric reason, which progresses by inventing increasingly sophisticated invariants enabling us to manipulate ever greater variations.

What relationship can this very brief historical survey of geometry have with the opportunities to be sure, right now, of creating a genuine non-standard architecture? What relationship can it have with both architecture and the non-standard? We will evoke an altogether classical definition of architecture: to order the diversity of space in such a way as to guarantee maximum freedom for the collectivity that frequents or colonizes it. Arranging means providing a diversity that is not naturally livable in with an invariant. Absolute space is an exterior that is scarcely more inhabitable than the hyper-grid of a totalitarian architecture. We are seeking devices that guarantee the invariants necessary to the supplest possible varieties. It is here that we are concerned with a non-standard architecture, to which we think that digital technologies might permit a threshold to be crossed, without the notion being completely new in itself. Because, in fact, if we set aside the extreme forms that architectures with isometric invariants (like Newton's cenotaph or the totalitarian spaces of a Hilberseimer) have constituted, architectural thinking has always turned, for preference, towards proportional invariants. To the point that a Le Corbusier still goes back to proportion when attempting to elaborate a universal system of industrial standardization. That he then invokes a harmonic, neo-Pythagorean conception invented all of a piece by 19th-century German ideologists[7], does not detract in the least from the pertinence of the concept of proportion in architecture; on the contrary, this modern error proves just how difficult it is to imagine architecture without proportion. Also, when the theorists of the Italian Renaissance attempt to interpret the perspective system invented by Brunelleschi in 1420, it is still to the system of proportions that they will repeatedly have recourse, striving in vain to reduce the projective coordinates by establishing simple ratios between the diminishing segments of a paved area seen in perspective, even though this is a canonic case of projective bi-relation.

The fact is that architecture was never to understand projective ratios except in a highly ambiguous way. Even though projective geometry was prepared and indeed invented by architects; a filiation that extends over two hundred years, from Brunelleschi to Desargues, and including Philibert De L'Orme, which is prolonged at least as far as Monge, and whose first area of application was the military fortifications at the École Mézières. Even though architects are the ones who worked out the projective coordinates, the stereotomic works integrating this geometry in the production of architecture itself always remained secondary: at the very most the magnificent vaults in the Hôtel de Ville in Arles[8], but more often than not simple additions such as the pendentives of Philibert De L'Orme. And the place of topological invariants, strap-work and the like, is presented under a still more problematic light: the knot[9] or foliated scroll[10] performing the role of a basic ornamental motif, a register from which, prior to very contemporary designs, these topological forms hardly ever deviate, aside from a few specific applications such as the extraordinary staircase schemes Philibert De L'Orme created for the Château des Tuileries.[11]

This formal analysis needs, of course, to be refined, but the more we consider the history of architecture from the CFAO angle[12], the more it seems to us that tradition has always incorporated, albeit in very different dosages, these four types of invariant: isometric, homothetic, projective and topological. What happens today is that we have the means at our disposal which allow the implicit system of hierarchy between these different registers to be repeatedly called into question, to the future profit of more sophisticated invariants, both projective and topological. Yet we don't believe in a merely topological architecture – an aleatory, fluid, moving or virtual, not to mention non-Euclidean one, or whatever – any more than we once did in an isometric architecture that was central, orthogonal and panoptic. We are on the lookout, much more, for a just and ordinary environment that incorporates the different registers of invariants, since in order to grant even more space to the grid/chaos alternation in the suburbs the media consensus is increasingly in favour of spatial ruptures in certain privileged locations. Generally speaking, and apart from a situation in which certain invariants are formulated by the actual context of the building, architecture will order the diversity of space that much better when it brings each of the four invariants into play by deterritorializing their traditional register of application: the isometry of central planes, the similitude of a proportional architectonics, the projectivity of complex solids, and the topology of intertwining ornaments. This reinterpretation of traditional registers takes in a rereading of historical urban typologies. An architecture based on variable invariants allows us to return, in effect, to typology in a way other than the neo-Platonist mode[13] of the identically or proportionally reproducible model.[14] The city thus becomes a field for the varying of historical invariants.

In point of fact, relationships in the city being determined, at least in part, by the relations of production; what is to be done in order for a non-standard architecture to become a social fact different from the latest form of distinction of a clientele which has the means to augment standard budgets? How do we prevent the non-standard from collapsing into original formalism? How do we see to it that the object is genuinely conceived and produced as a single instance in a series? How do we integrate the architectural object in the urban fabric? To all these questions there is, in our opinion, one basic response: the productivity of agencies of various architectures, of conception keeping track of fabrication. From this point of view, the question of non-standard architecture is no different from the basic problem of postindustrial societies, namely the productivity of services in general.[15] The architect is a worker whose mode of production is conditioned by digital technologies, but the development of these has nothing natural about it. In that respect the writing of software programs is at once the major genre of contemporary culture[16] and at the same time the privileged terrain of a confrontation of the forces which organize production in our societies. In this field it is a strategic concept that will determine the form standard architecture will take in the years ahead: this is the concept of associativeness.

What are we to understand by associativeness? Associativeness is the software method of constituting the architectural project in a long sequence of relationships from the first conceptual hypotheses to the driving of the machines that prefabricate the components that will be assembled on site. Designing on an associative software program comes down to transforming the geometrical design in a programming language interface. Thus, to create a point at the intersection of two lines no longer consists of creating a graphic element, but in establishing a relationship of intersection on the basis of two relationships of alignment. Here, the reader will recall that this involves two basic projective invariants, as well as two primitive gestures in space: aiming and intercepting. The whole interest of associative CFAO software programs lies in translating this geometrical relationship into a program which will see to it that the point of intersection is recalculated as it should be when we displace the end points of the segments of the lines we intersect. Of course, only an elementary link is involved here and all this only has architectural interest provided we are able to set up long sequences of subordinates on the basis of a small number of primitive elements called, in technical jargon, 'original parents'. The first consequence of associativeness is the need to rationally formalize the architectural project, taking great pains to distinguish antecedents and dependents, at the risk, if not, of creating circular references or all kinds of other logical incongruities. Associativeness constitutes, then, a filter obliging us to rationally think through the architectural project and to explicate its hypotheses. Ultimately, this ought to encourage clear thinking in both the procedures and concepts of architecture. We might also be surprised that this concept has awakened so little interest among those who once flaunted themselves as the champions of rational architecture.

What we have just described concerns the activities of conceiving the project alone. Now, the whole difficulty of non-standard architecture lies in the sheer quantity of data that has to be generated and manipulated in order to industrially fabricate components that are totally different to each other at a price that is not necessarily higher than if they were standardized. In order to efficiently manage these data flows and to guarantee full and entire associativeness between conception and fabrication, it is essential above all else to work on the same nucleus, or control program, which will enable us, among other things, to ensure size control of the components following the conception stage, and this up to and including the generating of the programs (code ISO) that will drive the digital machines ensuring the production of the objects. On these grounds the technical specifications of a CFAO associative system includes at least four basic elements. The first has to do with the need to handle vast groups of complex elements, all of them different, elements that it is no longer possible to design one by one. This causes us to have recourse to a process known in technical terms as the 'insertion of components'. The designing of a project using an insertion of components obliges us to first think up a 'model' of relation that can be applied in all the situations in which we will have to create a component of this type. The model is, as it were, an invariant that must cope with all the variations to which the terms we have established relations between will be submitted. That Platonism bears the seed of all the technological developments of our Western societies is an assertion that for us is no longer the object of theoretical speculation, but instead the result of empirical verification. And we have indeed experienced situations in which the implementation of this logic of components in a non-standard project has been able to generate gains in productivity of a factor of 100! Furthermore, it is only on the express understanding of gains in productivity of this order of grandeur that the term 'non-standard architecture' has meaning.

Another aspect of the technical specifications is the need to work in distended flows and in a state of provisional information up until the very last moment, and this in a delocalized way. It was Moholy-Nagy who said in the 1920s that the criterion of modernity of a work was of its being able to be transmitted by telephone. This is even truer today. The multiplicity and dispersion of interlocutors, the volatility of decisions, oblige us to begin formalizing the project on the basis of uncertain information. Some values that are capable of being easily corrected must be able to be given by default, some points must be able to be defined in a geometric location without receiving a definitive positioning on this location, manufacturing programs must be able to be brought up to date the evening before their execution. Prior to taking shape as constructed buildings, non-standard architecture proceeds from an abstract architecture that orders the flow of data necessary for digital production, and this in a much more automated way since there is no longer an intermediary between conceiver and machine. The modification of one of the original parents of the project has to automatically set in motion the updating of the entire sequence of information because human intervention is always subject to error. As it is, a truly non-standard architecture will only emerge on condition that it reproduces in the realm of construction what has already occurred in the realm of edition. Just as it is possible today to write and lay out graphic documents that can be put online on the internet by their conceiver and be printed on demand by a distant reader, so non-standard architecture presupposes that the conceiver of a building is capable of producing all the documents necessary for the distant production of architectural components without the a posteriori intervention of any office of control or office of business studies filtering out the errors from them. Lastly, in order for all this not to remain at the utopian stage, this automated sequence of data must include the documents that serve as backup to the economic transactions necessary to the production of the structure: specifications, estimate, production and delivery orders, assembly plans, etc.

To be sure, all these technical specifications turn associativeness into a mechanism that is at once very powerful and very complex. CFAO software programs are only beginning to implement computerized architecture in such spheres as mechanics. But there's nothing to suggest that this full and entire associativeness may never see the light of day, except in very compartmentalized and exceedingly limited industrial applications. Many factors of a social, legal and cultural kind are involved, which may be summed up in a single formula: in order for associativeness not to become mere technological prowess and for it to be inscribed within economic reality, it is necessary for conception and production to be strongly integrated. Indeed, what point is there in developing highly sophisticated software tools if we don't encounter users – and architects, in particular – who are ready to understand the functioning of these? The ability and rigour necessary to using such software programs means that they are by nature aimed at well-informed users endowed with a certain level of logical and geometrical reasoning. What use is it, too, to develop an associativeness between conception and fabrication if in practice order-placers and producers do not manage to establish relationships that enable them to make the most of the continuity of the flow of information? As long as each of the two parties doesn't encounter the arrangement that makes it advantageous to collaborate and not to artificially break this chain and blame the other party, associativeness will be a mere software producer's marketing ploy, or worse still, a strategic error of development. More than ever, architecture will benefit from the opportunities offered by the non-standard only on condition that it progressively and patiently constructs a genuine culture of digital production.

1 Conception Assistée par Ordinateur (Computer-Assisted Design).
2 On all surfaces developable on a plane, the sum of the angles of a triangle remains constant and equals 180°.
3 An Italian company, the market leader in facade facings for oddly shaped buildings of great size.
4 David Hilbert: *Fondements de la géométrie* (1899); see the chapter devoted to the theory of proportions.
5 To us it seems important to note that the theorem of the mystical hexagon was invented long before Pascal was connected with Port-Royal. There would thus have been a mystical process of Pascal's own that had nothing to do with his relations with his sister and her entering the convent. Was Guarini, who rejected the secular implications of Arguesian geometry, aware of this?
6 Félix Klein was to expound his general conceptions of geometry in the following texts: *Ueber die so-genannt Nicht Euklidisch Geometrie* (1871); *Au sujet des géométries dites non-euclidiennes: Programme d'Erlangen* (1872).
7 *Le Nombre d'or, anatomie d'un mythe*.
8 Probably built by Hardouin-Mansart around 1640.
9 Gottfried Semper, *Der Stil*, 1861.
10 Alois Riegl, *Stilfragen* (1893); French translation: *Questions de style*, Hazan, 1992.
11 See the reconstruction drawing in Philippe Potié, *Philibert De L'Orme, Figures du projet*.
12 Conception et Fabrication Assistée par Ordinateur (Computer-Assisted Conception and Fabrication).
13 At the level of problems, Platonist philosophy seems much more open than most of the interpretations given of it by epigones.
14 See the series of illustrations in which a regular hexagon, archetype of the central plan, is varied so as to progressively transform it into a figure certain Californian architects would not disown, while preserving the projective invariants of the theories of Brianchon and Pascal: a convergence of diagonals, an alignment of the intersections of opposite sides.
15 Paul Krugmann, *L'Âge des rendements décroissants*, Economica, and *La Mondialisation n'est pas coupable; vertus et limites du libre échange*, La Découverte. More conjunctionally, one may refer to the article by Patrick Artus, under the heading of 'Economiques des Rebonds' in *Libération*, March 31st 2003, called 'Des finances pour la croissance de l'Europe'.
16 We can only render homage here to the developers of the Missler Company, who go on developing the TopSolid software program on which the Objectile application is based. We wish to thank Christian Arber and Jean-Luc Rolland, along with their whole team of collaborators, foremost among whom we have to mention Jean-Louis Jammot and Charles Claeys.

PART TWO: PROJECTS

INTRODUCTION

Building, altering, demolishing, rebuilding – it is a time-honoured cycle. Accordingly, there have been many attempts before now to anticipate the changes buildings go through. Not a new phenomenon then, but today there is one major difference. Ours is an increasingly dynamic age. Economic and social changes are succeeding one another at an ever more rapid pace and the resulting changes in use require that buildings possess a great ability to adapt. The 29 projects we have chosen had to satisfy two key criteria, namely that they were designed recently and are now largely on site, and that they pick up on the changes each will inevitably undergo.

When compiling this section of the book we spent a great deal of time discussing how to select the projects and how to categorize them. In principle there are three possible ways for buildings to deal with time and uncertainty:
they can be polyvalent;
they can be part permanent (the 'base building') and part changeable (the 'fit-out');
they can be semi-permanent, e.g. industrial, flexible and demountable (IFD) buildings.
These three categories are treated in depth by Bernard Leupen in the first text of Part One (see pp. 12-20). However, the many projects we found interesting and sufficiently illustrative of the problematics of Time-based Architecture proved difficult to place under just one of these headings. Once again, reality is a lot less simple than those documenting it would wish. After several attempts at categorization, we dropped the idea of hard-and-fast divisions and arrived at the present sequence of projects. The only aspect in any way informing the order of presentation is the time factor. If the first projects – the B001 housing block and the Cathedral of Our Lady of the Angels – are pretty much built to last for ever without needing much in the way of modification, the ABT/Damen office building and the Spacebox are semi-permanent by nature.

We can discern several design strategies informing the efforts to achieve a greater adaptability. There are, for example, buildings so constructed as to admit changes of use. This may be effected with sliding partitions to produce different spatial configurations or by fully adaptable facade and floor systems. This ability of buildings to be inhabited in various ways is termed 'polyvalence'.

Another approach concerns buildings that can be simply altered internally or externally by making the distinction between a permanent and a changeable portion. A variation on this theme is buildings that can be easily extended. The building as a whole is the permanent portion to which new elements can be added.

In addition, buildings can be designed on the basis of a period of use specified beforehand. The principle behind this type of building is that there is nothing basically wrong with demolition or disassembly as long as it has been anticipated. If it is already known that a building's functional needs will change drastically after a particular time-span it can be useful to construct it specifically for that period. However, this need not always be a case of building for the short term. Buildings designed to a 'best-by date' may well last for centuries.

Each project in this section is accompanied by an in-depth description of the design strategy used and an explanation of why it rates as Time-based Architecture.

FORTRESS ON THE SOUND
B001, Malmö, Sweden,
Gert Wingårdh, 2001

For Gert Wingårdh, sustainable in the first place means well-considered. Armed with natural materials and robust building techniques, he designed for the B001 housing exhibition in Malmö, Sweden, a housing block that should last for hundreds of years. The theme of the exhibition was sustainability in all its aspects. Ralph Erskine and Santiago Calatrava were among the other architects invited to make designs that combined ecological insights with the latest technical discoveries.

Gert Wingårdh's building is a prominent feature of the residential area designed by Klas Tham. The housing block looks out over the Sound, the strait between the North and Baltic Seas. It consists of two parts, the tallest of which protects the district beyond, with its narrow car-free streets, from the cutting sea wind. In the central courtyard directly behind the 'fortress' stands the second, less-tall apartment building. The facades of the housing block as a whole are of a lightweight concrete brick plastered on both sides. The composition and thickness of this facade system renders additional insulation superfluous. The block's plinth is clad with limestone, as is the floor of the ground level. Its stairs are generously proportioned and have solid banisters.

Wingårdh claims that only architecture that has been crafted with care can stand the test of time. A century ago it was quite normal for architects to design not only the exterior but also the interiors of housing blocks in the greatest detail. Such authentic finishes are appreciated and cared for by residents today. Wingårdh sees in this the proof that an architect's active interest can lengthen a building's useful life. So here at B001 he has designed every detail of the kitchens himself.

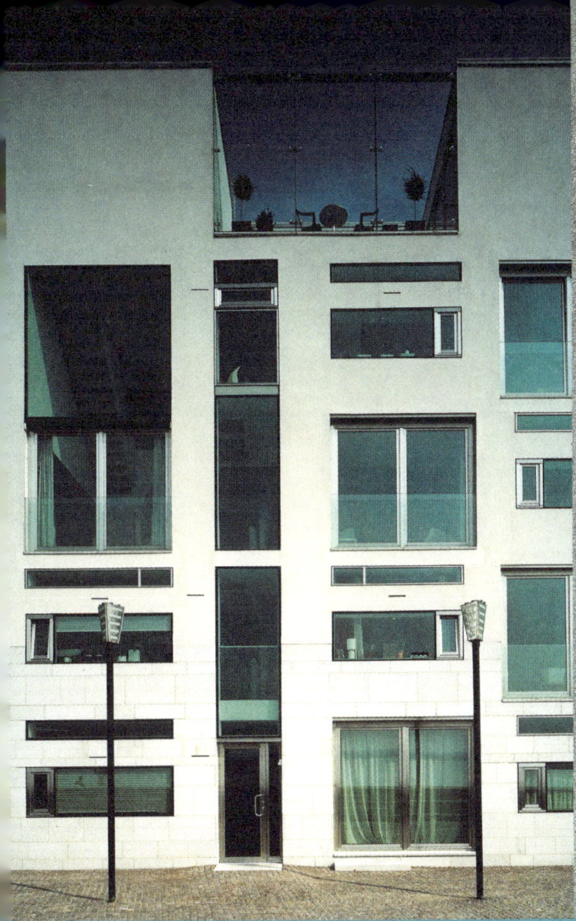

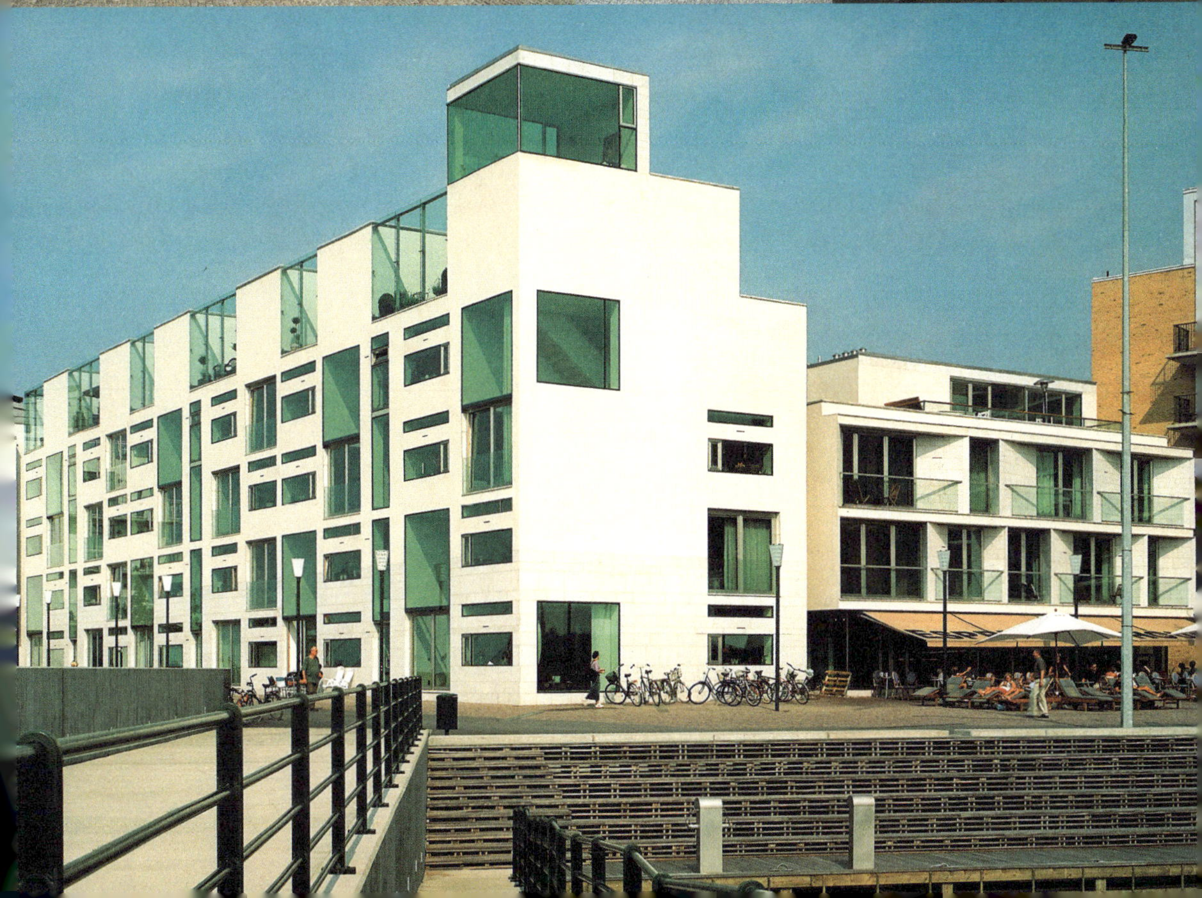

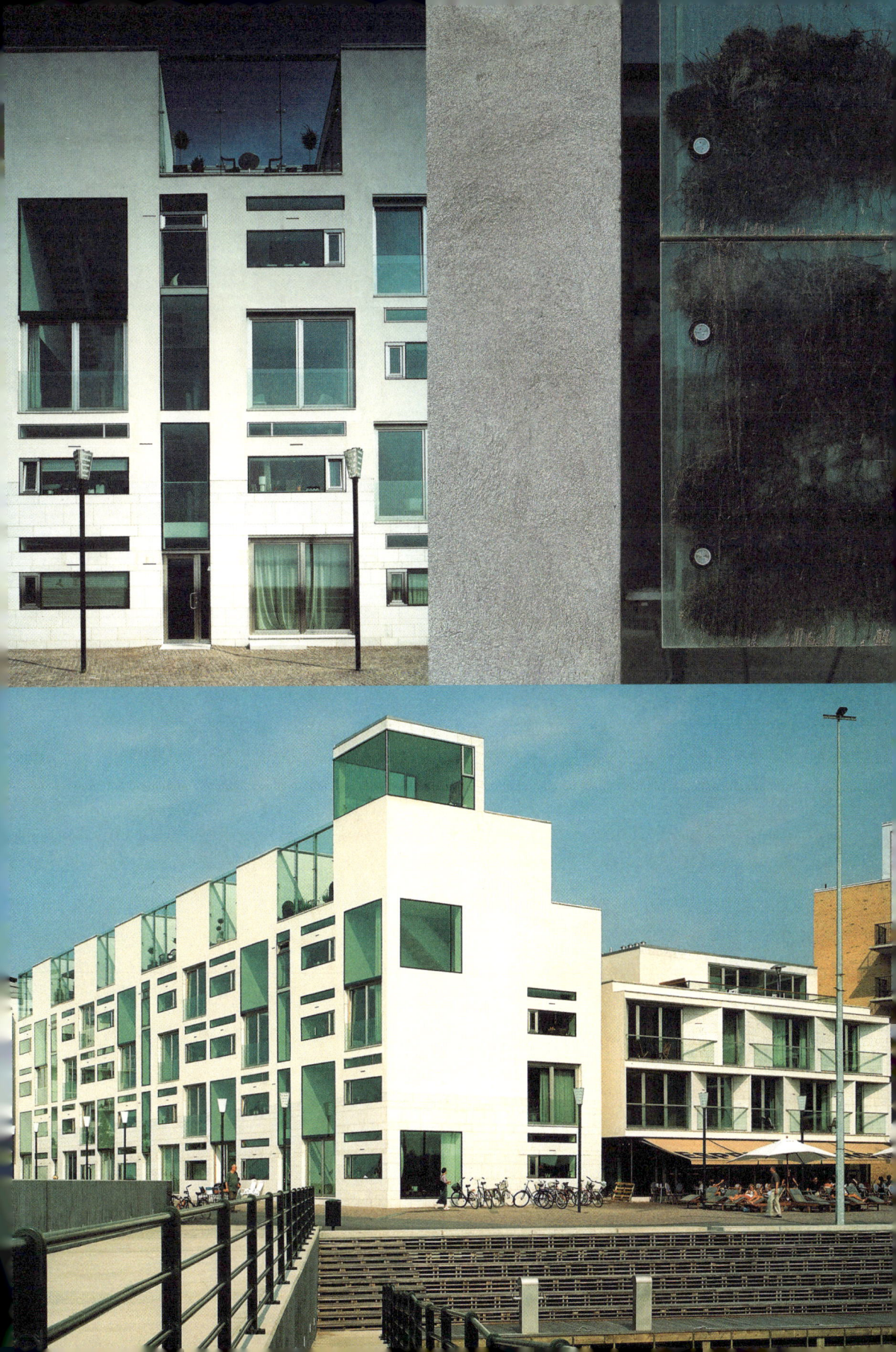

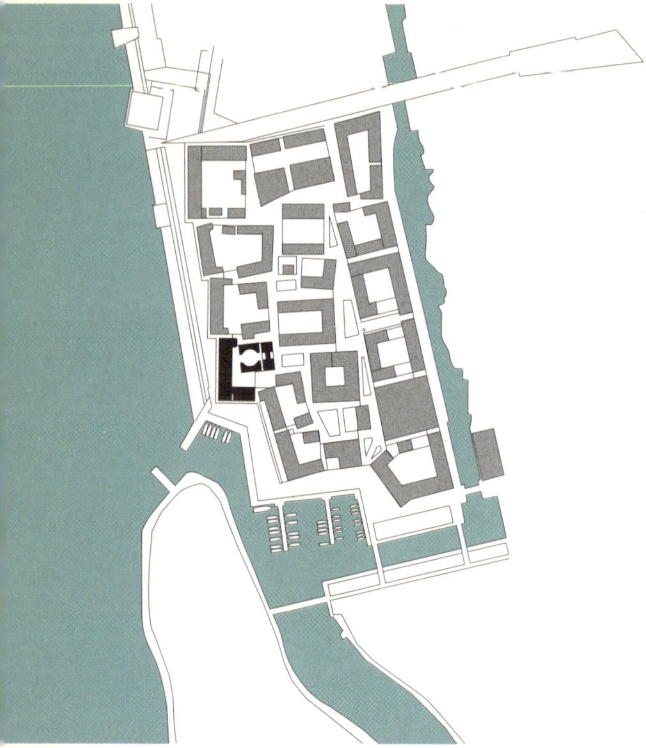

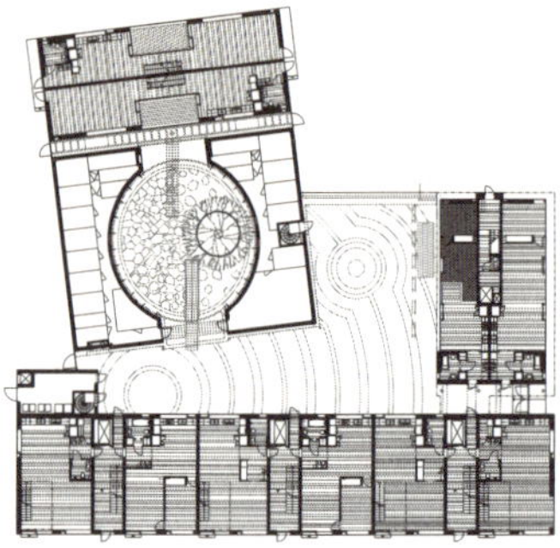

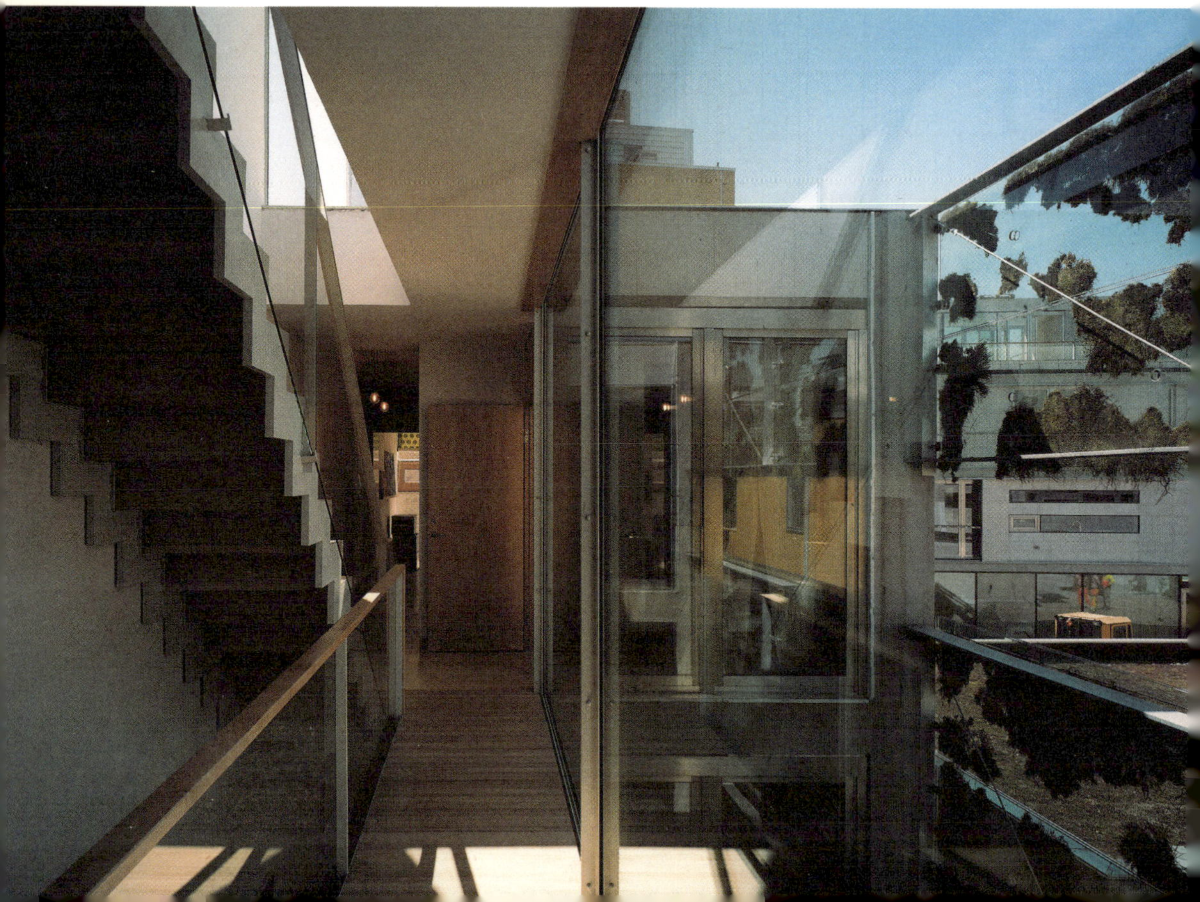

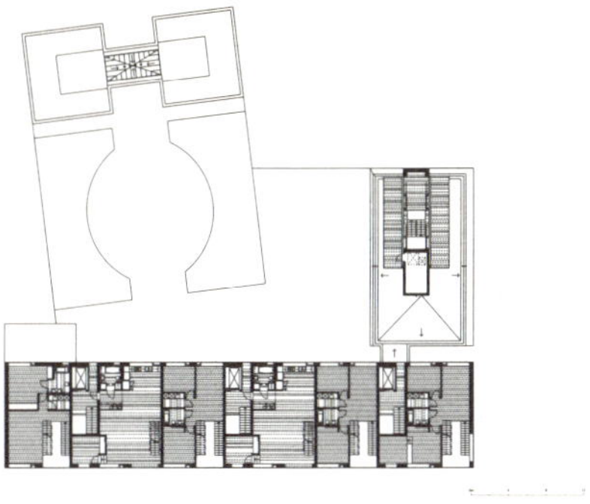
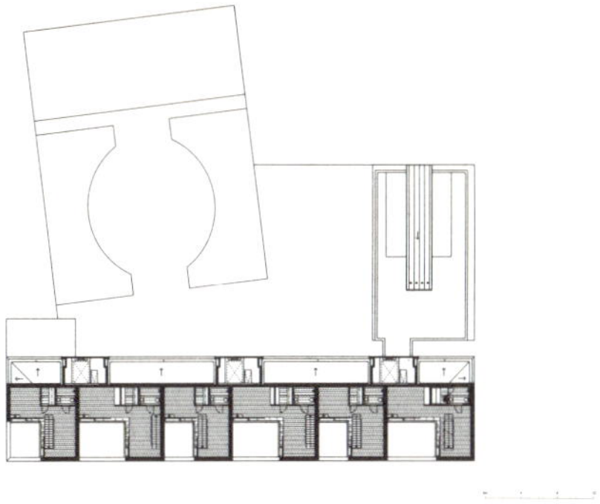
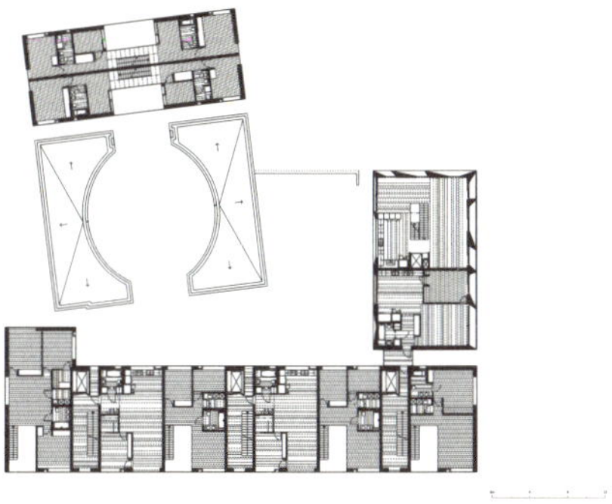
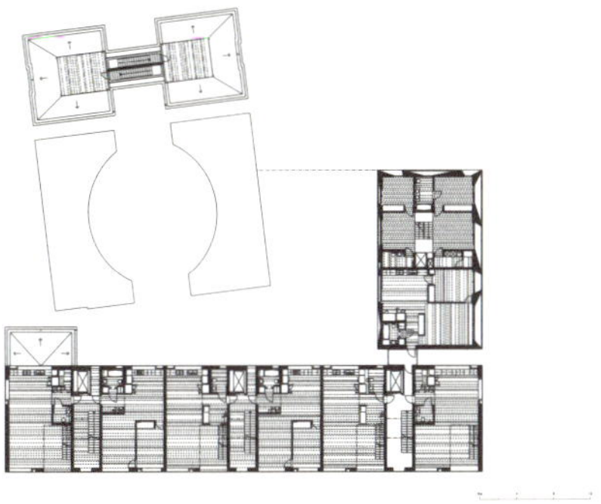
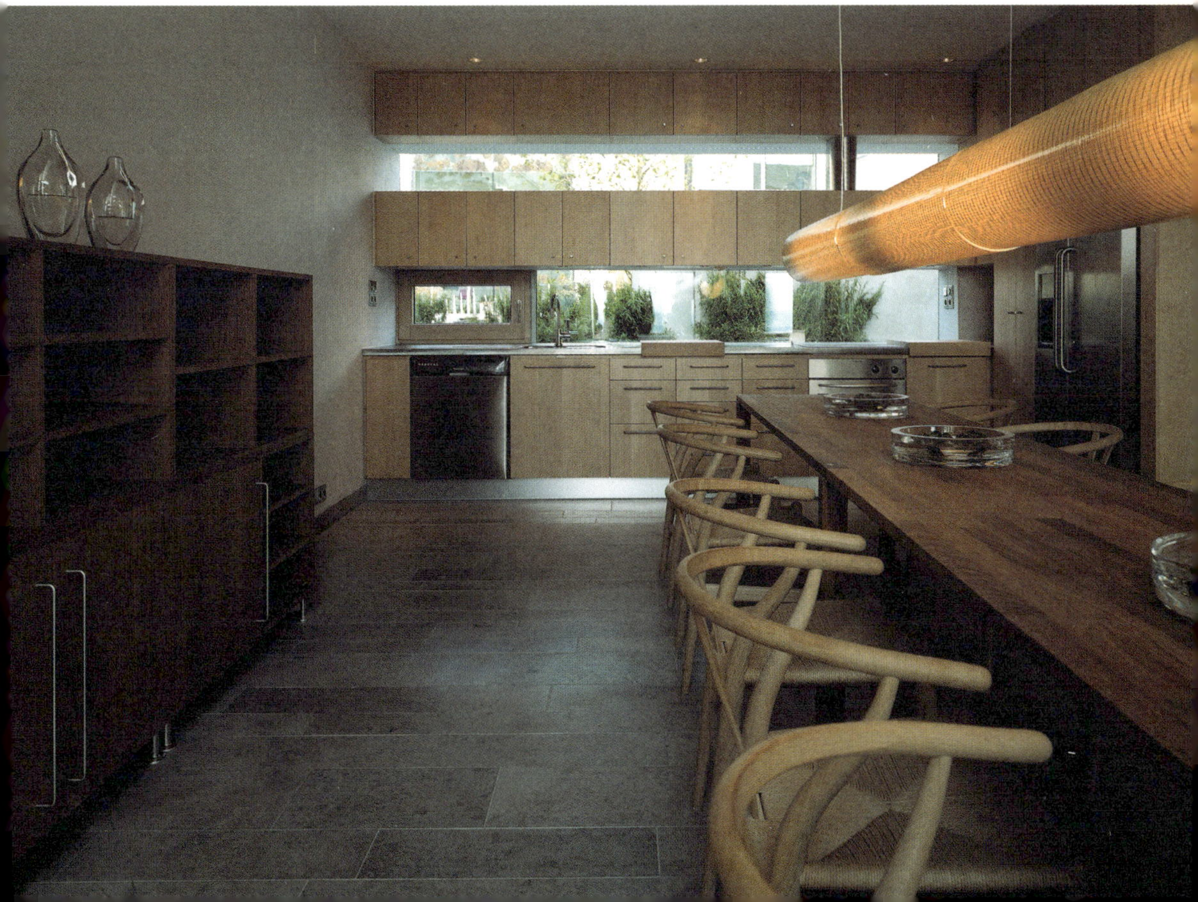

CATHEDRAL FOR A NEW MILLENNIUM
Cathedral of Our Lady of the Angels, Los Angeles, US, José Rafael Moneo, 2003

Just as many medieval cathedrals were built on the banks of rivers, so this modern cathedral stands along the traffic flows of the Hollywood Freeway. The Cathedral of Our Lady of the Angels is designed to stand for 500 years.
Its architect, Rafael Moneo, gave it a monumental, solid concrete structure with walls metres thick in places. But in an area given to earthquakes like California this is not enough. Whether the building will indeed last for centuries largely depends on the effect of the ingenious mechanism beneath it. The monumental volume is built on shock absorbers able to withstand quakes of up to 8.4 on the Richter scale. Armed with this isolating mechanism the concrete structure is able to move 70 centimetres in all directions. The materials used to flesh out the building are likewise trustworthy and sustainable: the roofs are clad with copper, the walls and floors with stone and the ceilings are of wood. The concrete bears the colours of the traditional Californian mission posts built in this area two centuries earlier.

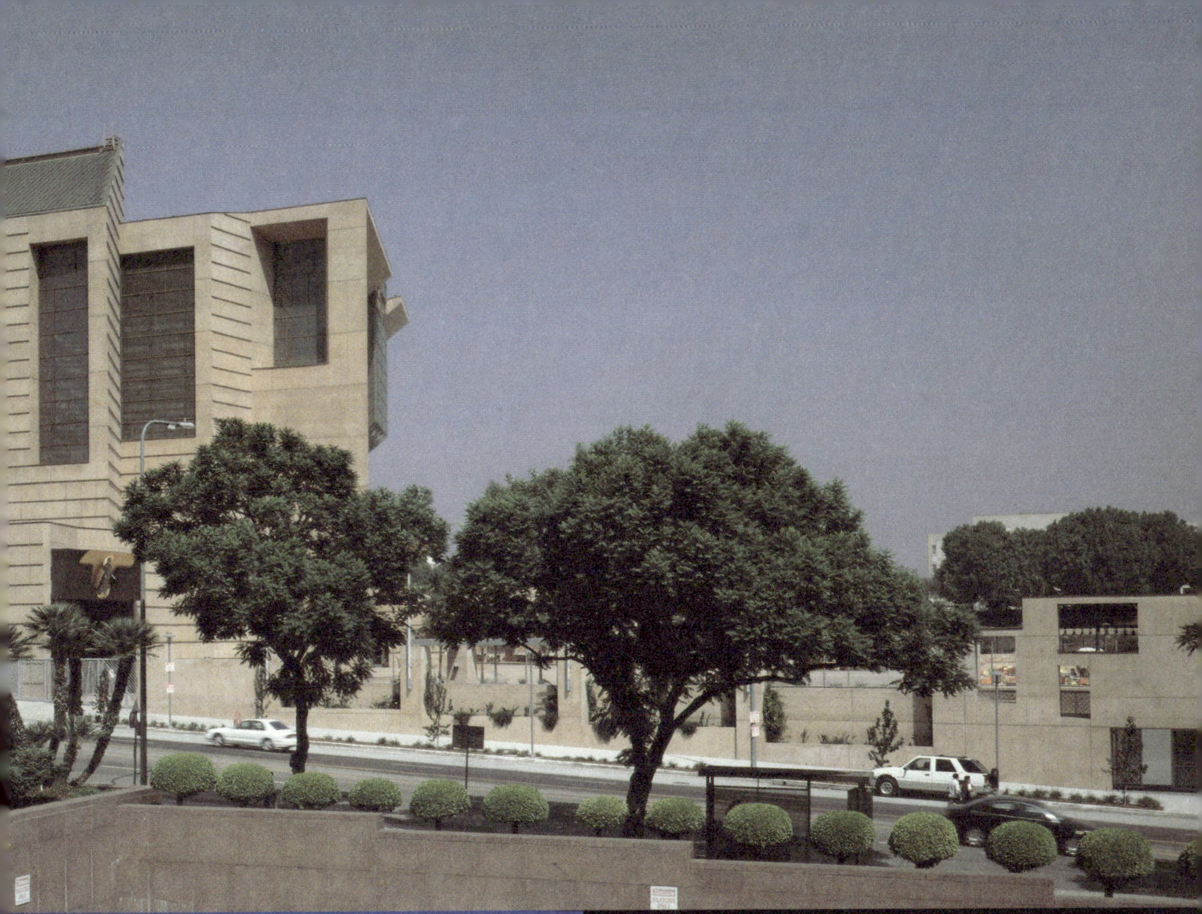

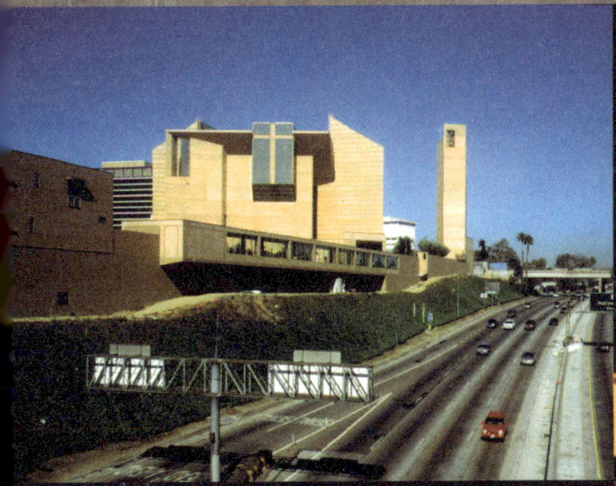

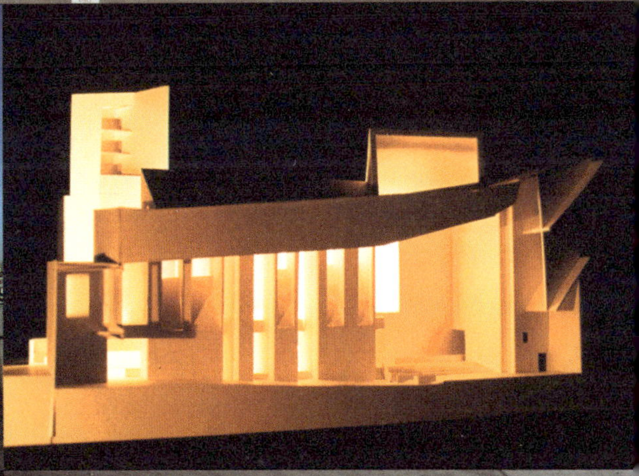

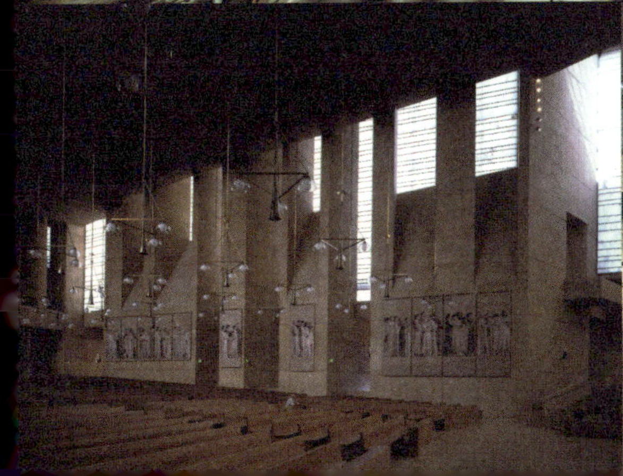

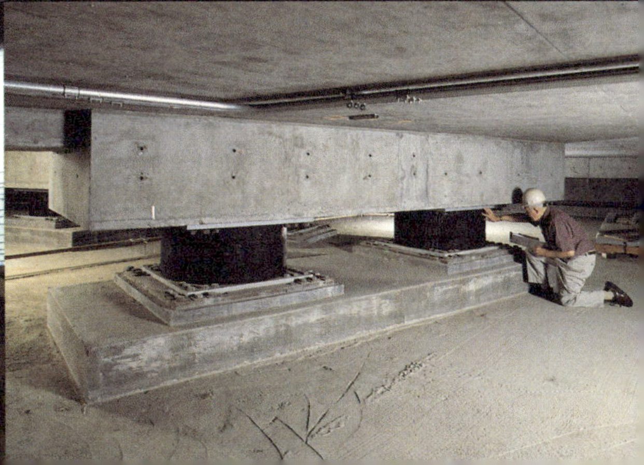

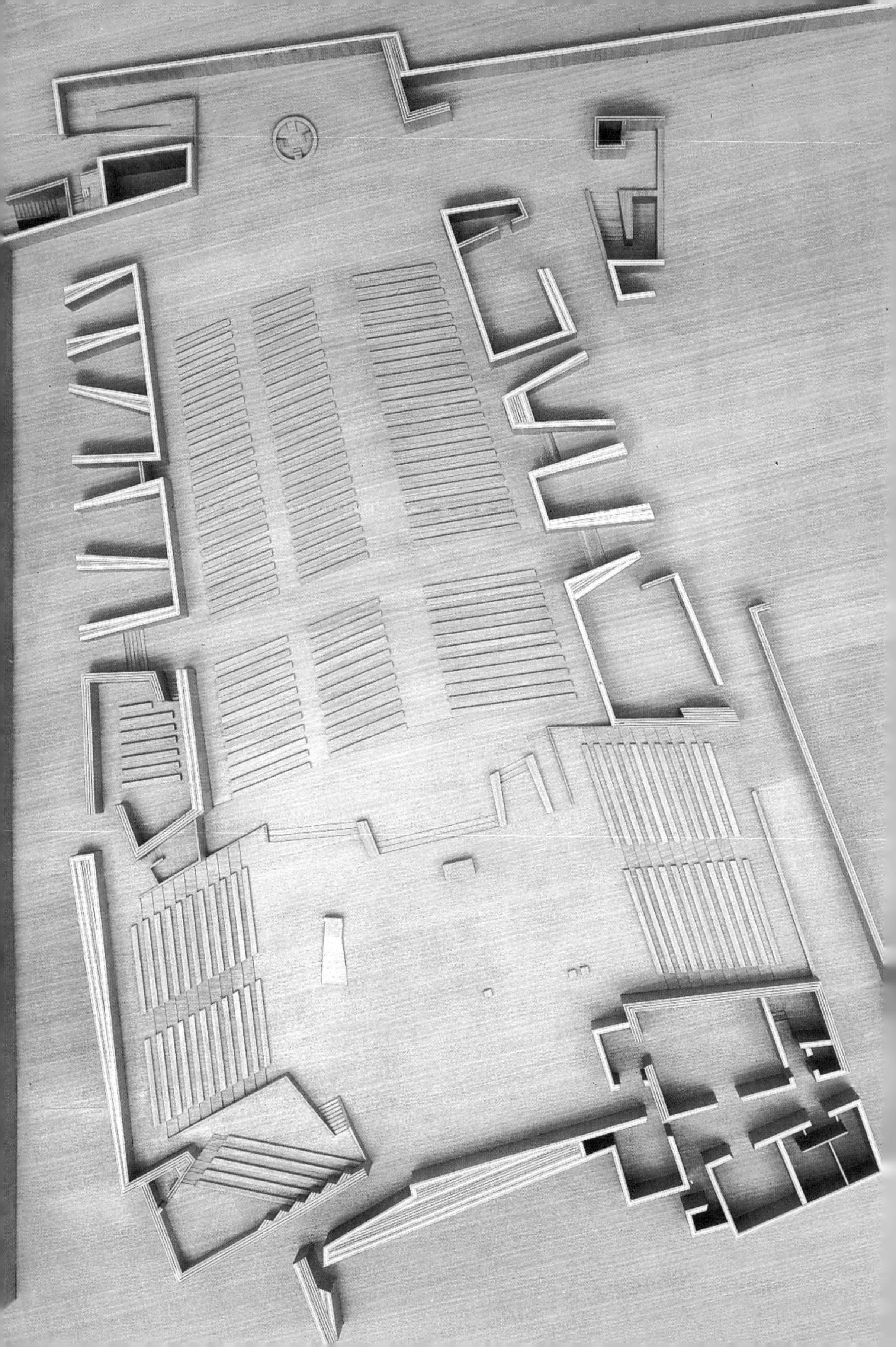

Los Angeles Cathedral. Section A-A'.

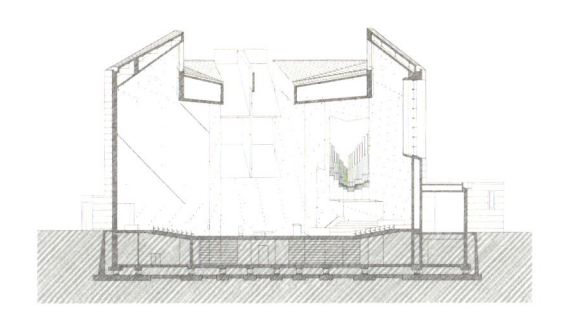

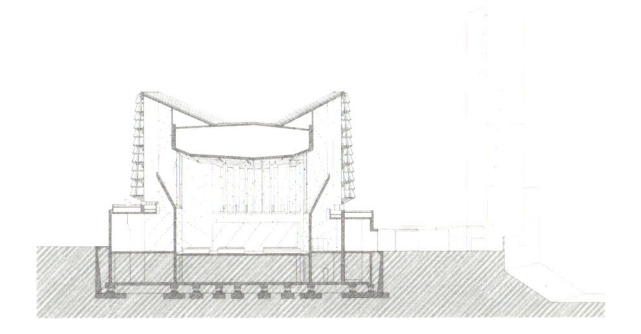

Los Angeles Cathedral. Section D-D'.

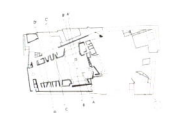

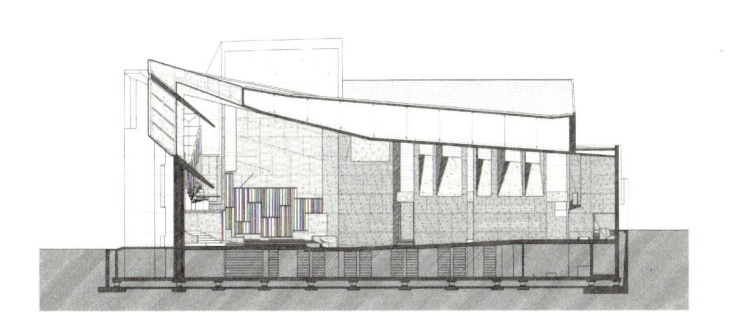

Los Angeles Cathedral. Section F-F'.

POLYVALENT HOUSES IN VIENNA

Housing on Grieshofgasse, 1996, and Wulzendorferstrasse, 1996, Vienna, Austria, Helmut Wimmer

The architect Helmut Wimmer designs buildings that can be occupied in different ways. This quality is not limited to the design of the floor plans; the facades too reflect the different and ever changing ways of use. Two housing projects, both built in Vienna in 1996, are rooted in these ideas. On Grieshofgasse Wimmer has designed dwellings with two living spaces of equal size flanking a central hall. Both living spaces can be divided in two using sliding partitions. The four compartments thus created can be variously linked via the central hall. As a result, each dwelling is suited not only for a small family but also for two one-bedroom flats with a shared bathroom.

In another part of the city, in Wulzendorferstrasse, Wimmer has realized a project similar in all respects but on a larger scale. Two annexes either side of the main living space can be opened up to it by sliding away partitions, so that these dwellings too enjoy great freedom of use.

Wimmer feels that the facades should show how individual units are used. The housing on Grieshofgasse has a double facade with a multicoloured cladding. Sliding panels between the outer, uninsulated glass skin and the internal skin of insulating glass can be used to screen off the interior. Residents were challenged to paint these panels as they saw fit, giving the building the most varied appearance from outside.

In the Wulzendorferstrasse housing, prominent white sun blinds make for a constantly changing exterior depending on the weather and the degree of privacy required. So in this project, too, the way the dwellings are used is indirectly reflected in the architecture.

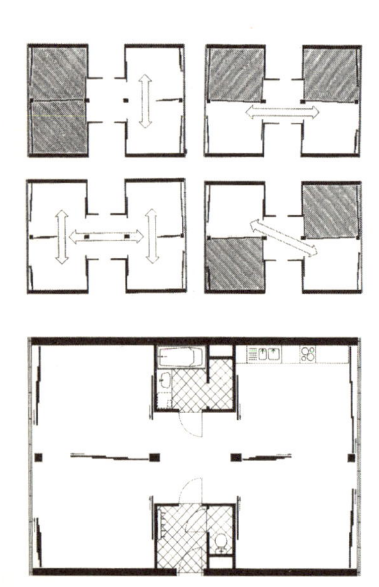

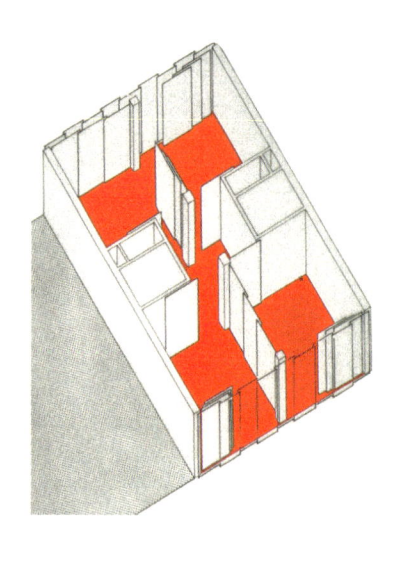

Grieshofgasse housing, 1996, Vienna

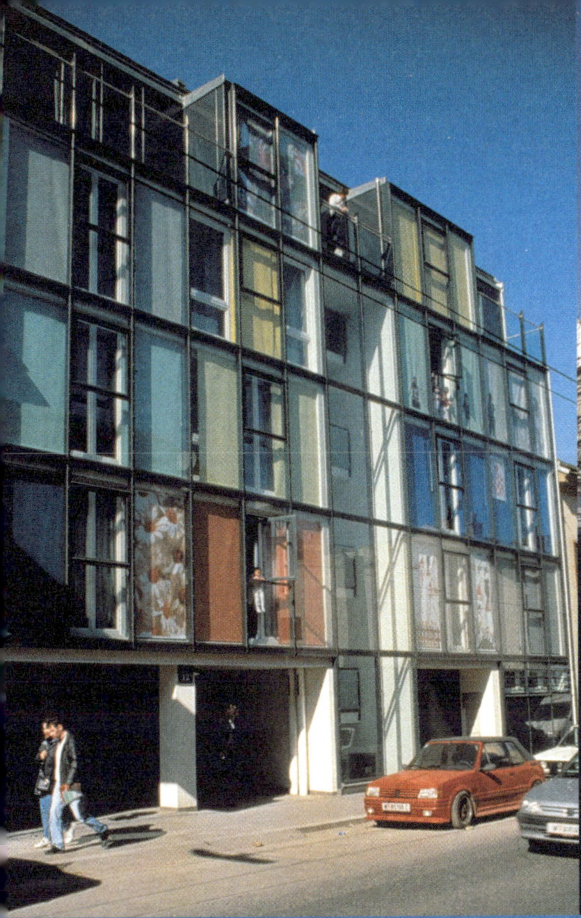
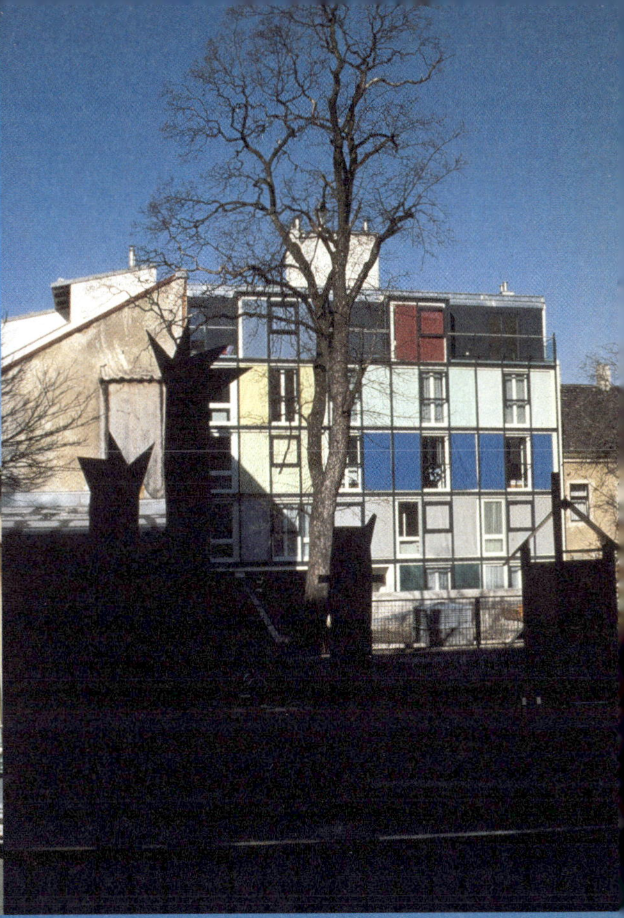
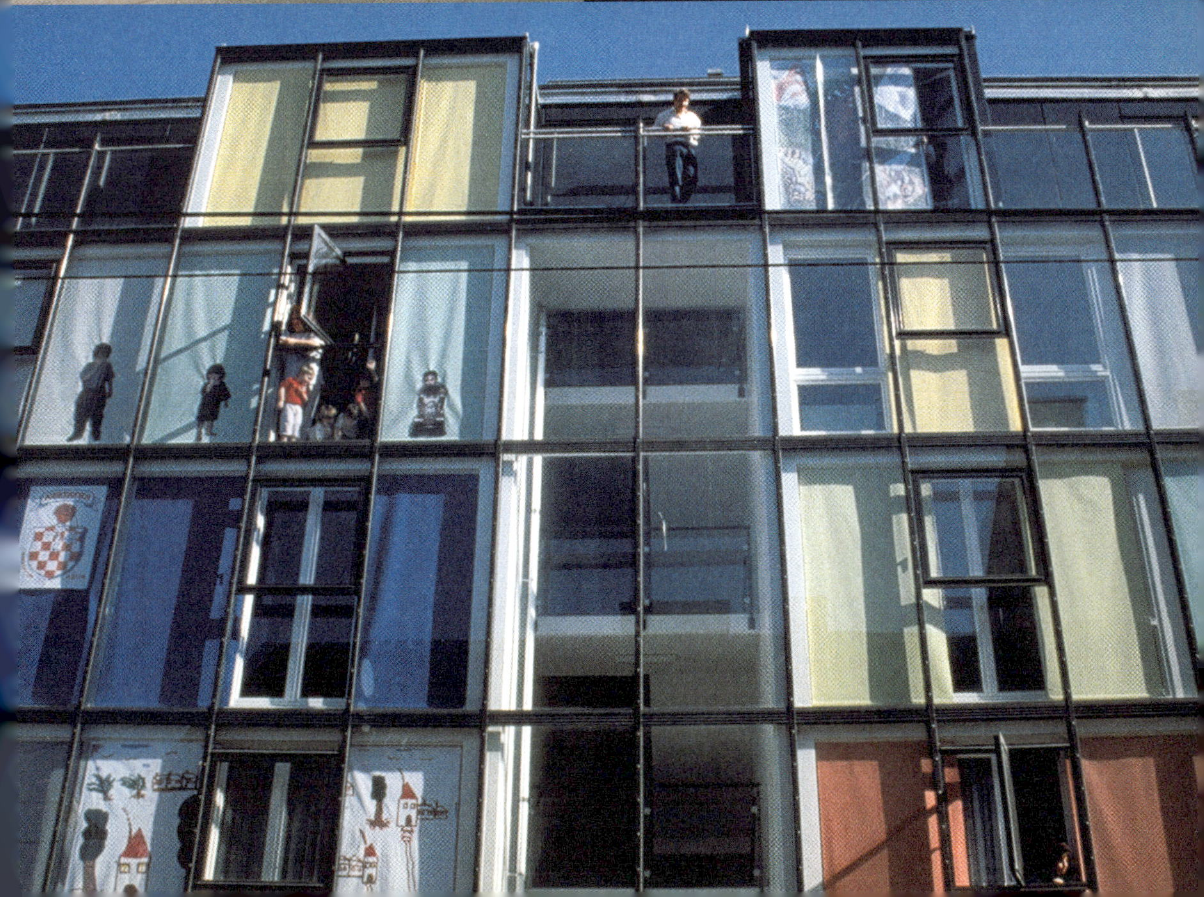

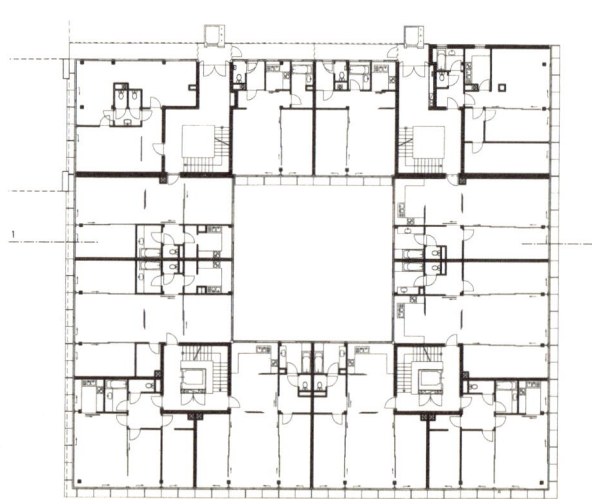

Wulzendorferstrasse housing, 1996, Vienna

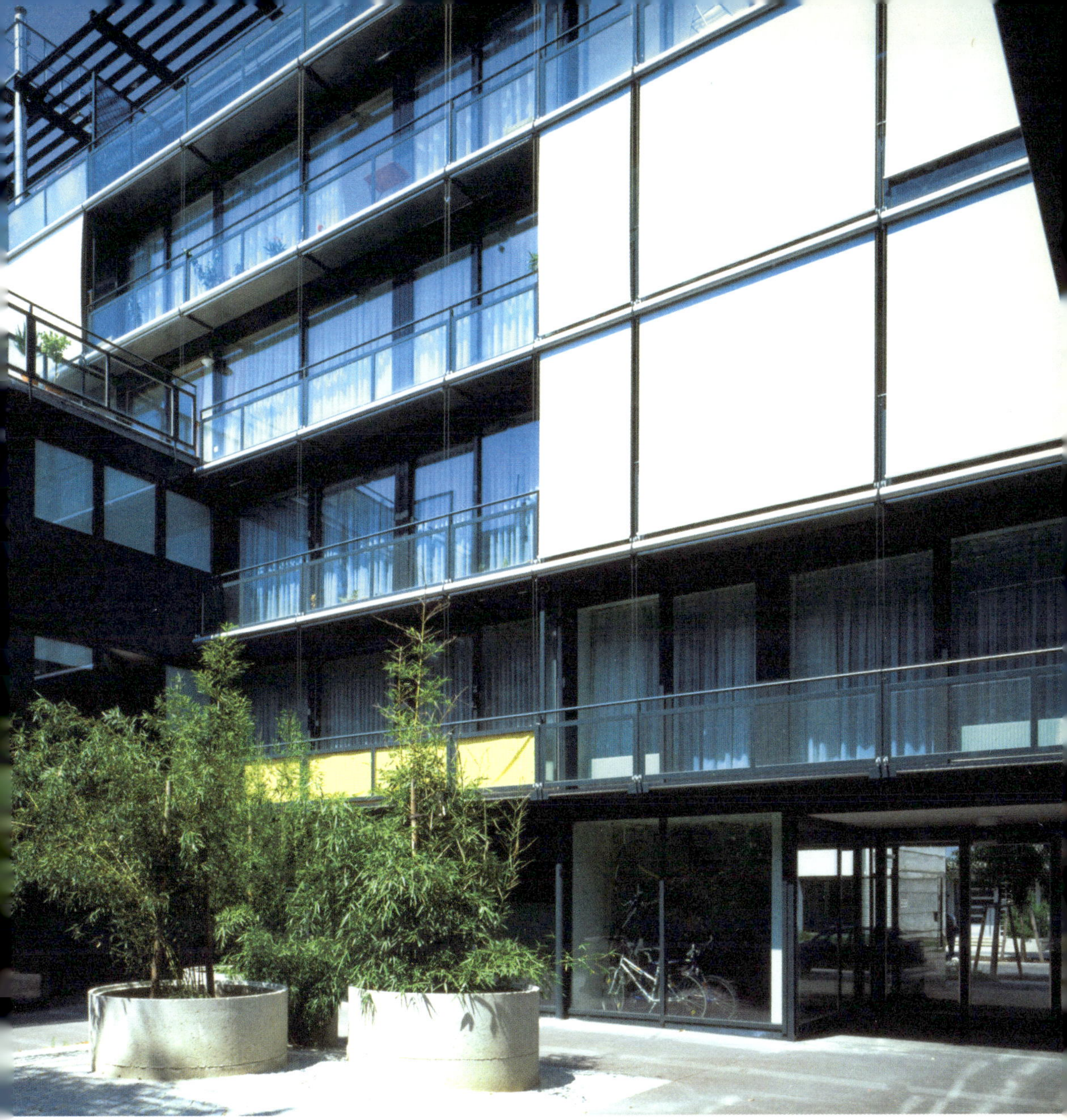

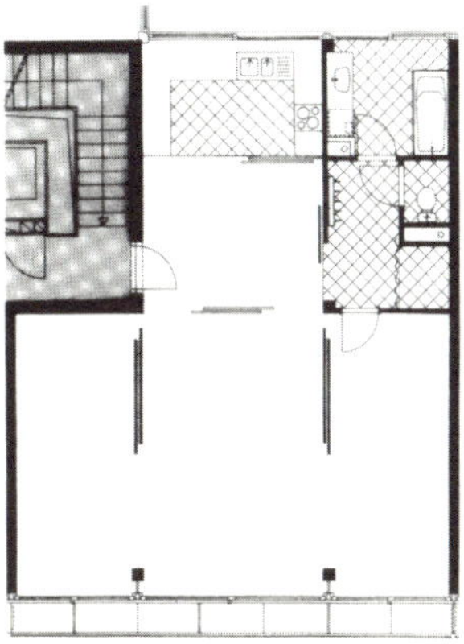

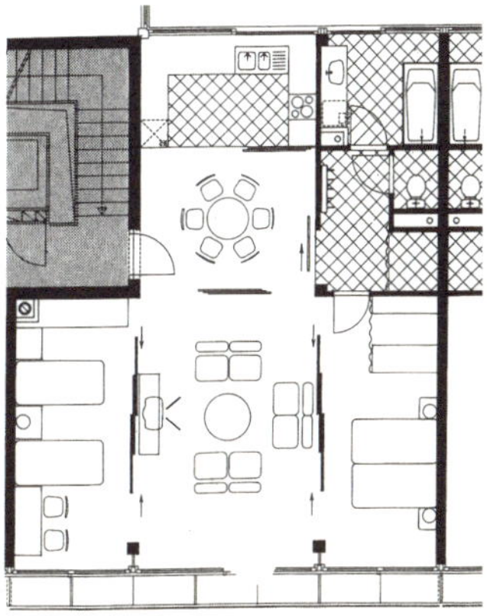

UNCONVENTIONAL DIMENSIONS

Casa Nostra, Graz, Austria, Riegler Riewe Architecten, 1992
Housing in Graz-Strassgang, Austria, Riegler Riewe Architecten, 1994

A building's potential can be increased not just by giving its spaces unconventional dimensions but also by adding new spaces. This is one of the key stepping-off points in the work of the Austrian architectural practice Riegler Riewe. Two housing projects, both in Graz, show in different ways how they develop this idea.

The housing project in Graz-Strassgang includes spaces with dimensions that deviate from the norm. For example, an oversized entrance can serve as a play area for the children or as additional storage space. In dwellings with an extra-large bedroom, the living room need not be confined to one place. An additional space likewise opens up new perspectives on use. In the Casa Nostra project in Graz Riegler Riewe designed homes with two kitchens so that the children can inhabit part of the house independently of the parents.

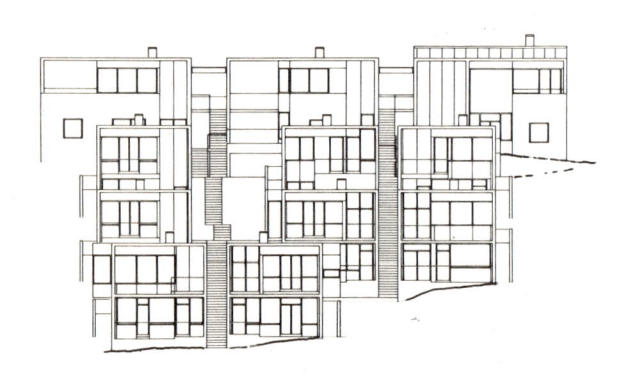

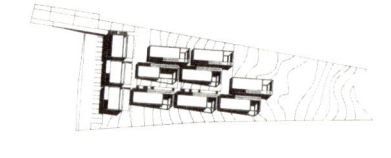

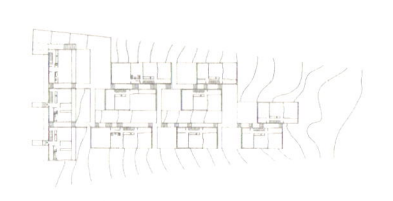

Riegler Riewe commissioned the Dutch artist Bas Princen to make a series of photographs of the interiors of Casa Nostra. Bas Princen is well-known for his photos of the recreational use made of temporary landscapes such as building sites and abandoned gravel pits. Unlike most photographs issued by architectural practices, which seek to exclude people and their possessions, those by Princen give primacy to everyday use.

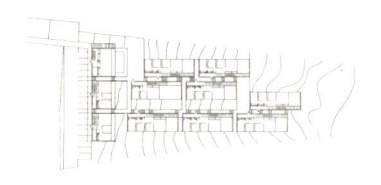

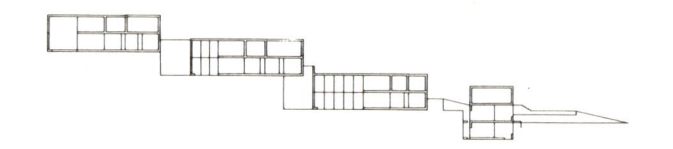

Casa Nostra housing, Graz, Austria

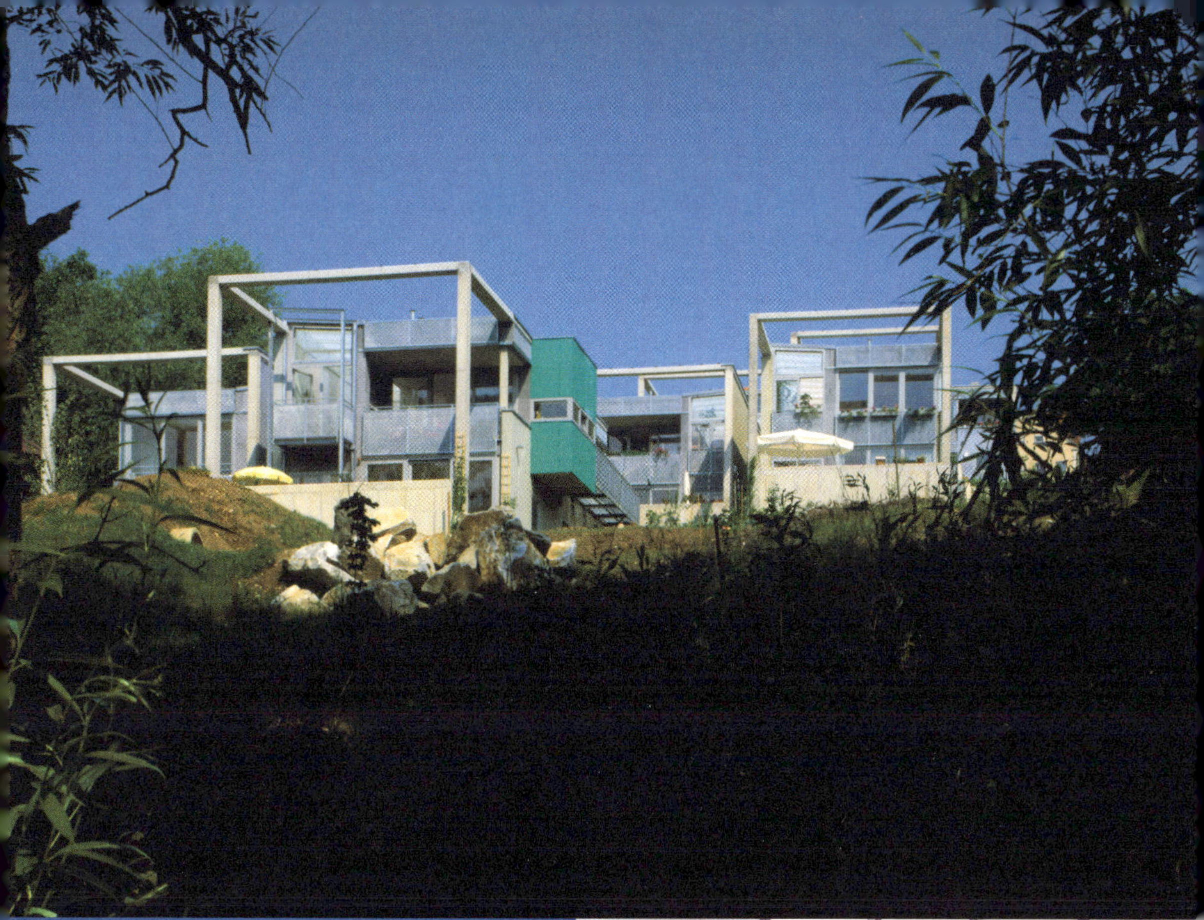
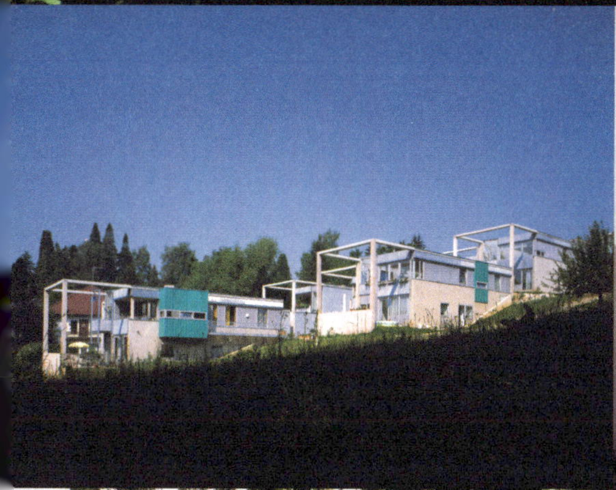
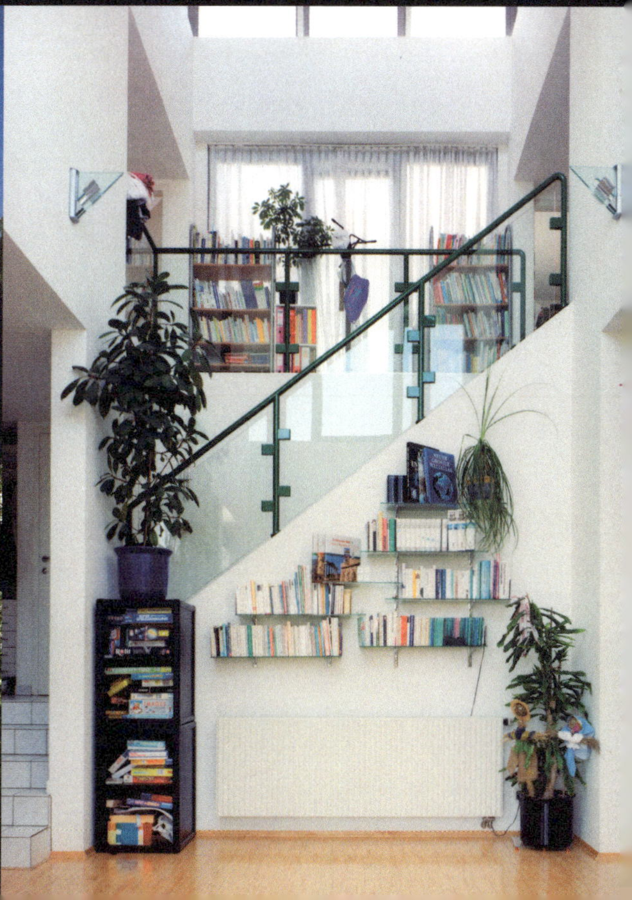
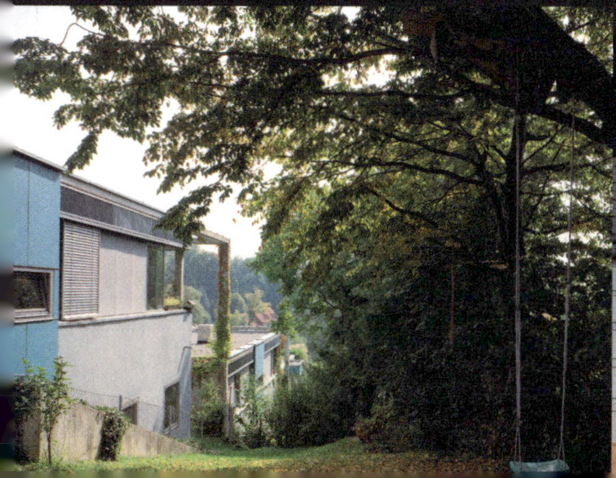

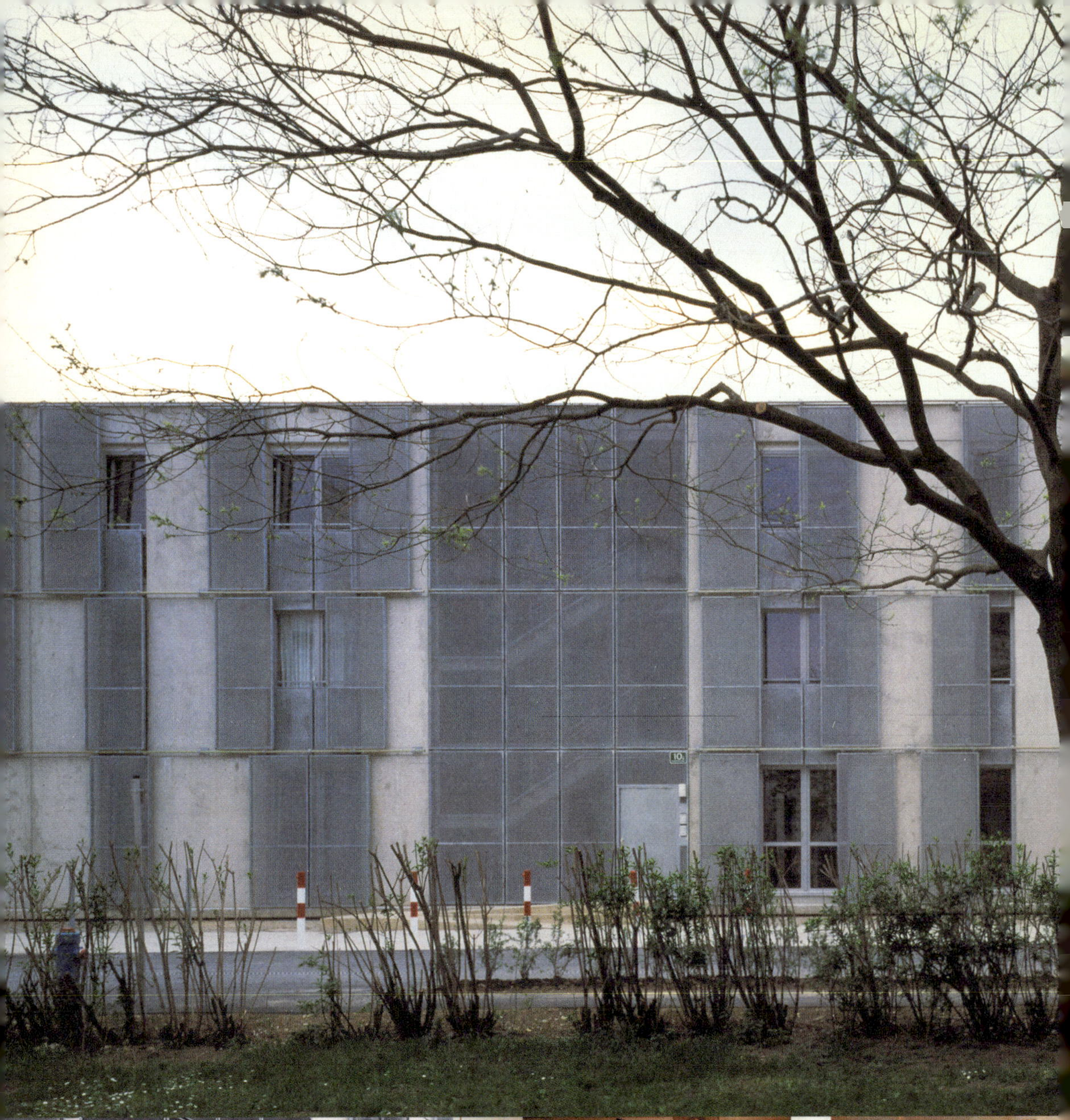

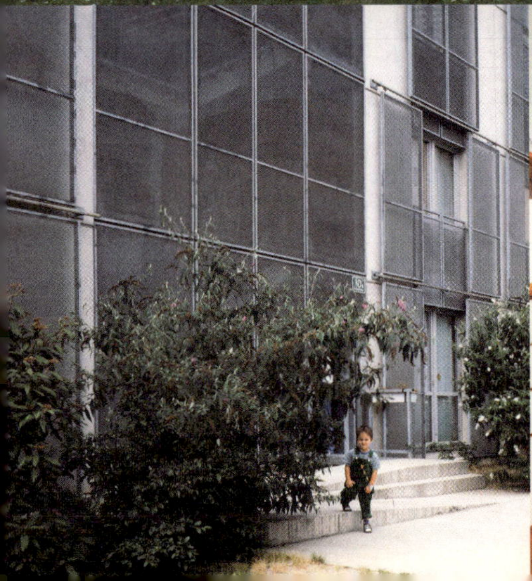

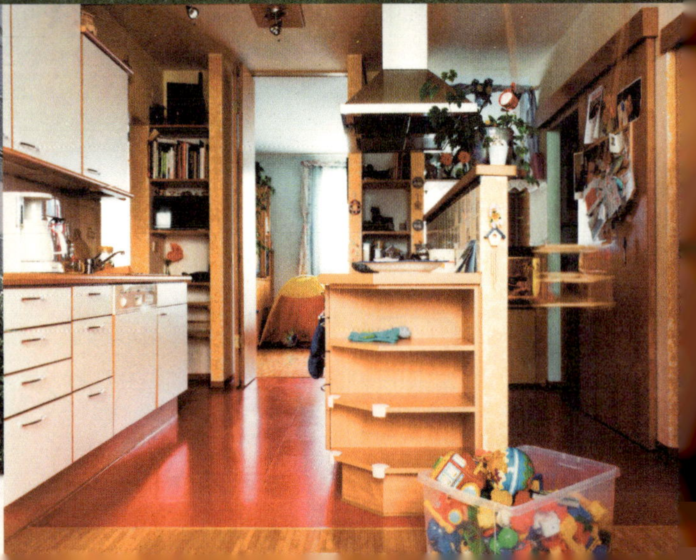

Housing in Graz-Strassgang, Austria

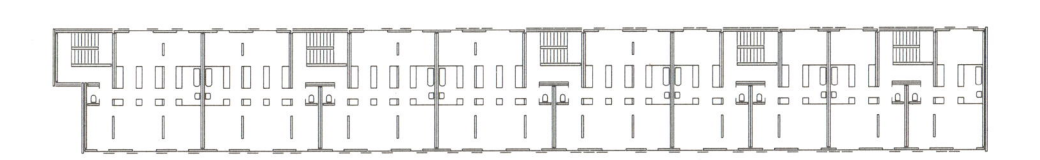

FLEXIBLE OFFICES

TBWA-Chiat/Day, New York, US, Gaetano Pesce, 1994

For TBWA-Chiat/Day in New York Gaetano Pesce designed a bright, cheerful office interior. Completed in 1994, it is one of the many examples of alternative work environments designed in the last ten years, based on the principle of the flexible office. Workers in a flexible office no longer have a regular desk but plug-in workplaces. Research had shown that in traditional offices the workspaces stood empty for most of the day, which is a waste of space and energy. Flexible offices mean more workplaces on smaller floor areas. Laptops are kept in special lockers or taken home. Besides open spaces there are others that are more enclosed. Large spaces are good for meetings and suchlike but when left empty they can double as offices that can be closed off. With the workplaces stripped of personal attributes, however, such offices could easily become neutral and impersonal. This explains Pesce's proposal to fit out the space as a living room. In Gaetano Pesce's own words, 'today office spaces no longer have defined and fixed functions. Current technology allows a greater liberty of movement and offers a larger selection of workspaces to office users. And this provides people with the ability to choose not only in which corner they want to settle down to work each day, but also the proximity to other staff members who share the workday. These choices can be dictated by professional priorities or simply by one's mood.

'In general, an office is like a big apartment that encompasses all of our everyday needs: a space that stimulates, and brings us joy, happiness and surprises. It is a space propitious to thought, meditation, and which is also able to inform us of historical qualities of the time we are passing through.'

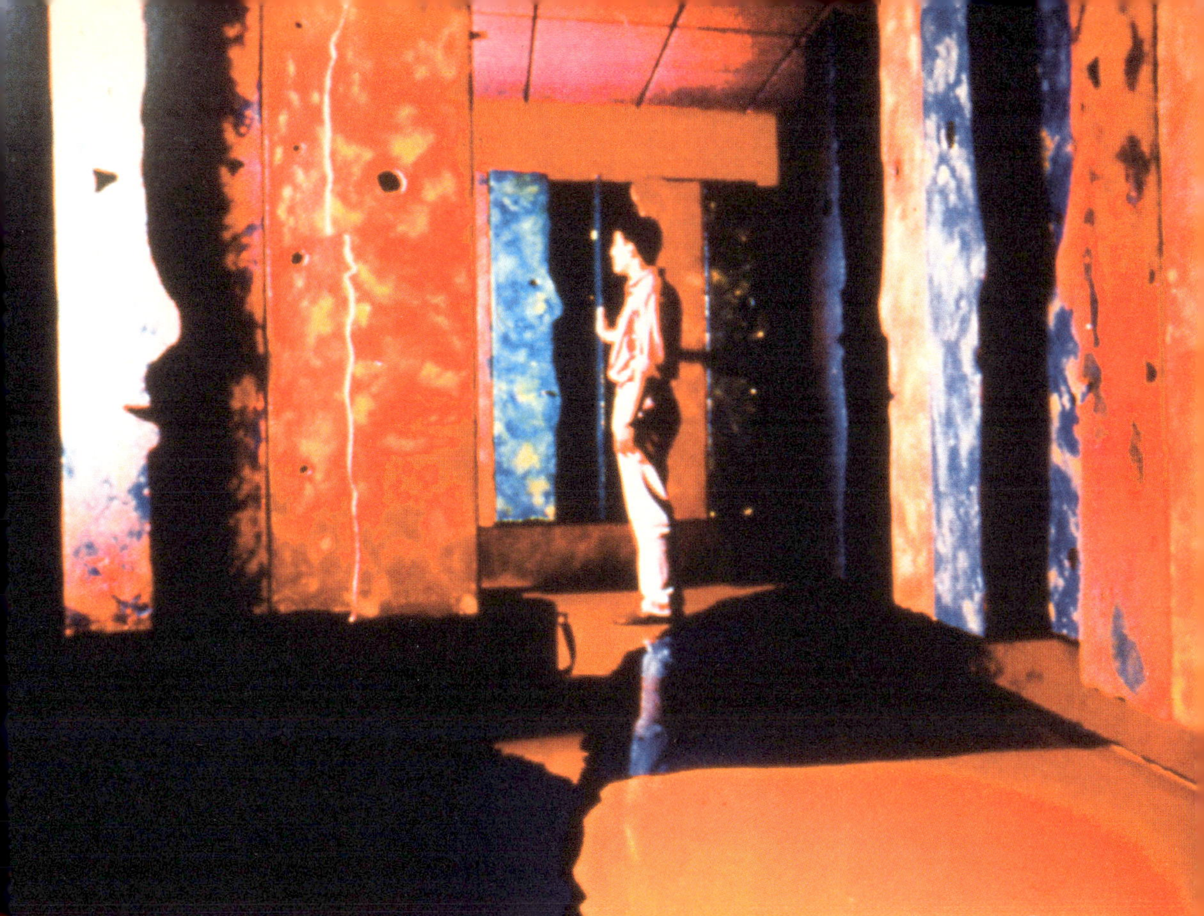

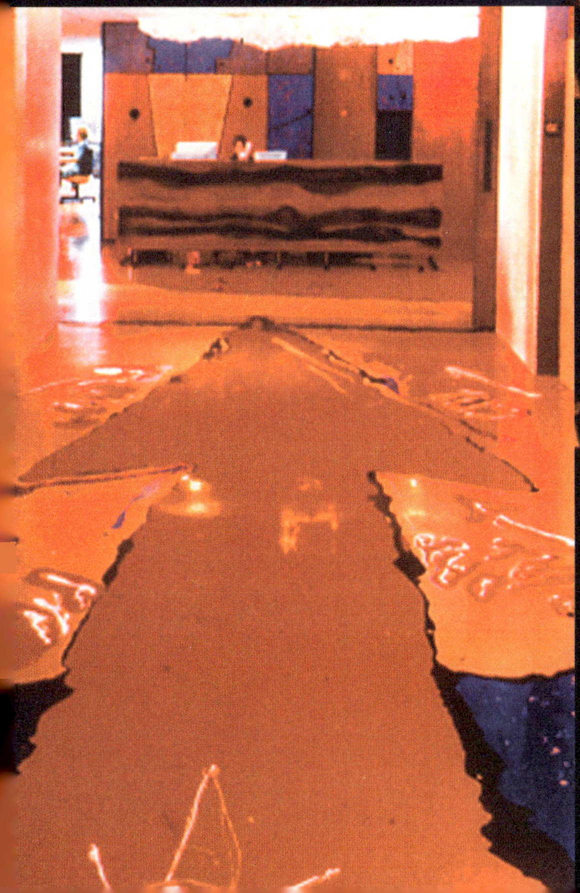

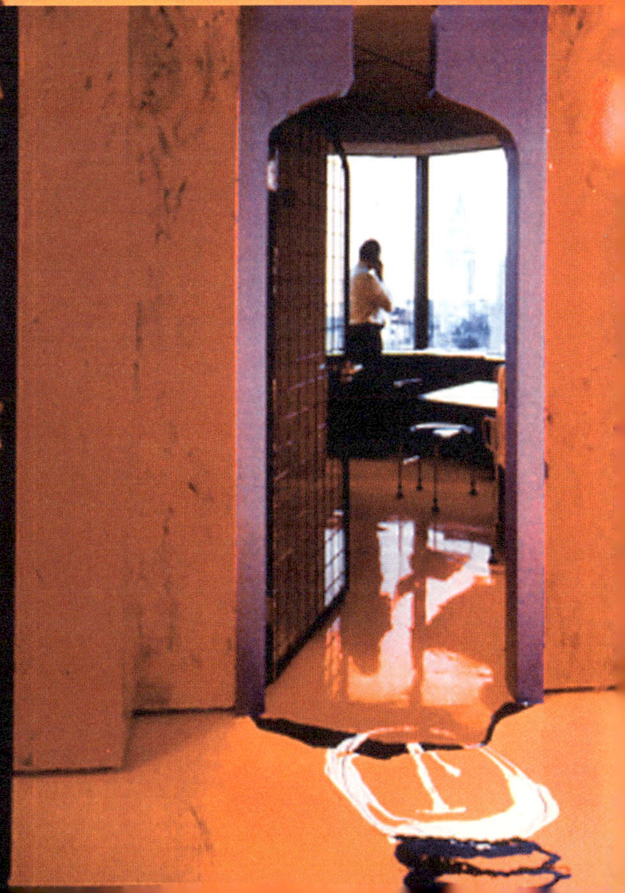

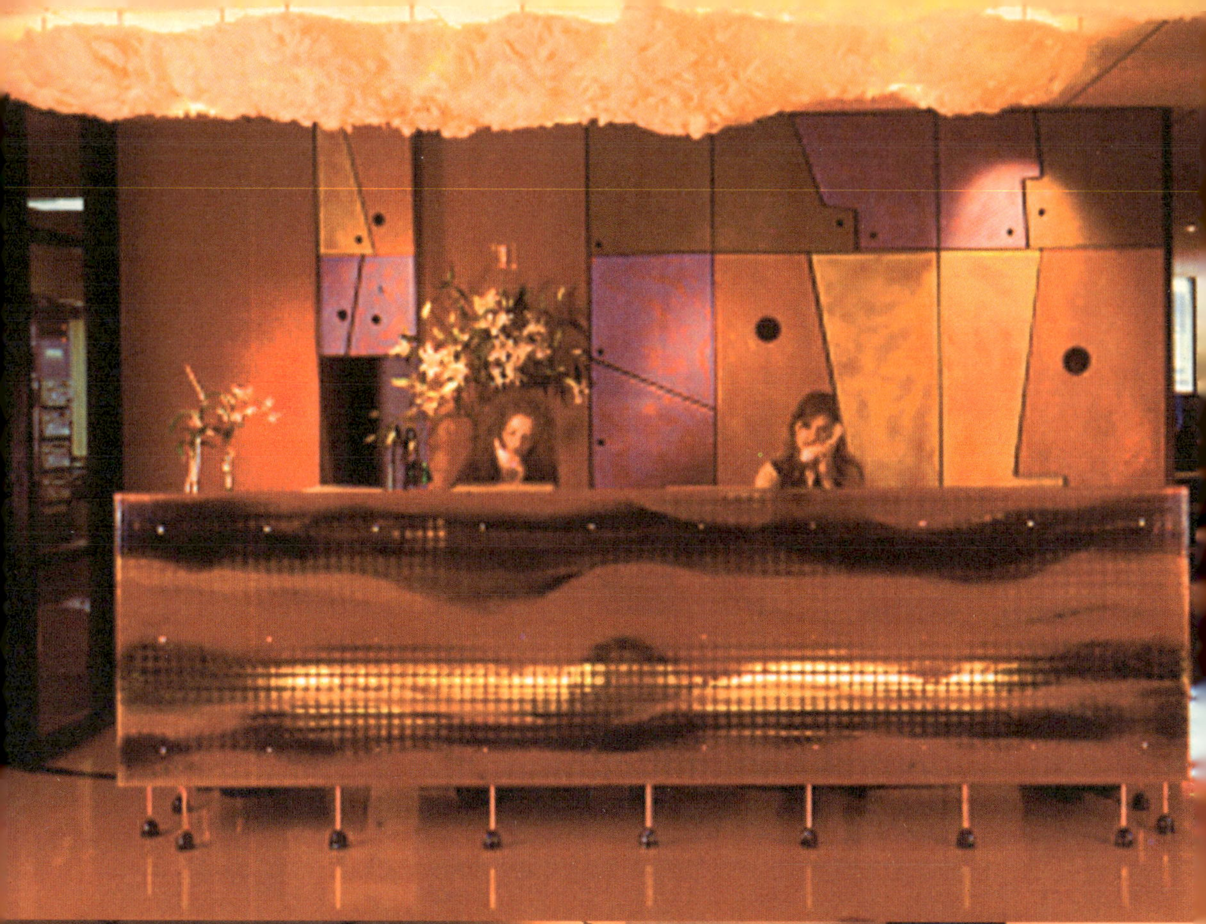
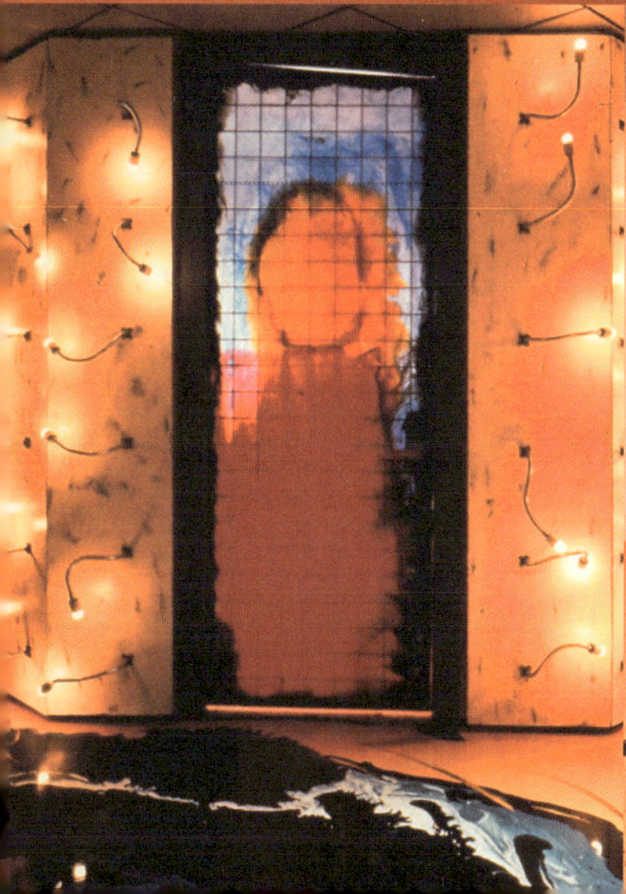
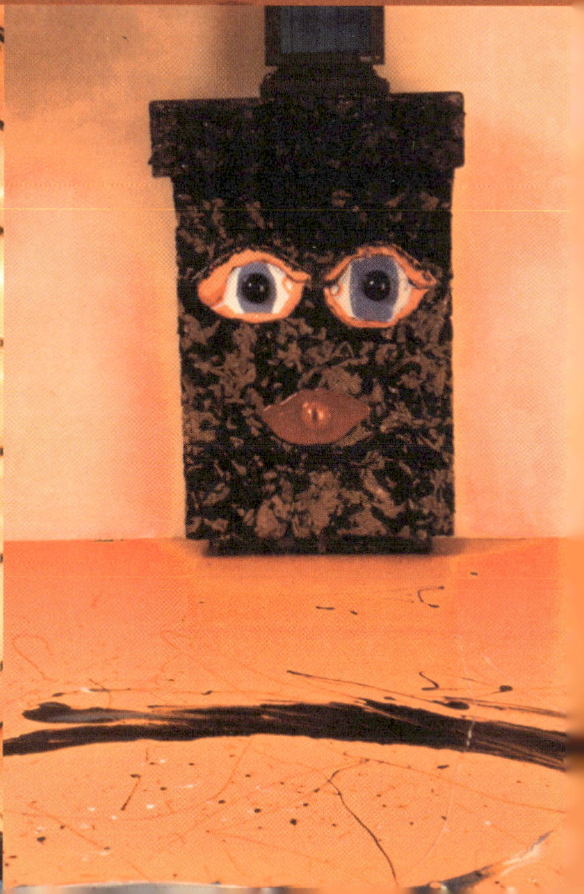

147

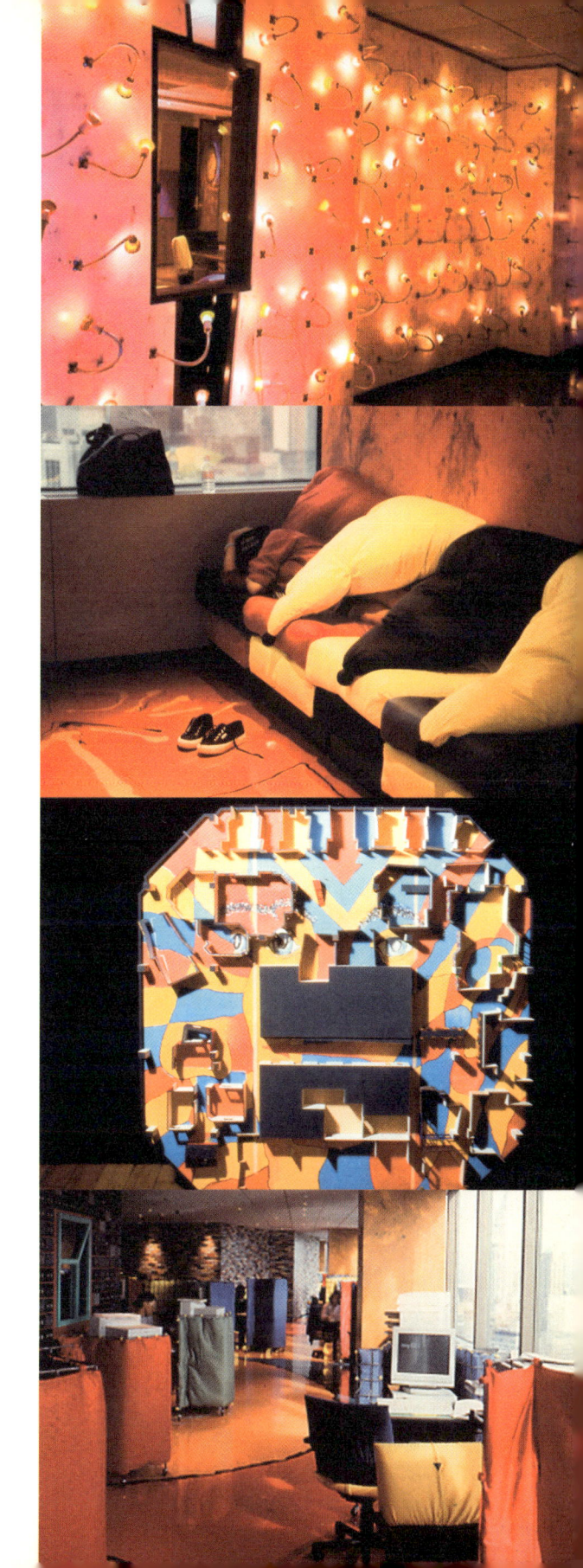

L'ESTRADE

Estraden House, Berlin-Prenzlauer Berg, Germany, Wolfram Popp, 1998

The first prototype of the Estraden House has been built in the Prenzlauer Berg district of Berlin. Its architect, Wolfram Popp, realized the project with his own development company. As the apartments have sold well, he now has plans to develop more Estraden Houses elsewhere in Berlin.

The Estraden House is marked by a freely subdivisible living space lined by 'estrades'. Estrade is French for platform. The Estrade in Popp's interpretation is a zone 180 cm across, running along the facade at a height of 40 cm. This conservatory-like strip threads between the interior and the surrounding balconies. Doors at the balconies can be fully opened up, bringing the living area into maximum contact with the world outside.

The second feature of this dwelling type is the large central living space which can be fitted out at the residents' discretion. This is flanked by a service zone containing the ancillary spaces – bathroom, kitchen, storage, entrance. These can be opened up to the main area using sliding panels. In the first Estraden House to be built, apartments of 80 and 100 square metres sit either side of a central stairhall. The second design provides larger units whose main living space can be divided into smaller zones using sliding panels or semi-permanent walls.

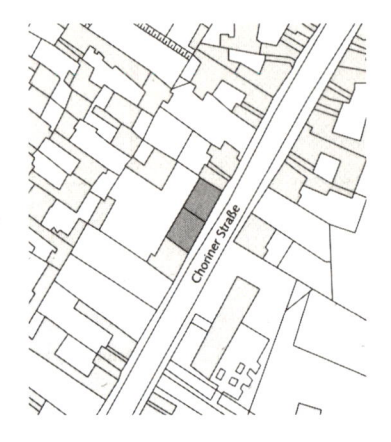

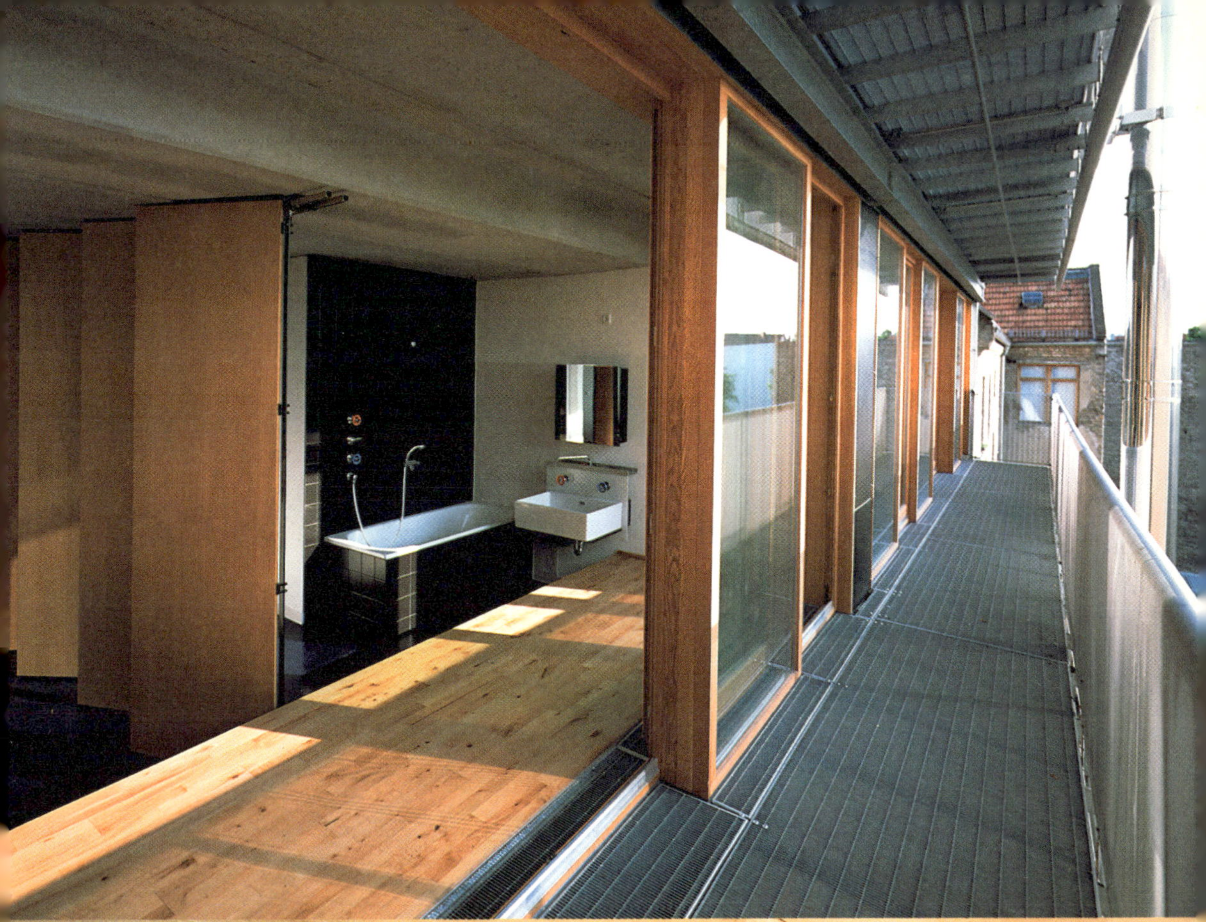

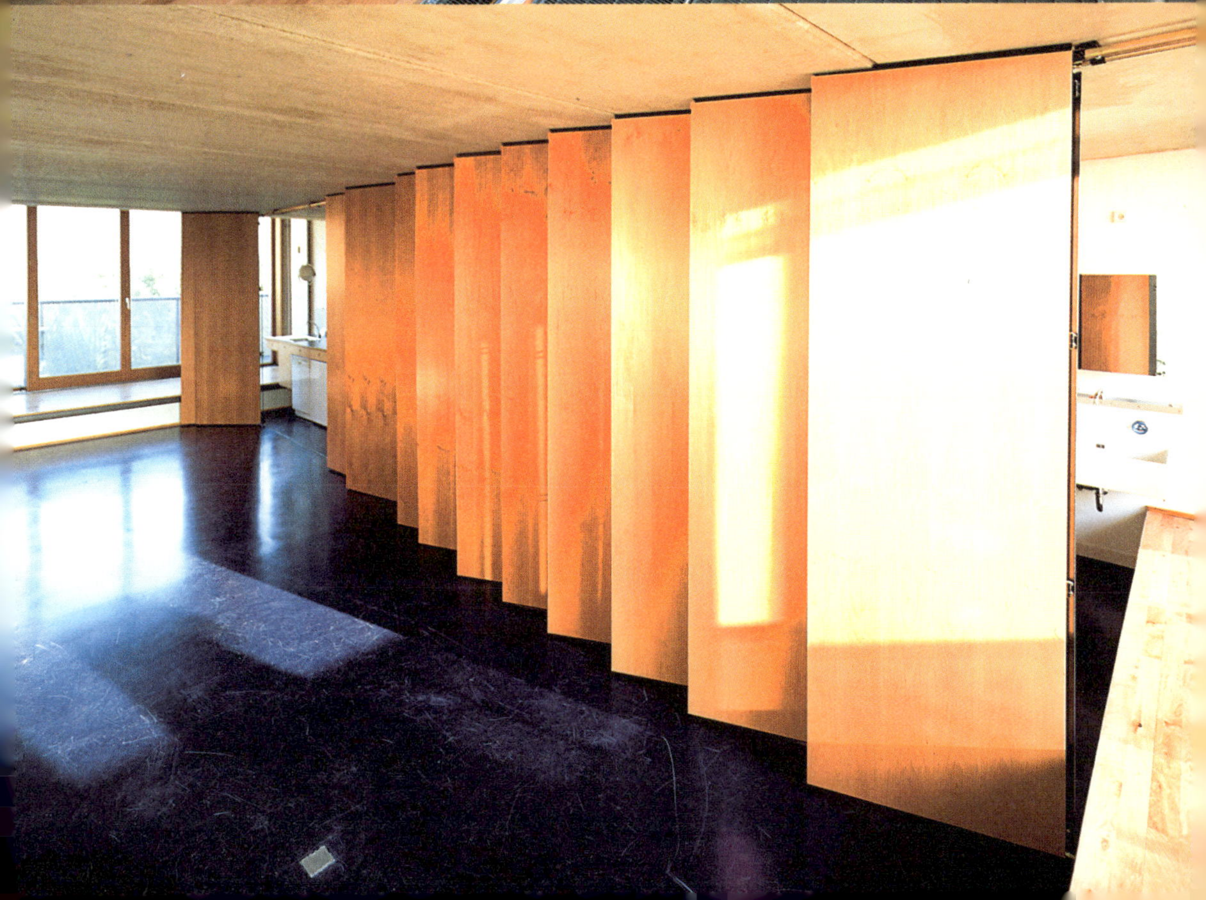

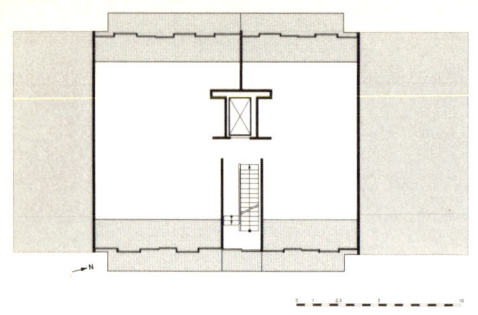

Basic type

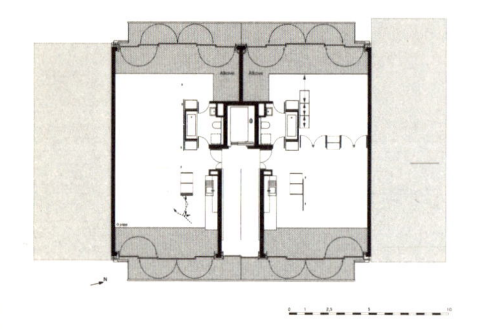

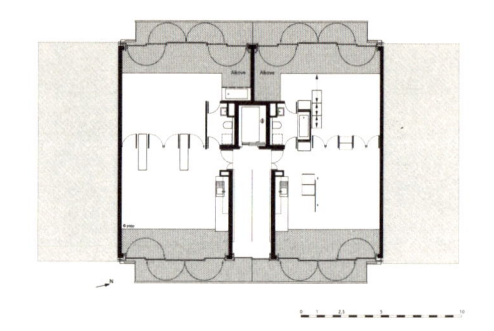

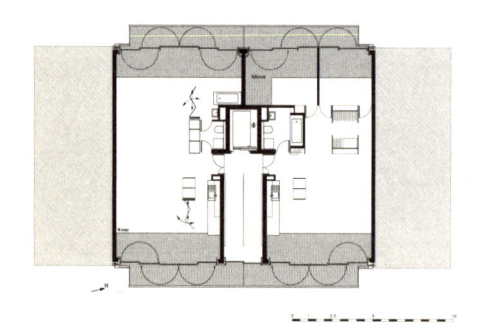

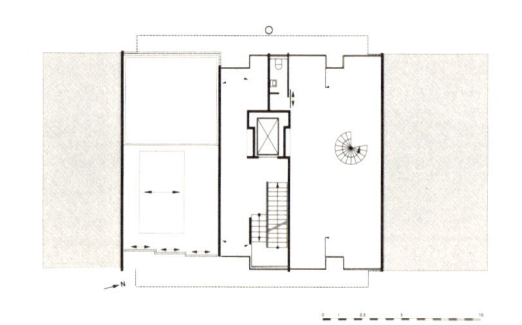

Four variants

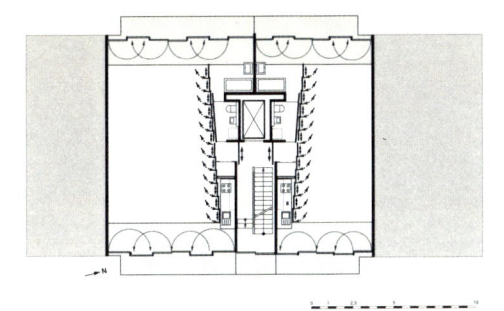

Basic type

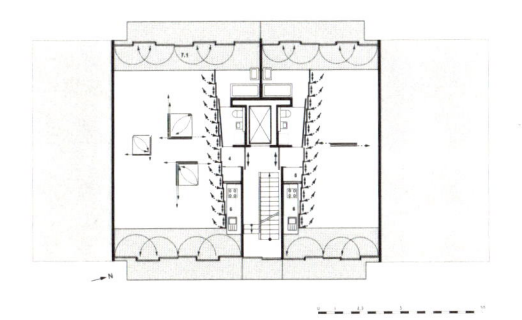

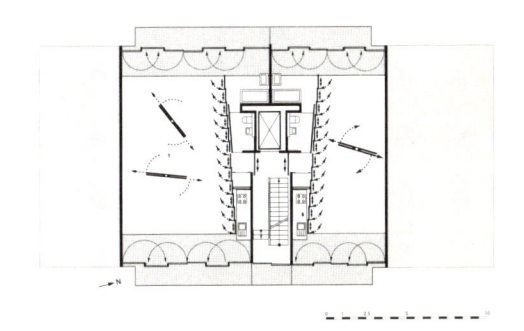

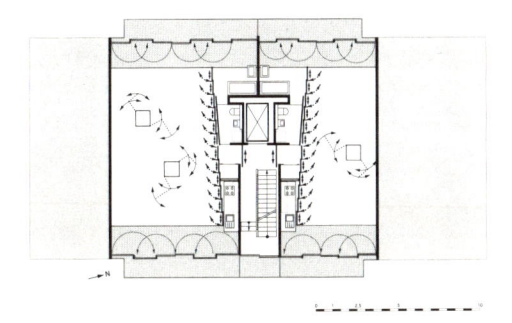

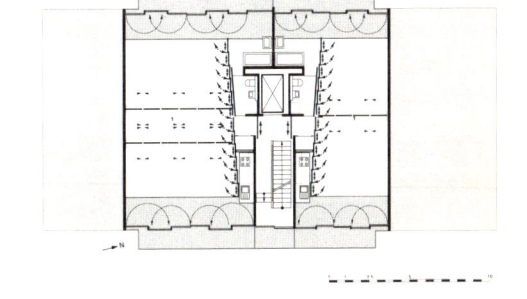

Four variants

151

DAY AND NIGHT ARRANGEMENTS

Manzana Cerrada, Carabanchel, Madrid, Spain, Aranguren-Gallegos, 2003

Affordability and flexibility were key design determinants for this housing block of 64 units in Carabanchel near Madrid. Its architects, Maria Aranguren and José Gallegos, chose a frame construction with cores for the wet services. The large unbroken space round the cores can be divided into smaller living areas using sliding partitions. An exceptional feature of the project is the raised central zone which includes the rooms for ablutions. There is space for cables, ducting and storage below the 60-cm-high floor. The bed can be slid away into this storage area to make extra space during the day for a workplace, for example. This gives the units two distinct arrangements for day and night. This is by no means a new way of saving space. Many housing projects of the 1920s and '30s were rooted in this idea, a good example being the one on Vroesenlaan in Rotterdam (1934). The architect, J.H. van den Broek, designed foldaway beds and sliding partitions to save space and thus provide affordable dwellings.

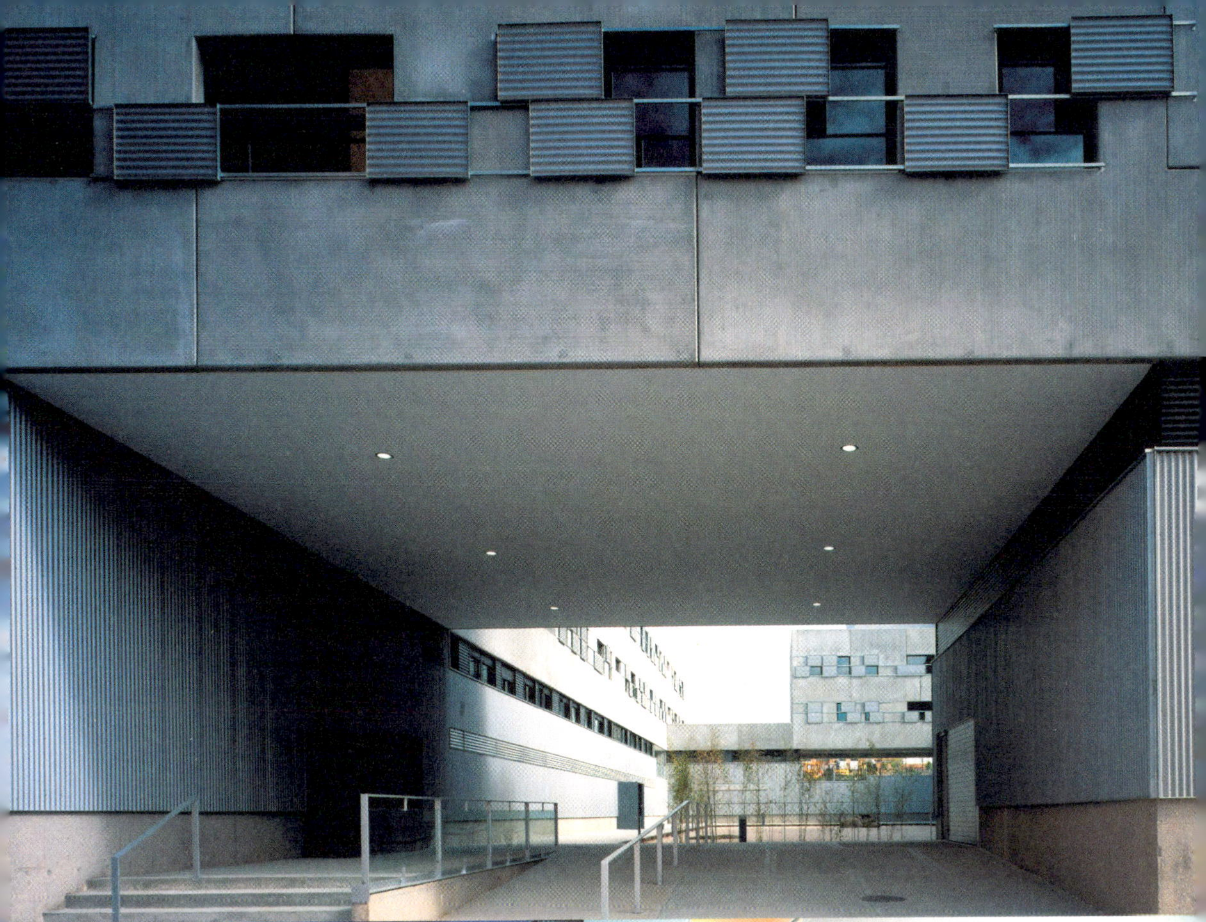

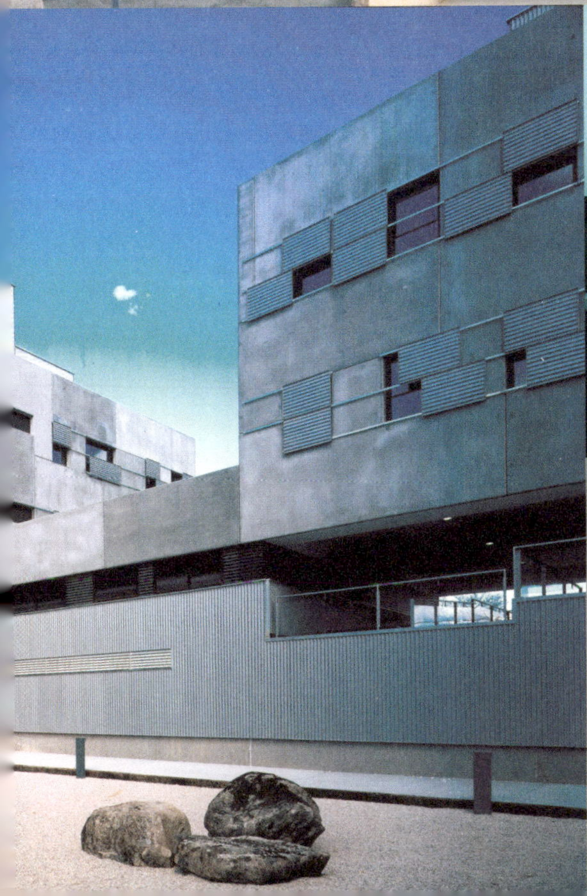

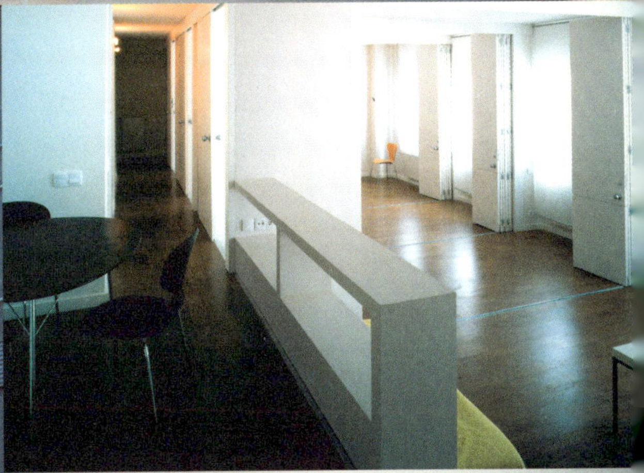

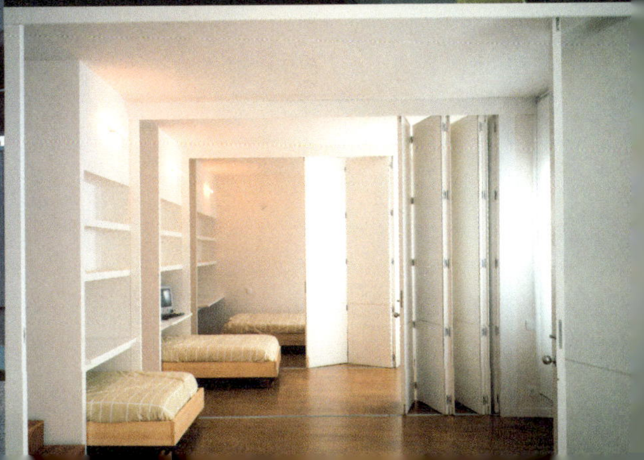

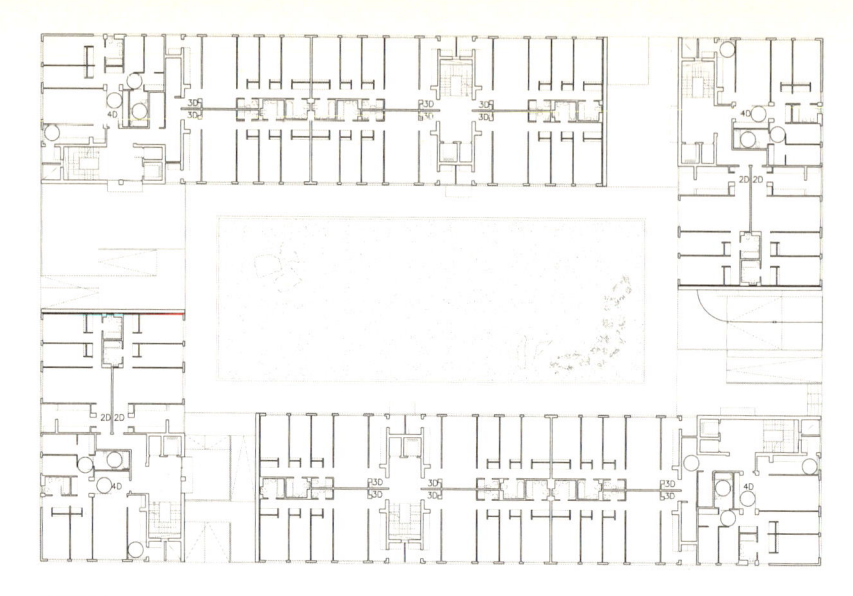

PLANTA 1

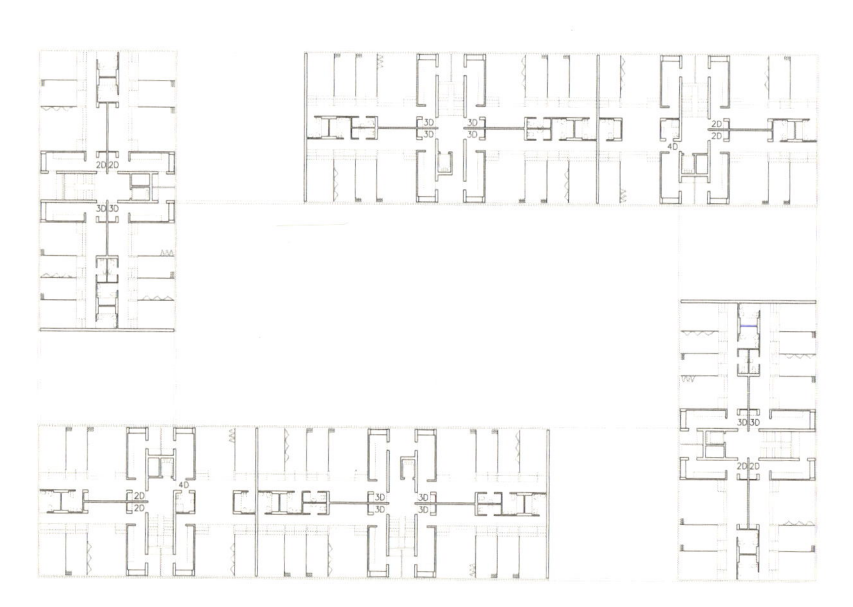

PLANTAS 2 Y 3

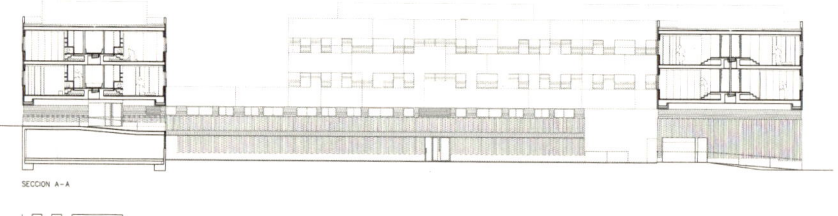

SECCION A-A

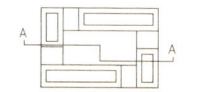

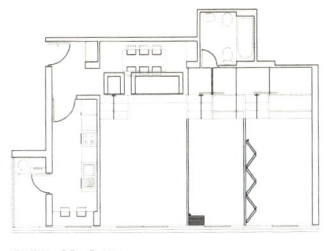

TYPE 2D DAY

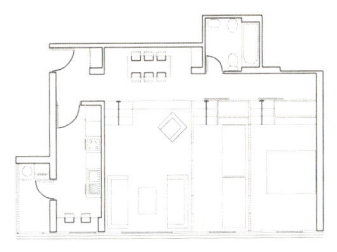

TYPE 2D NIGHT

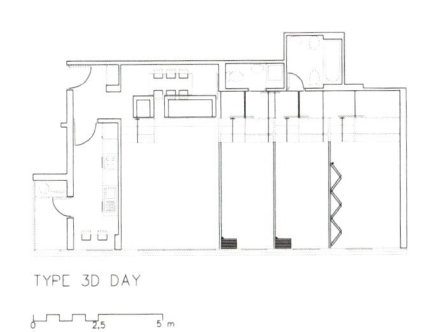

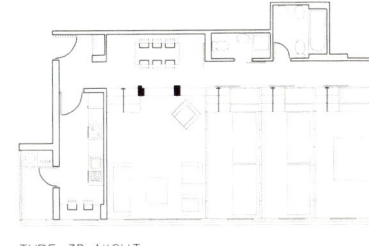

TYPE 3D DAY

TYPE 3D NIGHT

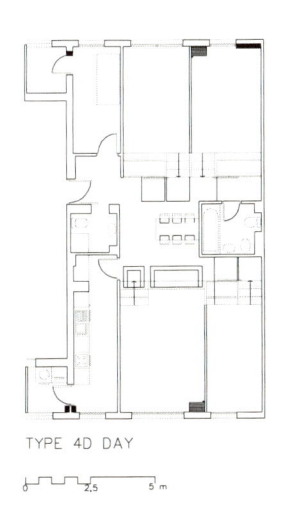

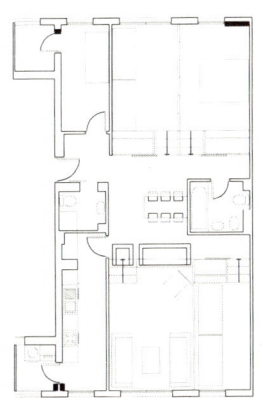

TYPE 4D DAY

TYPE 4D NIGHT

A MULTIFUNCTIONAL ENTRANCE ZONE

Codan Shinonome, Tokyo, Japan, Riken Yamamoto & Field Shop, 2003

Shinonome Canal Court, a large-scale building scheme of more than 2000 dwellings in combination with shops, offices and parking facilities, occupies a site five kilometres south-west of the centre of Tokyo in the Koto-ku district. To meet the extremely diverse domestic requirements of today's city-dwellers, this scheme offers, within an ostensibly rigid system, a wide variety of dwelling types ranging from one-room apartments of 43 m² to units for larger households with a floor area of 132 m². On top of that, the Shinonome project group gives the option of small-scale workspaces in the building. To this end it has developed the concept of Small Office/Home Offices (SOHOS). A SOHO is an apartment that can also be used for an office, studio or showroom.

The scheme consists of blocks enfolding courts, six in all, each with their own architect. Sub-plan 2, designed by Riken Yamamoto, has a ground-floor 'plinth' of offices and facilities and a high-rise portion with over 400 corridor accessed units. The larger units are provided with so-called F-rooms (foyer rooms) placed along the corridors and accessing the dwellings. As the fixed elements such as the kitchen and bathroom lie along the external facade, the living room can be attached to the F-room in numerous ways. The bathroom and kitchen have glass partitions allowing daylight to penetrate deep into the home. At the other side it is a similar story; 60 per cent of the access doors in the corridors are of glass as prescribed in the brief. The corridors in turn receive light from double-height wells hewn from the blocks at regular intervals. This way, the corridors come to lie along the facade as flush-floor living-streets.

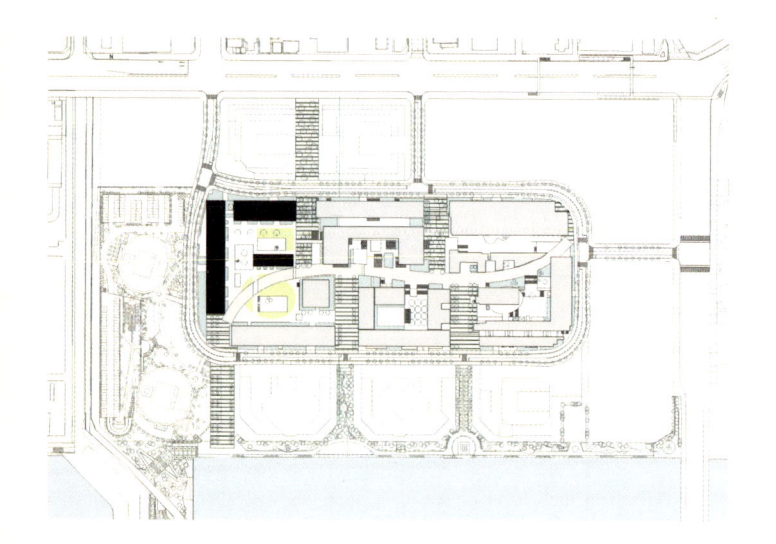

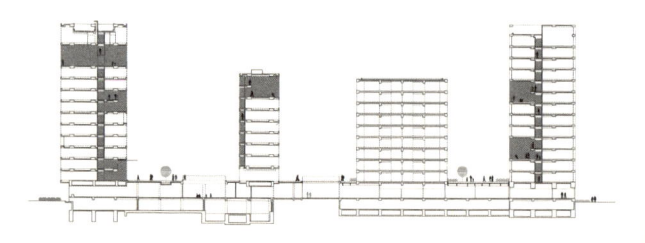

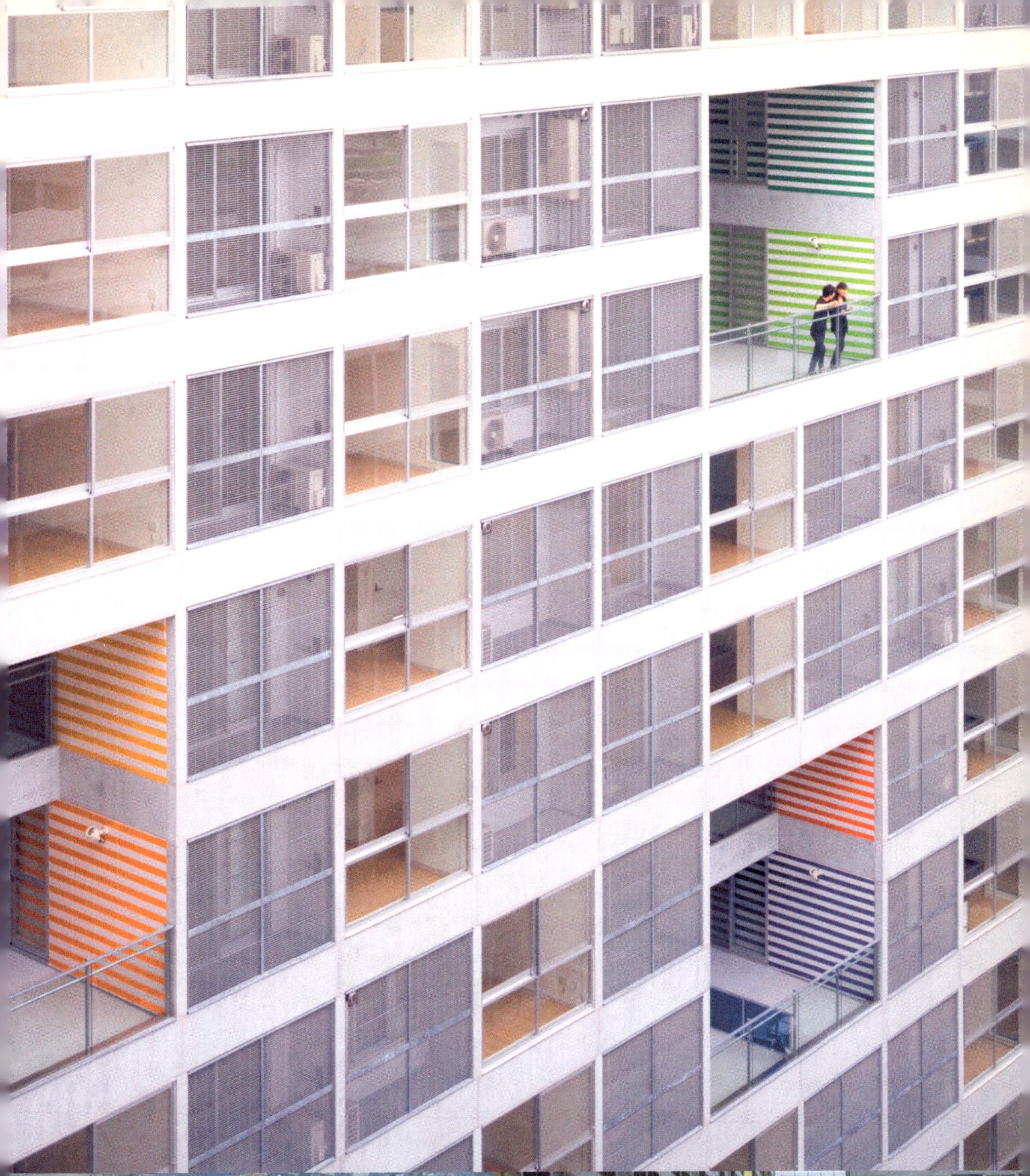
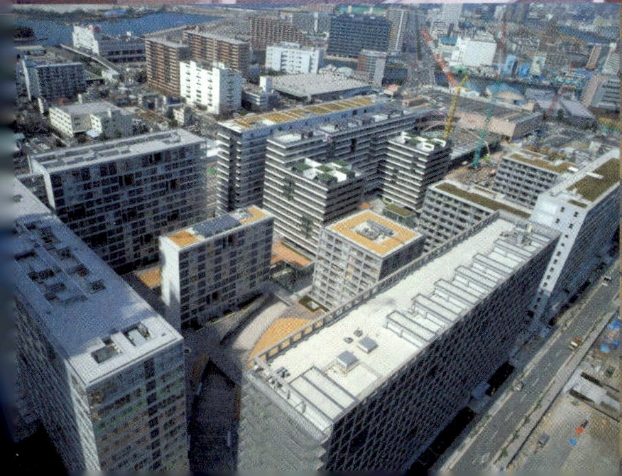
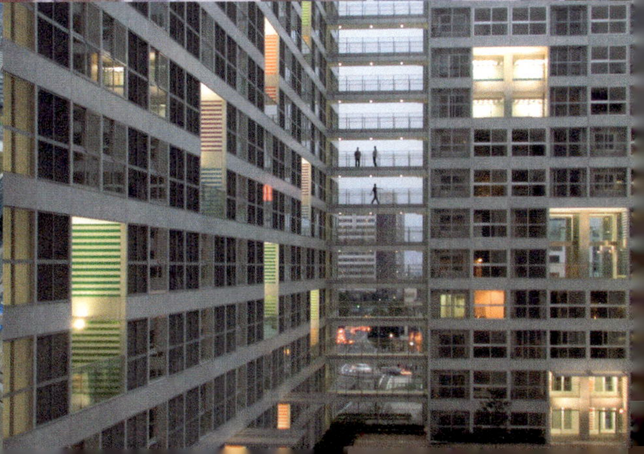

Typical floor plan 2-4

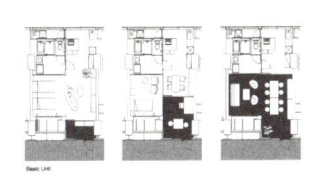

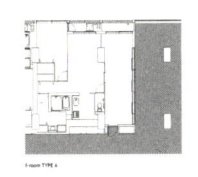

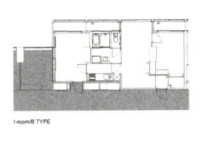

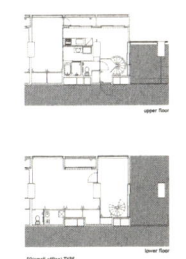

Unit plans

MON ONCLE REVISITED

Turn-on Urban Sushi, AllesWirdGut, 2002, Rotor House, Luigi Colani, 2004

Sliding partitions and computer floors are now established features in all kinds of buildings. Even floors of adjustable height are no longer confined to the theatre. For example, the Design Museum in Ghent has a mezzanine floor that can be raised or lowered depending on what the current exhibition requires.

Buildings whose complete interior can be rotated with a simple action have got no further than futuristic concepts – until now, that is.

The Austrian design studio AllesWirdGut has designed a home like an item of furniture, which can be freely divided along low-tech lines to suit the occasion. By rotating it a full circle, the object can, in turn, function as a bedroom, kitchen, bathroom and lounge.

Luigi Colani's Rotor House can be 'refurnished' in no time. It contains a 'rotor' divided into three segments comprising the bedroom, bathroom and kitchen and can switch from one to another in the shortest time.

These ideas are nothing new. Such designs belong to a tradition of dwellings with day and night arrangements which saw its most widespread application in the floor plans of homes designed in the 1920s.

Urban Sushi

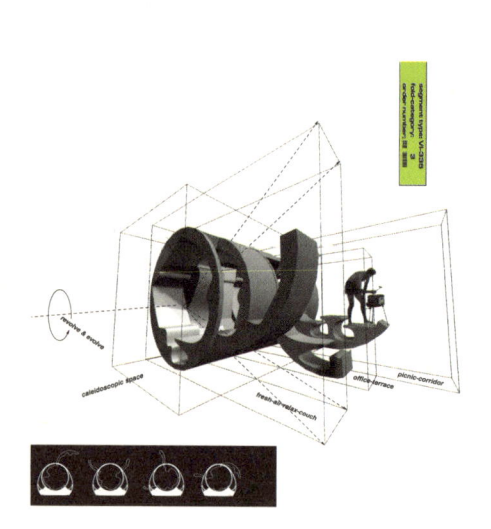

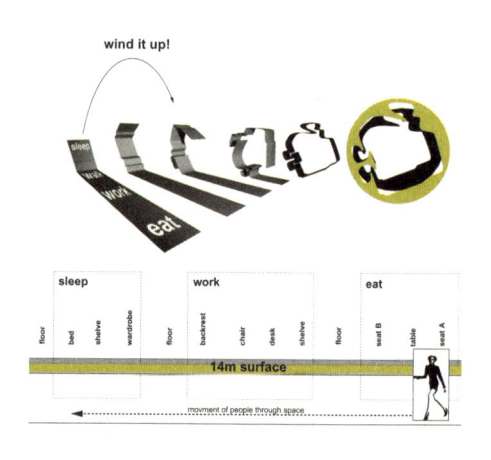

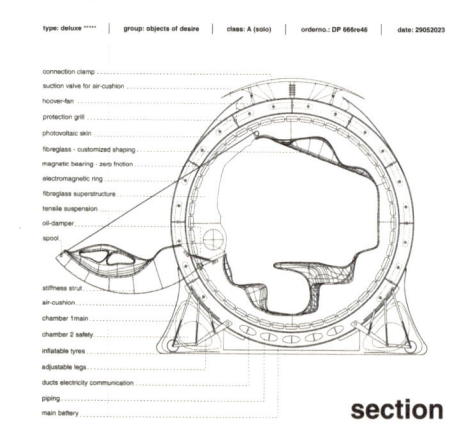

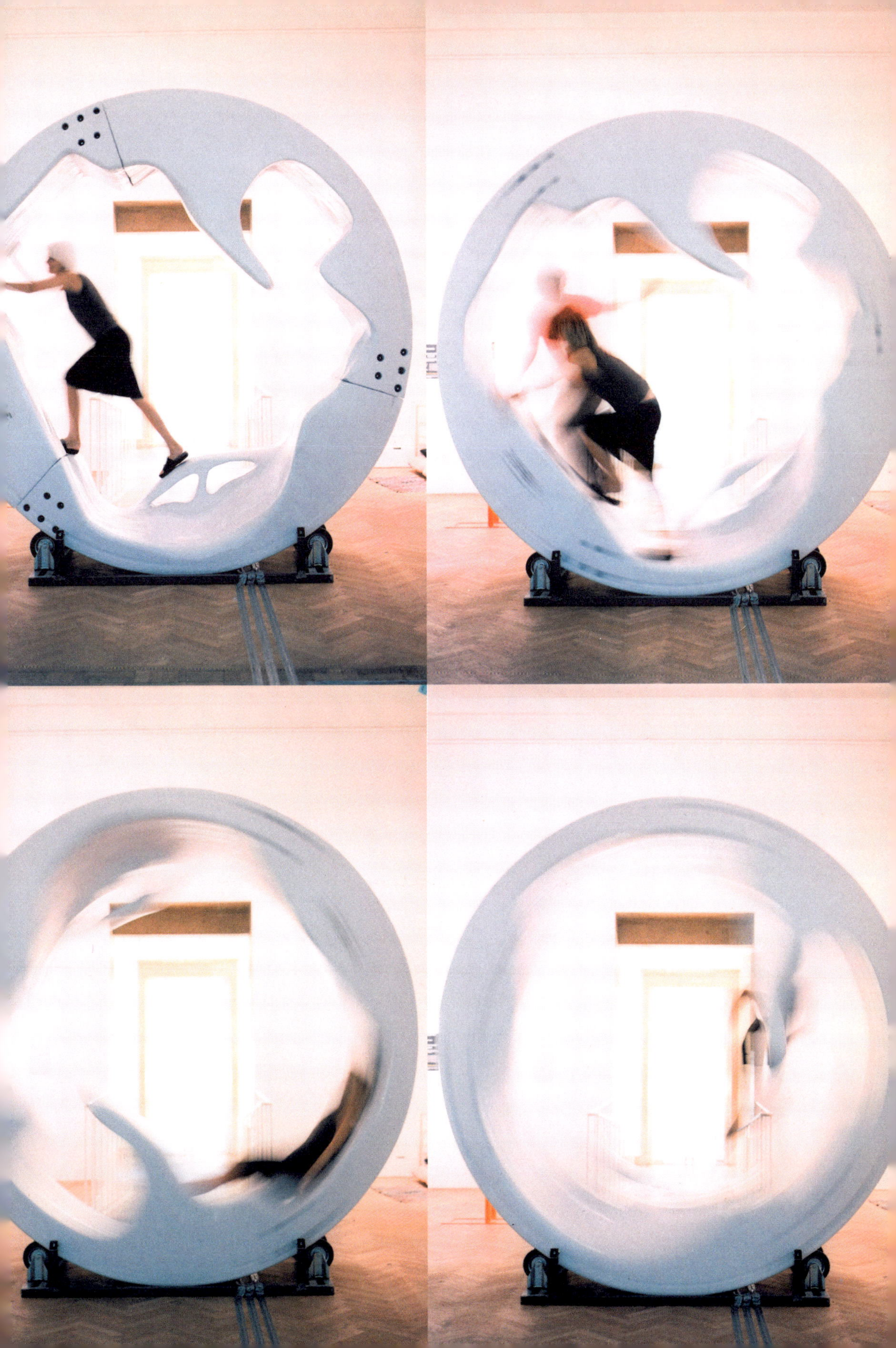

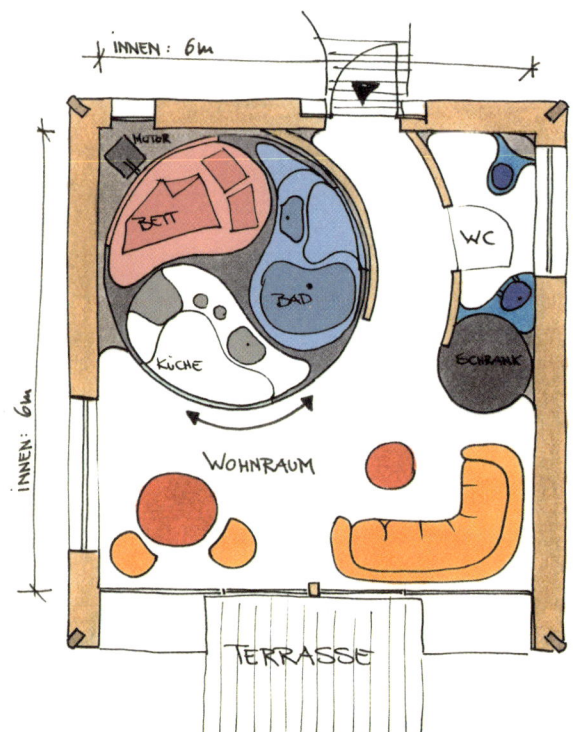

Rotor House

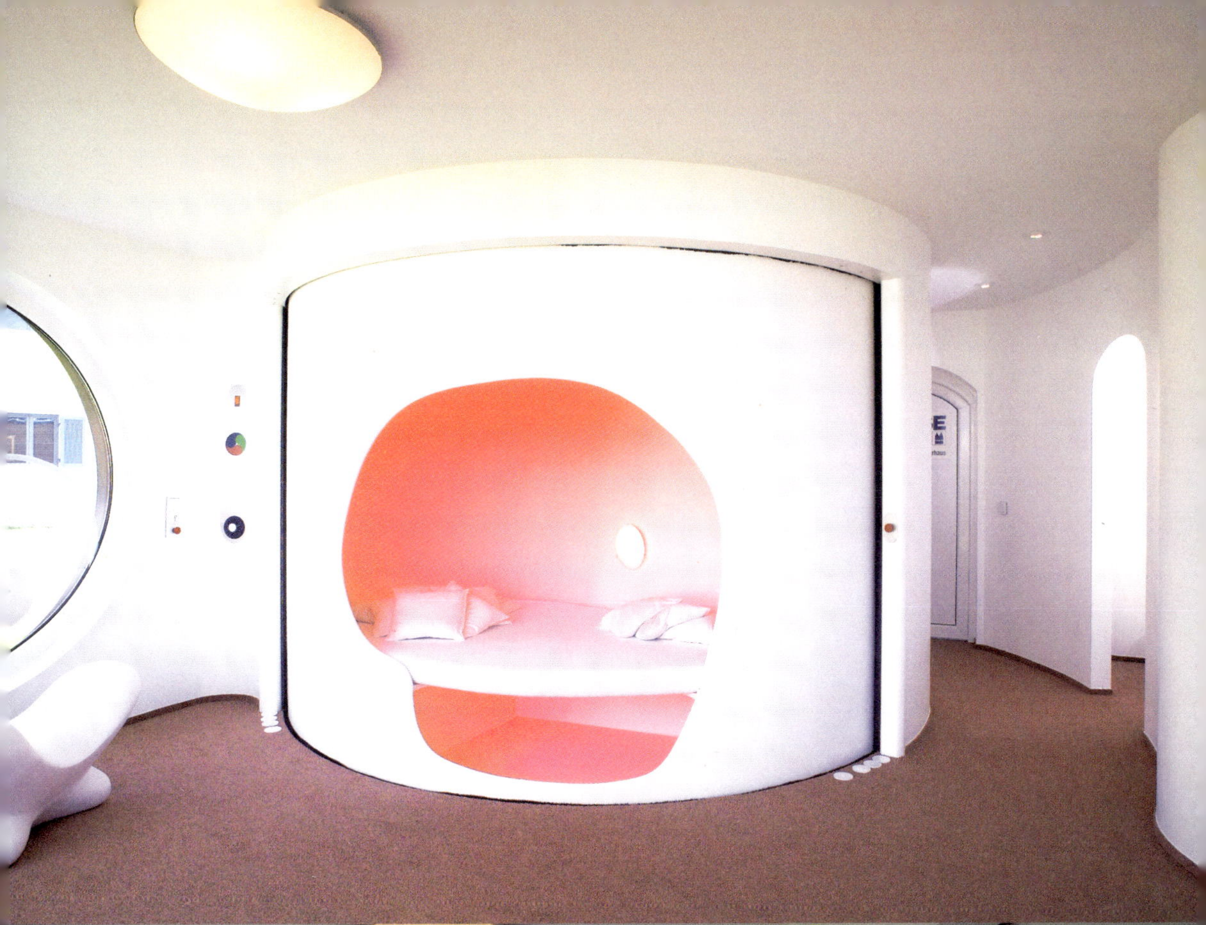

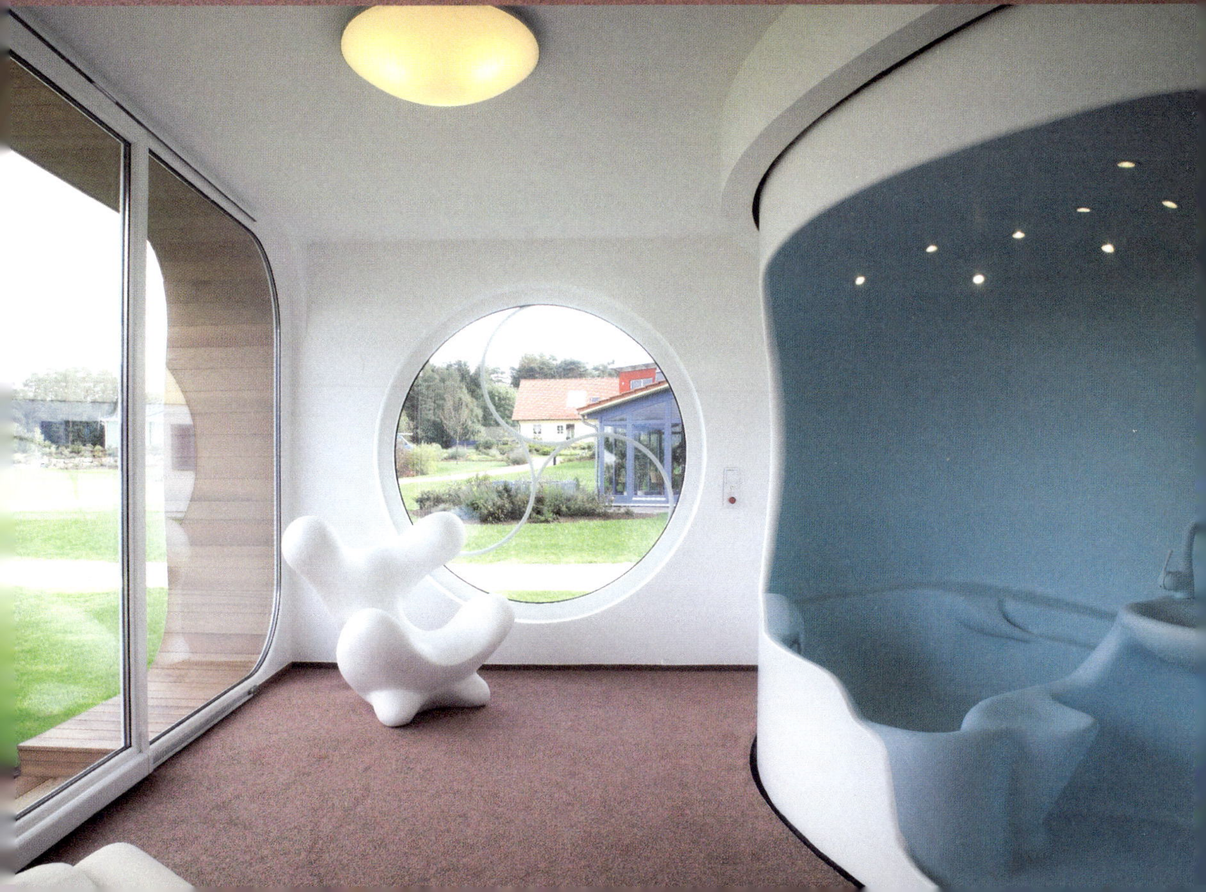

TWENTY-FIRST CENTURY WAREHOUSE

Spaarndammerdijk, Amsterdam, Netherlands, De Architecten Cie (F. Van Dongen), scheduled for completion in 2007

Frank Bijdendijk, director of Het Oosten housing corporation, suggests that we should build for hundreds of years (see Bijdendijk's contribution on pp. 42-51 of this book). Like the old warehouses, many of which in Amsterdam have been recast as apartments, work buildings should also be able to transform into housing in the future.

The architectural office Maxwan provided the urban design context for a 'warehouse of the 21st century' together with a quartet of scenarios. Each of these describes different relationships between living and working. The building was then designed by the architect Frits van Dongen of De Architecten Cie based on these scenarios. This 21st-century warehouse was given the name Amsterdam-Werk (Amsterdam Work).

The building has a ground-floor 'plinth' 6 metres tall and 30 metres deep, with above that a 17-metre-deep superstructure of four storeys. The floor-to-floor height of the superstructure decreases from over 4 metres at the lowest levels to 3.5 metres on the top floor.

Three aspects of the building enable changes to be made in the future: the access, the main load-bearing structure and the services design.

Access to the four storeys is by way of a mix of porches, galleries and corridors, allowing the superstructure a variety of subdivisions. In addition, the complex has a second ground plane, so that the higher levels are also accessible by car. This gives the superstructure still greater potential.

The structural facades, designed to a module of 1.2 metres, allow the interior to be subdivided in complete freedom. They consist of brickwork grids with an infill of glass panels that can be slid away. Should the building be used for apartments, these glass panels can do duty as French balconies.

The services likewise include amenities that look ahead to possible future changes. As housing generally needs heating and offices are more likely to require cooling, there is to be a floor heating system that can regulate the temperature for each 3.9-metre strip of floor using either hot or cold water.

Besides changes in the future, this built-in flexibility should also demonstrate its worth during the project's development. This has proved not to be the case in practice. When the office market collapsed at the end of the 1990s it at first seemed a simple matter to redevelop a percentage of the offices as housing. However, this strategy came in for major delays when companies in the vicinity of Amsterdam-Werk complained. According to the land use plan, they argued, the area was intended for businesses and offices. Modifying the land use plan is a drawn-out procedure in which discussion between parties is only possible at certain moments. So in the end, it was Dutch legislation that hampered the flexibility aspect.

scenarios

handel- kantoren

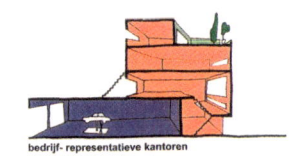

bedrijf- representatieve kantoren

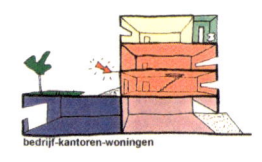

bedrijf-kantoren-woningen

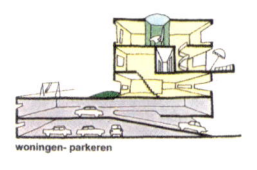

woningen- parkeren

165

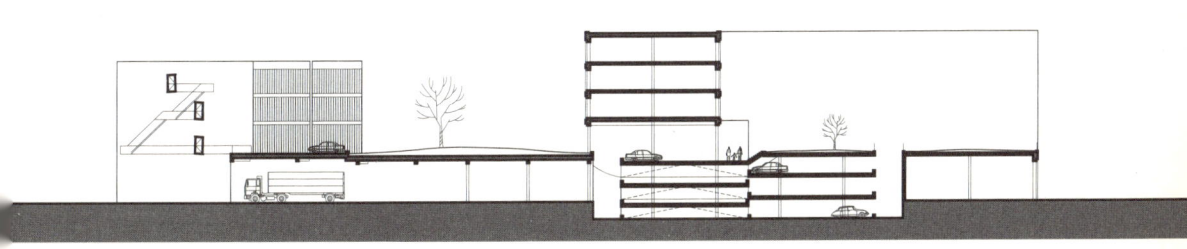

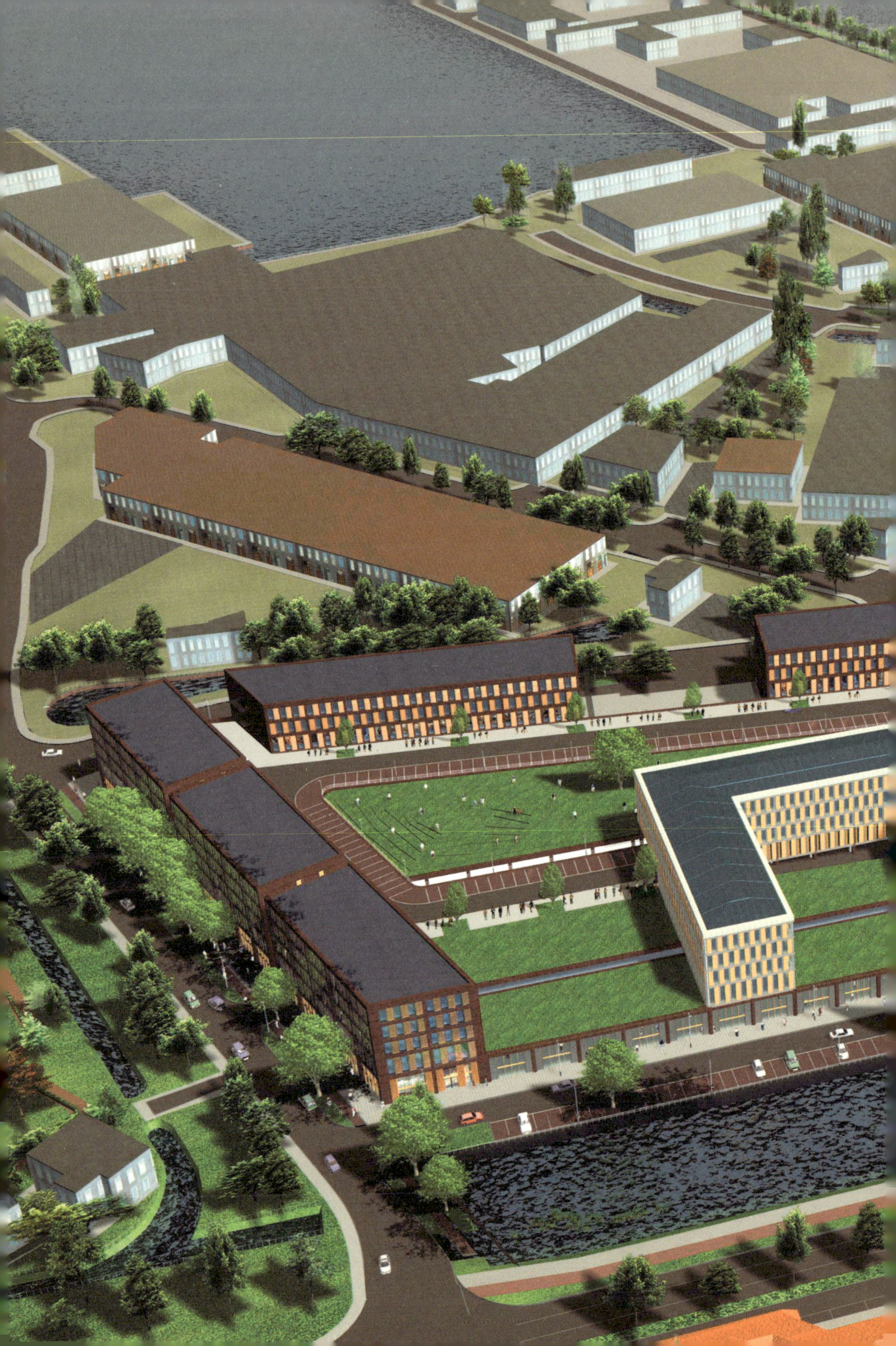

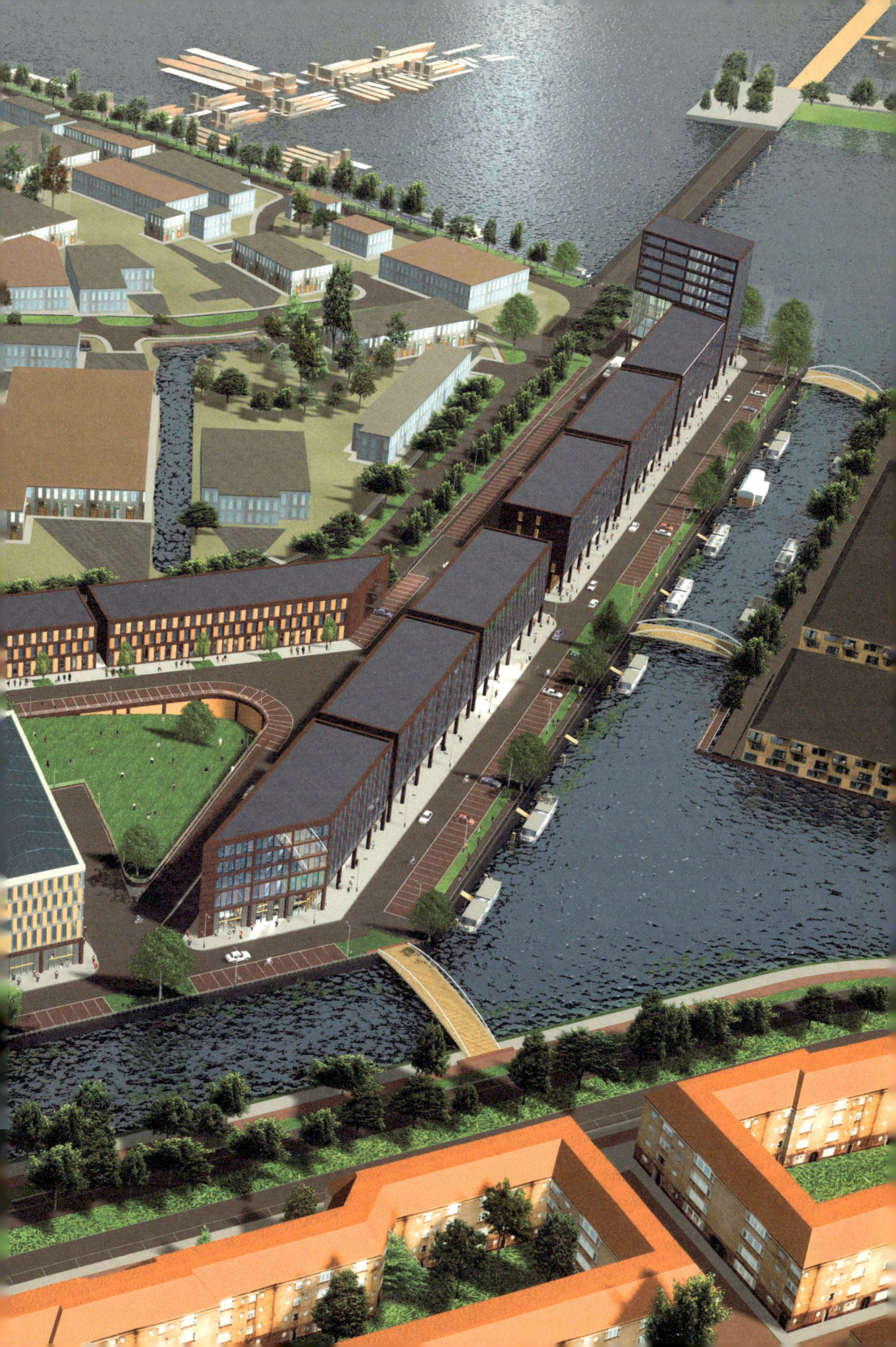

STRUCTURAL FACADES

Block A, centre scheme for Ypenburg, Netherlands, Rapp+Rapp, 2003

The firm of Rapp+Rapp was responsible for designing the central area of Ypenburg, a state-designated site for urban expansion near The Hague. The first housing block consists of a quadrangle of dwellings with a sports hall at its centre. The building has structural facades, normal enough for offices in the Netherlands but highly exceptional for housing. The advantage of structural facades is that the dwellings can eventually be made wider or narrower. The advantages were there even during the development stage, as the exact width, and with it the number of units per storey, could be modified right up to the end of the process without delaying the project as a whole.

The party walls consist of two separated metal stud walls each with an additional layer of plasterboard on both sides. The cavity in this double wall system is filled with insulating material. For all their light weight, these walls make excellent soundproofing material. The mix of functions makes exceptional demands on the way the services are laid out; these are kept separate from each other wherever possible. The sports hall services can be accessed from the galleries. The offices for their part have their piping and wiring in vertical shafts in the stair halls. The dwellings also have theirs running perpendicularly, deliberately avoiding the horizontality of the other functions lower down.

The building is suffused with high-grade materials, including Wittmunder peat-fired bricks, an artisanal German brick whose format and weight are greater than those of typical Dutch bricks. German bricklayers, used to working with this larger type, were eventually called in to build the facades. According to Christian Rapp, a careful choice of materials and thoughtful detailing are key conditions for an enduring architecture.

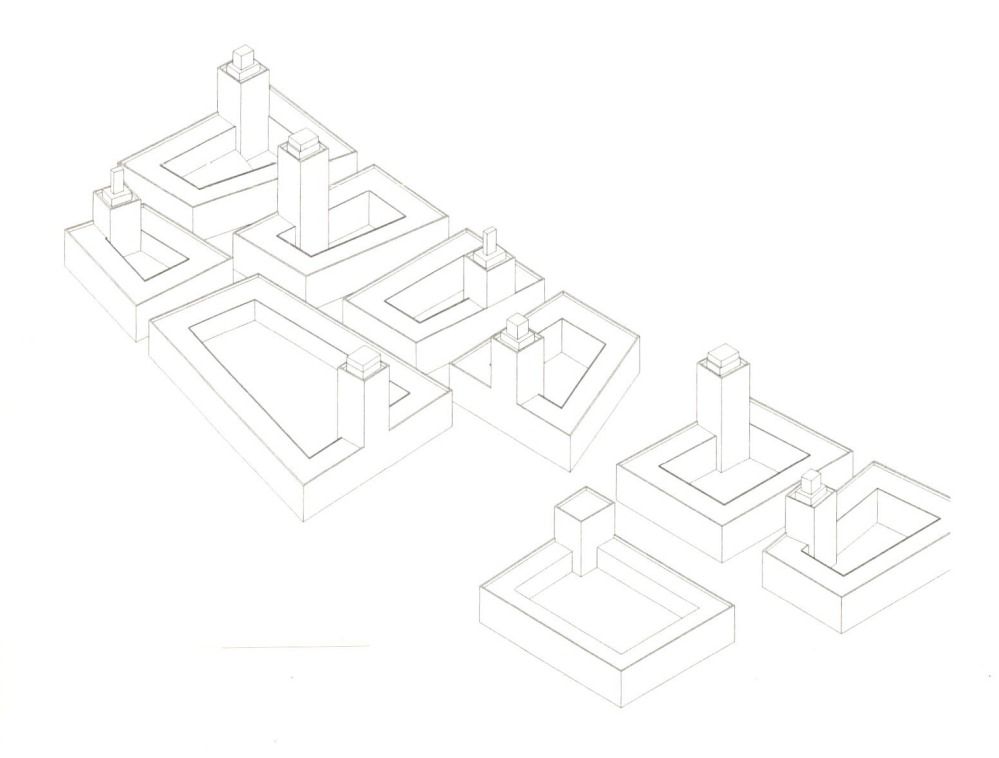

168

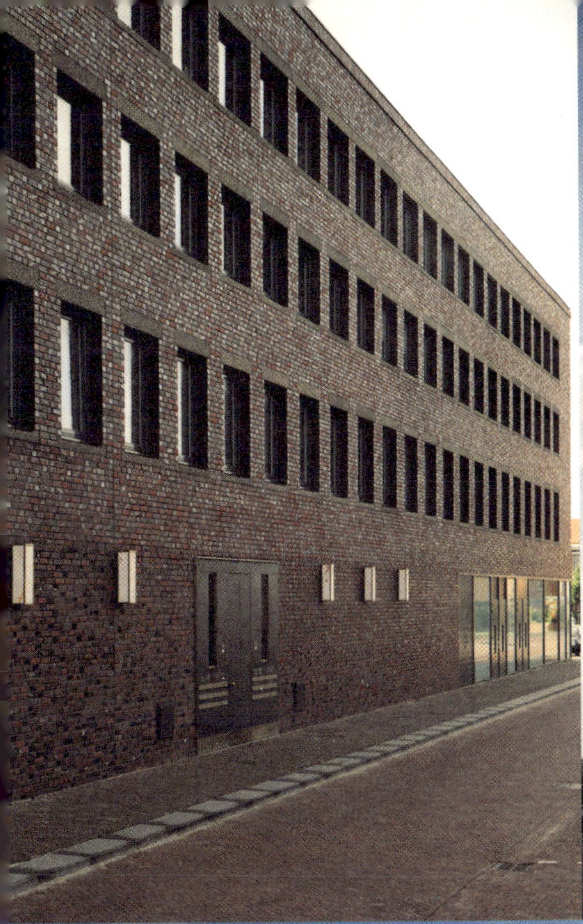
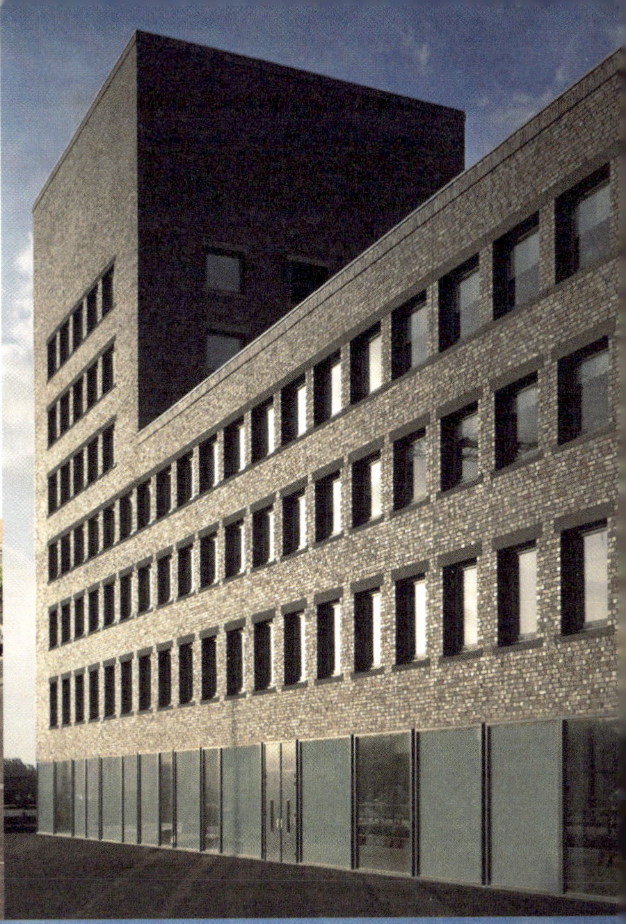
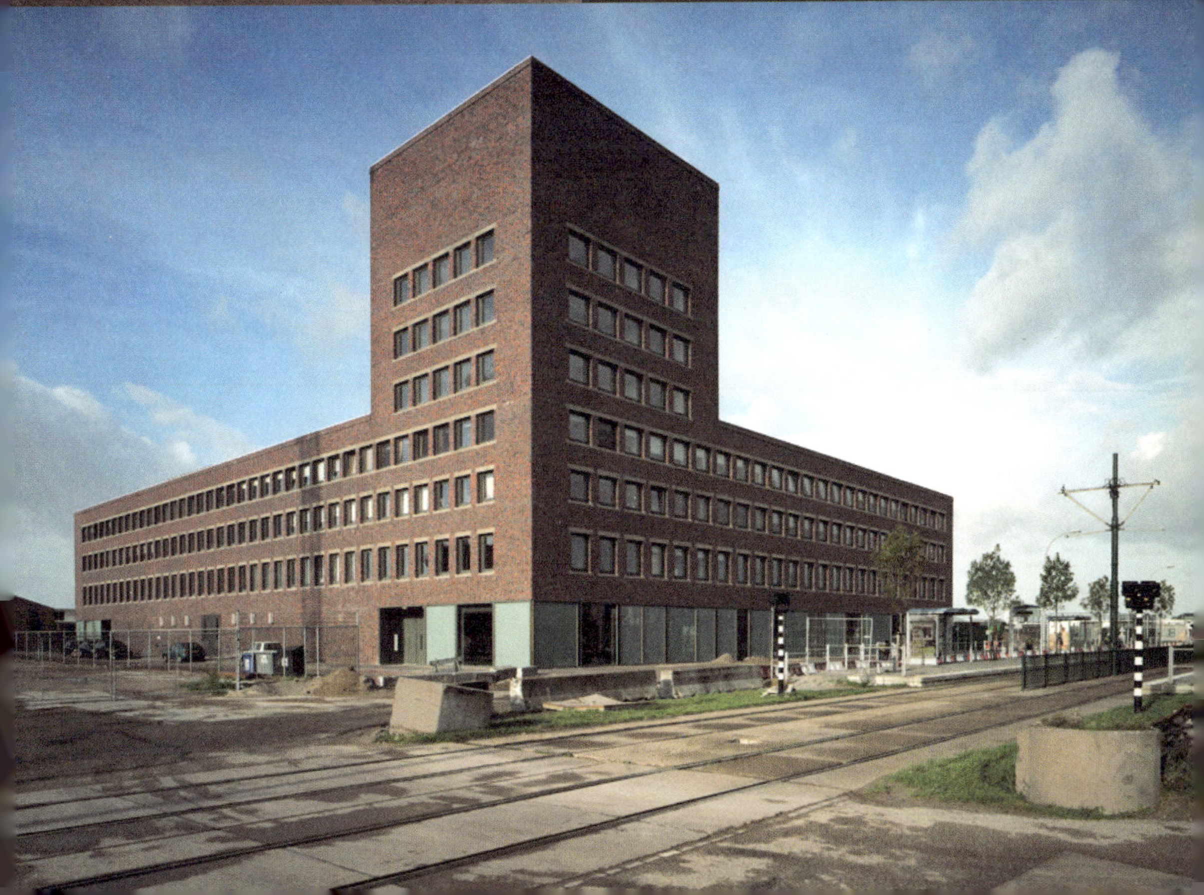

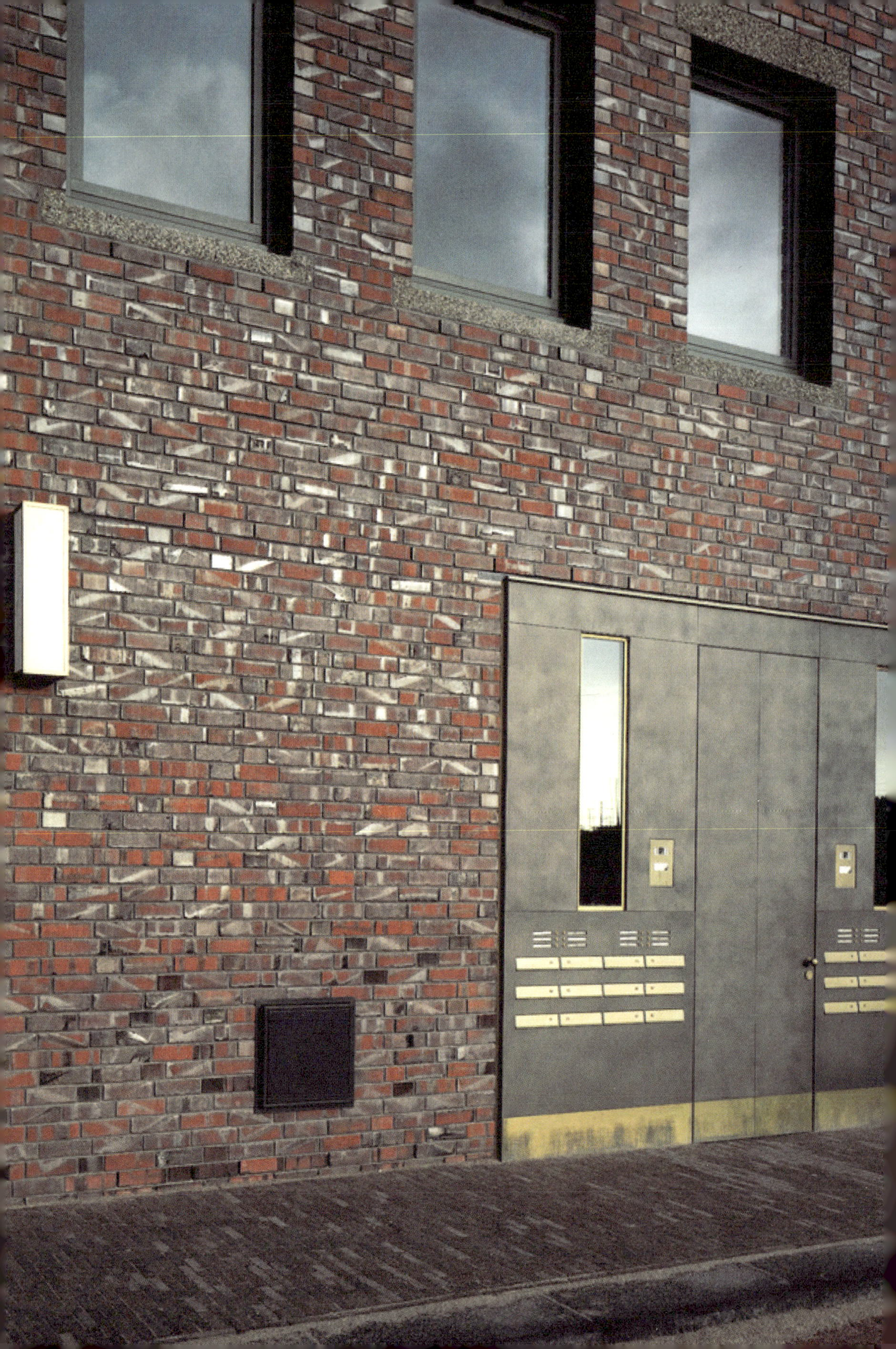

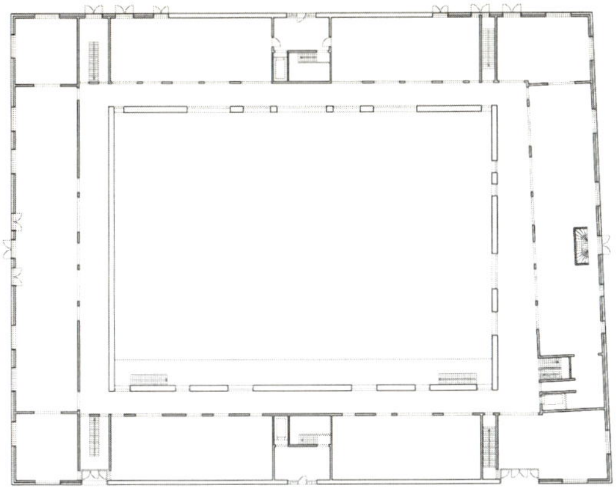

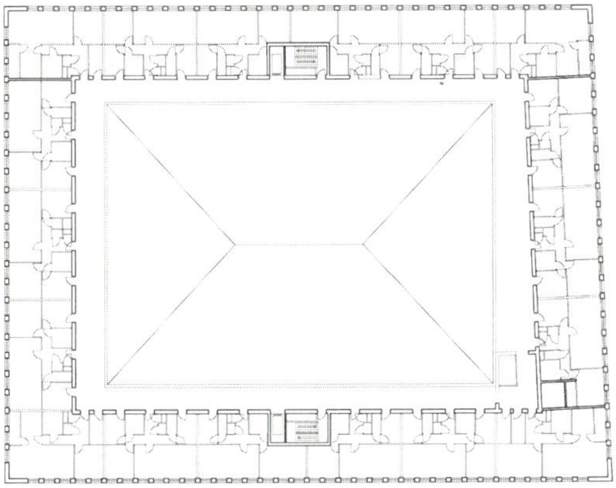

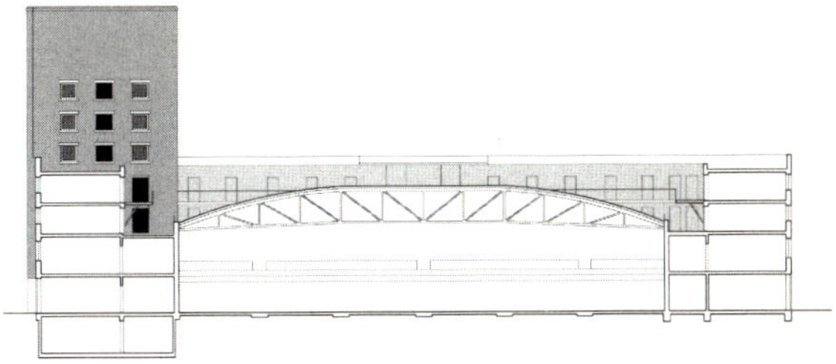

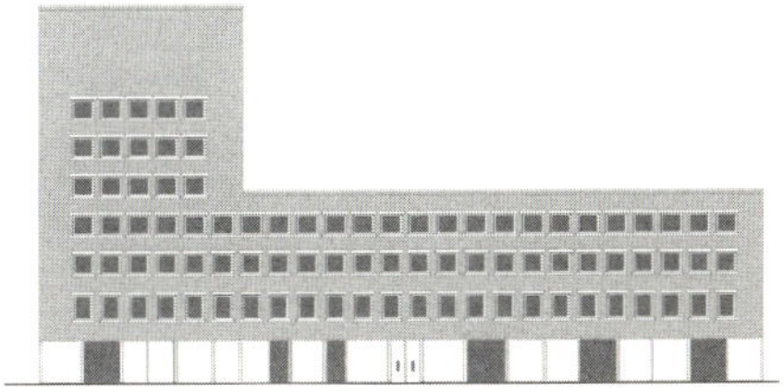

CITY GARDEN

Winter Palace, Aomori, Japan, Atelier Kempe Thill, 2002

The idea underlying Winter Palace, a competition entry by André Kempe and Oliver Thill, was to give the city of Aomori in Japan a large public park. Set in the centre of the city, it would not only benefit the houses surrounding it; the city as a whole could profit from the closeness of nature. Enfolding this 5600 m² public space is a 'ring-building' of housing and amenities. This consists of six storeys 7 metres tall, enveloped in a fully opening glass facade. The six storeys are entirely empty and act as stacked plots in which housing units can be placed as in a storage rack. A prefabricated building system keeps construction costs down and increases the speed of building; it also allows future occupants to assemble their homes as they see fit. Exceptional demands were made of its main loadbearing structure – all the more so as it needed to be earthquake-proof like all large buildings in Japan. This main structure consists of steel beams and joists, with concrete floors. Not just a 'constructional oversize', it is flexible in a second, quite different way. The steel construction of the facades protects the building against violent tremors. Stay cables in the facade give the building its stability, the net formed by these cables acting as a kind of support stocking.

Originally, the professional jury proclaimed the Winter Palace design winner of the international competition for a 'Northern Style Housing Complex in Aomori'. In the end, though, Atelier Kempe Thill had to make do with second prize and there are no plans to get the Winter Palace built. It was the mayor of Aomori who baulked at the idea of a building that flaunted its contents on all sides. What particularly upset him was the view of cars parked at front doors all the way up.

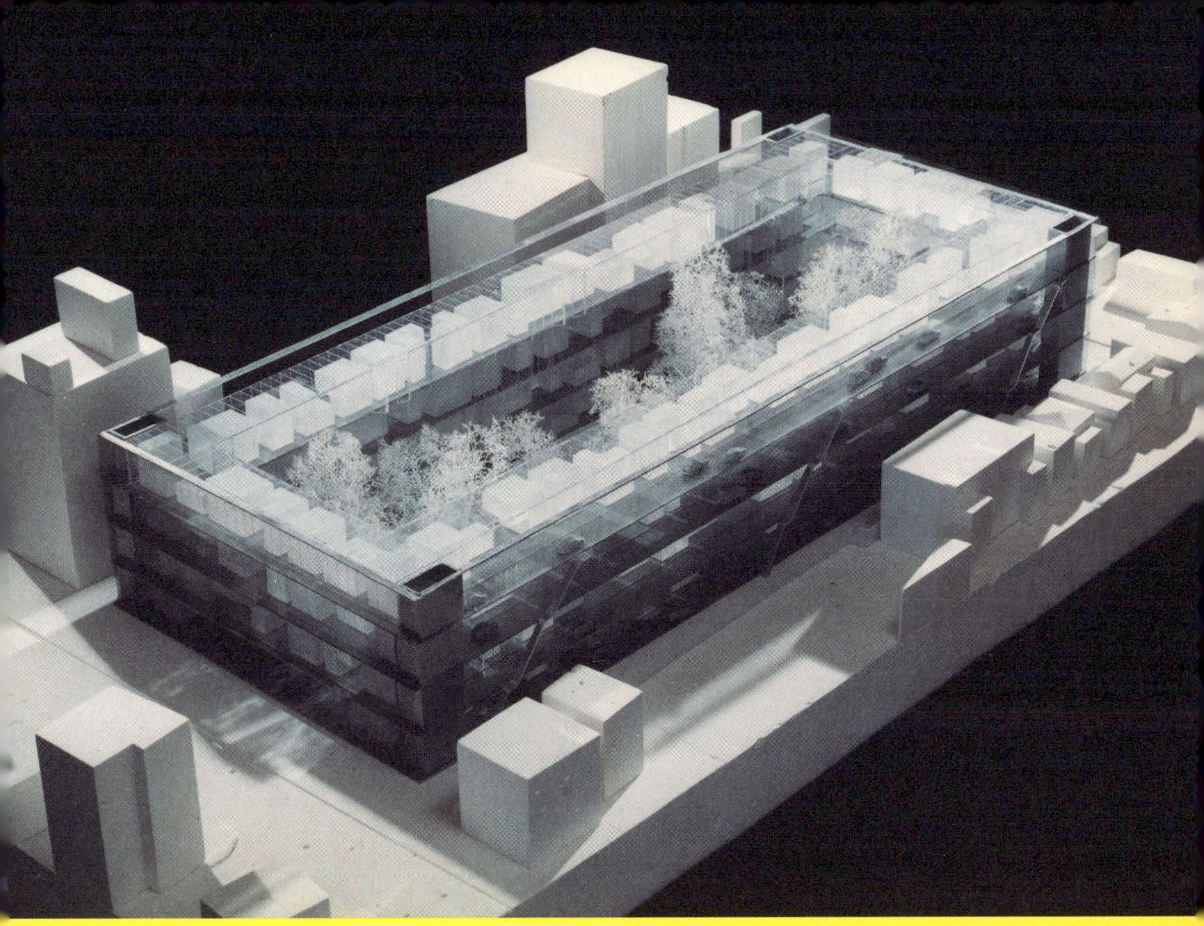

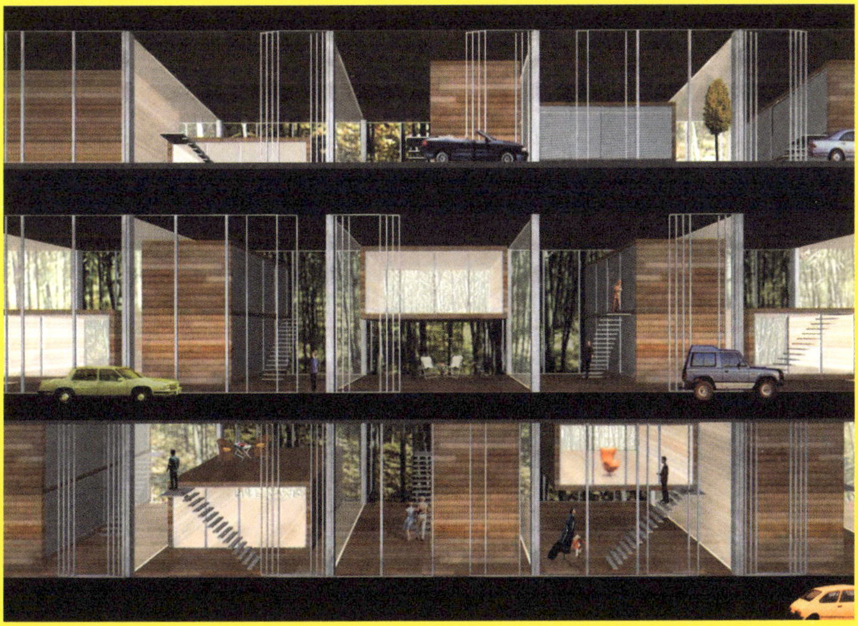

STRUCTURE

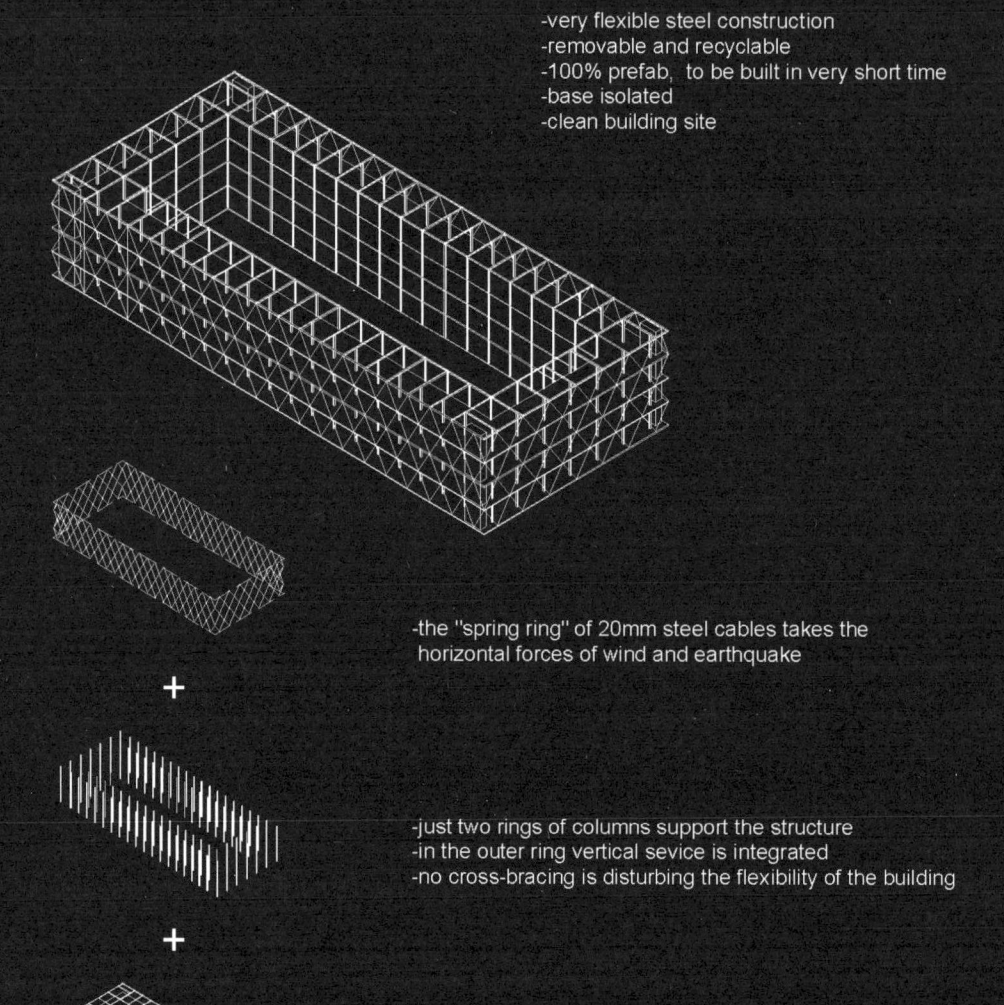

-very flexible steel construction
-removable and recyclable
-100% prefab, to be built in very short time
-base isolated
-clean building site

+

-the "spring ring" of 20mm steel cables takes the horizontal forces of wind and earthquake

+

-just two rings of columns support the structure
-in the outer ring vertical sevice is integrated
-no cross-bracing is disturbing the flexibility of the building

+

-the floor consists of steel beams and pre-cast concrete elements

BASIS   COURTYARD - TYPE   GARDEN - TYPE

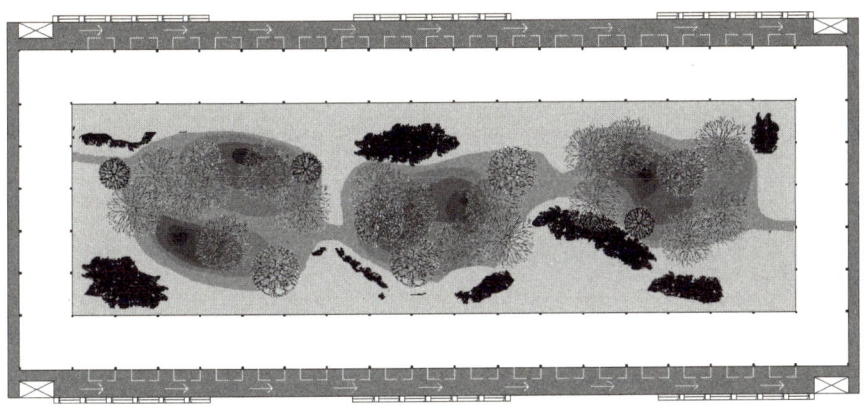

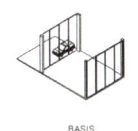

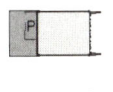

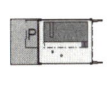

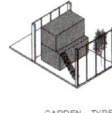

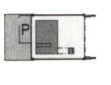

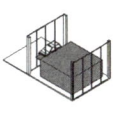

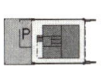

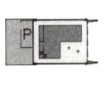

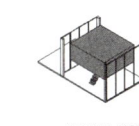

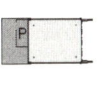

ROOF TERACE - TYPE   L - SHAPE -TYPE   HANGING - TYPE

BASE BUILDING AND FIT-OUT

Next 21, Osaka, Japan, Yositika Utida and Shu-Ko-Sha arch. & urban design studio, 1994

Commissioned by the Osaka Gas Company, Next 21 was built as a look ahead to the housing of the future. The building is an experiment in energy-saving and water management. Respecting a great many environmental measures, it integrates greenery into the roof and the facades. In addition, the building's lifespan has been increased by separating base building and fit-out. As propagated by the 'Open Building' international network the individual living units can be easily adapted without needing to change the building's shared structure (see N. John Habraken's essay on pp. 22-29). The U-shaped apartment building is like a small city, its 18 units reached off three-dimensional streets. The shared structure comprises the vertical and horizontal access, the basement parking facilities and the gardens on the roof and round the building. Residents could choose their own architect to design a home for them with the help of cladding units and fit-out kits specially made for the project. The facade system consists of aluminium panels and a wide selection of windows and doors, all of which can be assembled without the aid of scaffolding. In the end, the 18 units were designed by 13 different architects during and after construction of the concrete base building.

Base building and fit-out have been so assembled that should a unit undergo alteration this will have no negative effect on the shared structure and the other units. For example the cable run is separate from the main load-bearing structure. The cables and piping for electricity, water and sanitation are housed in the lowered floors of the galleries and corridors. In the dwellings themselves, the suspended ceiling contains the ventilation system, with the smaller runs occupying the space in the raised floor. Osaka Gas actually carried out modifications to some units by way of demonstration. Now it is a question of waiting for residents to spontaneously make the first sweeping changes.

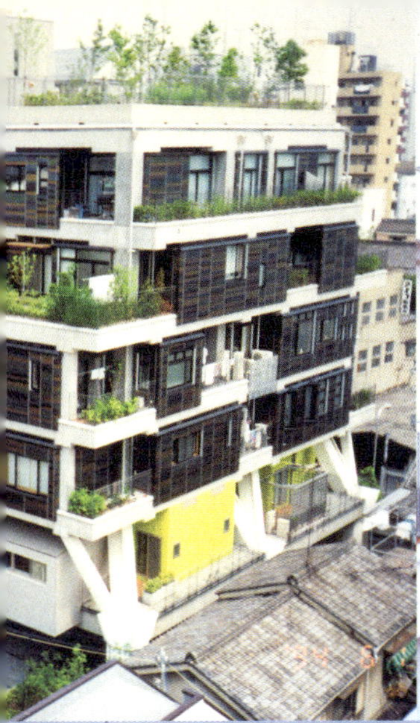

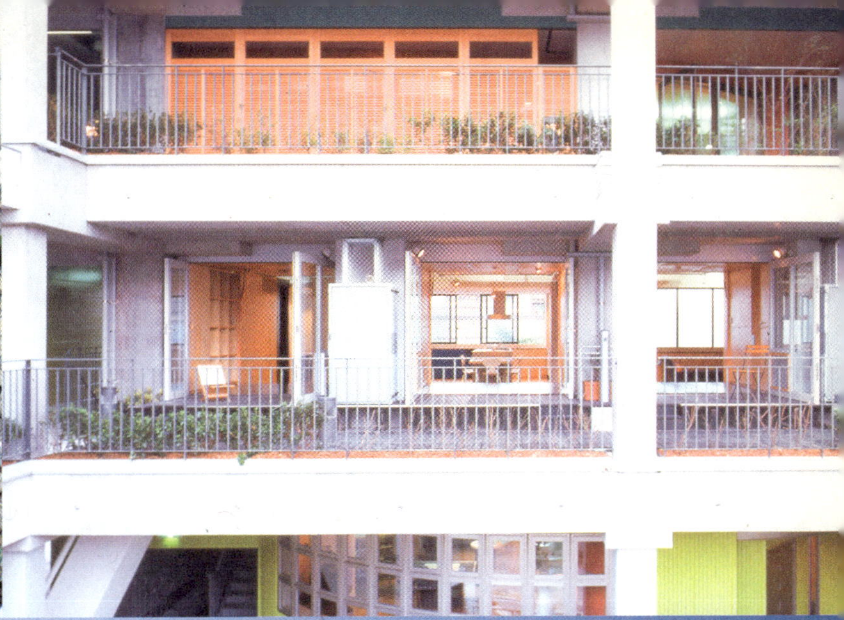

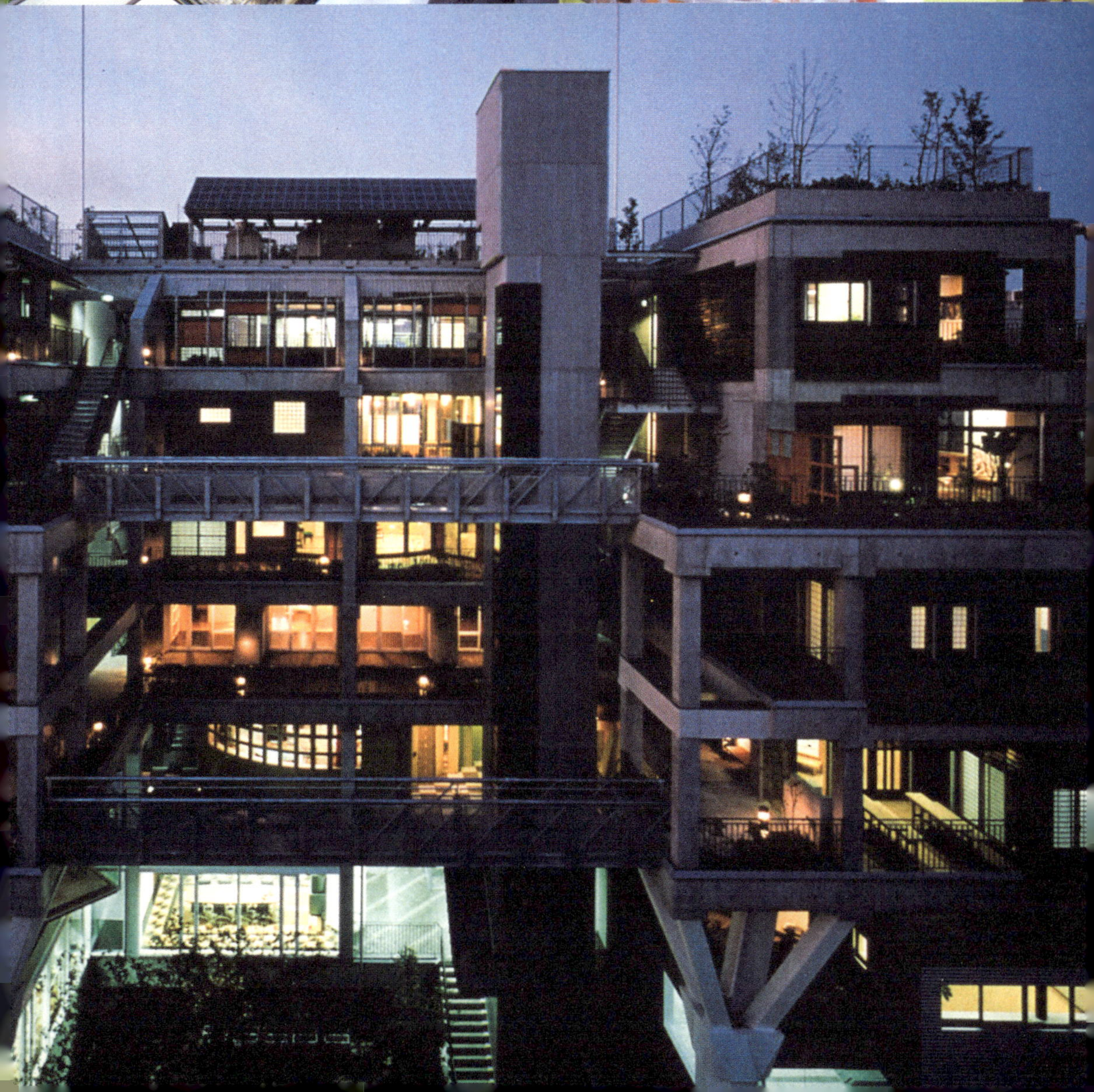

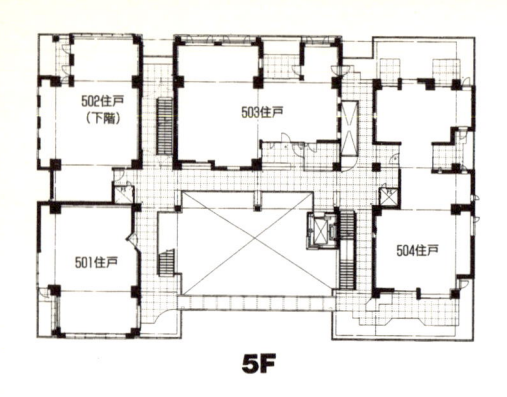

5F

502住戸
(下階)
503住戸
501住戸
504住戸

4F

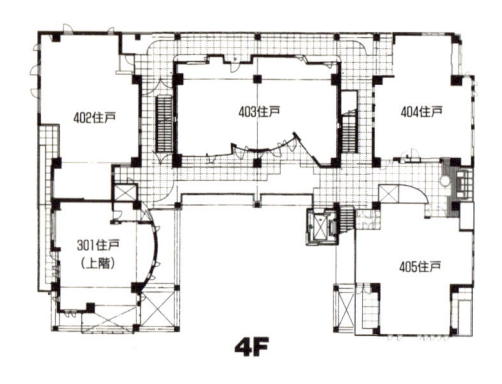

402住戸
403住戸
404住戸
301住戸
(上階)
405住戸

3F

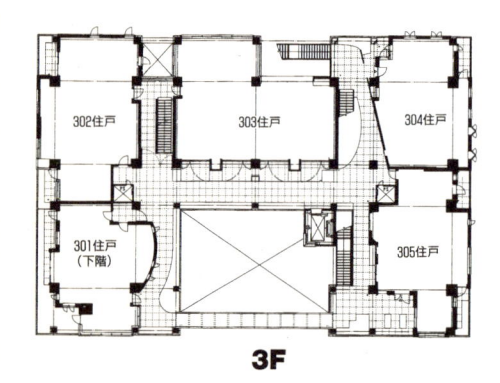

302住戸
303住戸
304住戸
301住戸
(下階)
305住戸

2F

NEXT21ホール
201住戸
202住戸

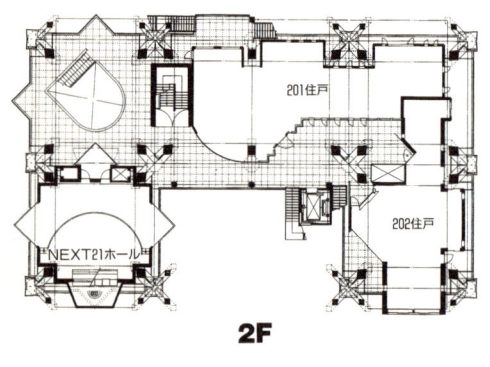

178

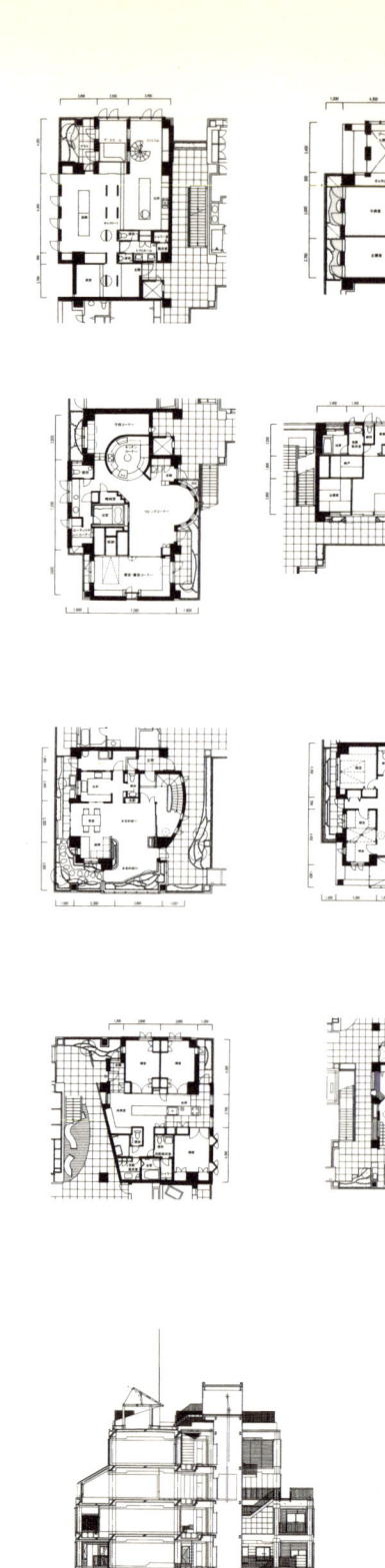

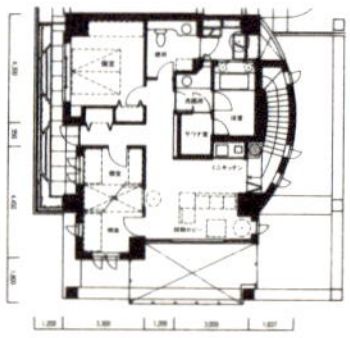

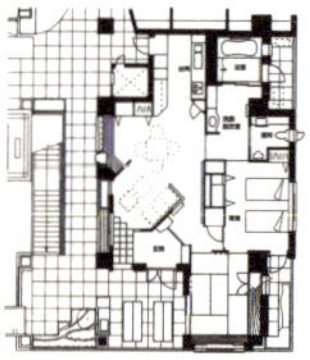

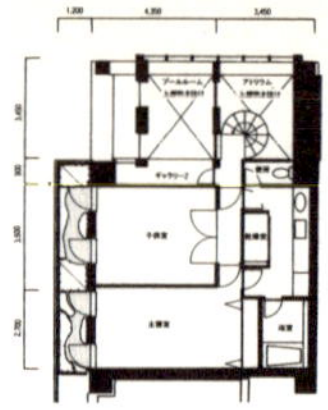

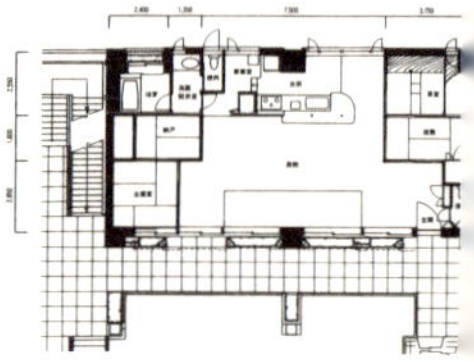

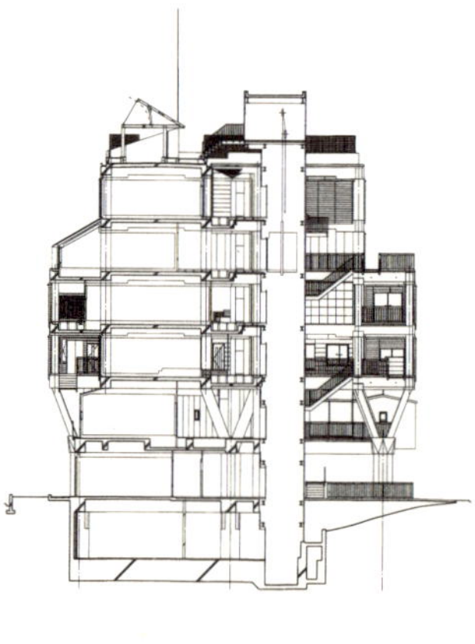

179

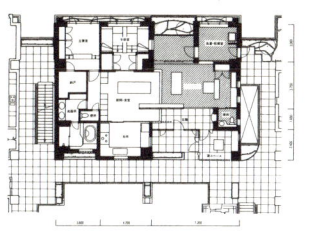

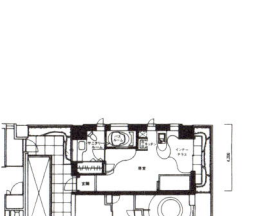

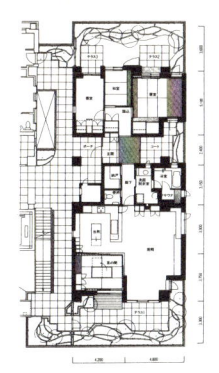

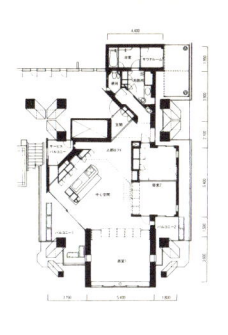

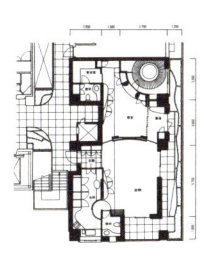

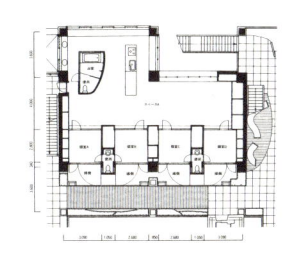

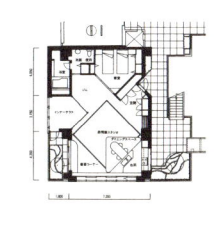

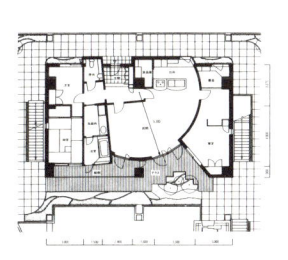

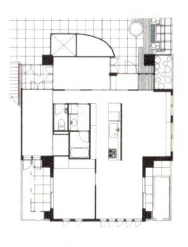

WORK BUILDING IN A GREENHOUSE
Crystalic, Leeuwarden, Netherlands, GD Architecten, 2002

In the drive to economize on energy, a number of buildings have been realized in recent years that can be described as a building inside a greenhouse. Crystalic is a fine example of this type. The climate between the glass outer skin and the actual building serves as an energy buffer to prevent heat losses. This sheltered environment functions not just as a place for the office staff to meet; it also houses a number of supplementary services such as a childcare centre, a copyshop, auditoria and a café.

The cloche-like envelope acts as a raincoat so that the building itself need not be wind- or waterproof. This meant that the office building could be simply constructed as a timber frame clad with MDF panels and can therefore be easily modified should this prove necessary. The climate buffer also means that the building can be accessed from outside along galleries. The facades on the galleries can be provided with additional doors at regular intervals, increasing the possibilities of internally subdividing the offices. Crystalic is intended for startup companies in the IT sector and each of these, no matter how small, can present itself in the facade along the gallery.

The building admits to an ingenious climate-control system. Screens for solar shading on the inside are separated from the glass sheath by a cavity half a metre wide. At the upper and lower edges of this cavity are push-out windows which when opened and closed create a draught in the cavity that carries surplus heat upwards. Condensers prevent the heat from being lost. In summer the collected heat is stored in the ground, in cold weather it is used directly for heating the offices. To further combat overheating in the 'greenhouse', solar cells have been placed in the south facade as a permanent anti-sun measure. An additional advantage of the glass envelope is that it shuts out the noise from the nearby provincial road.

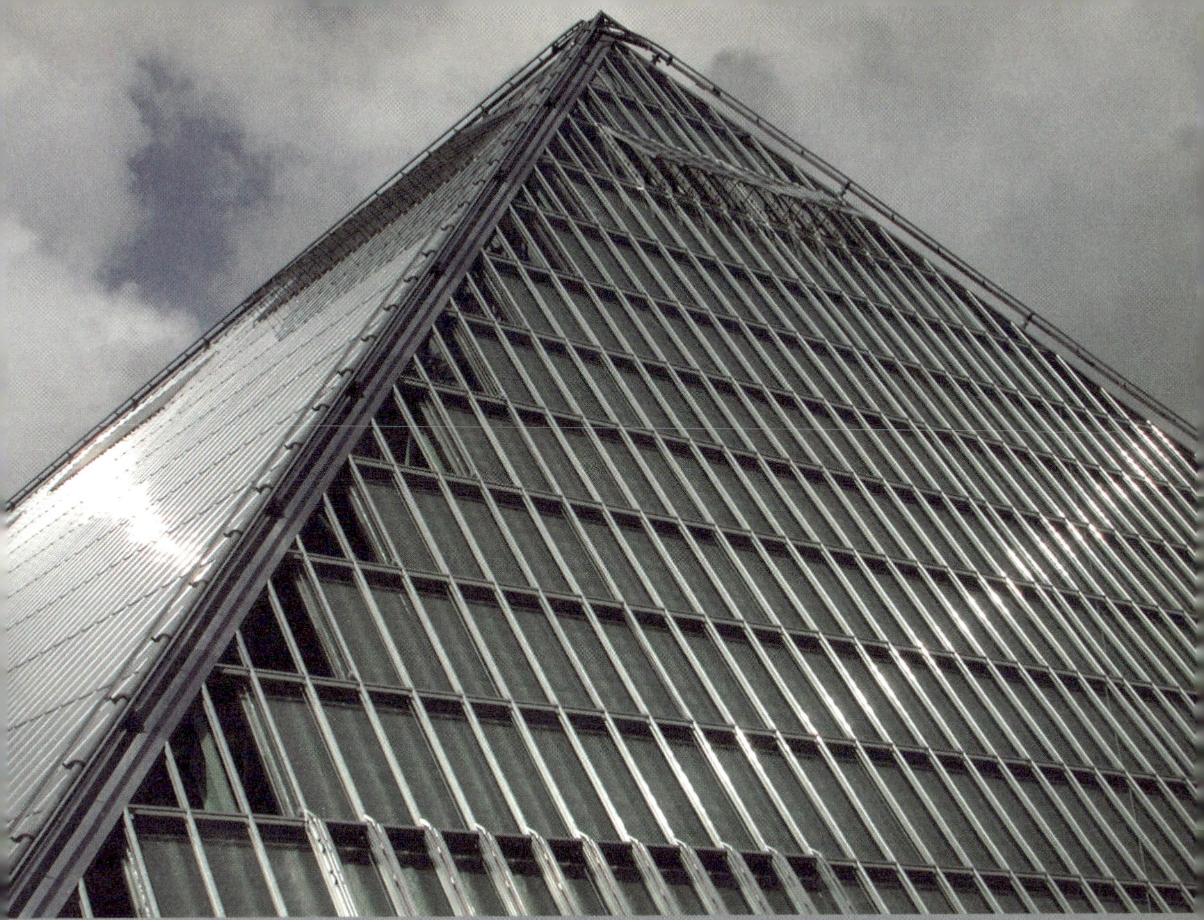

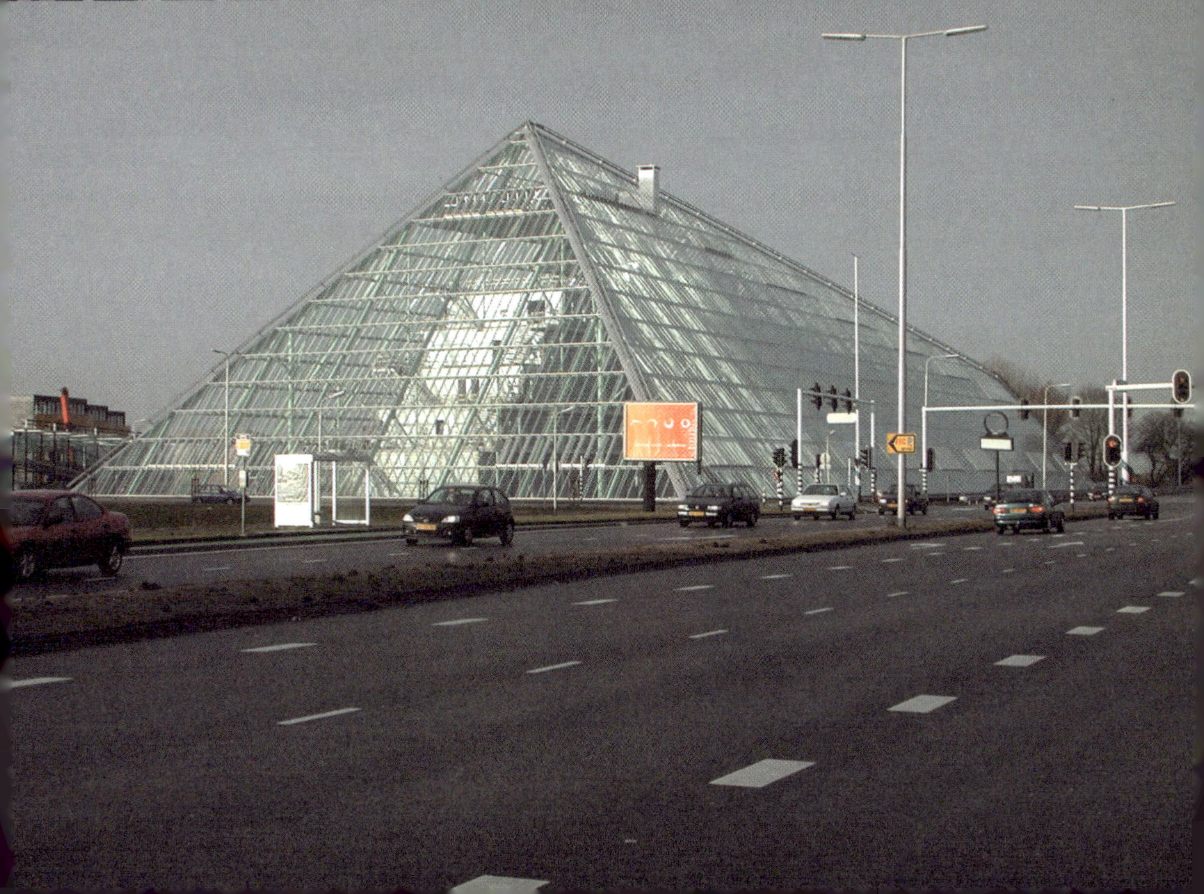

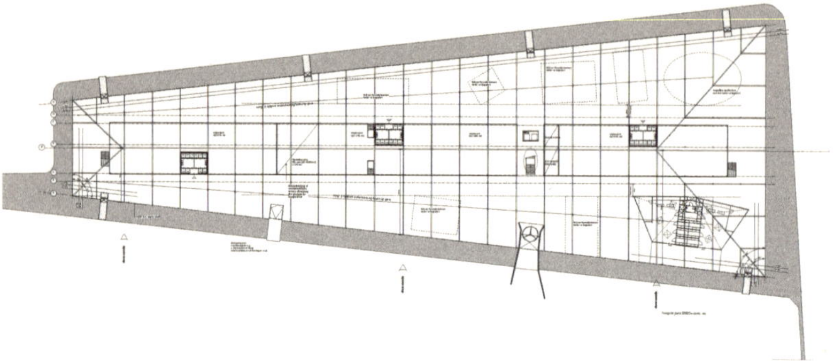

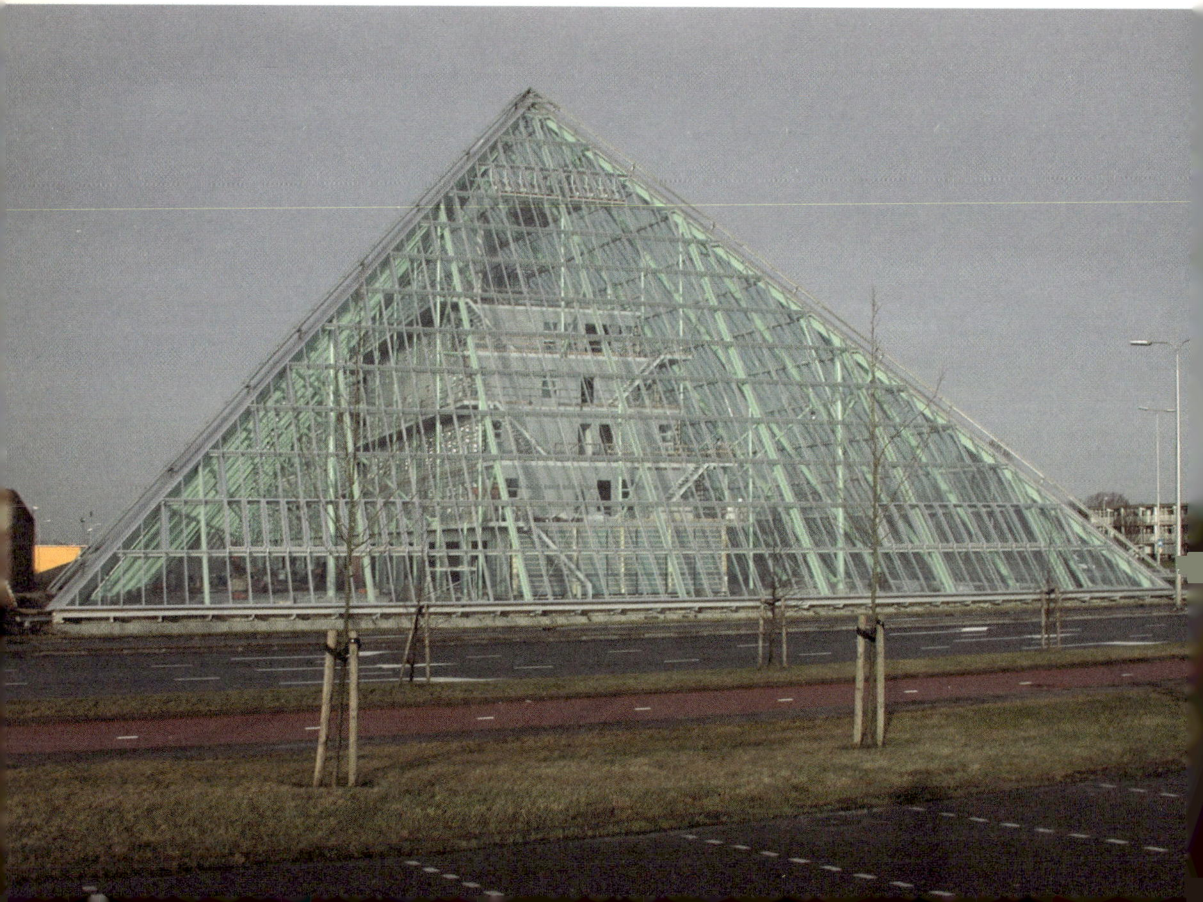

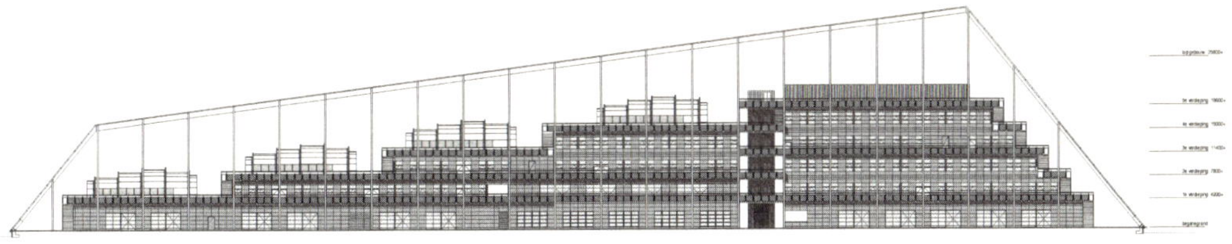

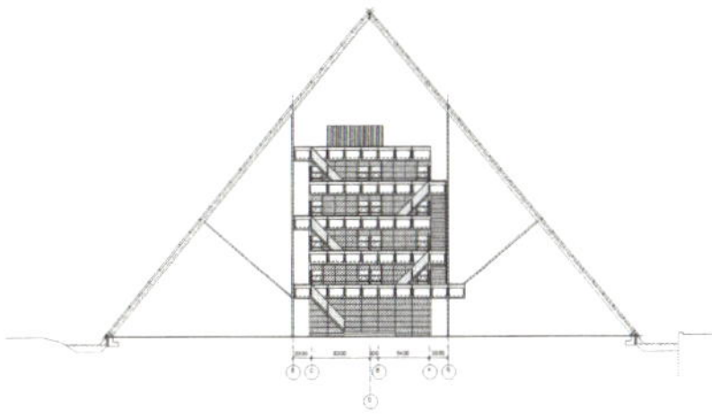

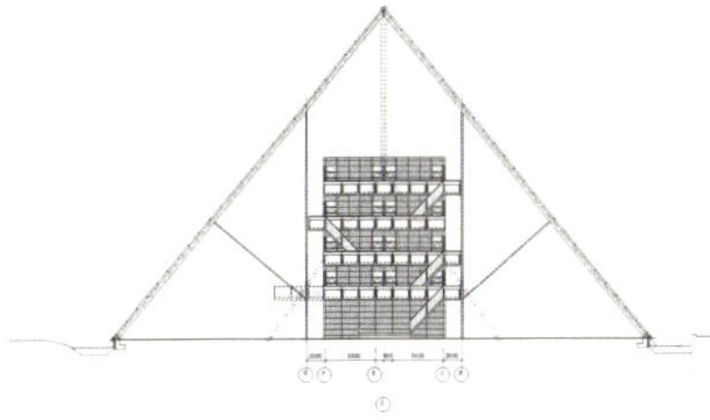

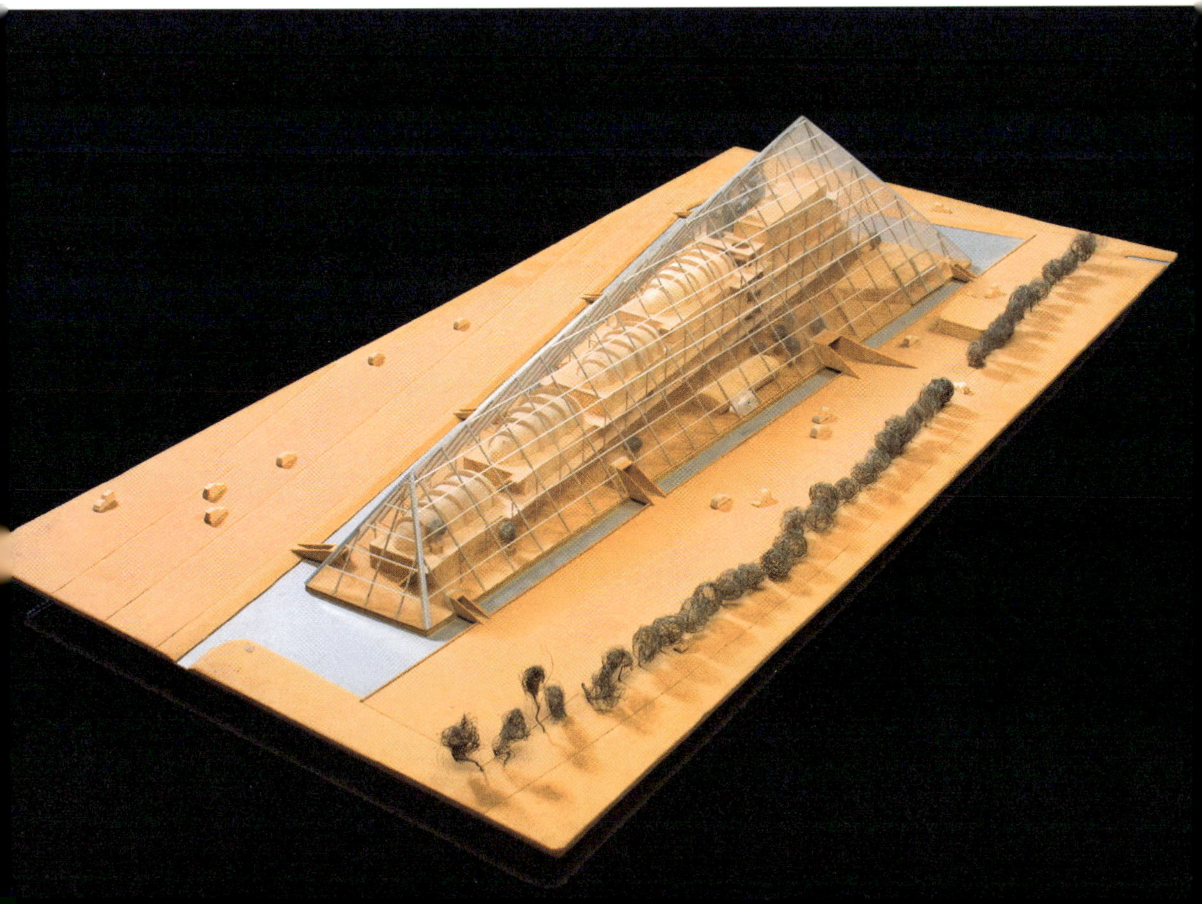

HOUSING ON IJBURG

Lux, London, UK, Maccreanor Lavington, 1997
Block 4, IJburg, Amsterdam, Netherlands, Maccreanor Lavington, 2003

The London-based architects Gerard Maccreanor and Richard Lavington bought a plot in that city with the money they had won in the Europan competition. As they had no idea what the market wanted they designed for it a building with a neutral facade able to front offices as well as housing. Armed with this scheme, they found two clients. For one of these, the London Electronic Arts and London Film-Makers Co-op, they developed the design as the Lux Building, which has since been built.
The principle of a neutral facade also figures in their design for Block 4 (2003) of the IJburg island settlement in Amsterdam. At present its facades front housing units only. Those on the ground floor can eventually be converted into shops and restaurants. They can be linked by opening up the walls between them (part of each concrete party wall is unreinforced). A share of the upper units are also able to take on other duties. Each unit has two front doors opening onto the stairs, so that part of the dwelling can be used for work and entered separately.
The future potential uses of Block 4 were used as a sales argument. The extra investments eventually incorporated in the cost price will be recovered in time, certainly if the ground floor is ultimately given over to shops, restaurants and other non-dwelling functions.

The Lux, London, UK, 1997

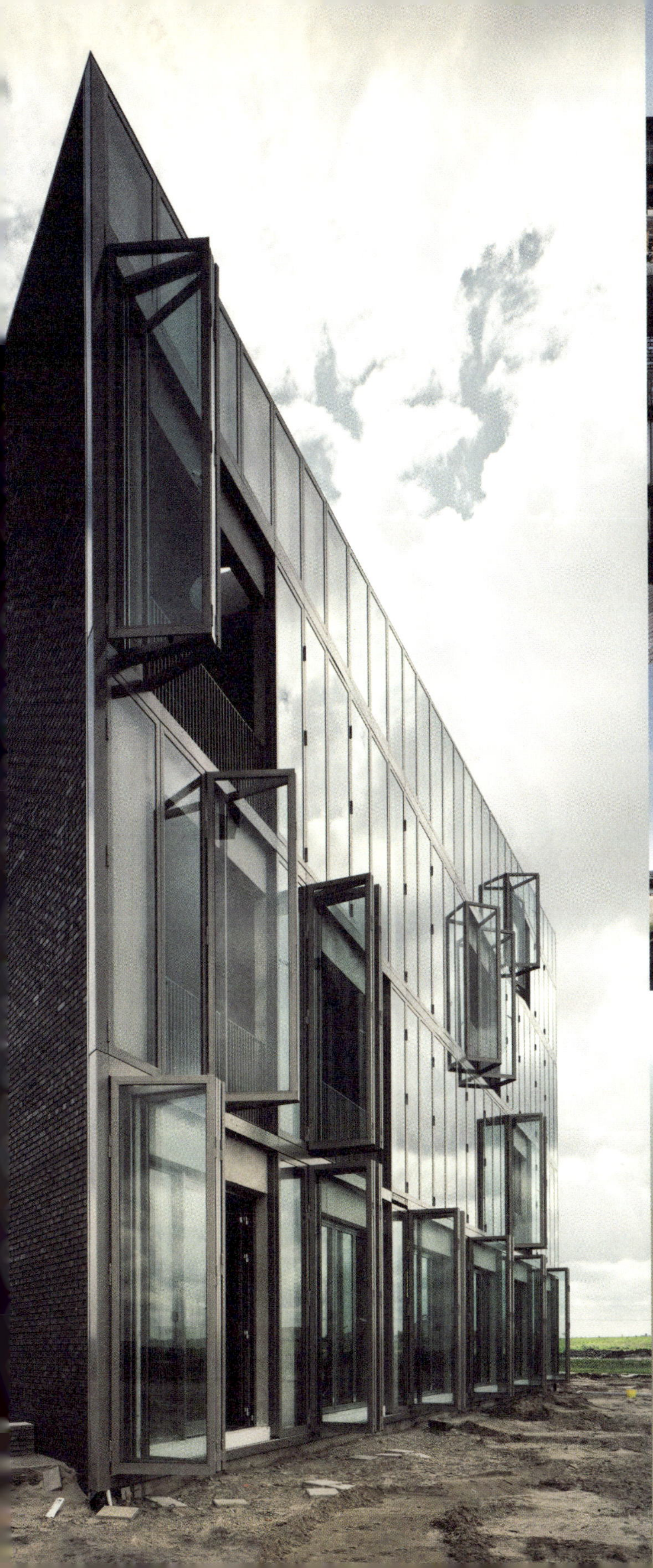

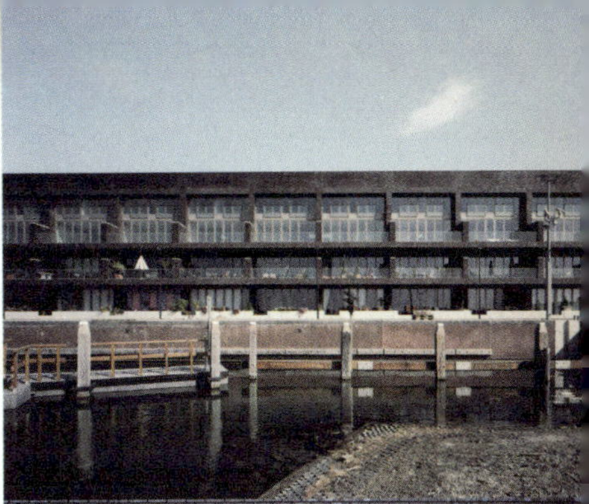

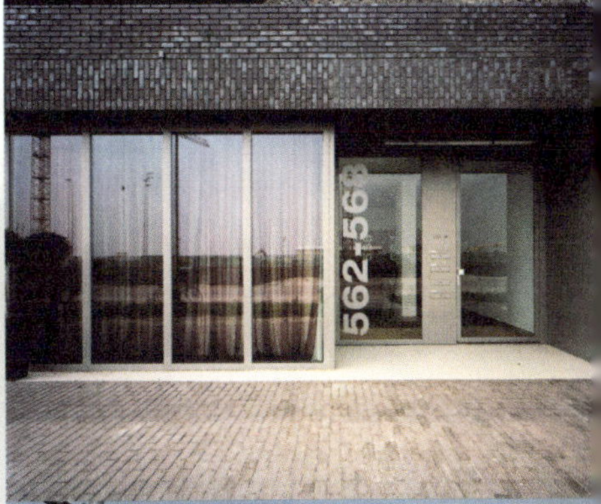
562-568

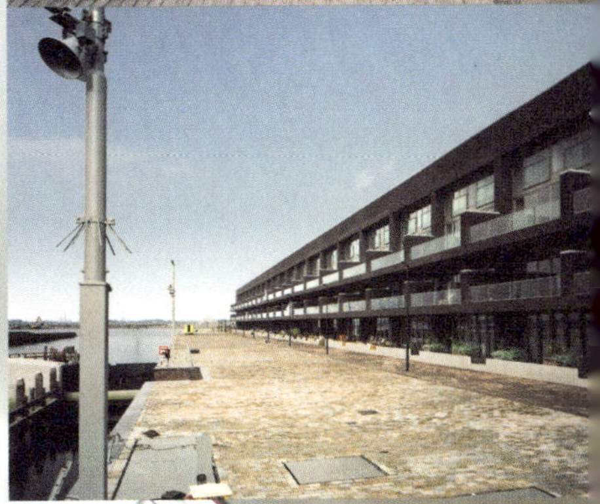

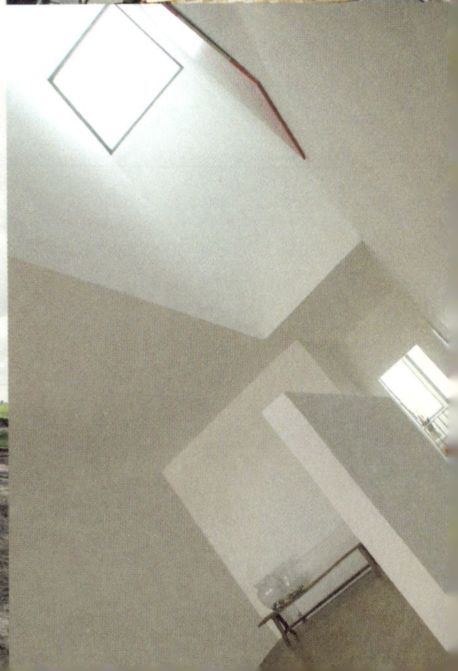

NOORDGEVEL

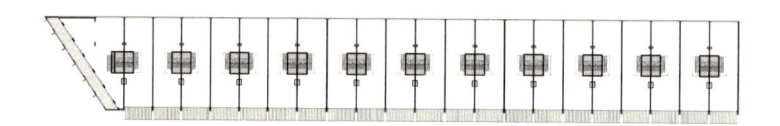

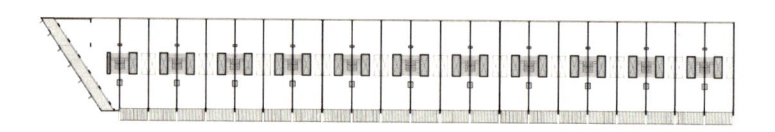

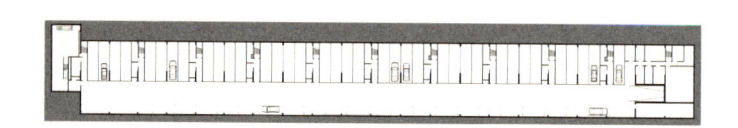

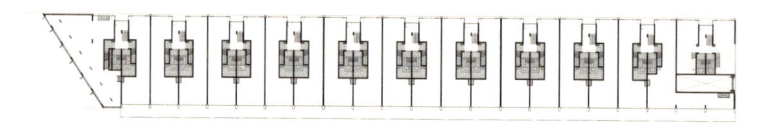

ZUIDGEVEL

187

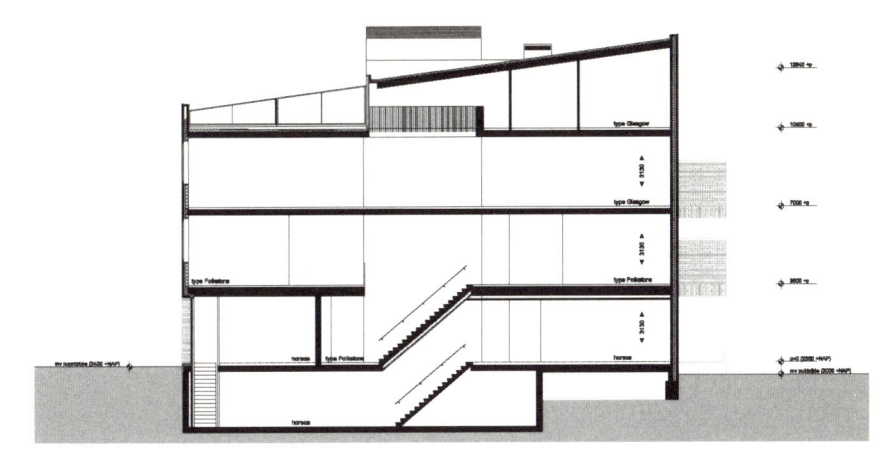

BILLBOARD FACADE

INIT Building, Amsterdam, Netherlands, Groosman Partners, 2003

INIT is a large mixed-used commercial building occupying a municipal wharf in the former Stork factory grounds in East Amsterdam. Not only very large, it is also compact, and targets a broad group of potential occupiers. Its access system is such that the building can be variously subdivided. Each unit can be reached in several ways via one of the many porches and a grid of corridors. The units themselves can be internally organized as their occupiers see fit.

As the building is to appeal to a broad target group architect Gert de Graaf of Groosman Partners sought to prevent the exterior from being dominated by one of the larger occupiers. At the same time he wanted to prevent it becoming an anonymous building where occupying companies were unable to present themselves to the outside world. To this end he opted for a double facade.

A double facade consists of a glass skin placed in front of an insulating wall containing areas of double glazing for views out (see 'Sources'). The cavity zone between the two facades is free of wind and rain and stays at a moderate temperature. One major advantage over a single glass skin is that the internal wall encasing the building is scarcely affected by the climate outside. This means less climate control and a simpler construction (and thus cheaper detailing) for the inner facade, making this easy to modify.
In the INIT Building the inner facade is given over to advertising space for the occupying firms. All shared facilities are expressed in the outer skin. This requires active management, as all individual presentations need regulating dynamically from a central point if there is to be a constantly changing exterior.

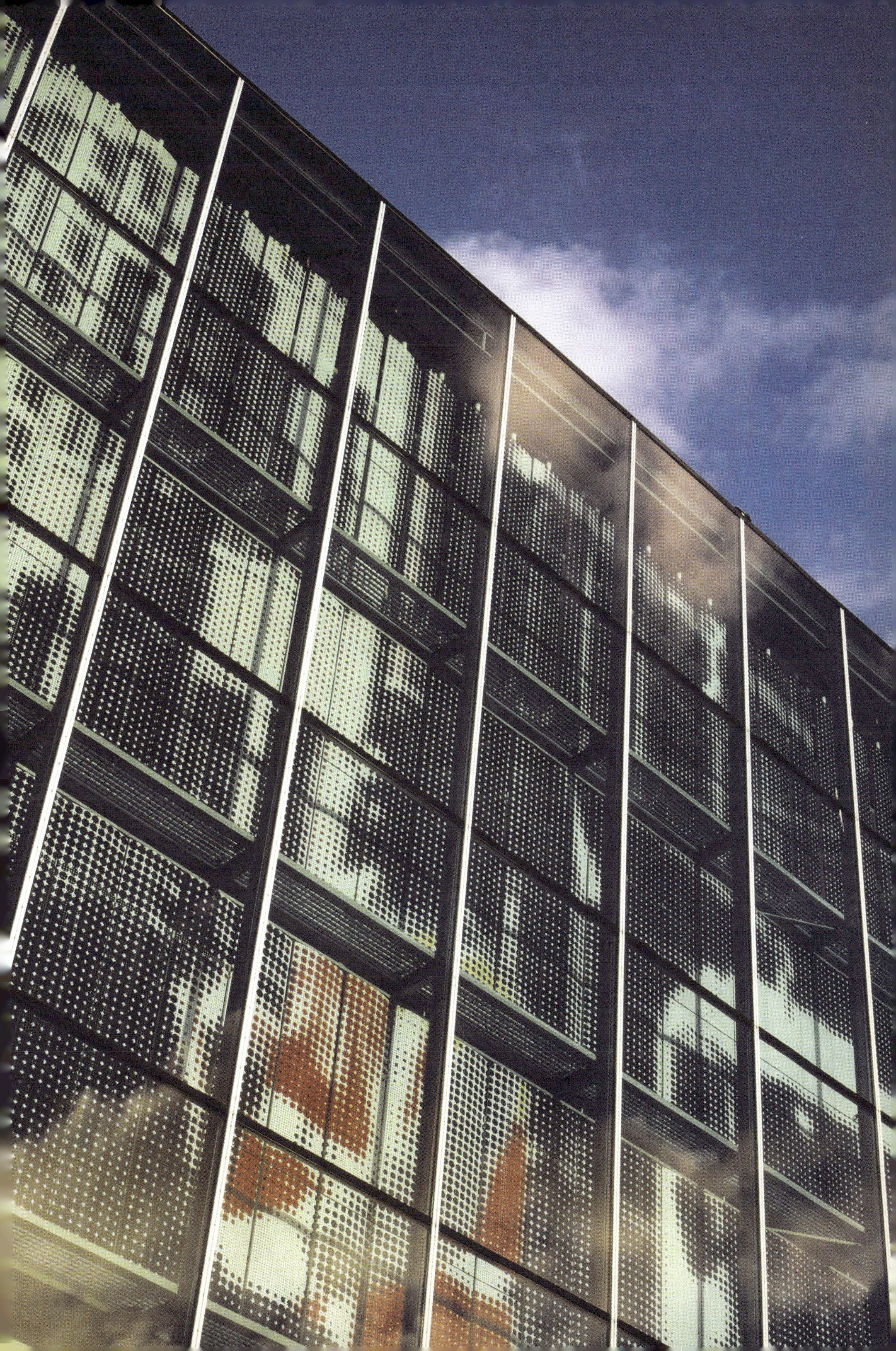

::: INIT OPENBAAR GEHEIM. ONDERIN, VERPAKT ALS DE PIT IN DE PERZIK, DEELS VERZONKEN IN DE DIEPTE, HUIST DE STADSREINIGING DIENST BINNENSTAD CLEAN HONDERDEN, KLEINE PRACHTIGE VOERTUIGEN ZULLEN ALS BEZIGE

[P]
[PLANOPBOUW]

[22]

- KANTOREN GEMEENTEWERF_
- ENTREE EN CIRCULATIERUIMTE_
- VERGADERCENTRUM_
- REPRESENTATIEVE RUIMTES_
- SERVICE-UNITS_
- PARKEERGARAGE EN EXPEDITIE_
- GEMEENTEWERF_
- WERK-UNITS_

INIT NIVEAU 0_   INIT NIVEAU 1_

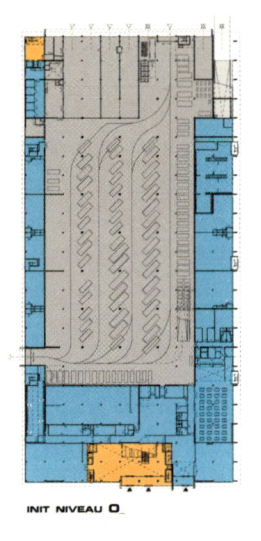

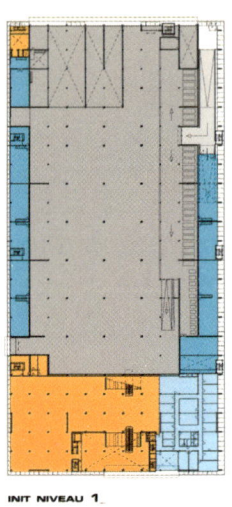

BIJEN GEZELLIG HEEN EN WEER ZOEMEN. DE VUILNISMANNEN ALS ENGELEN DIE DE EINDELOZE VUILNISBERG VAN DE STAD LACHEND TE LIJF GAAN. DEZE PLEK. MIJN GEBOUW IS KLAAR. DE MAQUETTE IS GEREED. HIJ STAAT DAAR.   ⟶

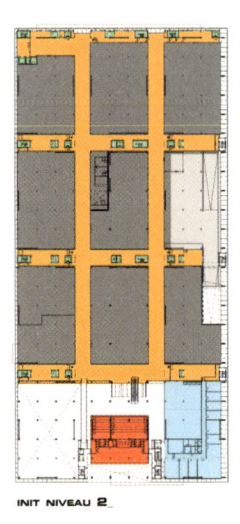

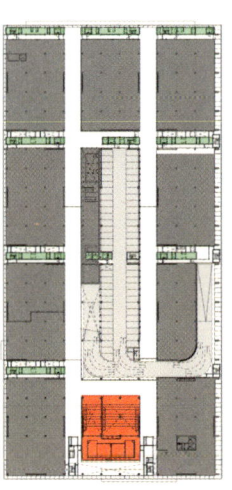

[23]

INIT NIVEAU 2_   INIT NIVEAU 3, PARKEERLAAG 1_   INIT NIVEAU 3, PARKEERLAAG 2/3_

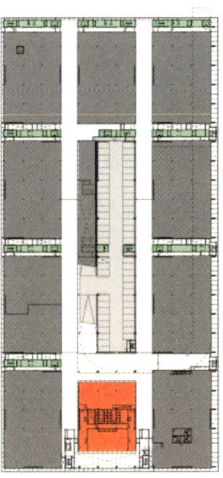

190

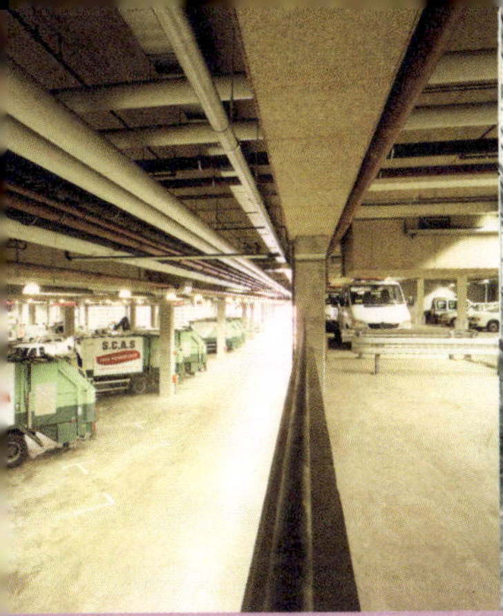

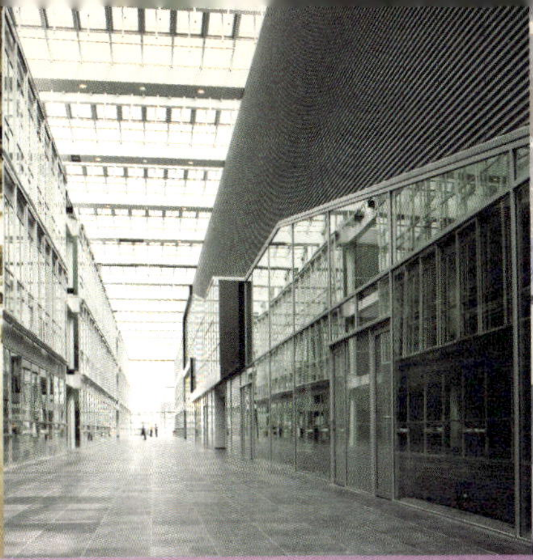

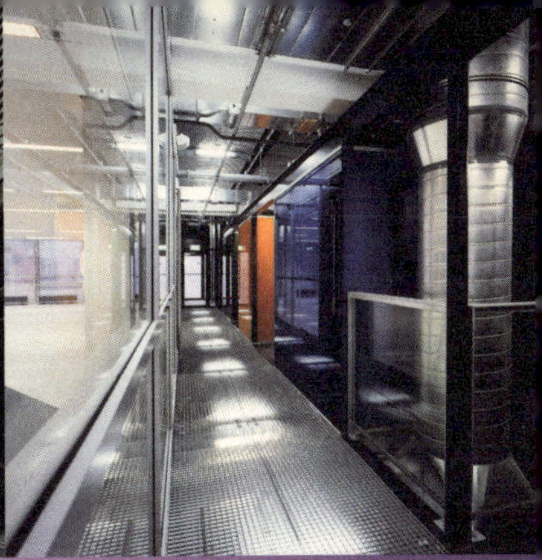

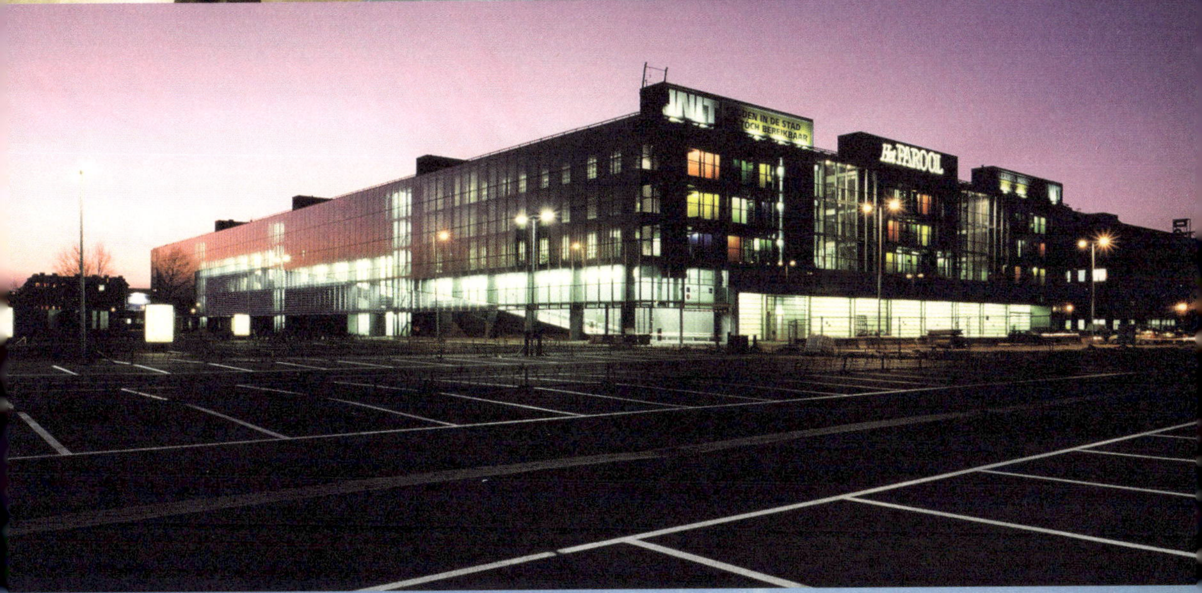
Het PAROOL

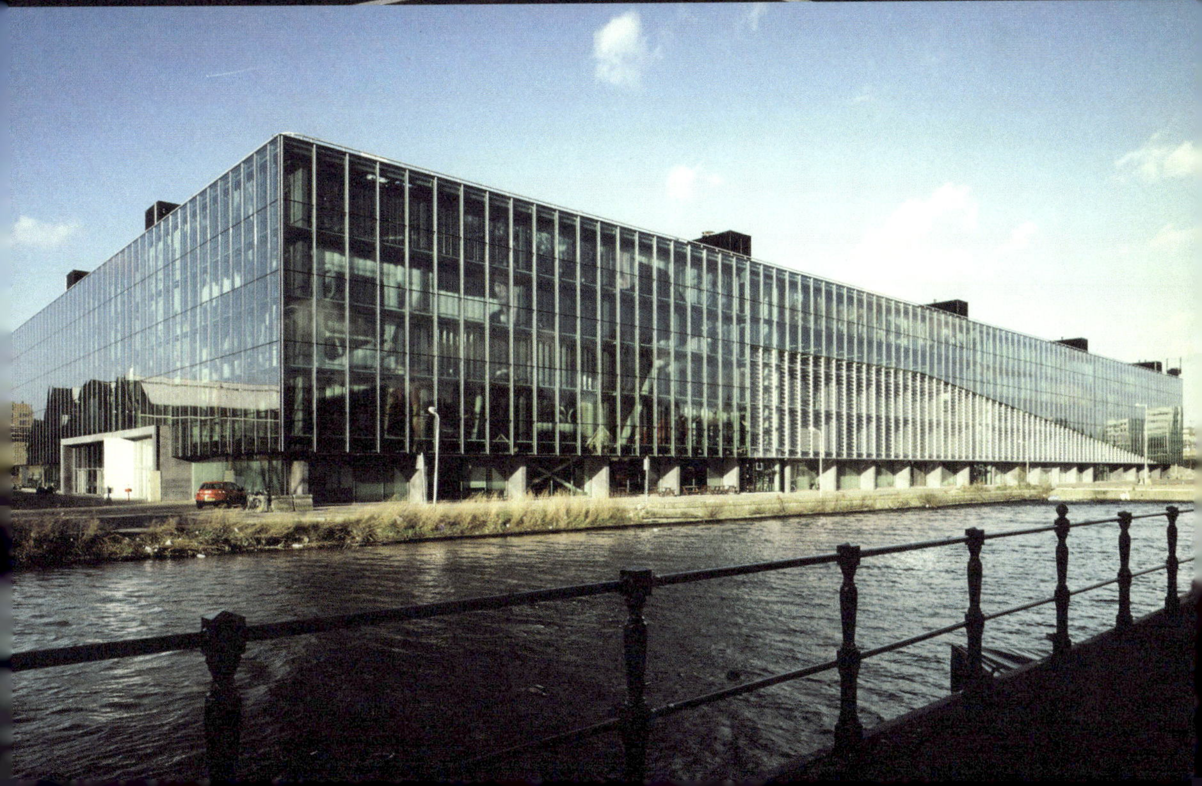

LAYERED STRUCTURE

INO, addition to the Insel University Hospital, Switzerland, Itten + Brechbühl AG, 2004
Process managed by the Canton Berne Building Department

Modern hospitals are complex buildings with elaborate services. Not only is medical technology advancing hand over fist, ideas on the methods of treatment are constantly changing too. All this is happening so fast that the construction of new hospitals is regularly delayed as the latest insights require that modifications be made to the design. Understandably, the costs of replacing the fit-out, or even of demolishing what has just been built, are not covered.

This is why the facilities group at the Insel University Hospital chose a method in which construction of the building was put out to tender and built in three distinct stages. First to be tackled was the primary system consisting of the main loadbearing structure and the facades, with an expected lifespan of 100 years. Then came the secondary system – services and dividing interior surfaces – with a lifespan of some 20 years. Lastly, the tertiary system for everything with a lifespan of less than five years, was separately tendered and built. The contractors for each of these systems received both the brief for the components in question along with the drawings of what was already on site. As it is not known exactly how the primary system will be fitted out, it has been designed with space in mind for future modifications. Floors in the main loadbearing structure include squares of 3.6 m² that can be easily punctured. The columns convey the ducting between storeys and have additional 'sleeves' incorporated in the floor at the base.

A special feature of the procedure for selecting the architect to design the primary system, was that only architects with no previous experience in designing hospitals were to apply. The traditional 'functionalist' design stance was regarded as obstructive to devising a flexible structure.

Sleeves in the floor round the columns facilitate future modifications to the building services.

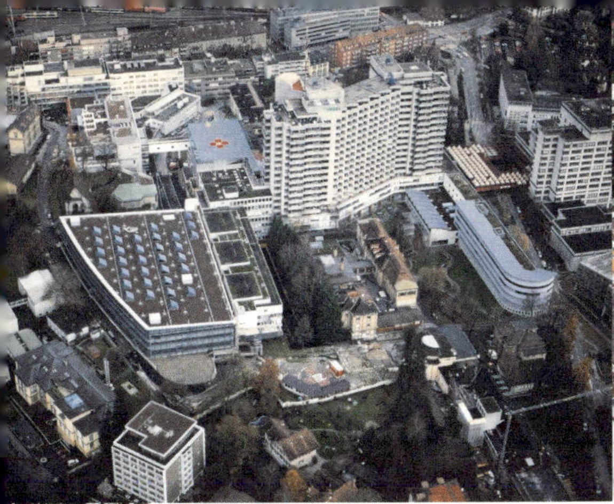
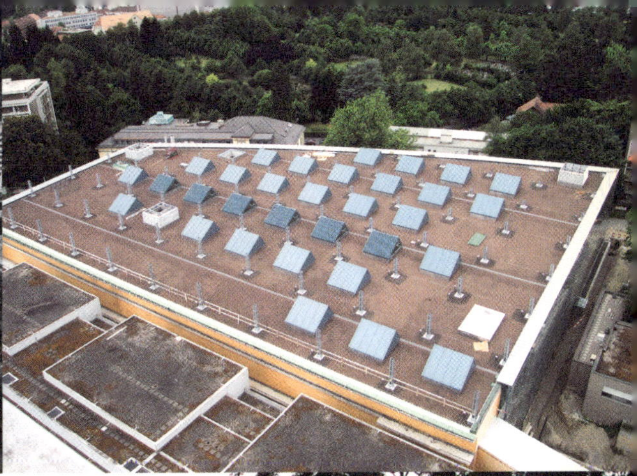
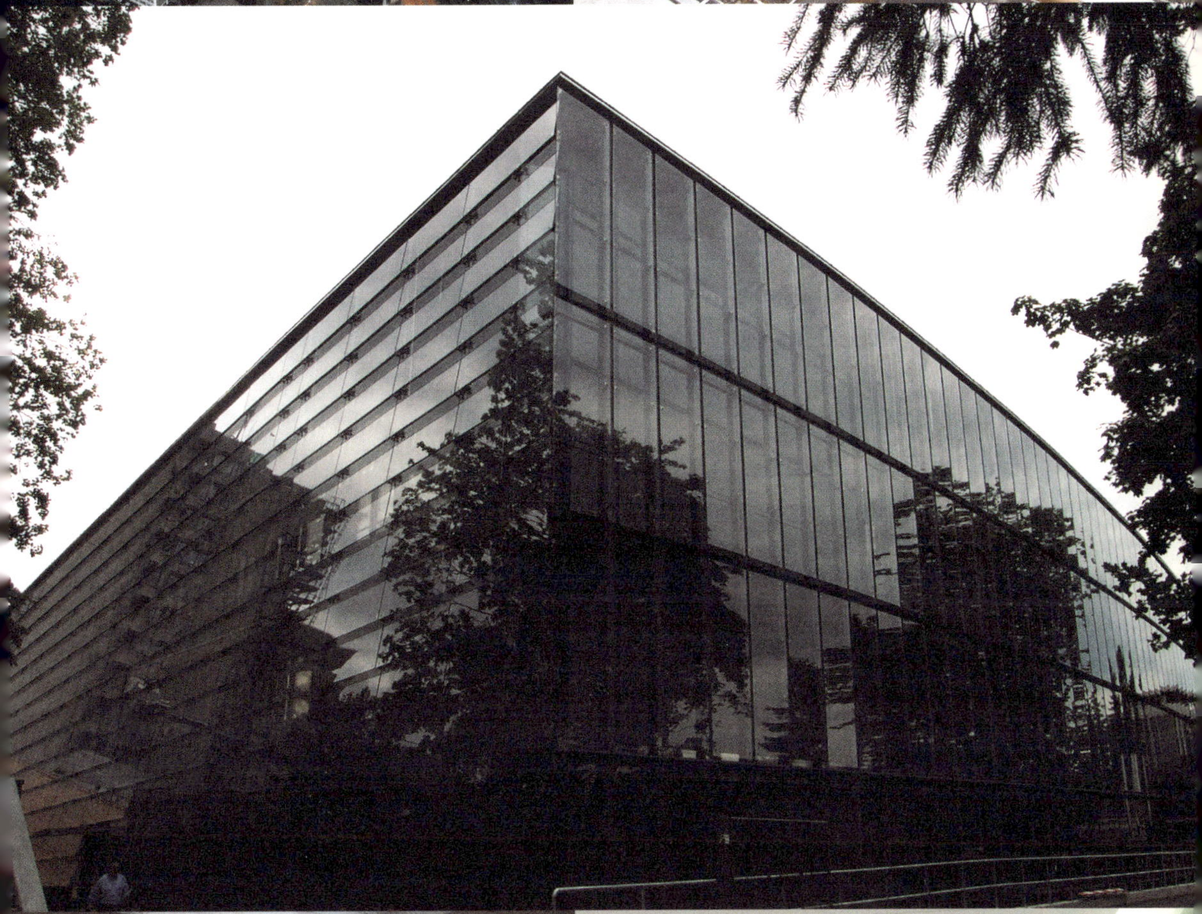
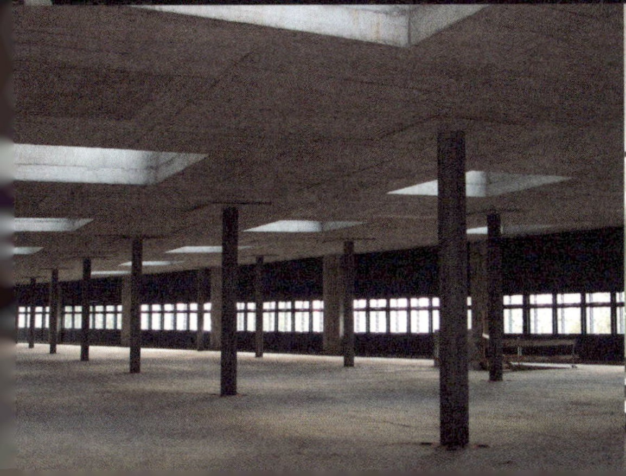
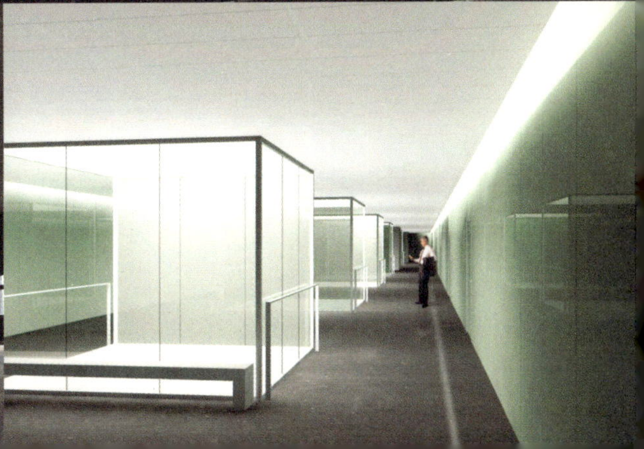

2.Etappe ◀▶ 1.Etappe

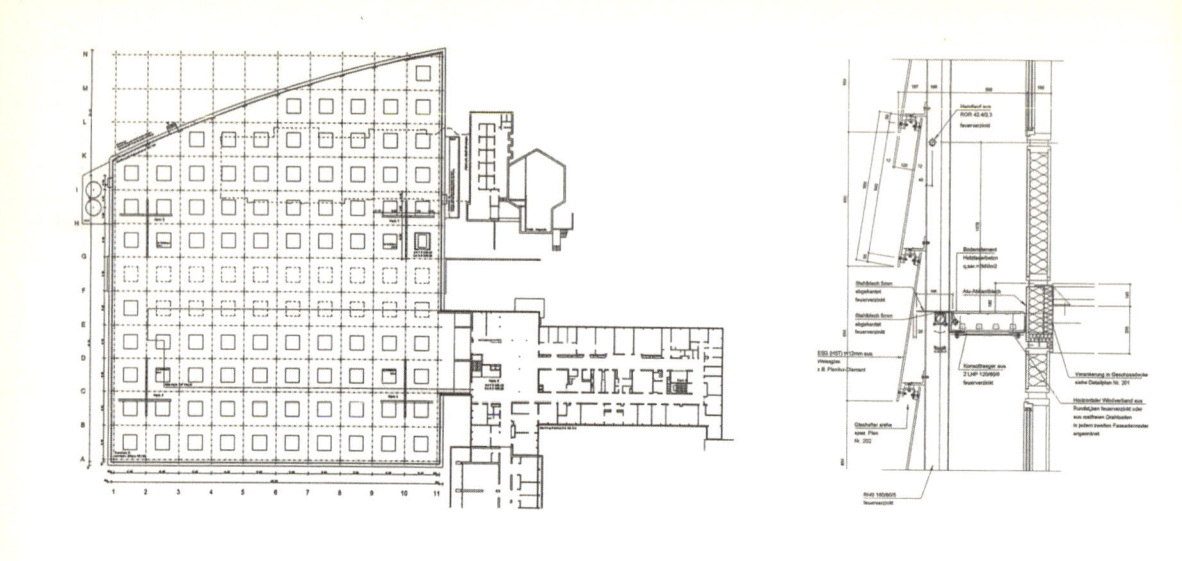

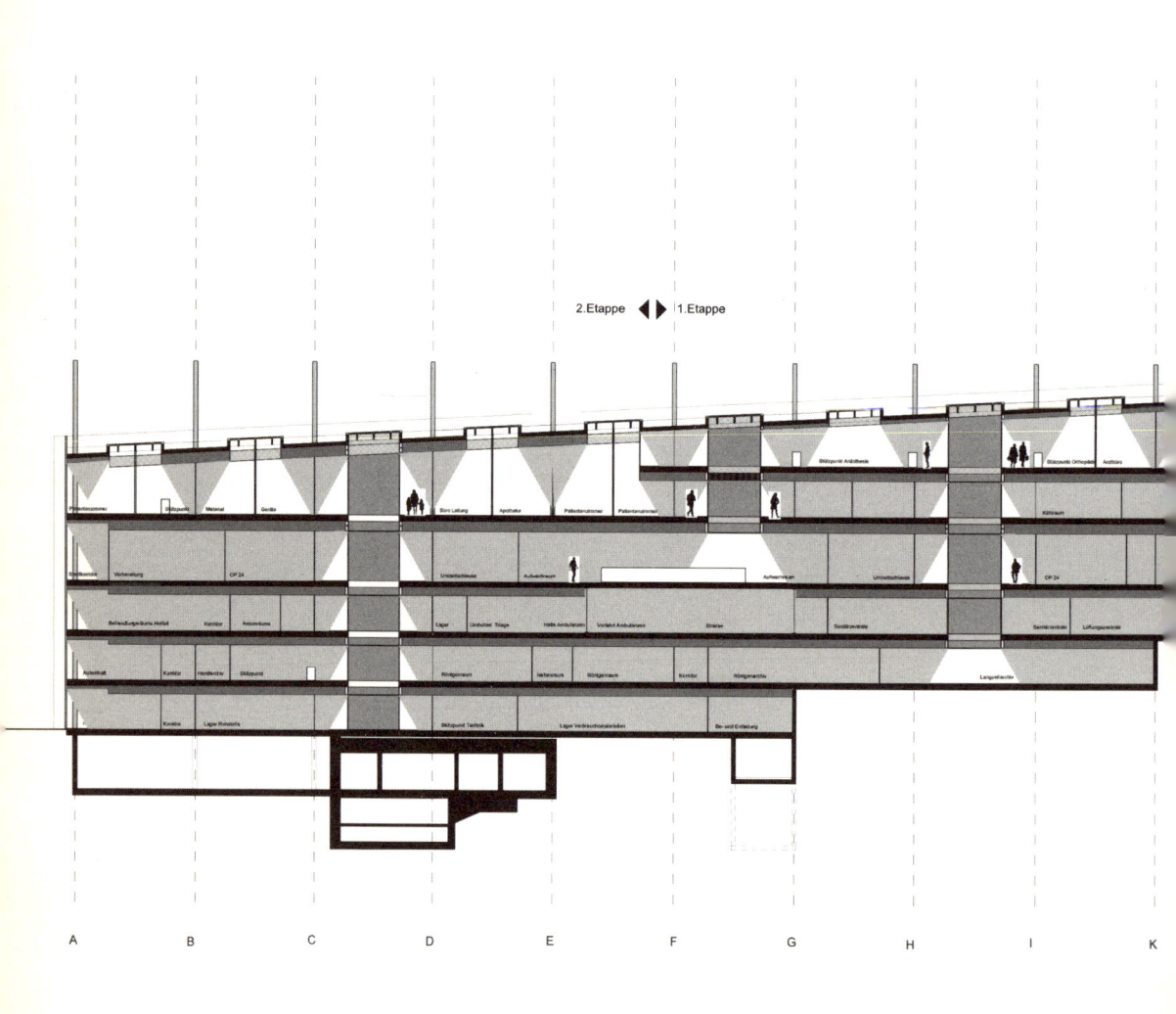

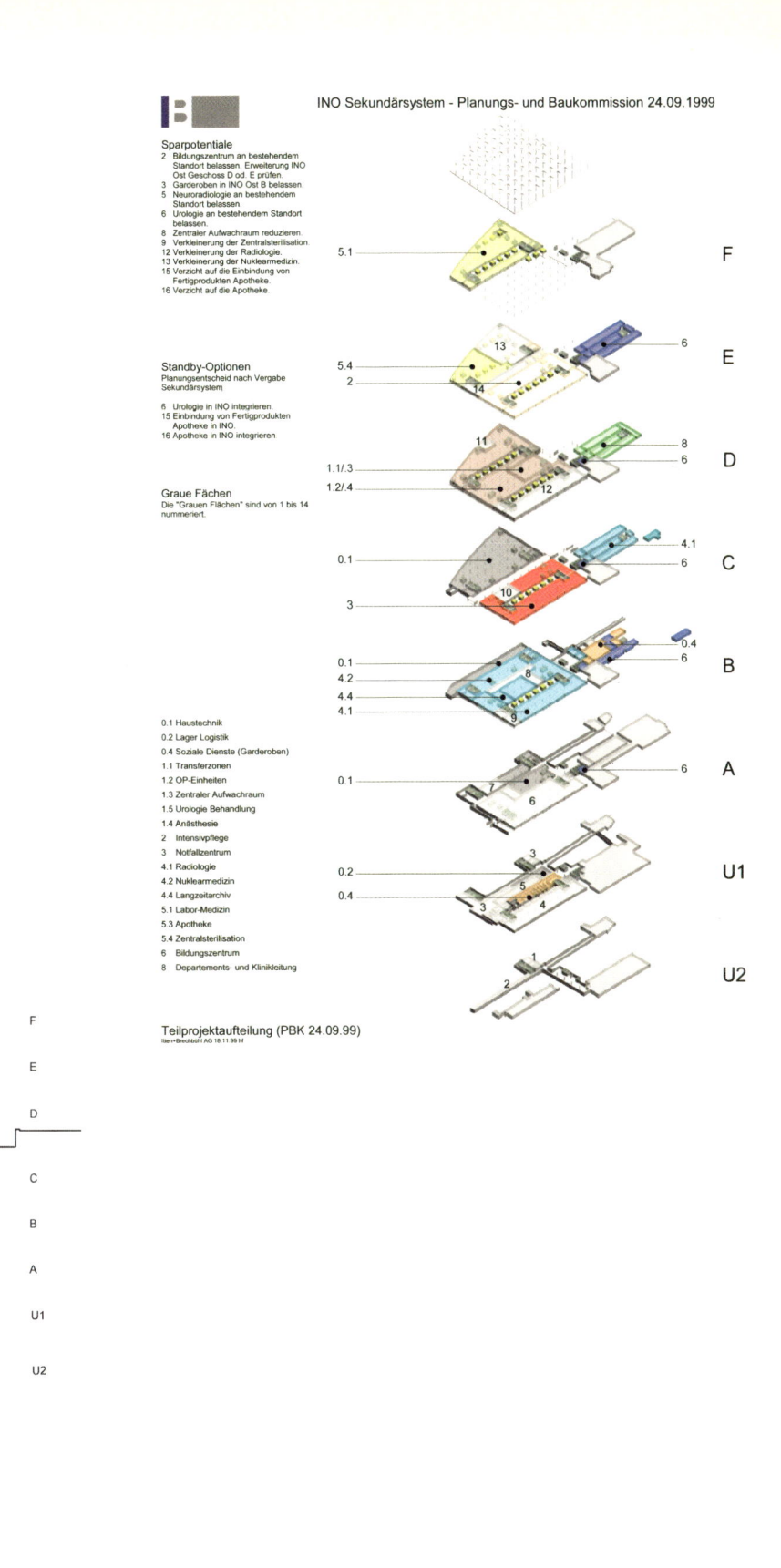

INO Sekundärsystem - Planungs- und Baukommission 24.09.1999

Sparpotentiale
2 Bildungszentrum an bestehendem Standort belassen. Erweiterung INO Ost Geschoss D od. E prüfen.
3 Garderoben in INO Ost B belassen.
5 Neuroradiologie an bestehendem Standort belassen.
6 Urologie an bestehendem Standort belassen.
8 Zentraler Aufwachraum reduzieren.
9 Verkleinerung der Zentralsterilisation.
12 Verkleinerung der Radiologie.
13 Verkleinerung der Nuklearmedizin.
15 Verzicht auf die Einbindung von Fertigprodukten Apotheke.
16 Verzicht auf die Apotheke.

Standby-Optionen
Planungsentscheid nach Vergabe Sekundärsystem

6 Urologie in INO integrieren.
15 Einbindung von Fertigprodukten Apotheke in INO.
16 Apotheke in INO integrieren

Graue Fächen
Die "Grauen Flächen" sind von 1 bis 14 nummeriert.

0.1 Haustechnik
0.2 Lager Logistik
0.4 Soziale Dienste (Garderoben)
1.1 Transferzonen
1.2 OP-Einheiten
1.3 Zentraler Aufwachraum
1.5 Urologie Behandlung
1.4 Anästhesie
2 Intensivpflege
3 Notfallzentrum
4.1 Radiologie
4.2 Nuklearmedizin
4.4 Langzeitarchiv
5.1 Labor-Medizin
5.3 Apotheke
5.4 Zentralsterilisation
6 Bildungszentrum
8 Departements- und Klinikleitung

Teilprojektaufteilung (PBK 24.09.99)

195

LIVING ON A PLUG-IN FLOOR

Oostelijke Handelskade, Amsterdam, Netherlands, DKV architecten, 2006

This forthcoming apartment building (christened Nieuw-Australië) consists of two parts. The new-build portion is partly draped over an existing warehouse ('Australië'). The DKV firm of architects designed freely subdivisible lofts for both the new-build and the reused warehouse building. The latter with its extra-tall spaces and cast-iron columns is ideal accommodation for 'shell units'. The new-build is similarly overdimensioned and freely subdivisible.

To give the floor plans maximum flexibility the architect has focused finely on the cable runs. The vertical run and the mechanical services are strategically sited in service ducts in the facade zone. Individual units can be 'plugged in' from inside these shafts. The units have a raised floor system suitable for pulling horizontal cable, which gives the first occupants complete freedom in fitting out the space. For their convenience the architect has compiled a catalogue of parts, such as facade glazing elements and sliding partitions, complete with variant floor plans. They can make their dream home come true in what is as yet an entirely empty shell. The infrastructure provided also enables occupants to rearrange the fit-out between whiles; it is relatively simple to move a bathroom for example. Needless to say, the raised floor system brings longer-term, more sweeping changes within reach.

ORIËNTATIE

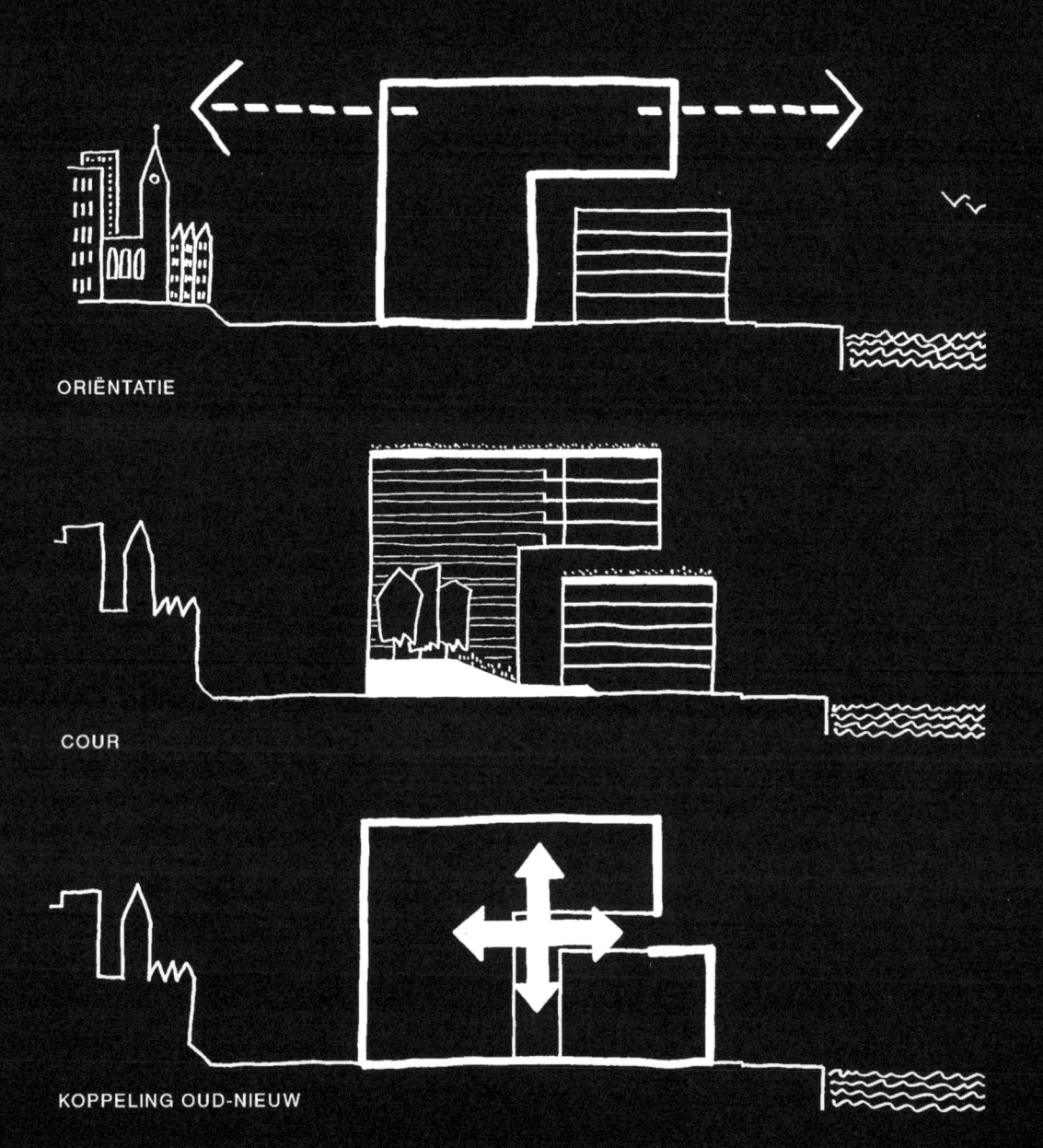

COUR

KOPPELING OUD-NIEUW

198

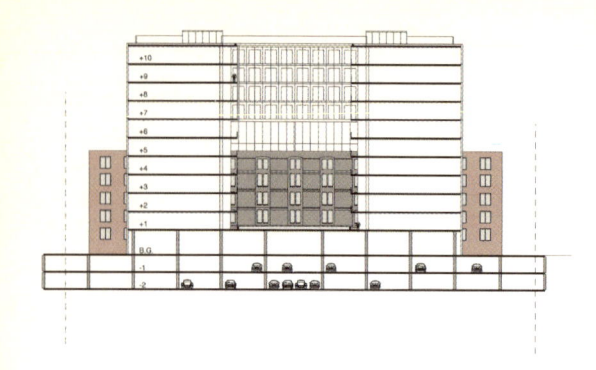

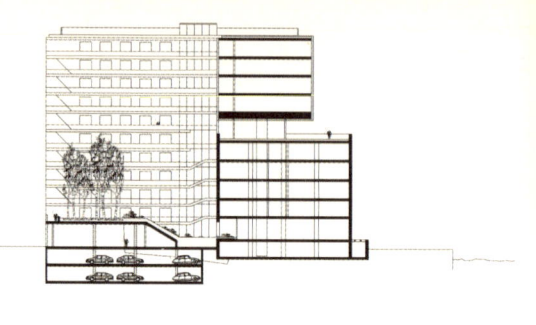

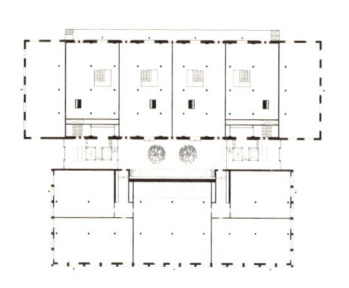

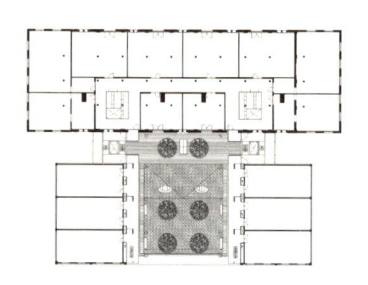

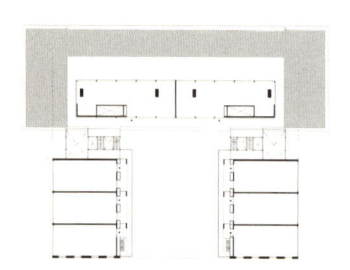

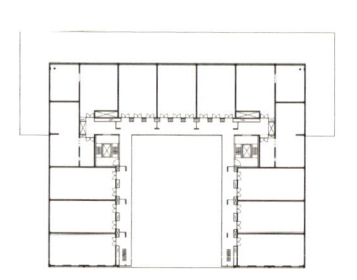

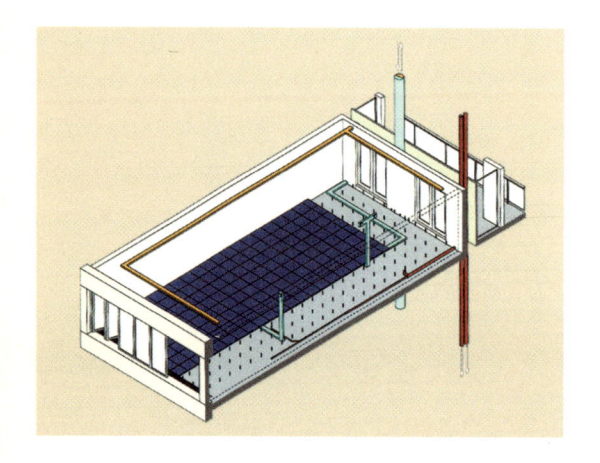

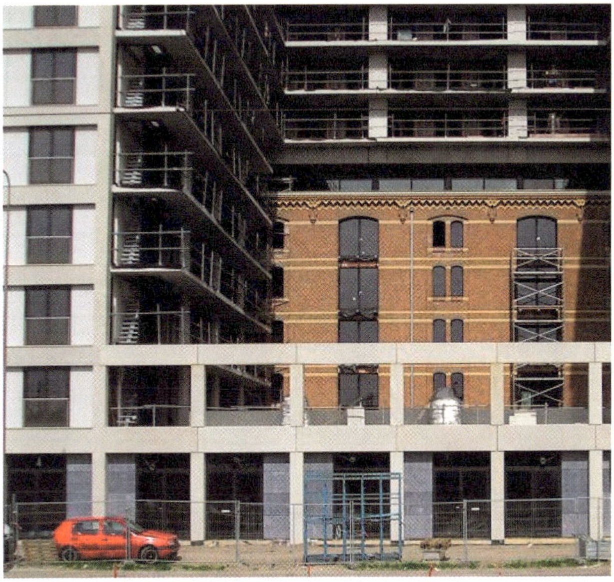

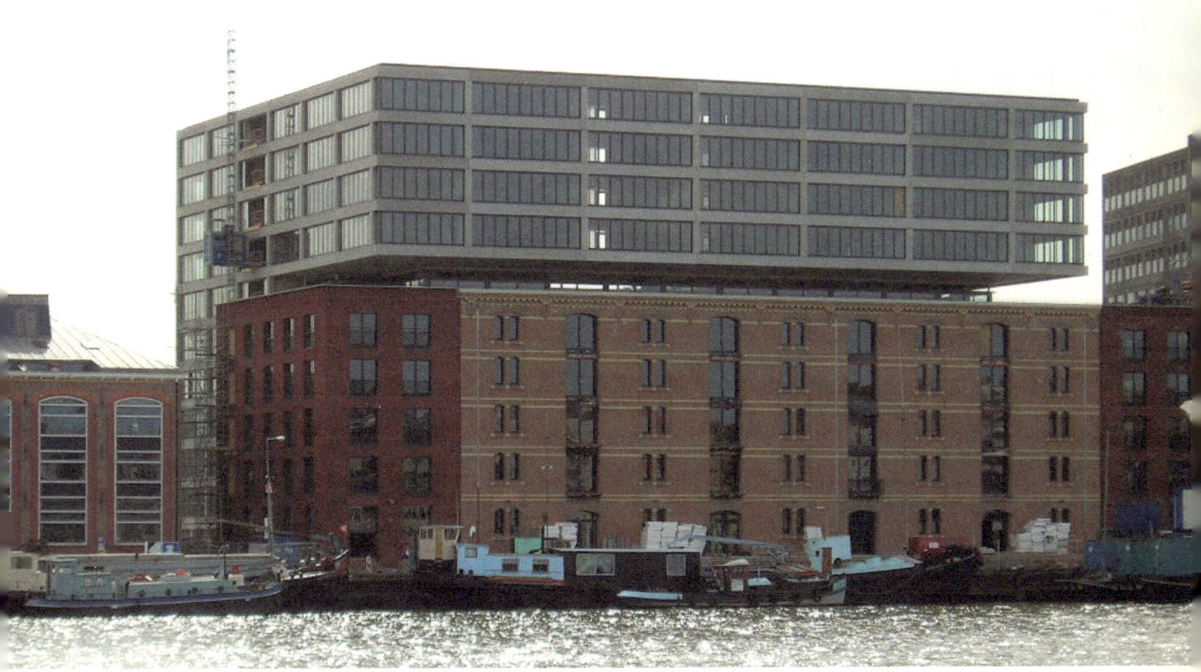

BETTER AND CHEAPER IN BOLIGER

Bedre Billigere, Boliger, Denmark, Juul & Frost, 2004

'Better and cheaper' – that was the slogan of the competition to design 300 housing units in Boliger in Denmark. Juul & Frost were the winners with units of a rational and rigid layout but not a trace of functionalism. The 300-strong complex consists of three-storey housing blocks shot through with living-streets at all levels. Affordability goes hand in hand with adaptability in this design. Inside each unit, open space surrounds a core of sanitary facilities. Adaptability and affordability prove to combine well in the facades too. Originally these were to have been of more expensive material but a reduction in expenditure resulted in aluminium cladding panels. An advantage brought by this new material in combination with Steckdoppel hollow core transparent panels is that it can be easily modified, say to provide an extra window.

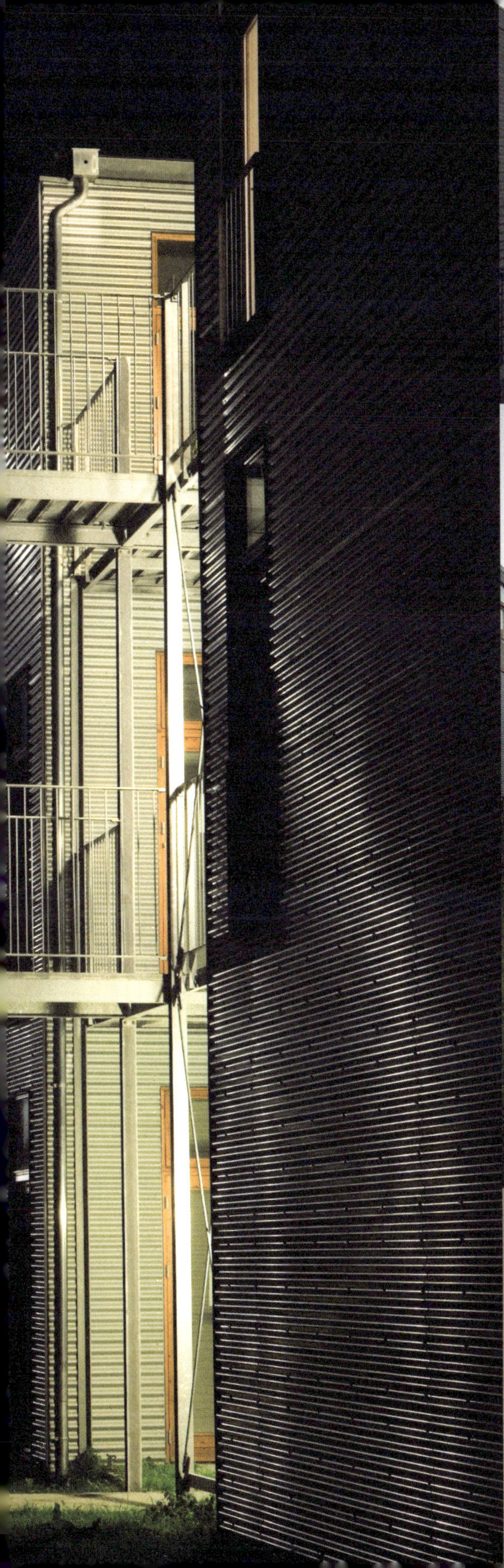
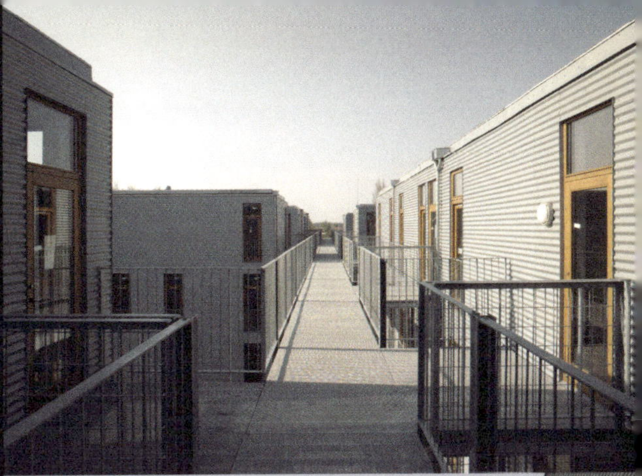
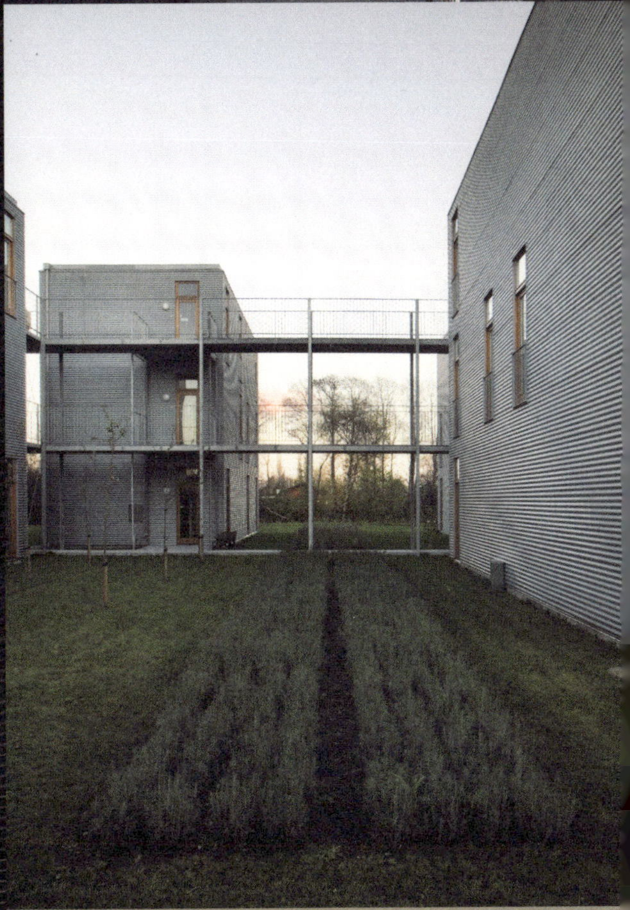
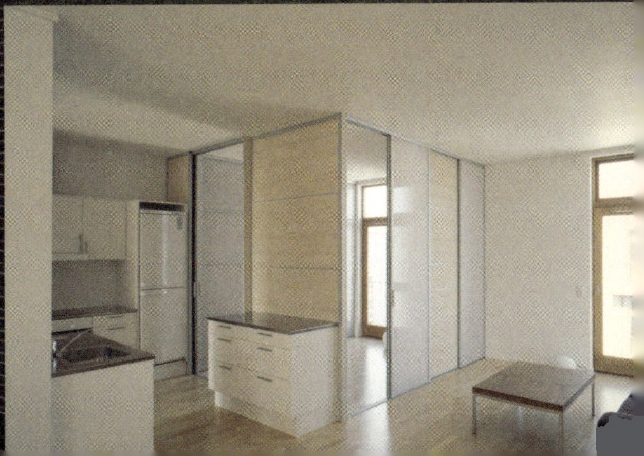

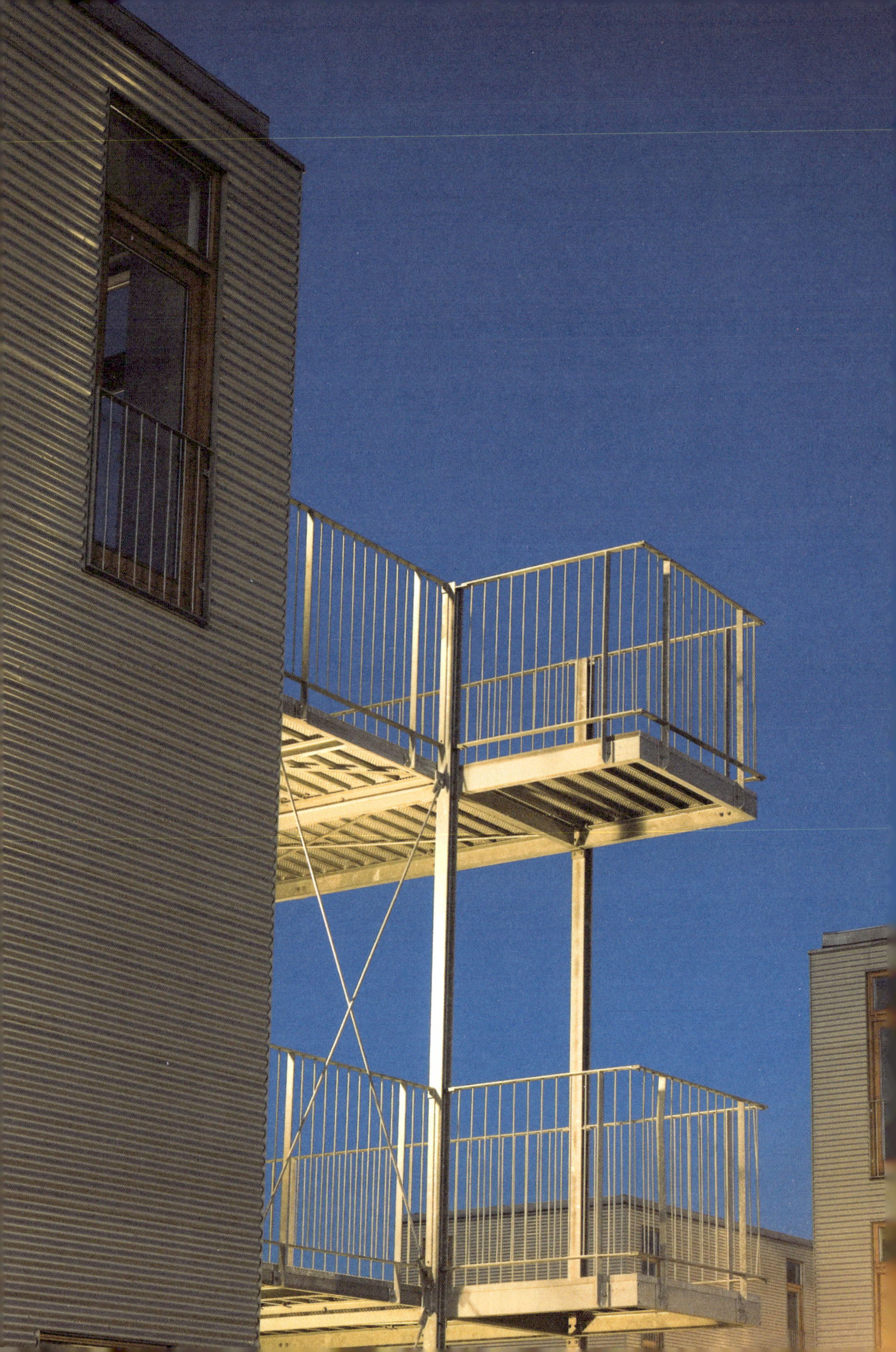

203

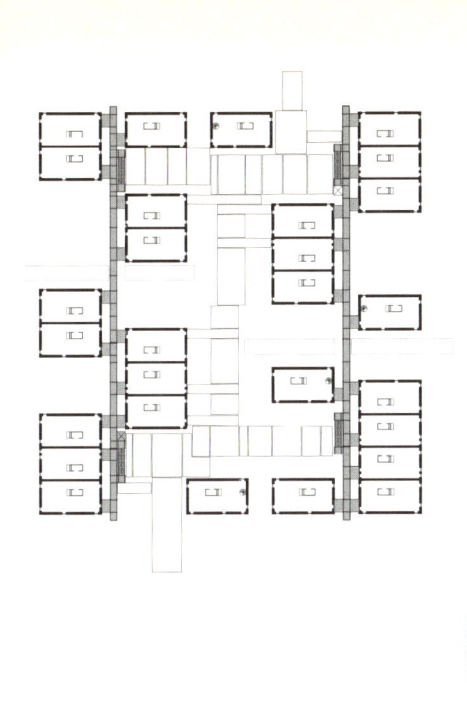

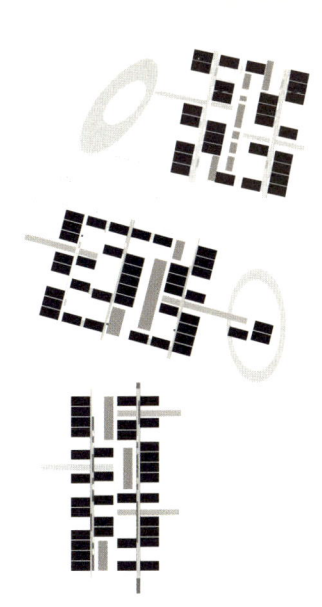

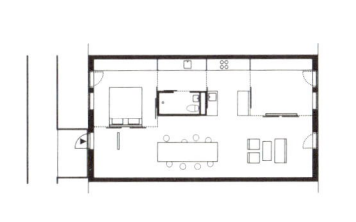

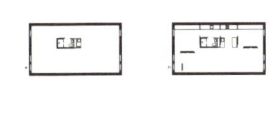

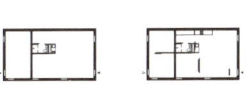

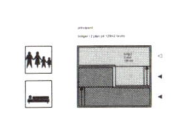

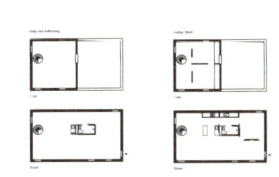

PREDICTING THE FUTURE

INHOLLAND University (formerly Ichthus University) and future extension, Rotterdam, (EEA) Erick van Egeraat associated architects, 2000
Temporary building, INHOLLAND University, Rotterdam, 2004

'All buildings are predictions, all predictions are wrong,' according to Stewart Brand in his book *How Buildings Learn* (see 'Sources'). This is something that has confronted the management of INHOLLAND University.
Though the school, designed by (EEA) Erick van Egeraat associated architects, looks like a single building it is in fact two separate ones joined together. An additional core of stairs and lift allows the one building to be used distinct from the other. This had been done to meet the eventuality of low student enrolment figures. But the deliberately built-in oversize in the access system failed to end up accommodating a second user. The very reverse turned out to be true: the building is now much too small. A large park of construction sheds now abuts the school a mere four years after delivery. The sheds housing the considerable overspill of students differ in colour only from the site construction sheds serving those building the extension to INHOLLAND.

The book *How Buildings Learn: What Happens After They're Built* describes how buildings change over time and is rife with anecdotes about buildings with an often unexpected life history. This is Stewart Brand again: 'A building is not something you finish. A building is something you start'. Maybe the extra stairhall can be integrated in the new extension so that this 'investment in the future' can be repaid after all.

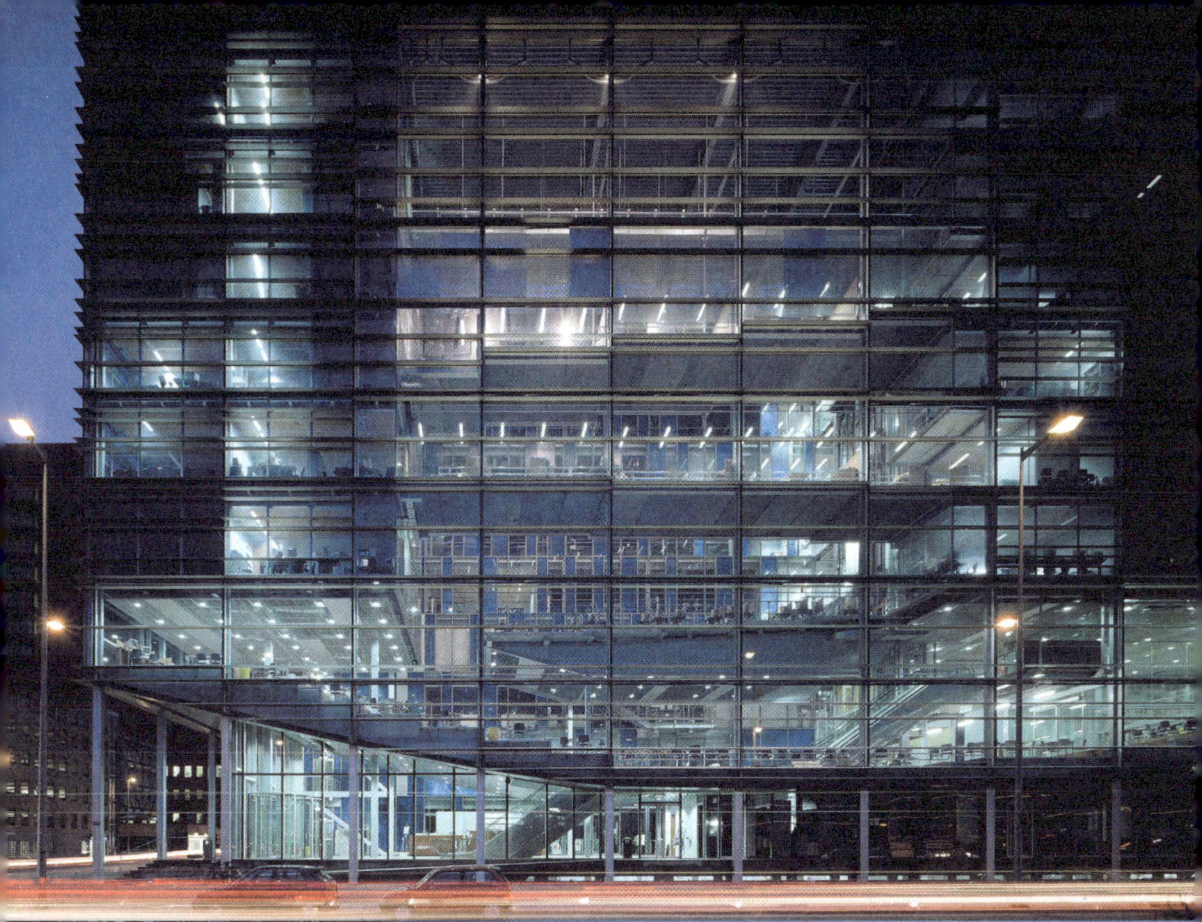

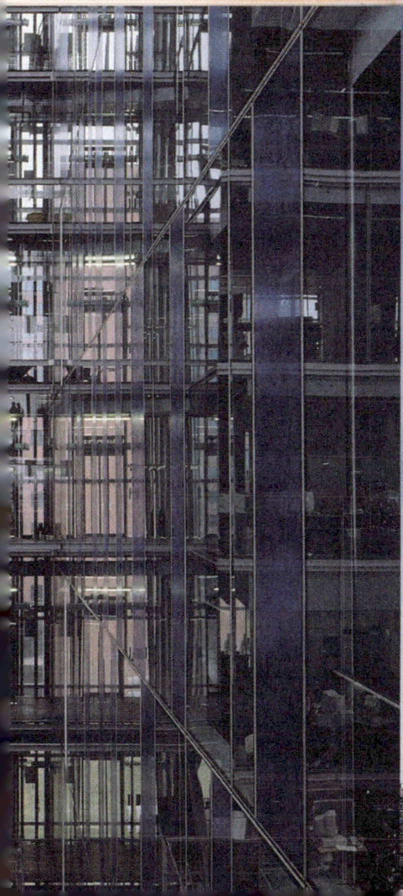

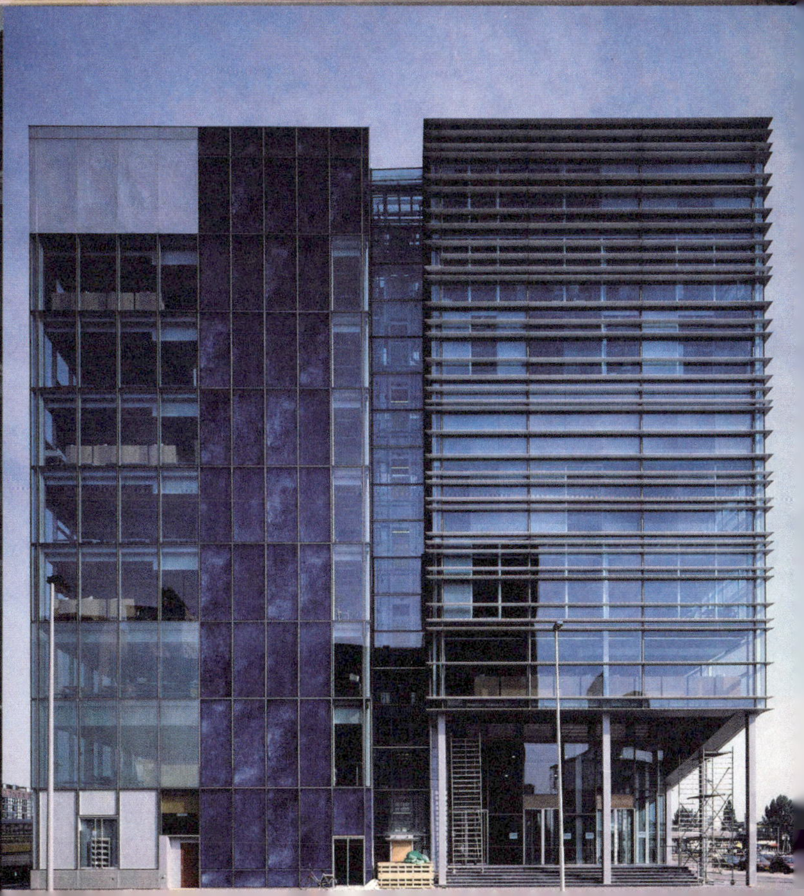

206

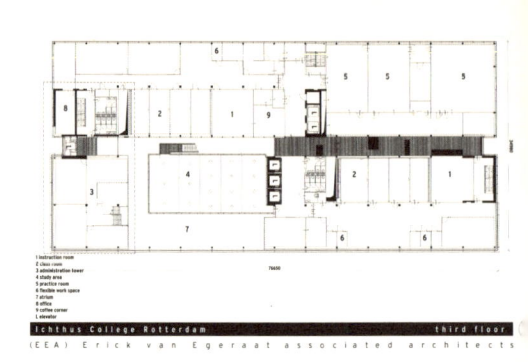

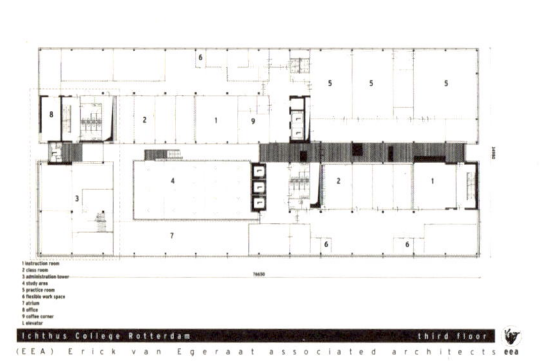

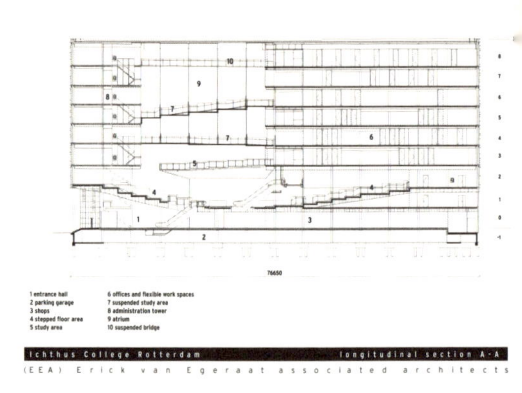

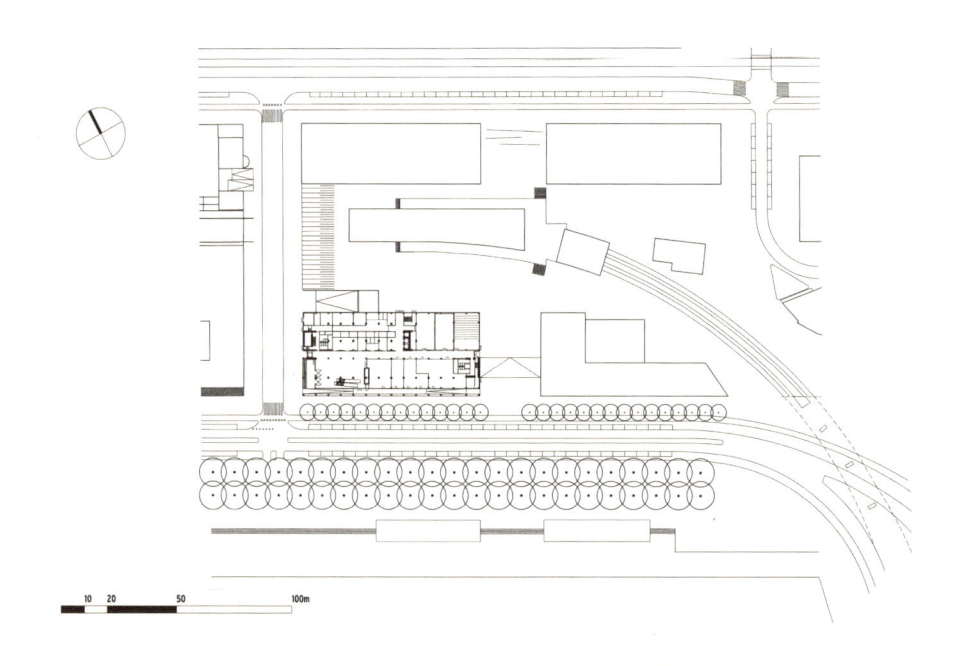

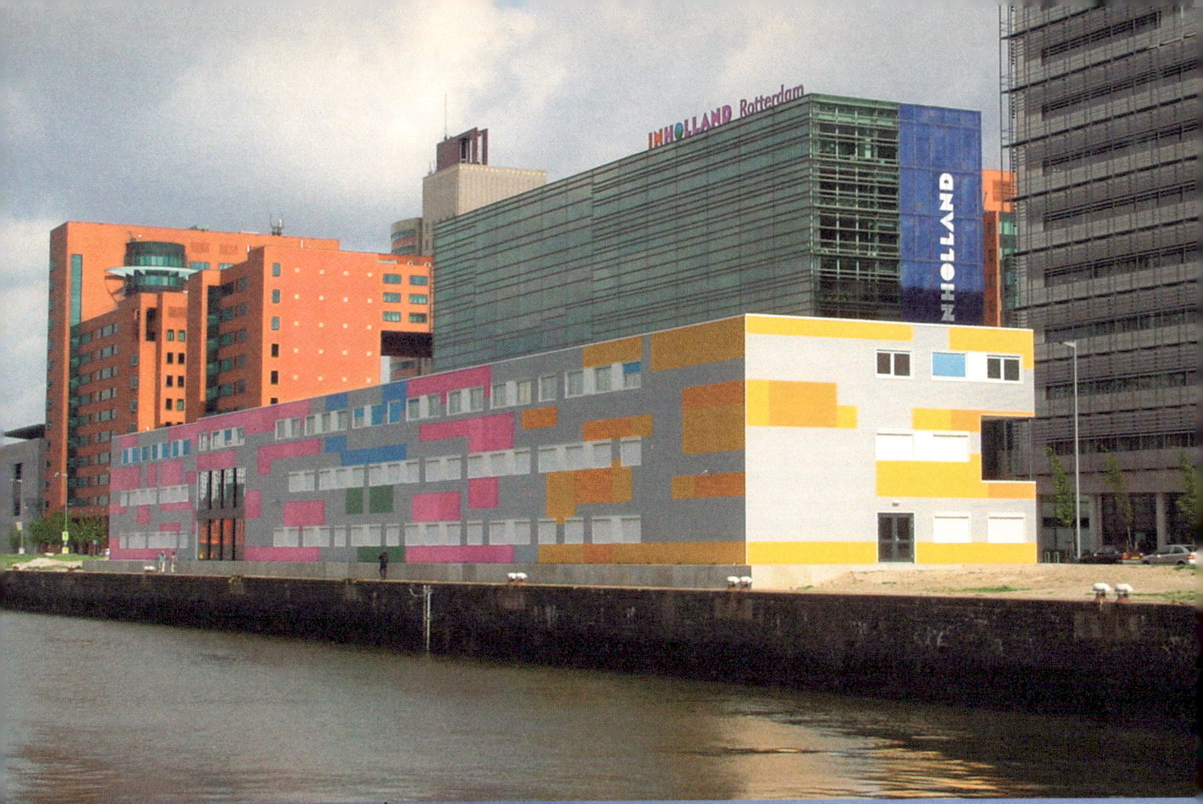
INHOLLAND Rotterdam
INHOLLAND
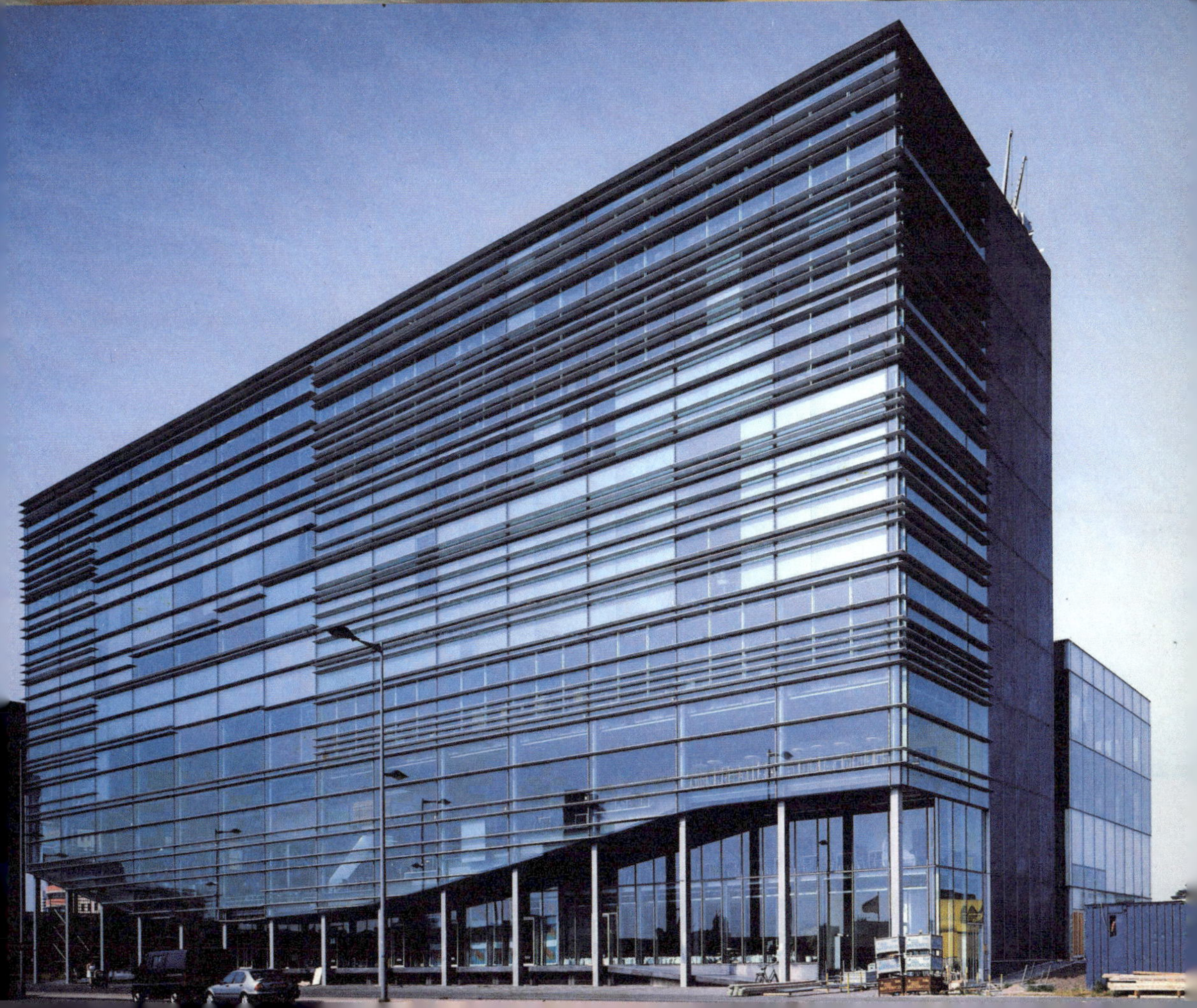

NEUTRAL EXPRESSION
De Nieuwe Veiling, Hoorn, Netherlands, RUIMTELAB, 2002

Multi-company buildings are all too often marked by a neutral, matter-of-fact architecture. With their design for 'De Nieuwe Veiling' in Hoorn north of Amsterdam, the RUIMTELAB architectural practice seeks to show that an unknown programme with a constant change of occupants can still make for expressive architecture. De Nieuwe Veiling stands on an industrial estate (De Oude Veiling), which like many of its kind built in the 1960s and '70s in the Netherlands is going from bad to worse. Its buildings are dilapidated and are of a low architectural quality. Few entrepreneurs are still prepared to invest in commercial buildings like these, preferring newly built premises. The upshot is many unoccupied properties and a decline in standards of the public domain. To put an end to this downward spiral the town council took the initiative of developing a large new multi-company building in the centre of the estate where a fire had destroyed some of the old premises. RUIMTELAB designed a sculptural building with a facade that shows what is happening inside.

The sculptural aspect of De Nieuwe Veiling derives from its setting. Differences in height and setbacks in the relatively large building accommodate it to its small-scale neighbours. Most company buildings these days have a definite front and back. This one opens up to all four sides. Even the roofscape is accessible. The building is geared to consumers and therefore is fully accessible to cars. A share of the parking space is on the roof. This gives not only short walking distances to the building's entrances but places more facade surface area in direct contact with the public realm. This second ground plane makes possible all sorts of fit-outs now and in the future. Multi-occupancy buildings have to be flexible to cope with all the companies moving in and out. Flexibility makes special architectural and structural demands on the construction and on the services. However, these demands often percolate through to the space plan and the facade, resulting in a none too expressive architecture. To prevent this from happening, De Nieuwe Veiling has been wrapped in a diaphanous skin. This so-called double facade incorporates the main entrance to the building. A double facade is not only interesting in energy-saving terms, but allows the individual companies to present themselves to the outside world. The inner leaf is suitable for the advertising purposes of individual firms; the outer leaf represents the building's activities as a whole. Stair towers and corridors complete the picture and add a dynamic, inviting aspect.

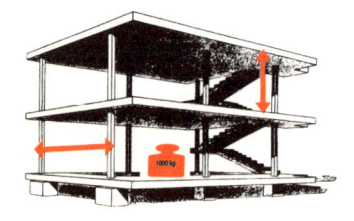

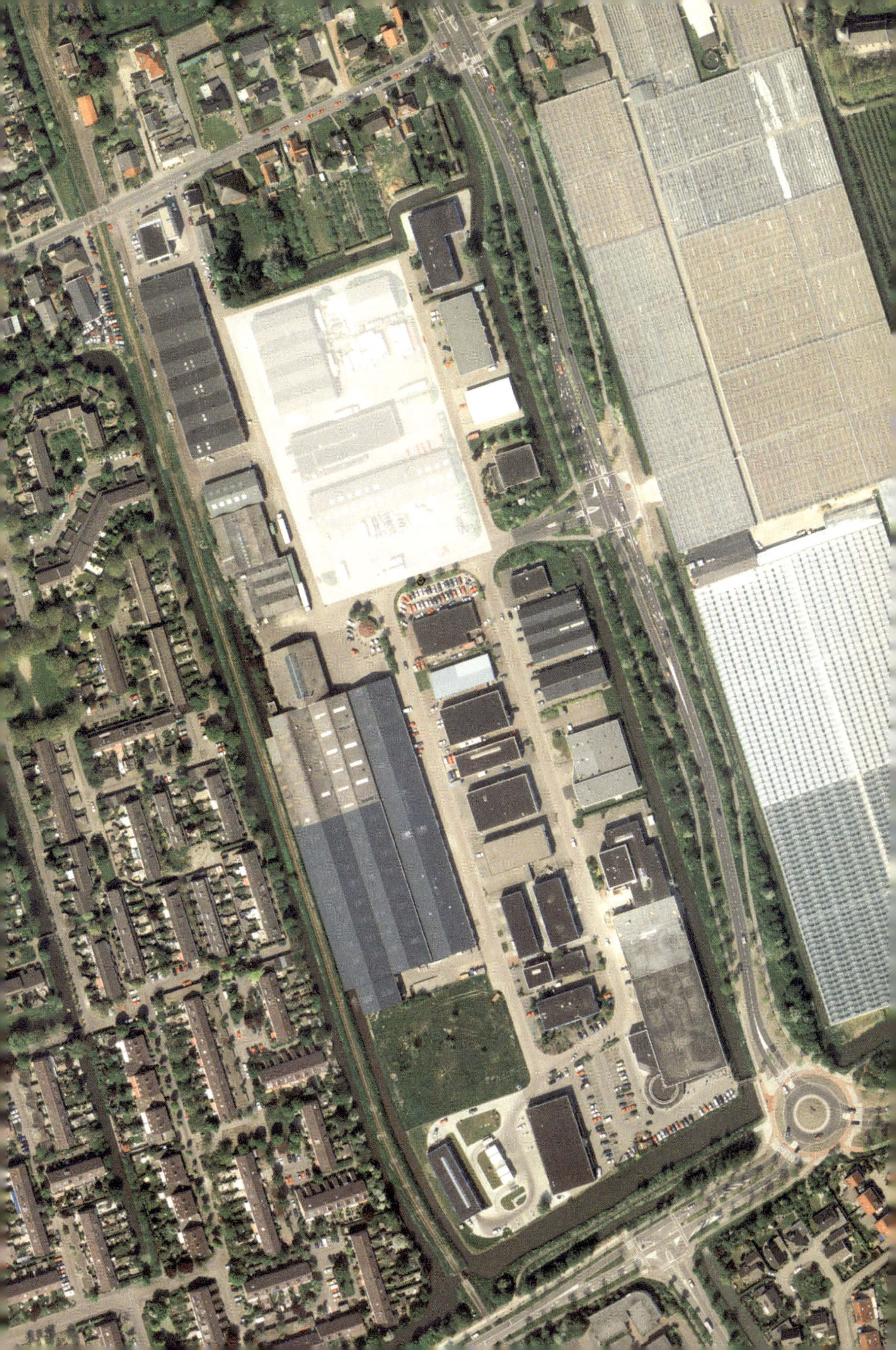

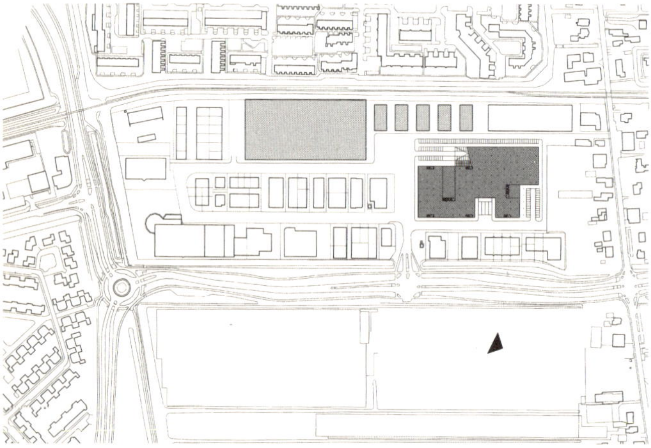

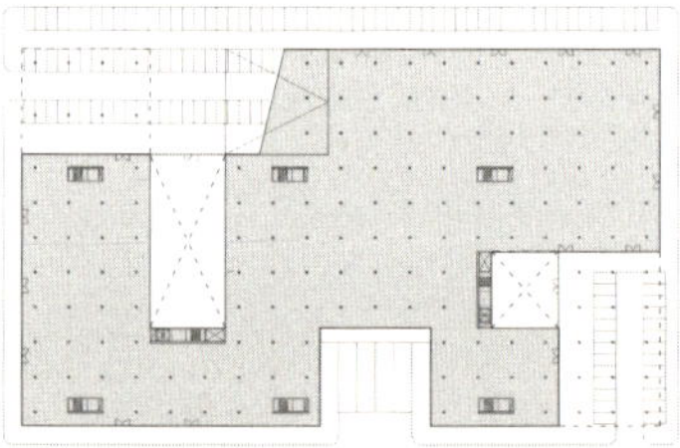

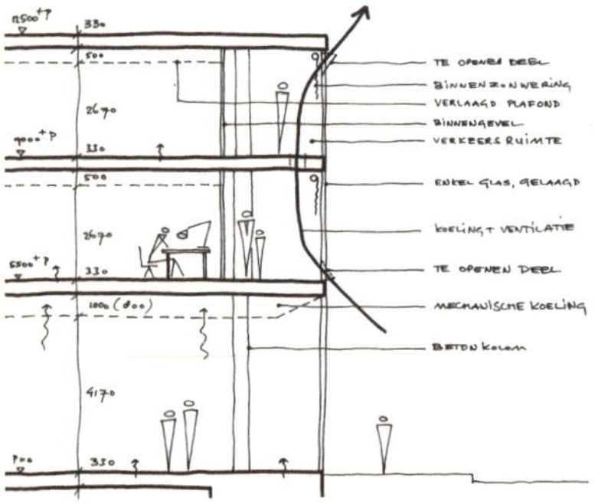
TE OPENEN DEEL
BINNENZONWERING
VERLAAGD PLAFOND
BINNENGEVEL
VERKEERSRUIMTE
ENKEL GLAS, GELAAGD
KOELING + VENTILATIE
TE OPENEN DEEL
MECHANISCHE KOELING
BETON KOLOM

A-A

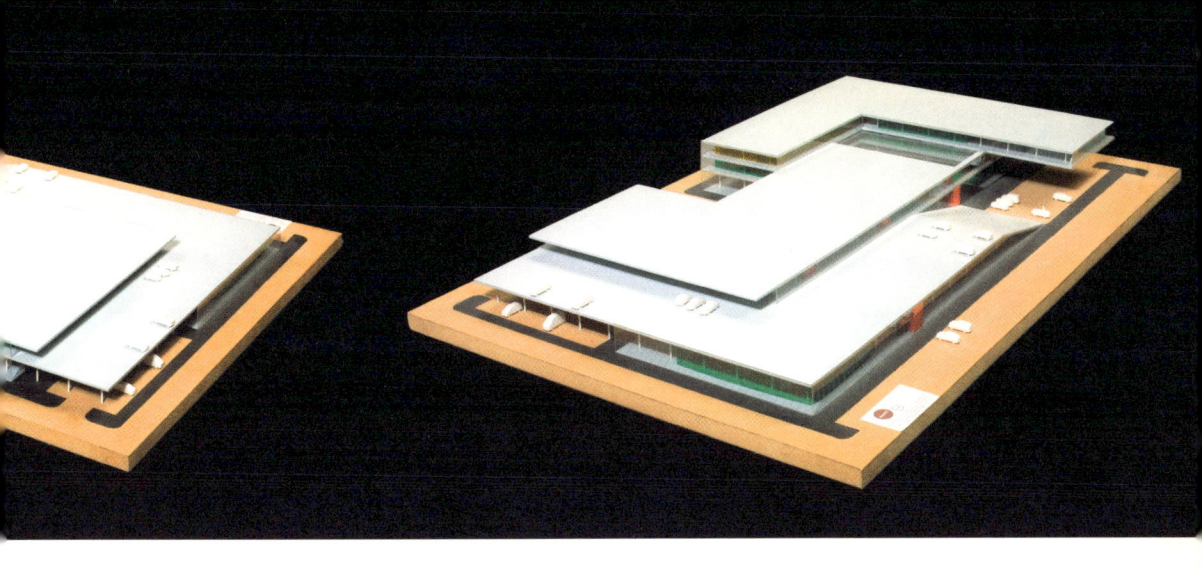

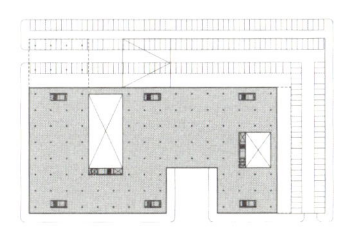

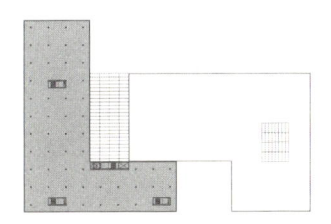

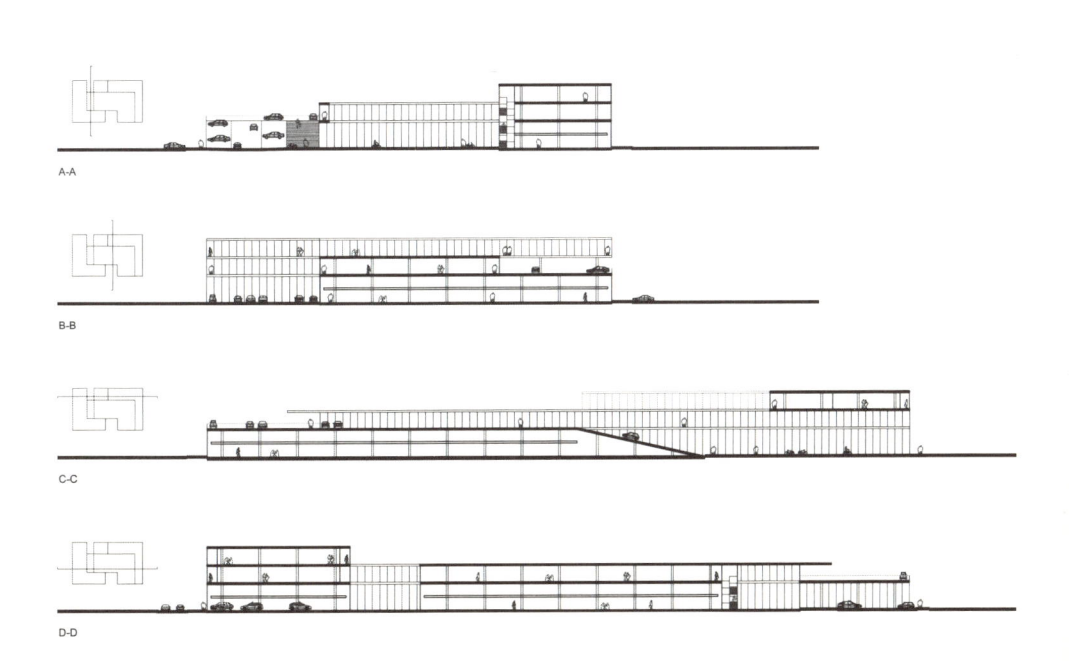

B-B

C-C

D-D

DEVELOPERS' FREEDOM

Multifunk, IJburg, Amsterdam, Netherlands, Ana-architecten, 2005

Amsterdam is in the process of developing the new residential district of IJburg on an artificial island in the IJ Inlet north of the city. Steigerdam, the settlement's central axis, is to be graced with the Multifunk building. This consists in part of small-scale units that lock into the freestanding houses of the Zuidbuurt district of IJburg. The portion on Steigerdam is bigger, with a tall ground floor and four upper storeys. The means of access, the zoning of cables and piping, the design of the exterior spaces and the additional height are all factors that can facilitate the transformation from housing to offices should that be necessary. The tall portion is accessed through porches combined with corridors. With two lifts planned for each porch plus the access 'oversize' of the corridors, parts of the building can be set aside for offices.

At the end of the 1990s the planning schedule for the ambitious IJburg programme stagnated in the wake of the economic downturn. Many plans on IJburg had to be redeveloped but not Multifunk, which is now being built to the original design. Originally 80% of the complex was earmarked for offices. This has been reduced to just 20% with the most minor of modifications. The extra costs necessary to make the building flexible have already been repaid by the rapid progress the project is making.

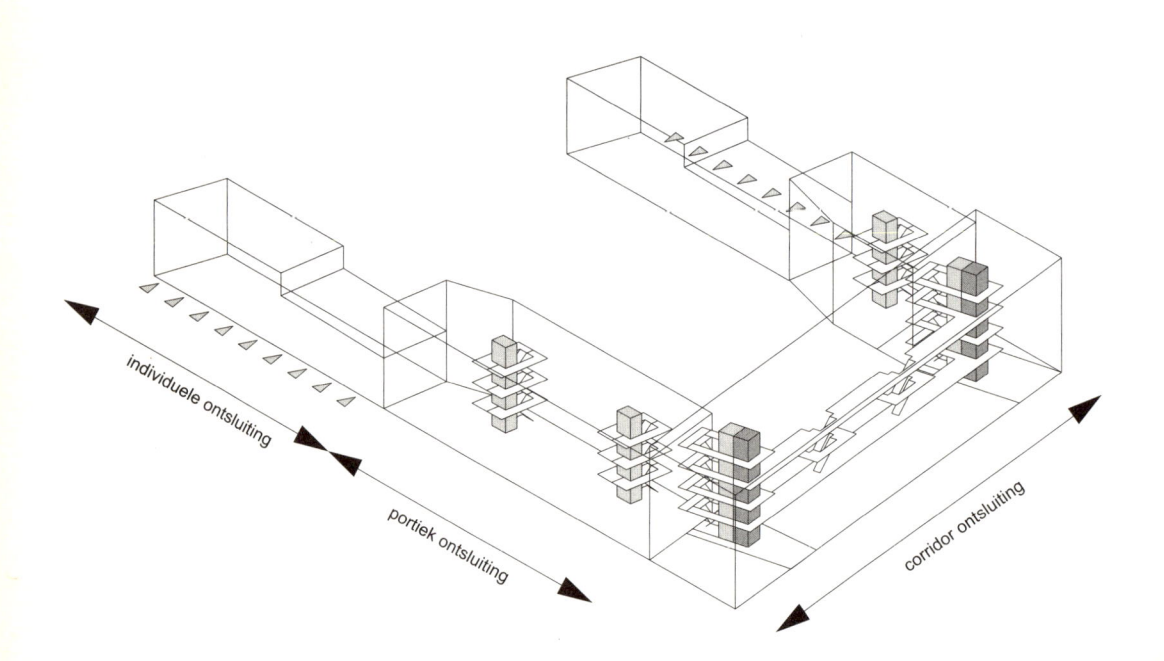

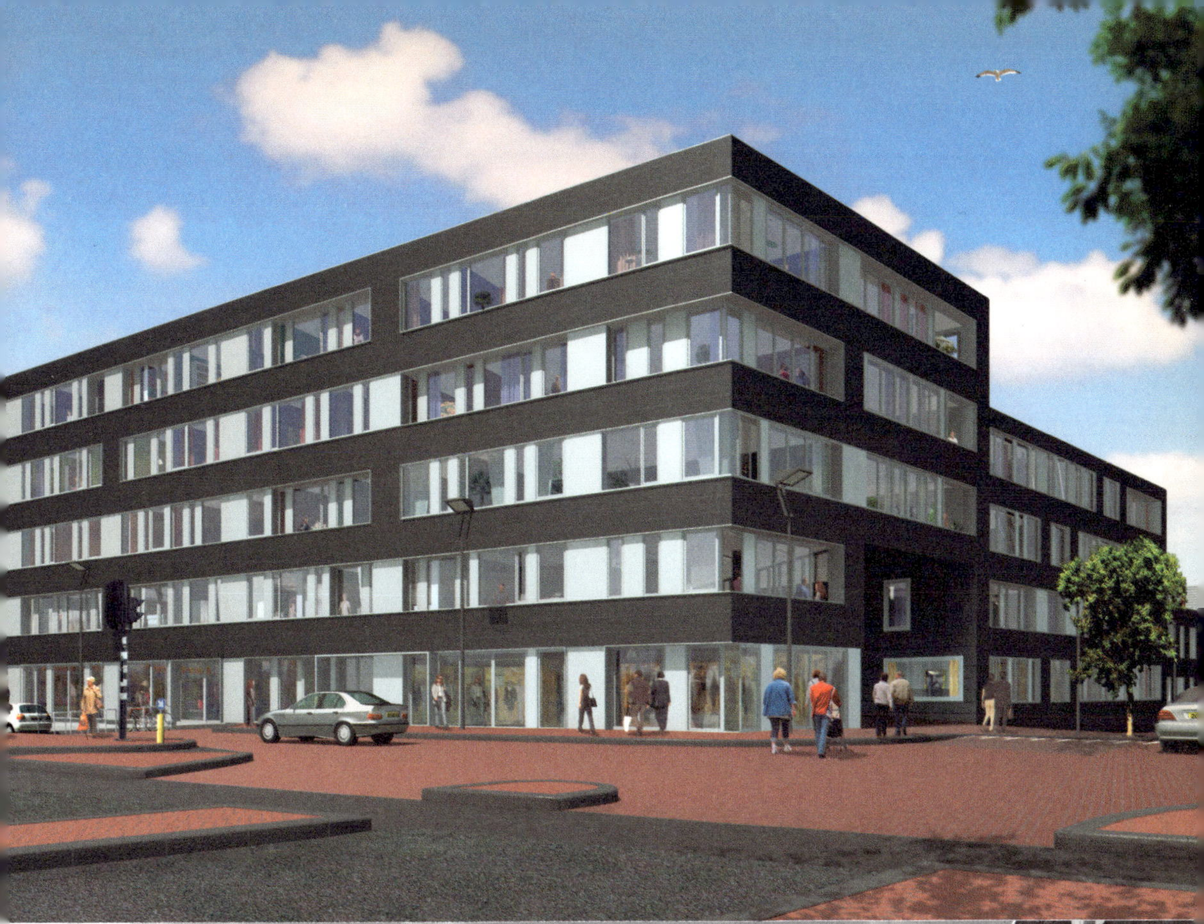

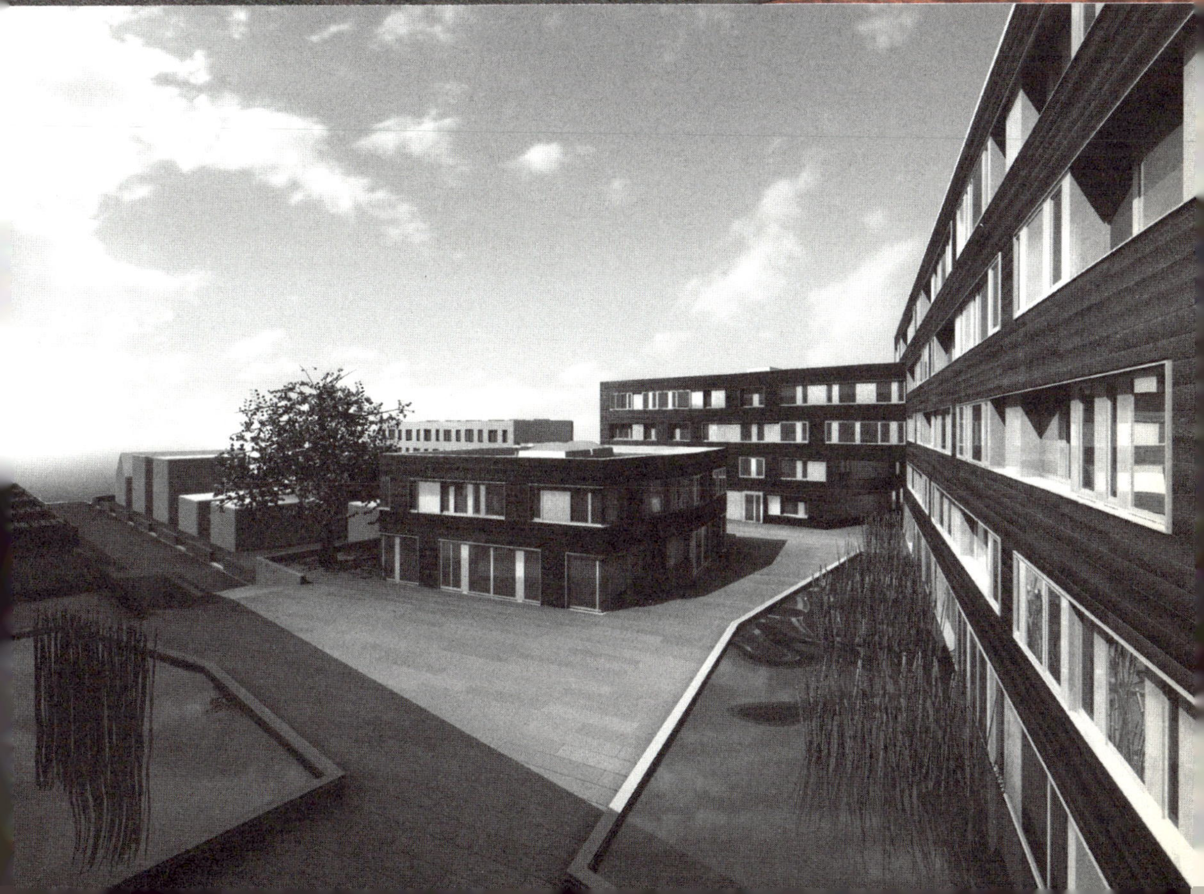

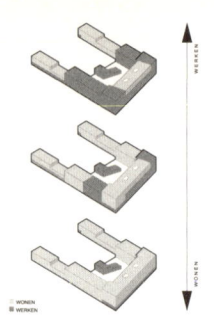

Flexiblity on the level of the building

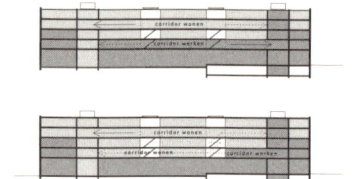

Flexiblity on the level of the access

Flexiblity on the level of the dwelling

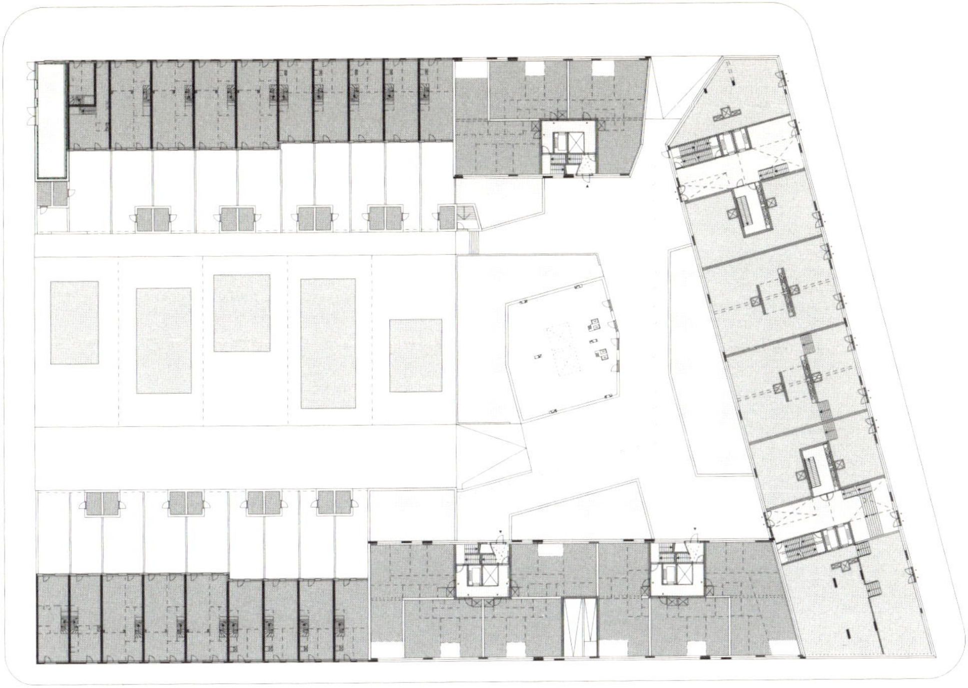

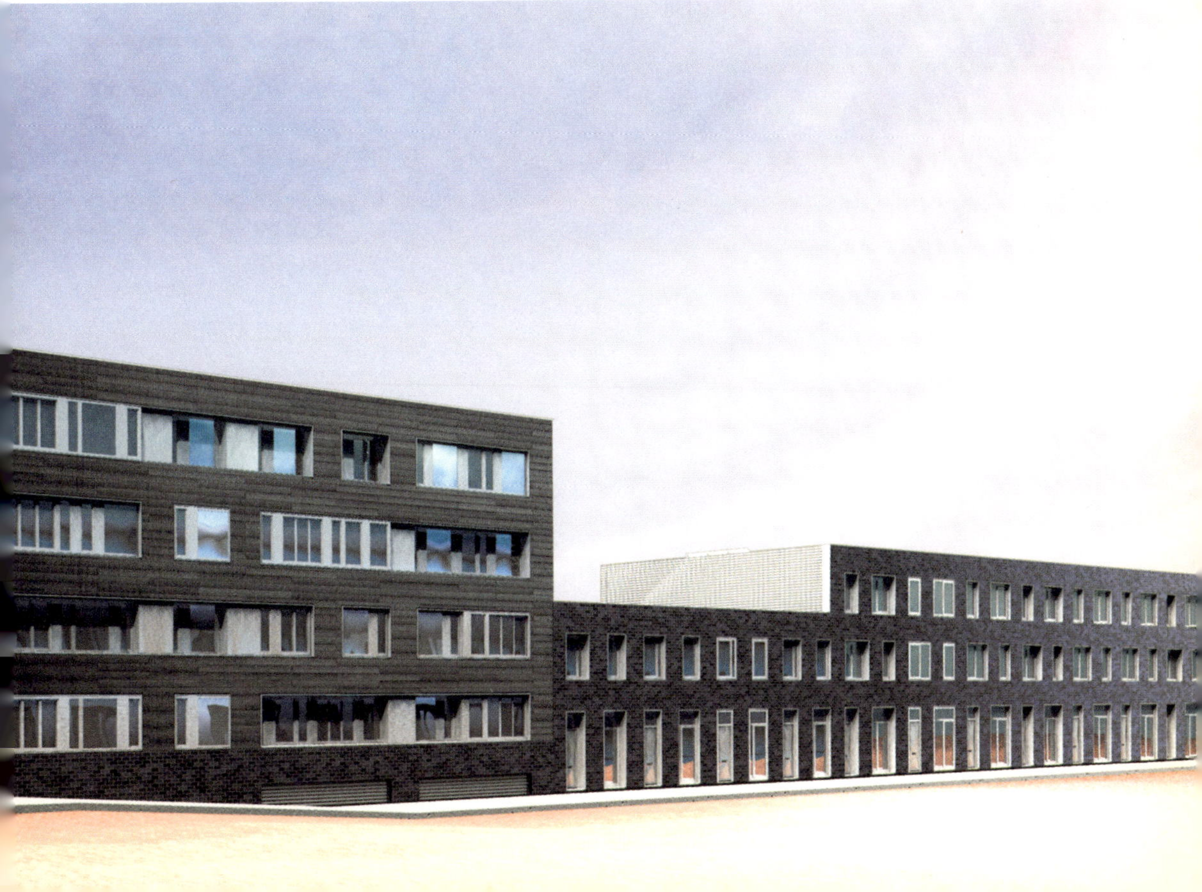

ELEMENTAL CHILE

Housing, Temuco, Chile, Pasel.Künzel architects, 2004

The residential district designed by Ralf Pasel and Frederik Künzel in Temuco is based on a growth scenario. First, the cores of amenities – three storeys high, more than a metre wide, eight metres deep – are bedded into site. These contain the kitchen, the cells for ablutions, the entrance and the stair. As the cores can be closed off, they can serve as a startup unit from where occupants can fit out the spaces between them. These intervening zones are not entirely empty. The three types of dwelling on offer all consist of a startup unit with a single living level in the remaining space. In 'Be Connected', the living room is on the ground floor and the dwelling can be expanded vertically. 'Best of Both Worlds', with the living on the middle storey, allows you to set up a garage or small business unit on the ground floor. The third type, 'Site Seeing', can be extended downwards and is suitable for siting against a slope.

On the macro planning level the district as a whole can be annexed over time. The small footprint of each of the dwellings leaves a proportionally large amount of public space. That space can be used communally or divided into small private gardens. As all dwellings are accessed at ground level and the ground floor is suitable for a workshop, garage or shop, a lively residential area should ensue. This project for 450 dwellings in Temuco is Pasel.Künzel's follow-up to winning the international Elemental competition. Their entry proposed constructing 160 units on a one-hectare site in Santiago de Chile. The dwellings in Temuco are at present under construction and the first occupants are expected to move in during the autumn of 2005.

30 viviendas

colegio 800 alumnos

225 viviendas

159 viviendas

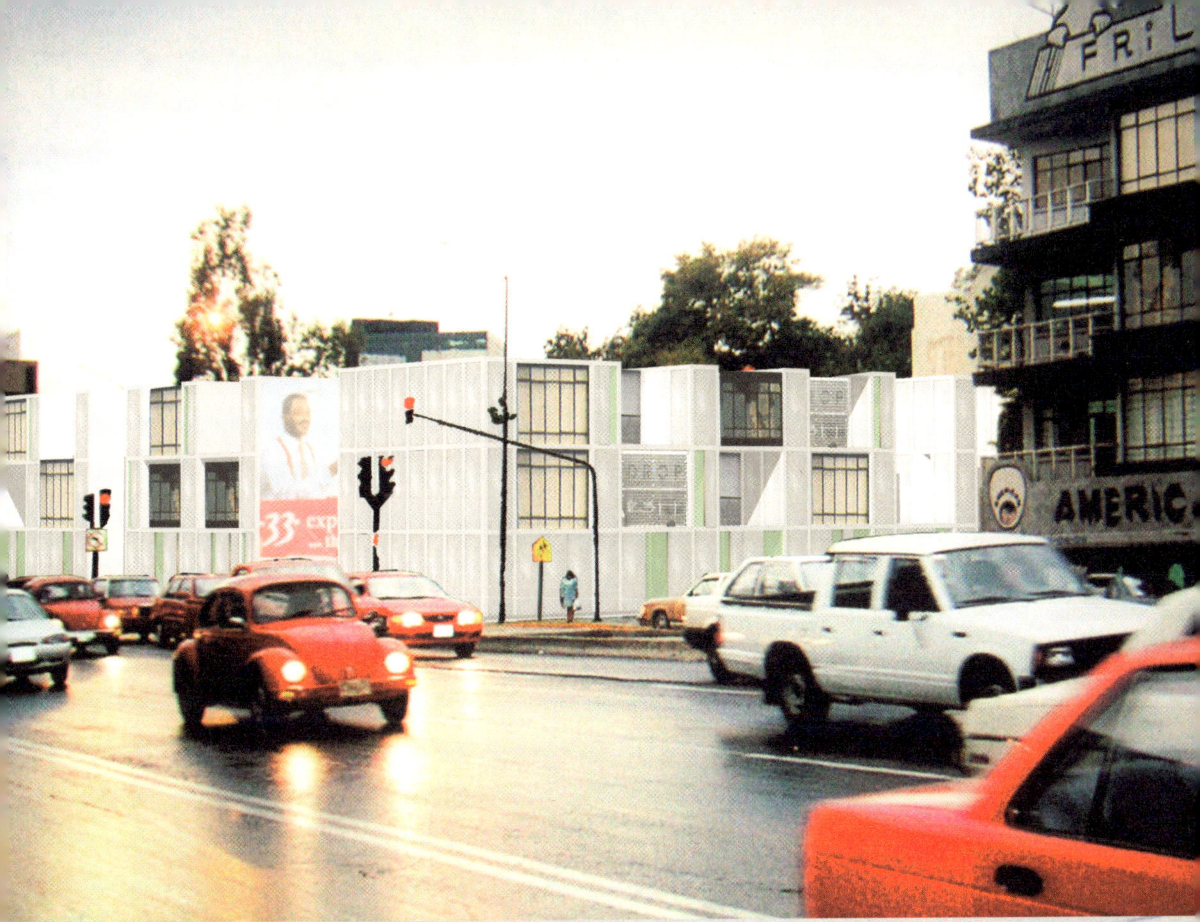
AMERIC
33 exp

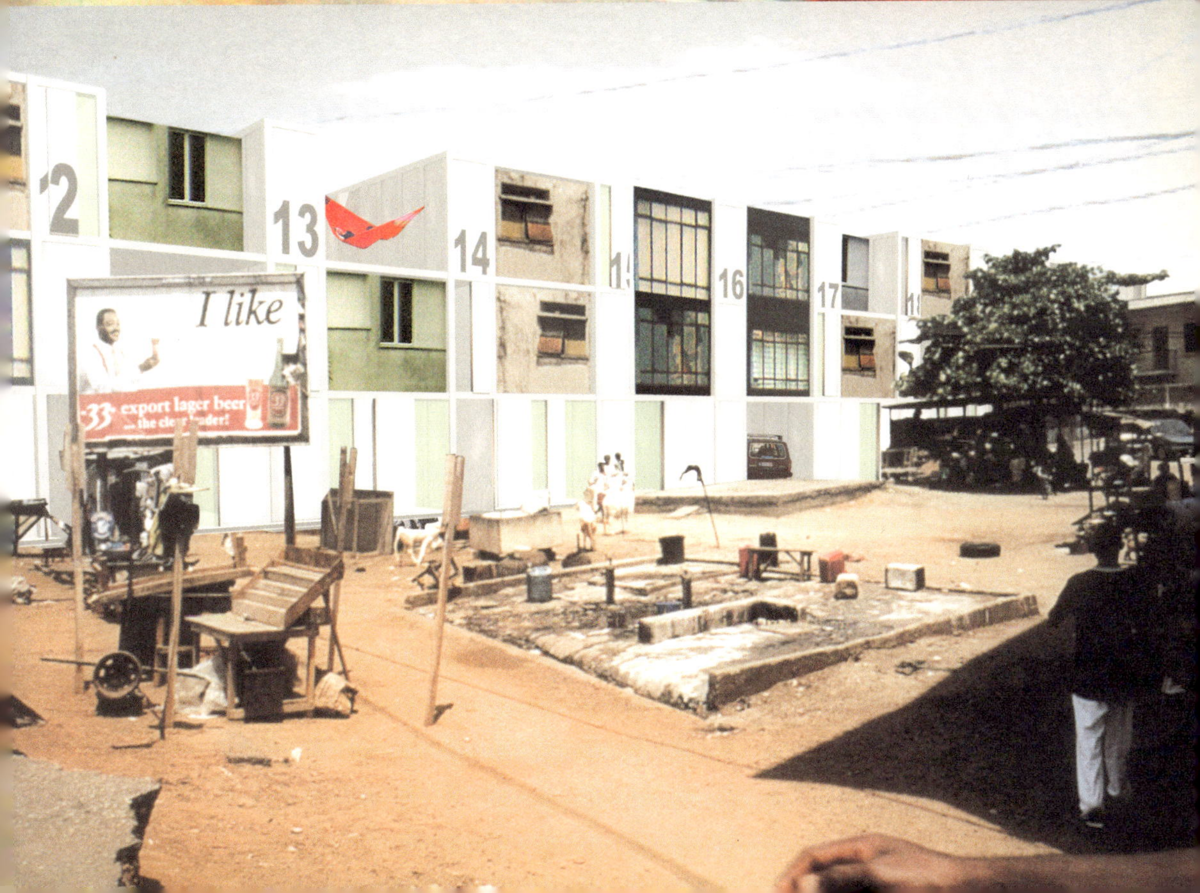
12
13
14
16
17
I like
33 export lager beer

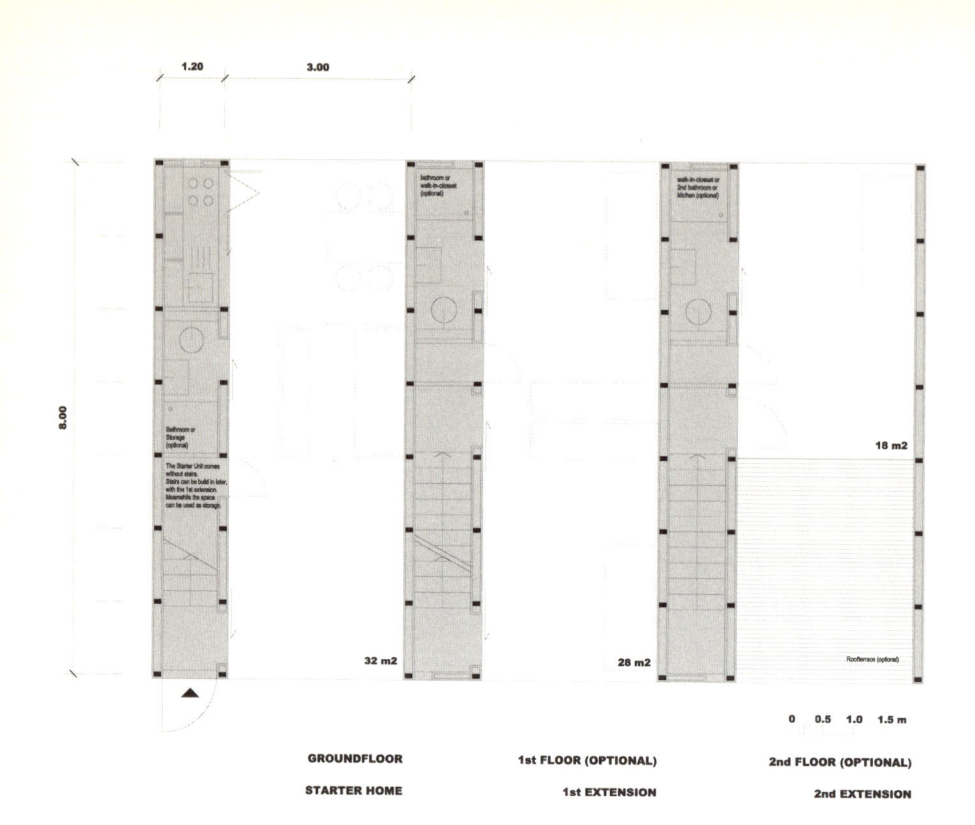

| 1.20 | 3.00 |

8.00

Bathroom or Storage (optional)

The Starter Unit comes without stairs. Stairs can be built in later, with the 1st extension. Meanwhile the space can be used as storage.

bathroom or walk-in-closet (optional)

walk-in-closet or 2nd bathroom or kitchen (optional)

32 m2

28 m2

18 m2

Roofterrace (optional)

0 0.5 1.0 1.5 m

GROUNDFLOOR   **1st FLOOR (OPTIONAL)**   **2nd FLOOR (OPTIONAL)**

STARTER HOME   **1st EXTENSION**   **2nd EXTENSION**

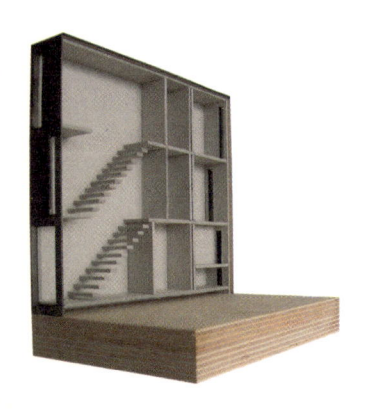

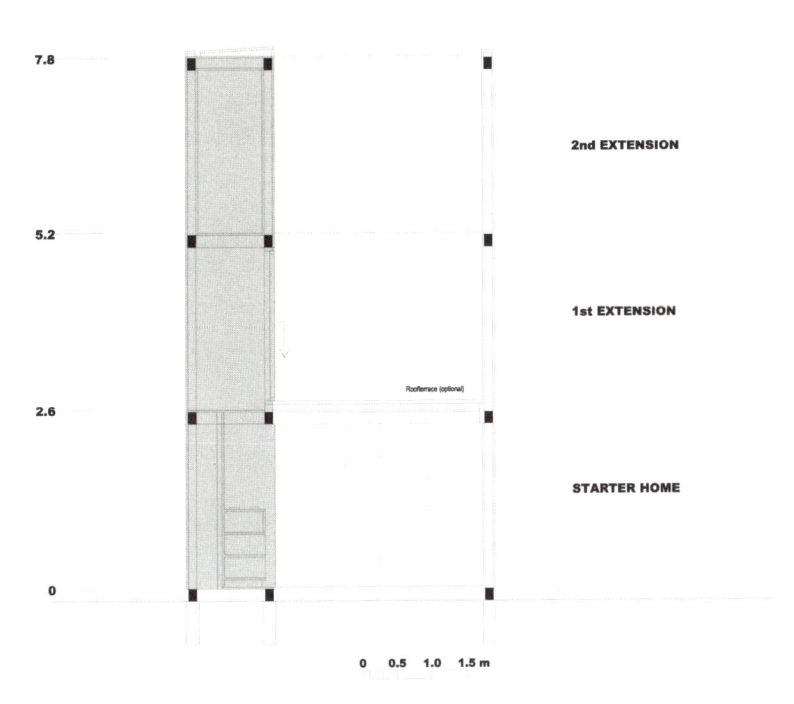

7.8

5.2

2.6

0

0   0.5   1.0   1.5 m

2nd EXTENSION

1st EXTENSION

Roofterrace (optional)

STARTER HOME

GROWTH HOMES

Groeiwoningen, Almere, Netherlands, Architectuurstudio Herman Hertzberger, 2002

Flexibility can mean the capacity of a building's interior to adapt, but the term can also be used to show that a building can be extended without difficulty. These 'growth homes' designed by Herman Hertzberger are a good example of that latter category. All the units in this project have the same basic unit plus a variable zone that can be fitted out at the occupants' discretion.

The majority of occupants chose a glass-enclosed zone, although a few tried out other scenarios such as an extra living room on the ground floor or an additional bedroom upstairs. Both the architect and the developer expected occupants to modify the zones in the fullness of time and add them to their house, but there have been few alterations as yet. Interestingly, one of the zones was built without the glazing at the occupants' request. So modifying is about excluding as well as including.

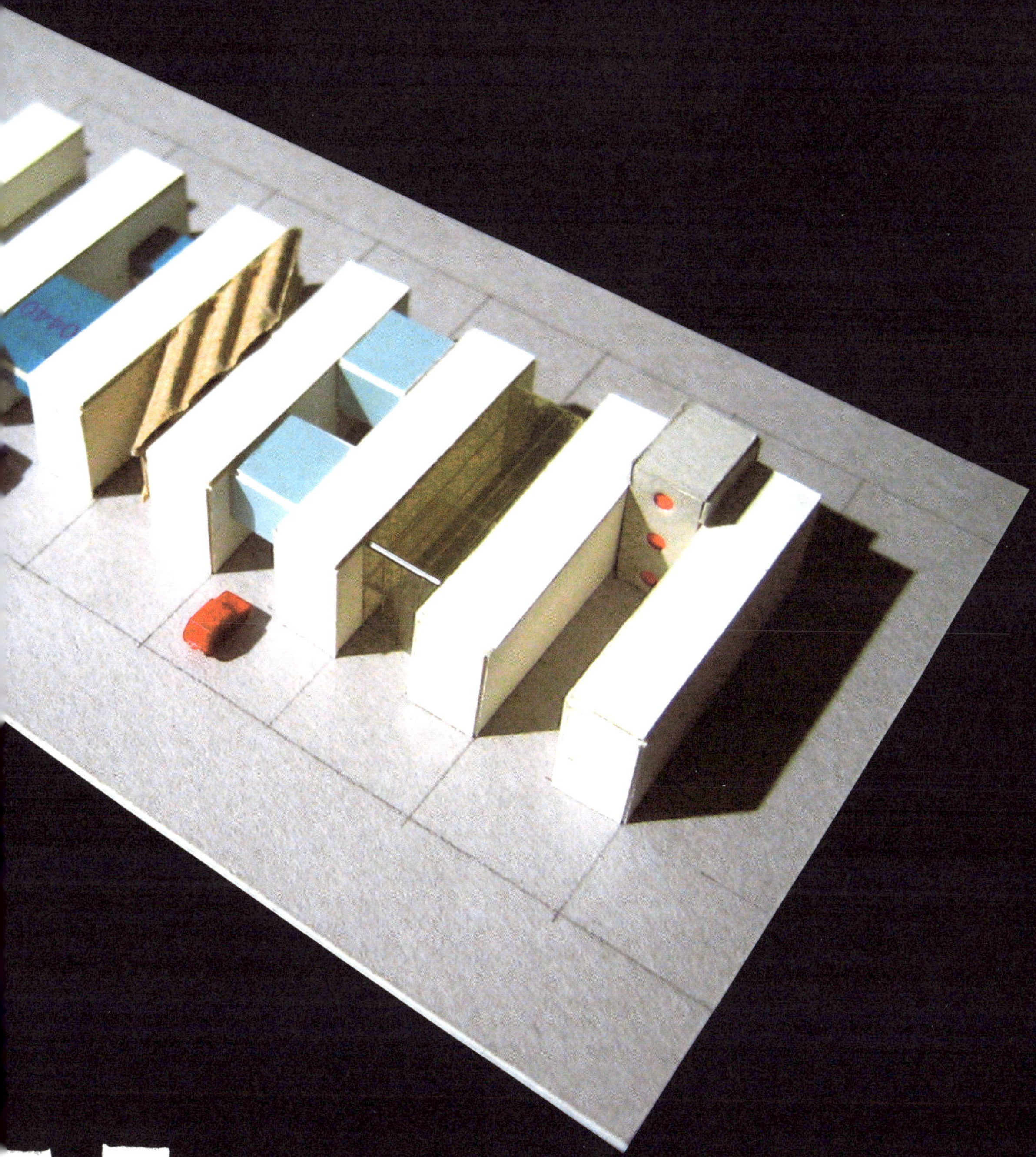

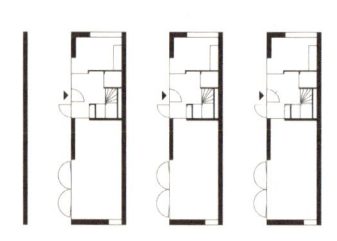

Ground floor

0 1 2 3 4 5   10

First floor

222

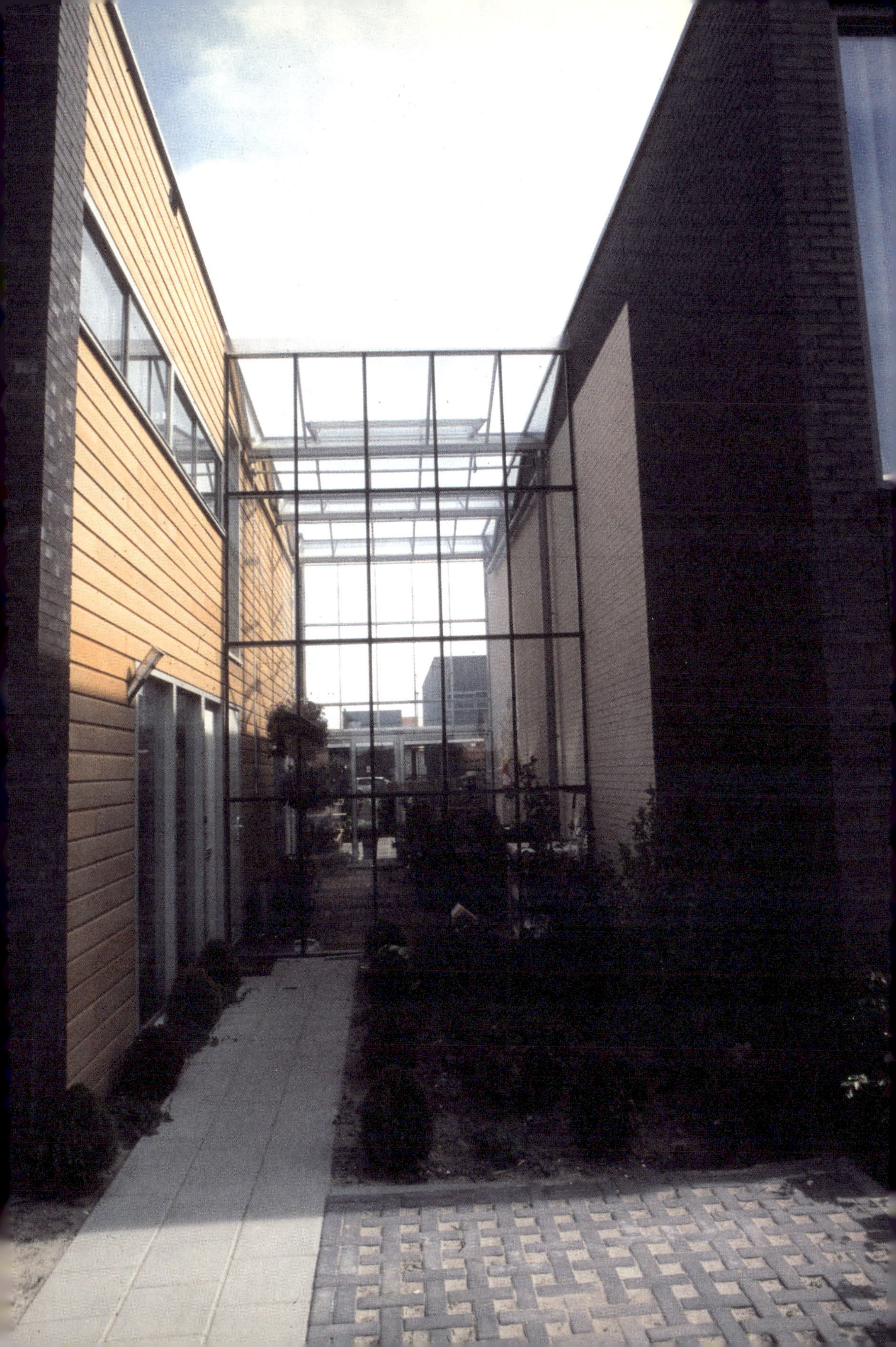

ONCE A FACTORY

A-Factory, Amsterdam, Netherlands, Neutelings Riedijk Architects, 2002
Interior of former factory shed, George Witteveen & Ramin Visch
Project development: TCN properties

The building now housing the 'A-Factory', a mixed-use building for small enterprises, began life as a bicycle factory and was later a distribution centre for the pharmaceutical industry. Originally it was to be demolished to make way for redevelopment. On further consideration it was decided that the concrete construction of the factory shed and the architecture of the offices were too fine to simply tear down. Neutelings Riedijk Architects landed the commission to renovate the complex and design three adjoining pavilions.

NRA proposed scooping four courtyards from the factory shed so as to be able to design offices with sufficient daylight and views out. The interior architects Witteveen & Visch have fitted out the office landscape for the firm of Ogilvy. Further features include the tall arches of the roof structure, masses of glass, jutting rooms for working and meeting and a single flat floor with all service ducts and terminals stashed beneath it. There are also the four large courtyards mentioned above.

The A-factory illustrates what can be meant by cultural durability as described in the essay by bOb Van Reeth (see pp. 110-115). The deviant subdivisions, great heights and large areas of glass make this an attractive building for businesses in the creative services sector. Advertising agencies, graphic designers, film companies and architects like to work in an unconventional setting. In the words of the developer, it pays to renovate an existing building if it has outstanding architecture.

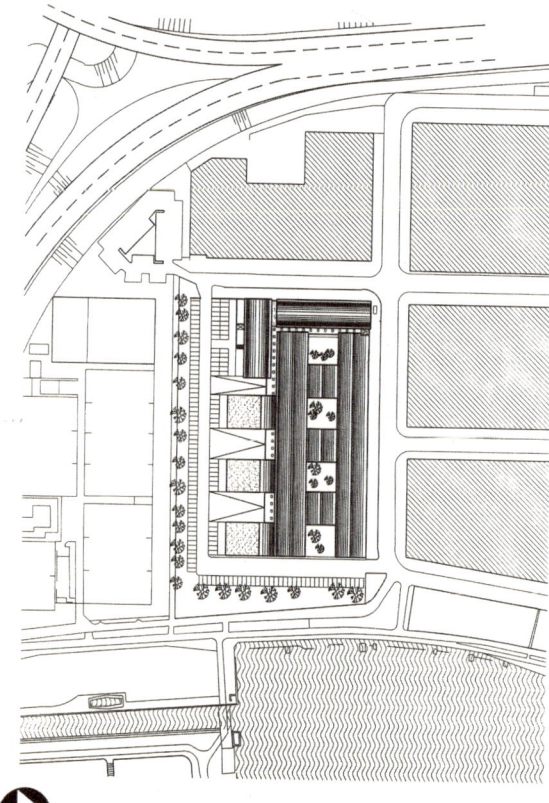

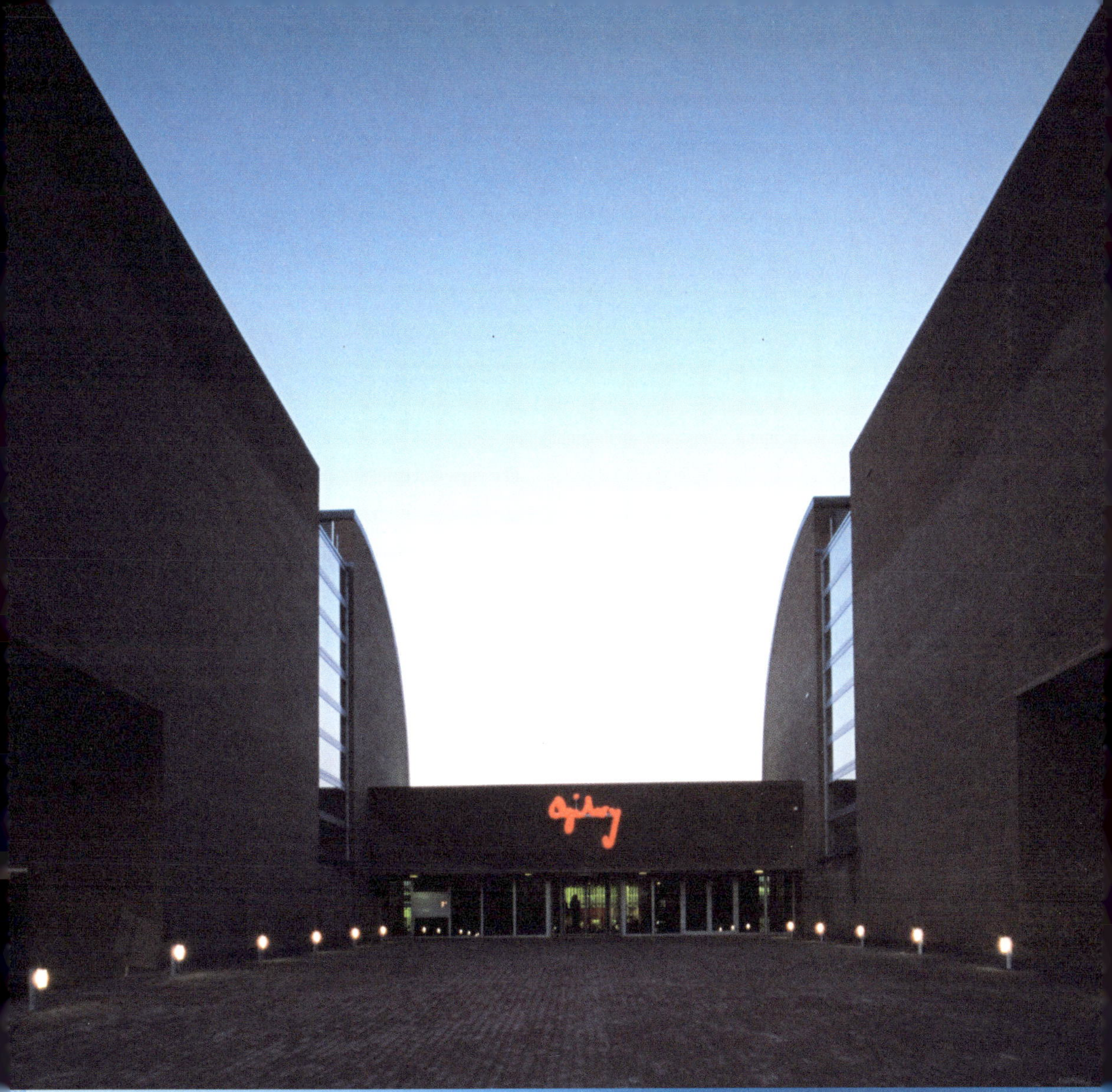

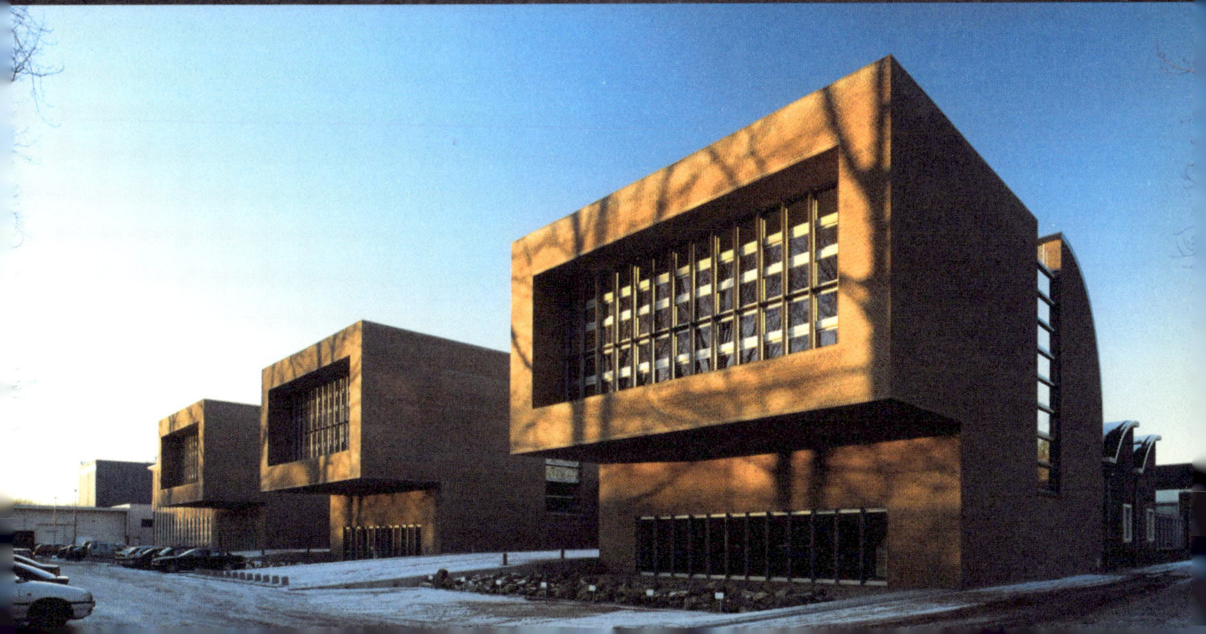

226

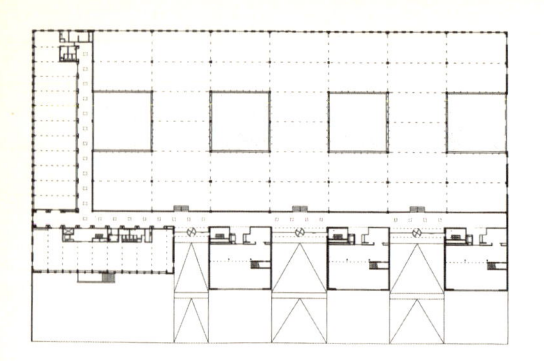

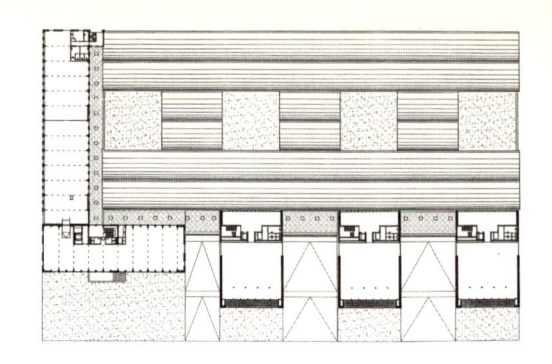

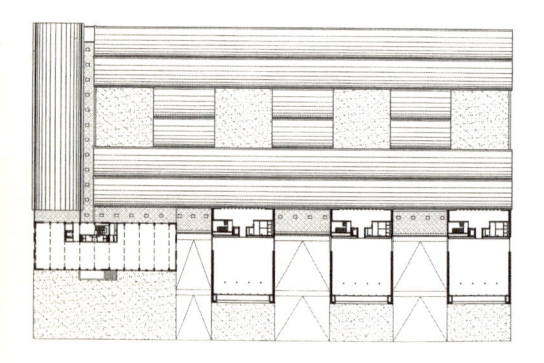

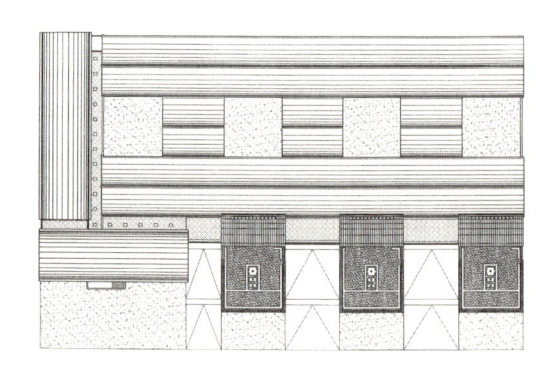

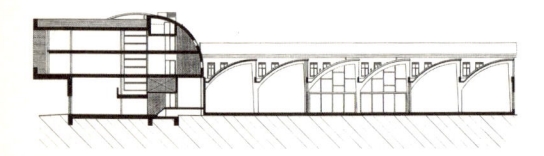

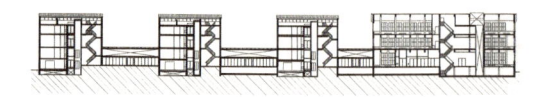

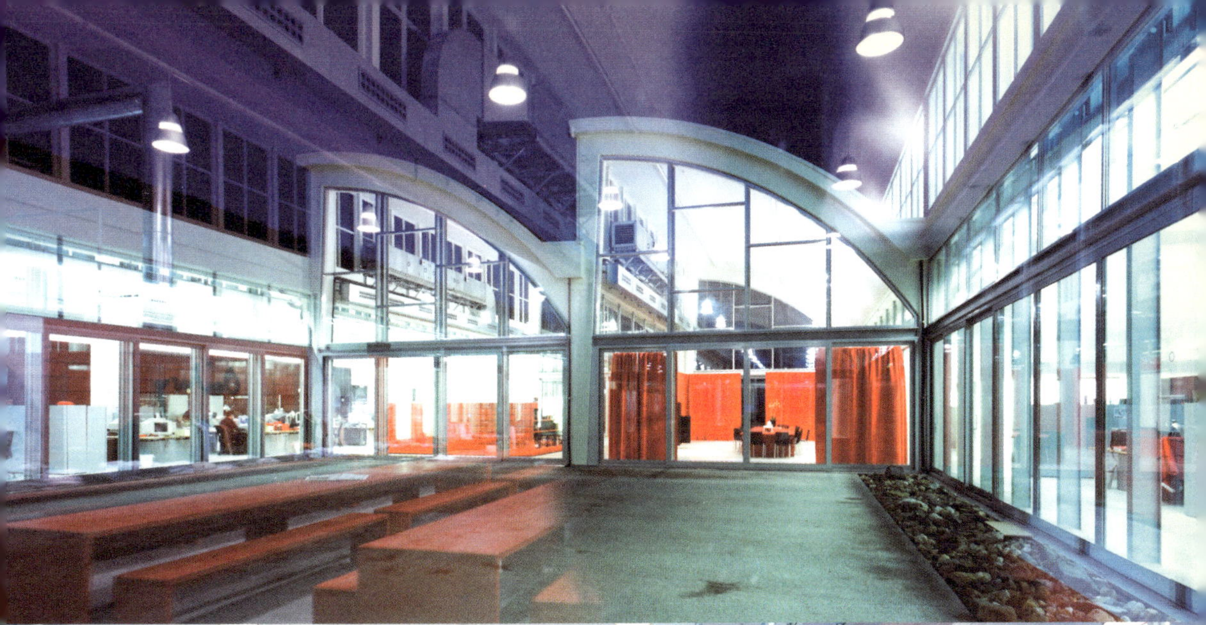

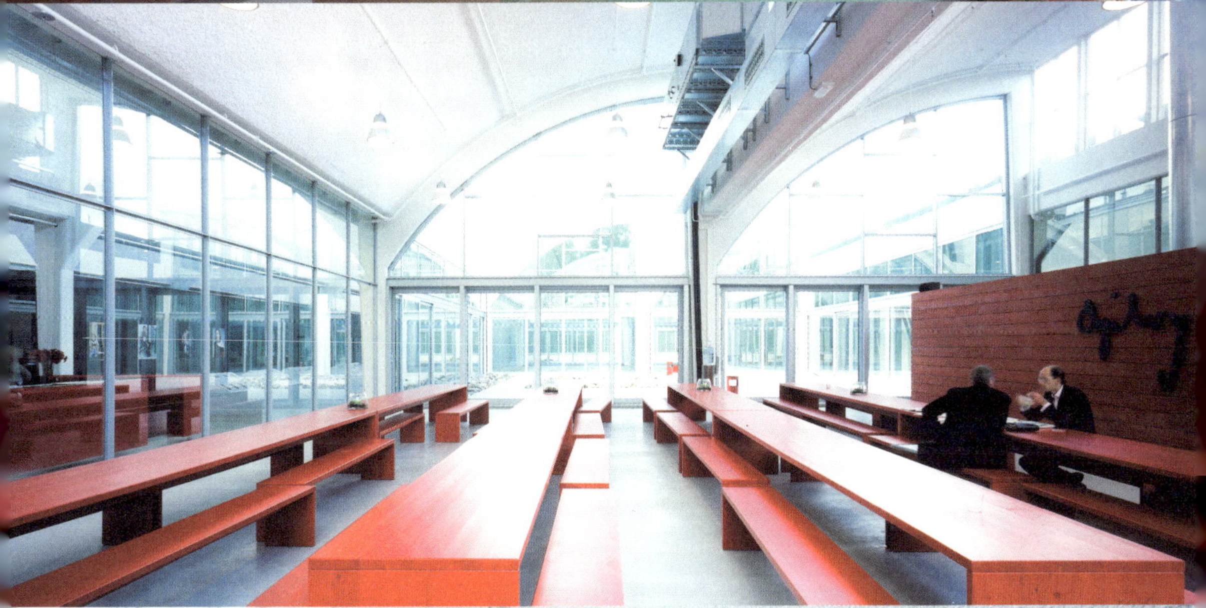

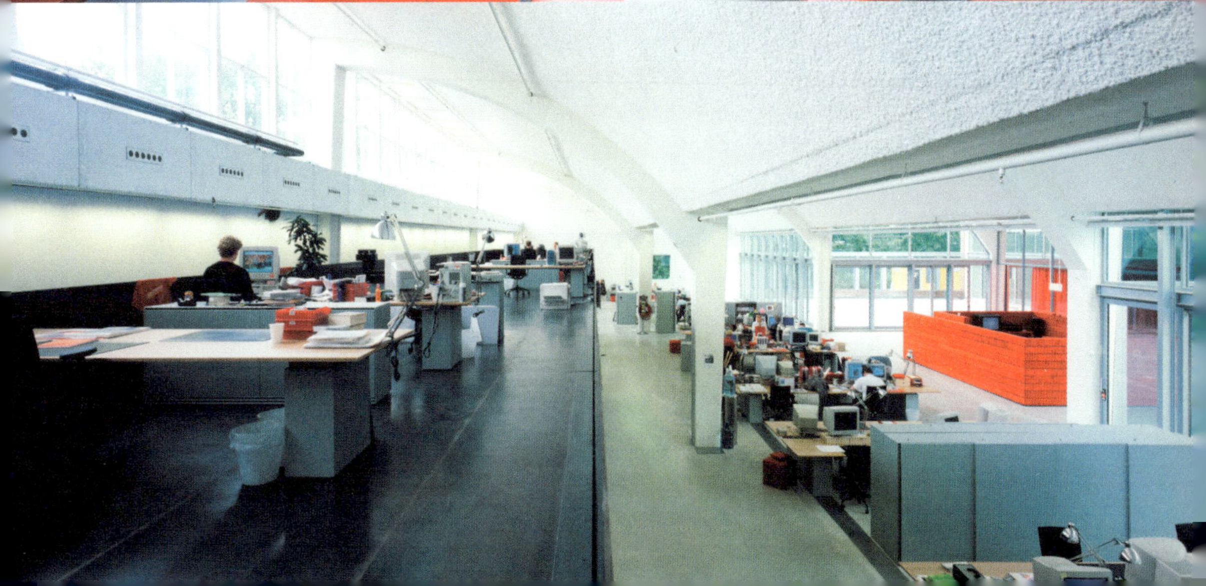

A CHIC MAKESHIFT CLASSROOM

Schoolparasites, Hoogvliet, Rotterdam, Onix, Barend Koolhaas and Christoph Seyferth, 2004
Instigated by WiMBY!, coordinator of the Rotterdam-Hoogvliet International Building Exhibition

Many school buildings in the Netherlands are equipped with one or more makeshift classrooms, cheap prefabs, there to solve temporary problems of accommodation. As with all stopgap solutions few demands are made on these classrooms. They are to meet the most slender of functional requirements quickly and cheaply. After all, they are just stopgaps until the real thing arrives. And this is where it often goes wrong; temporary classrooms are often less temporary than was originally planned. Intended for a period of three to five years at the most, it is not exceptional for them to do duty as fully-fledged accommodation for ten or even fifteen years.

This was what prompted the WiMBY! foundation to get alternatives designed as part of the Rotterdam-Hoogvliet International Building Exhibition. Together with three schools requiring temporary extra space in the Rotterdam urban redevelopment area of Hoogvliet, WiMBY! commissioned young designers to develop a classroom not only suitable for short periods but also able to function for a longer period of fifteen years – in other words, a high-grade makeshift classroom. This produced the three 'Schoolparasites', as these prototypes are called. Each is tailor-made for a particular use. The design by Onix is a music room, that by Christoph Seyferth is meant for cookery classes and Barend Koolhaas's design provides rooms for individual tuition. All three are equally suitable for use as a standard classroom. Each designer chose a different construction technique. Onix designed a demountable and fully relocatable timber unit, Seyferth designed steel precast elements and Koolhaas opted for elements of timber-frame construction clad with corrugated sheet.

It is the intention that these prototypes are to be further developed for use in other Dutch schools. Their ability to be disassembled and moved about depends on a specific type of detail developed in close collaboration with a producer. Not only that, the construction costs can only be lowered if the models are produced in series. Whatever the outcome, the schoolchildren in Hoogvliet are benefiting now from these 'Schoolparasites'.

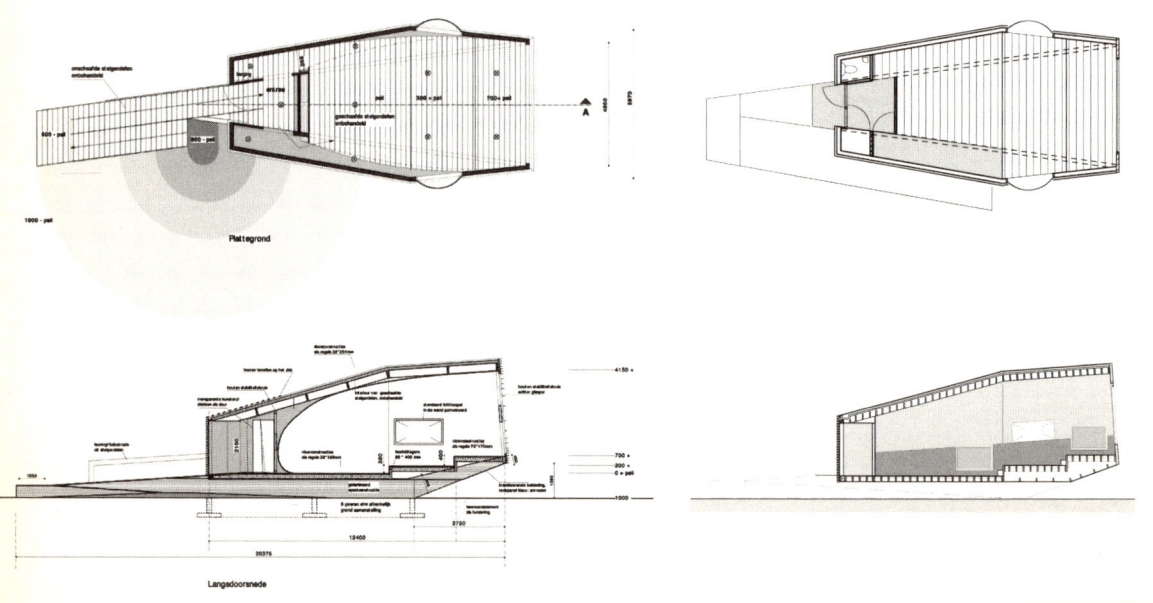

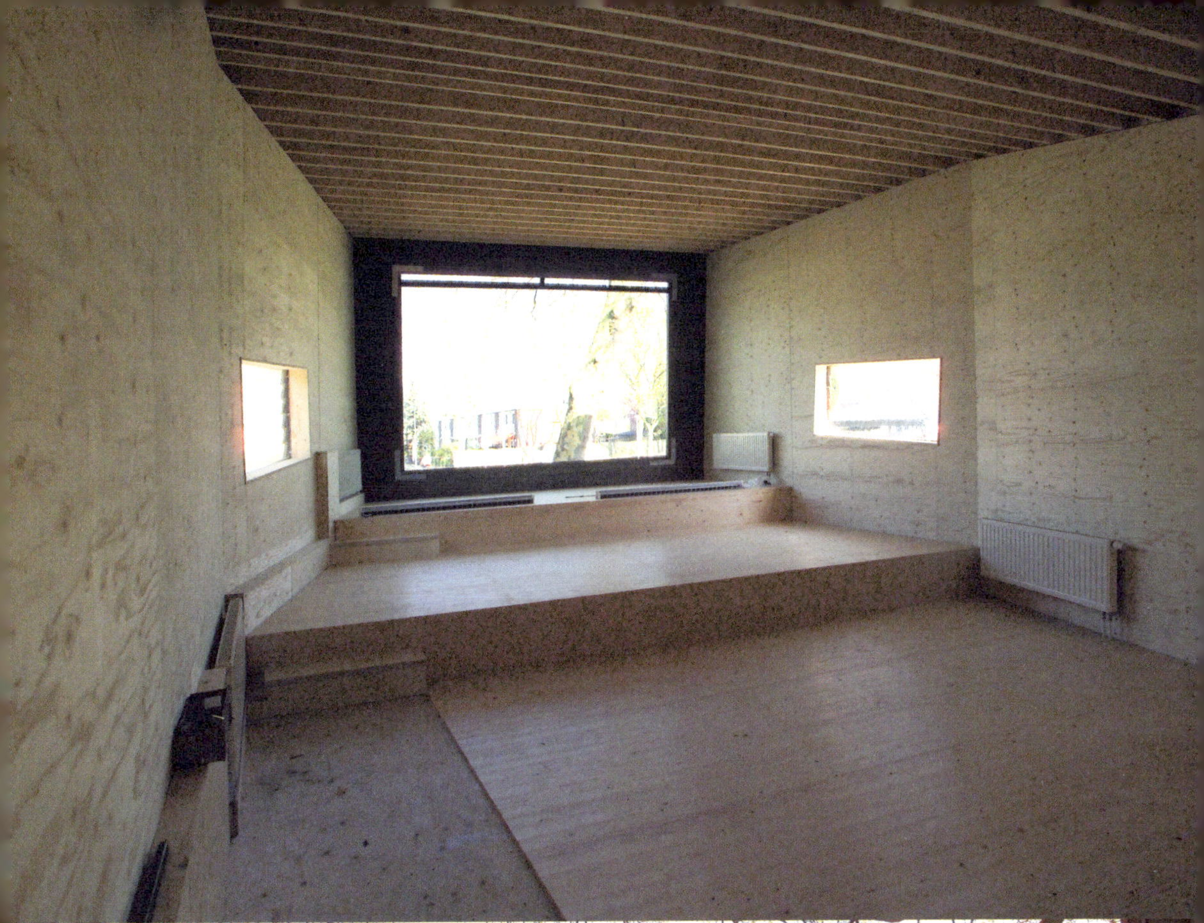

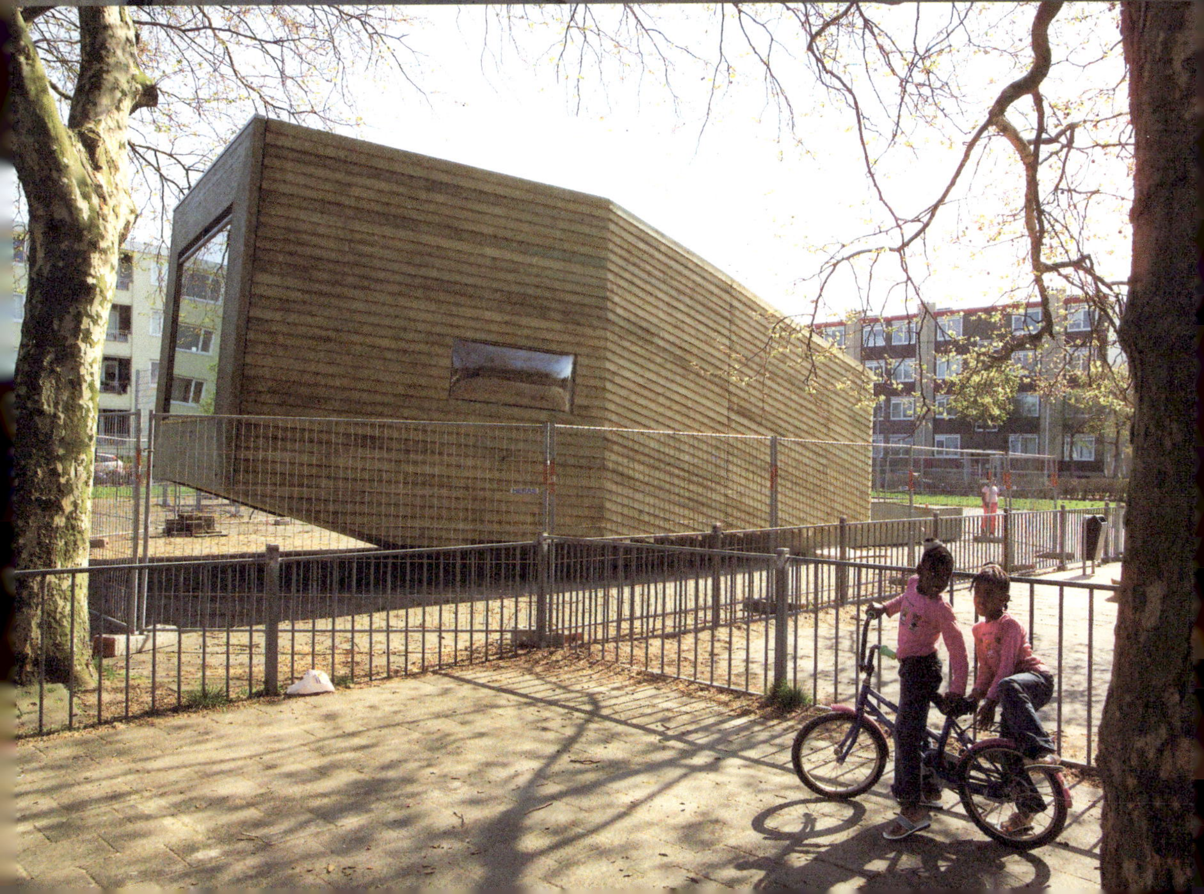

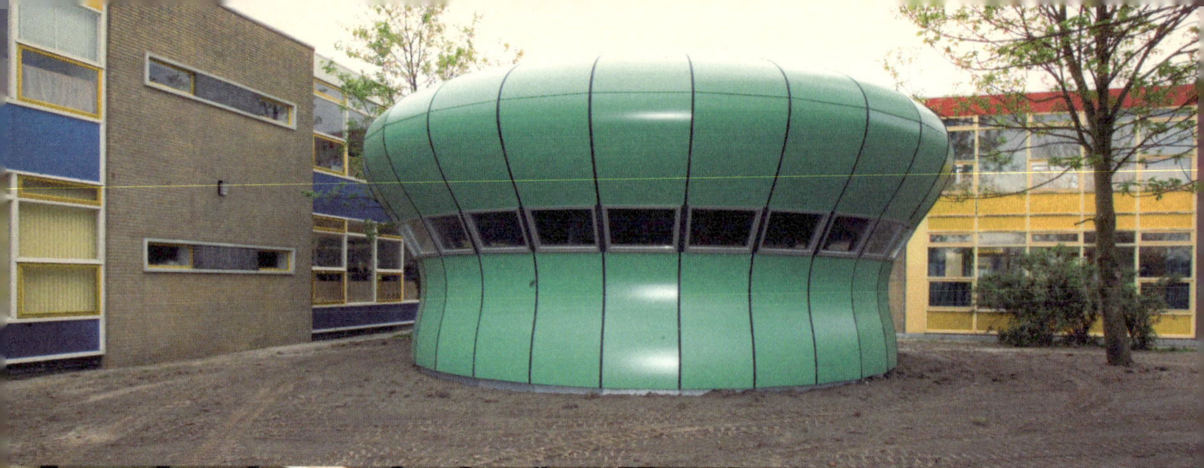

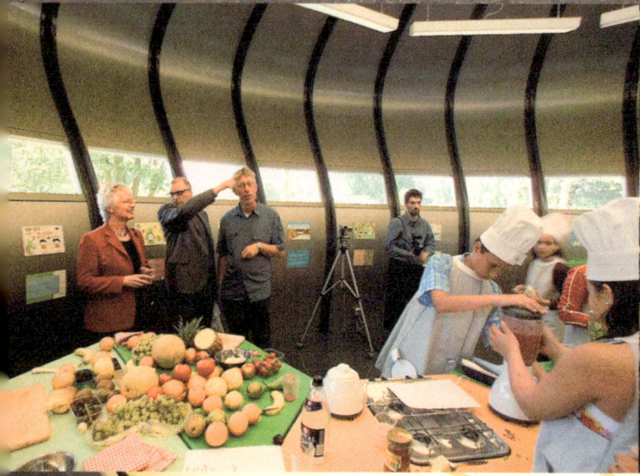

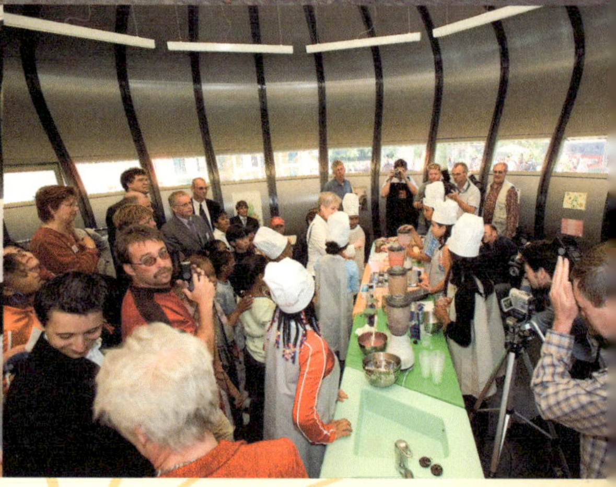

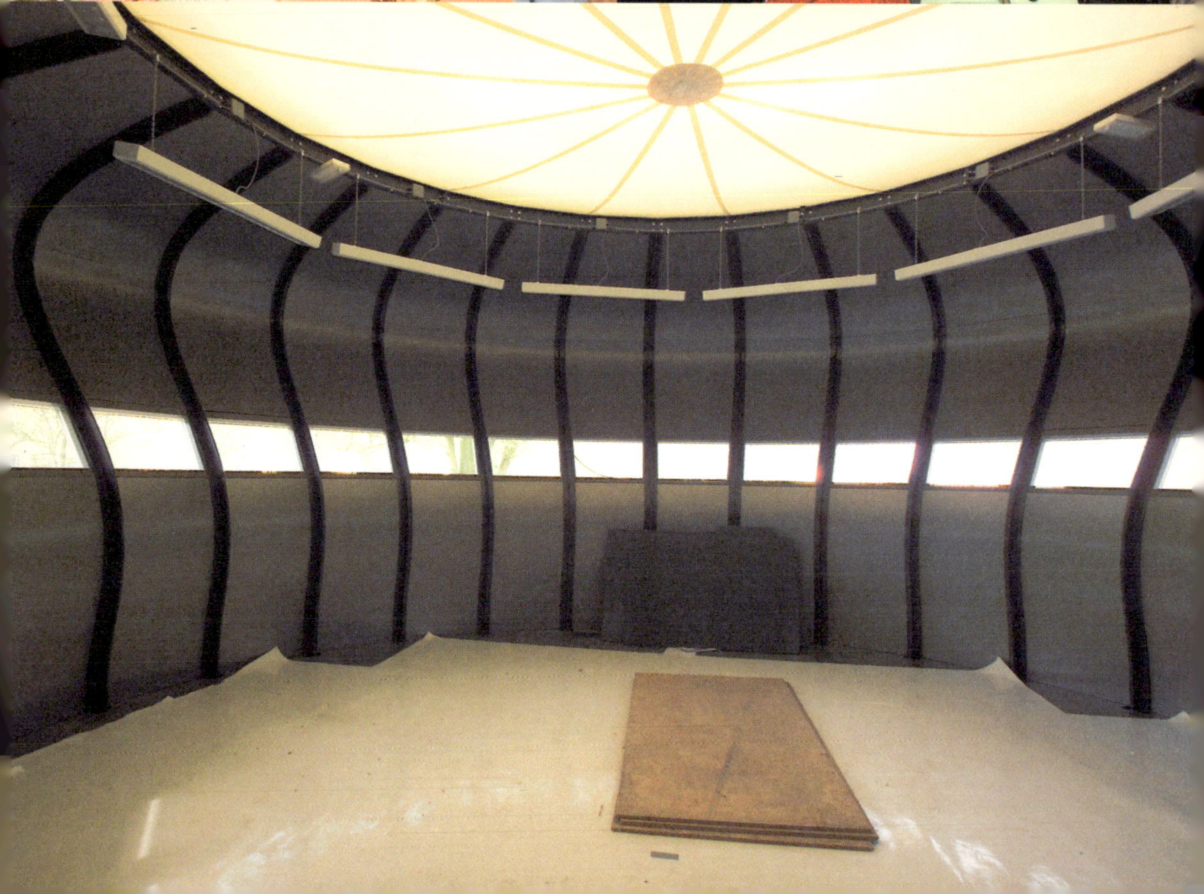

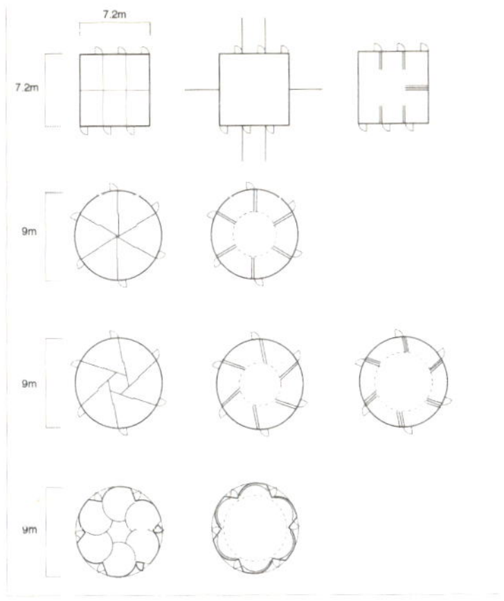
7.2m
7.2m
9m
9m
9m

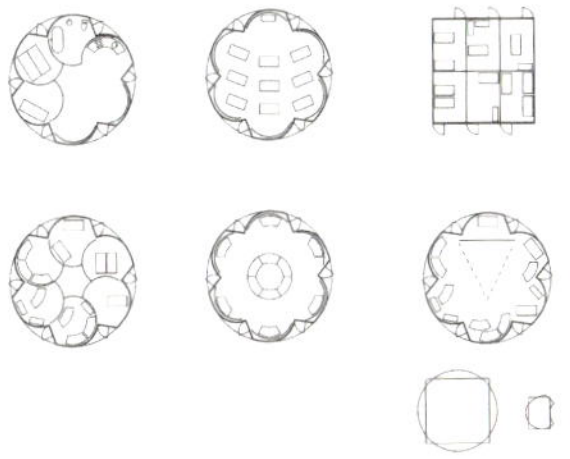

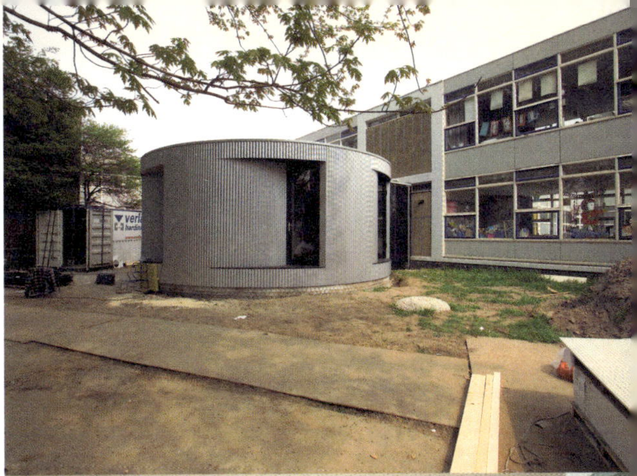

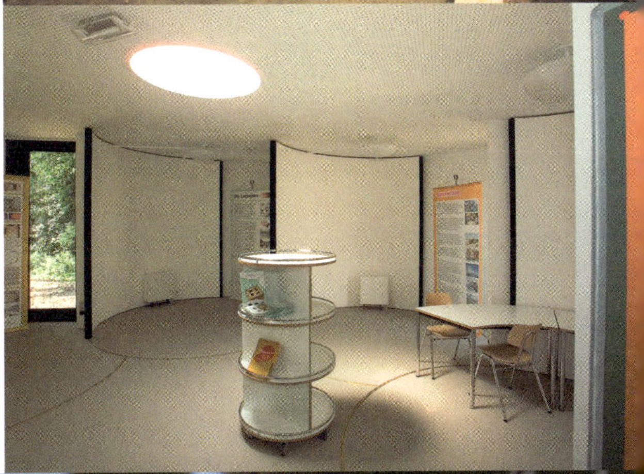

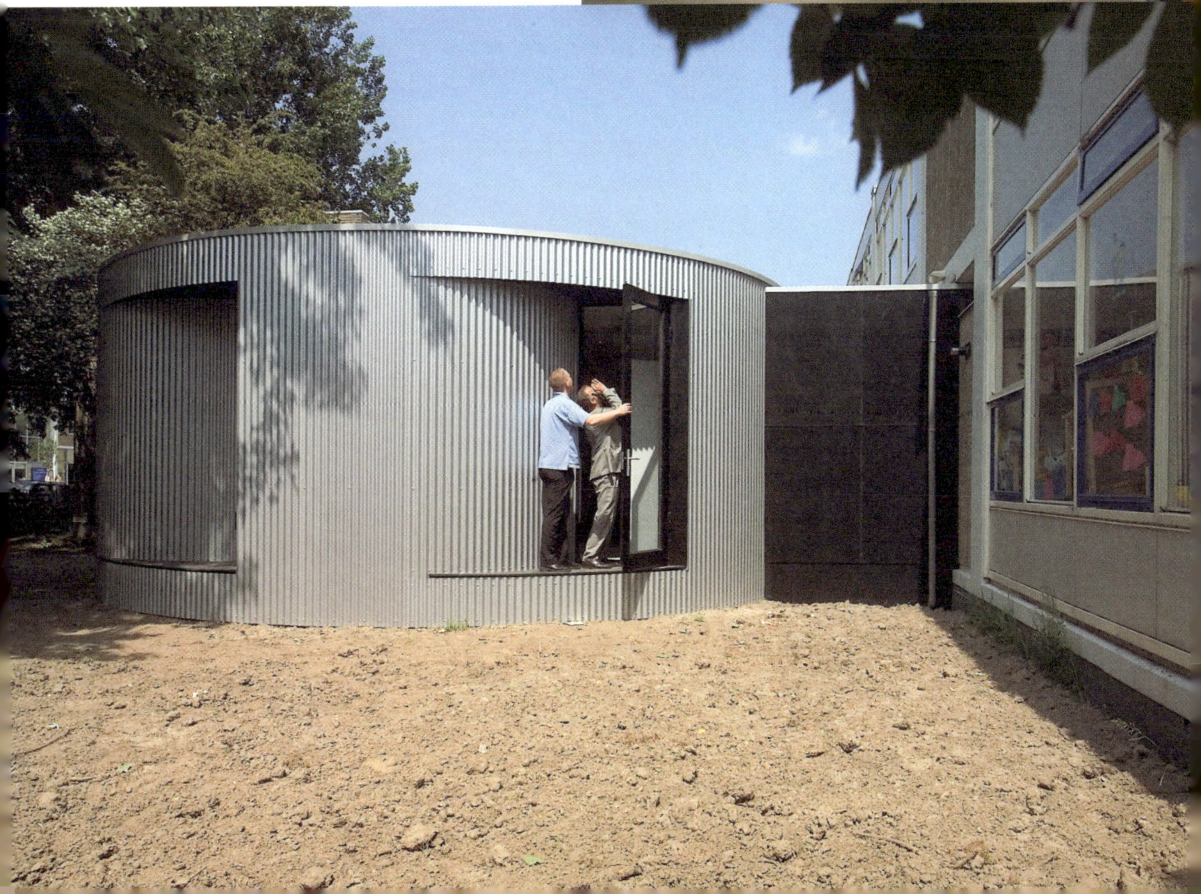

STUDENT HOUSING

Spacebox, Mart de Jong, architectenbureau De Vijf, 2003

There is an acute shortage of student accommodation in the Netherlands. There are enough plans for new-build housing for students but so many projects are taking so long to materialize that the coming decade will see many students forced to live in temporary buildings. The 'temporary' student flat is a phenomenon that has been with us since the 1950s. Time and again, temporariness proves to be an expandable commodity. In such projects as Gimmie Shelter on the campus of Delft University of Technology the structural best-by date was exceeded to such as extent that in the end the floors were virtually giving way beneath the occupants' feet. The Spacebox is another project to be designed to circumnavigate the glacial speed of planning processes. A demountable system with sound architectural and structural detailing, it can spend a short or longer period in one place and then be moved for redeployment elsewhere.

Interior designer Mart de Jong created the Spacebox, a compact, self-sufficient live/work studio with a surface area of 18 square metres and weighing something over two tonnes, standardly equipped with a shower, toilet and kitchen. The residential units are supplied ready for use and are lowered into place using a small crane. In no time at all, you have a building with up to three living levels atop a temporary foundation of Stelcon concrete pads.

The most groundbreaking aspect of the Spacebox is its materiality; the unit is made of composite materials until now only used in the shipping and aeronautical industries. The big advantages of these materials are their long lifespan, light weight, high stiffness and extremely high insulation values for sound and heat.

Mart de Jong expects that once the student housing shortage has been solved, his Spacebox system can be simply redeployed for a second form of use. He sees possibilities in small modifications that allow units to be strung together into two- or three-room apartments. This makes the Spacebox a fine example of flexible architecture, picking up on the current need for temporary living space, with an eye to a possible future as apartments.

At present there are units in operation in Delft and Utrecht and projects in preparation in Eindhoven, Hilversum and Liverpool (UK).

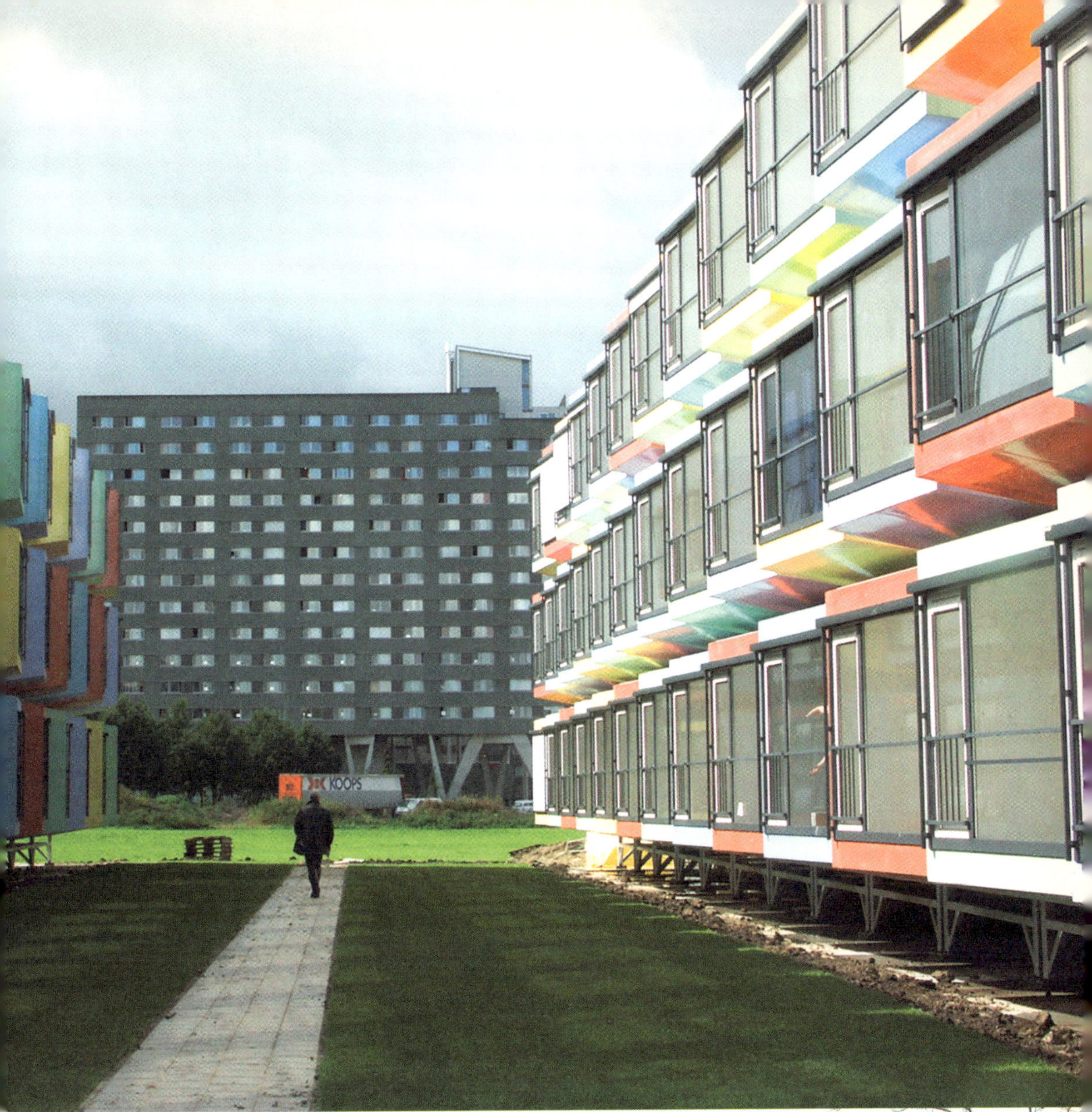

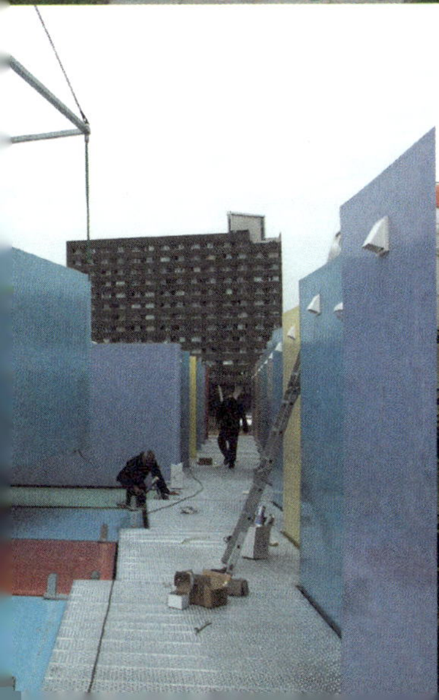

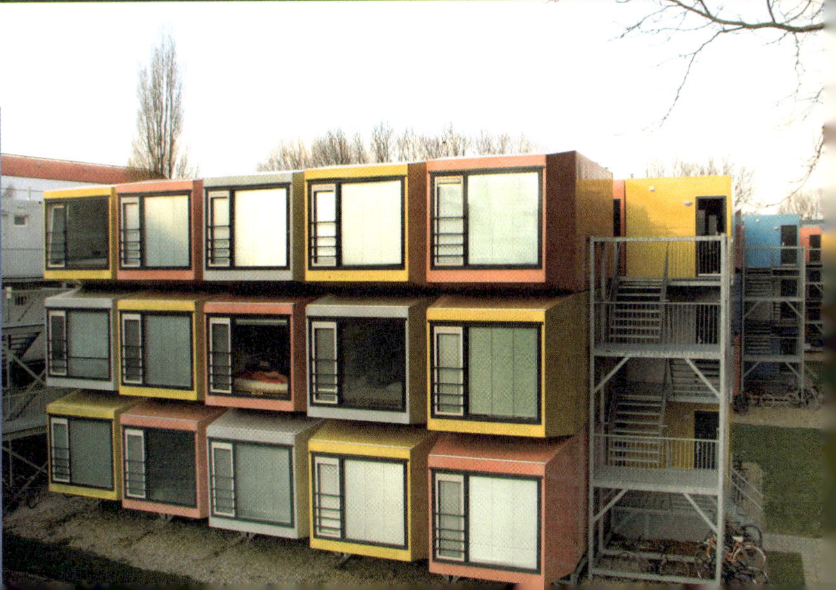

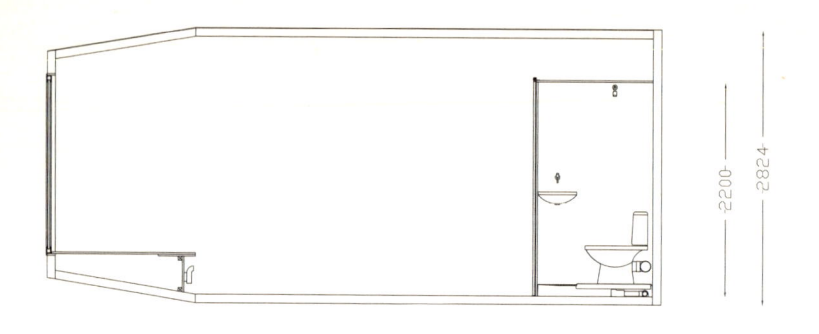

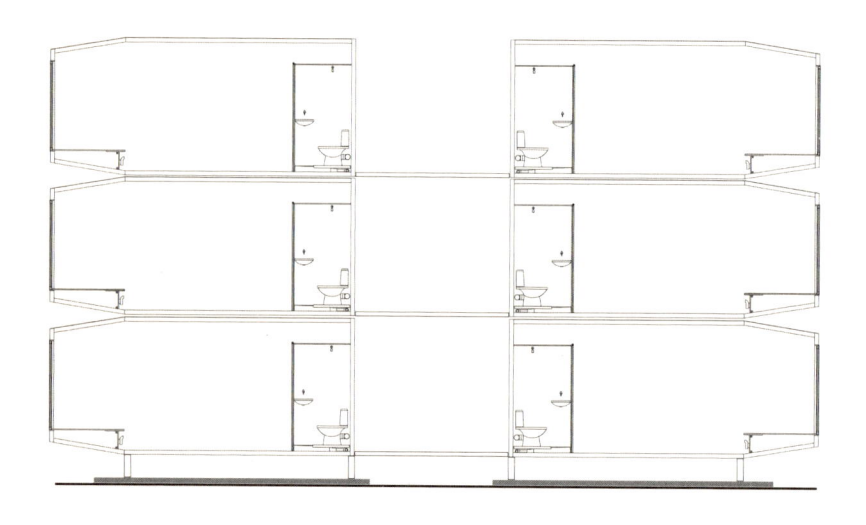

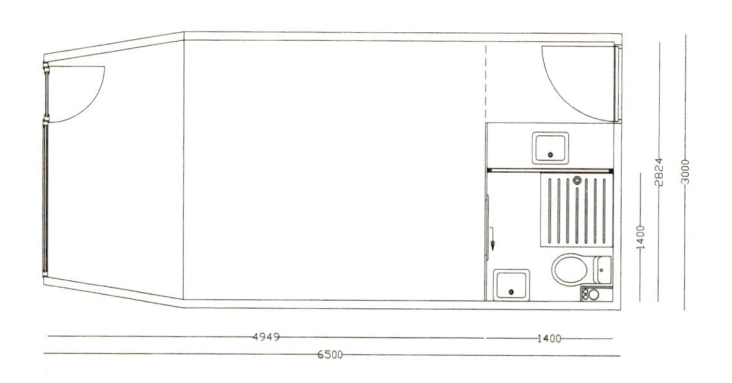

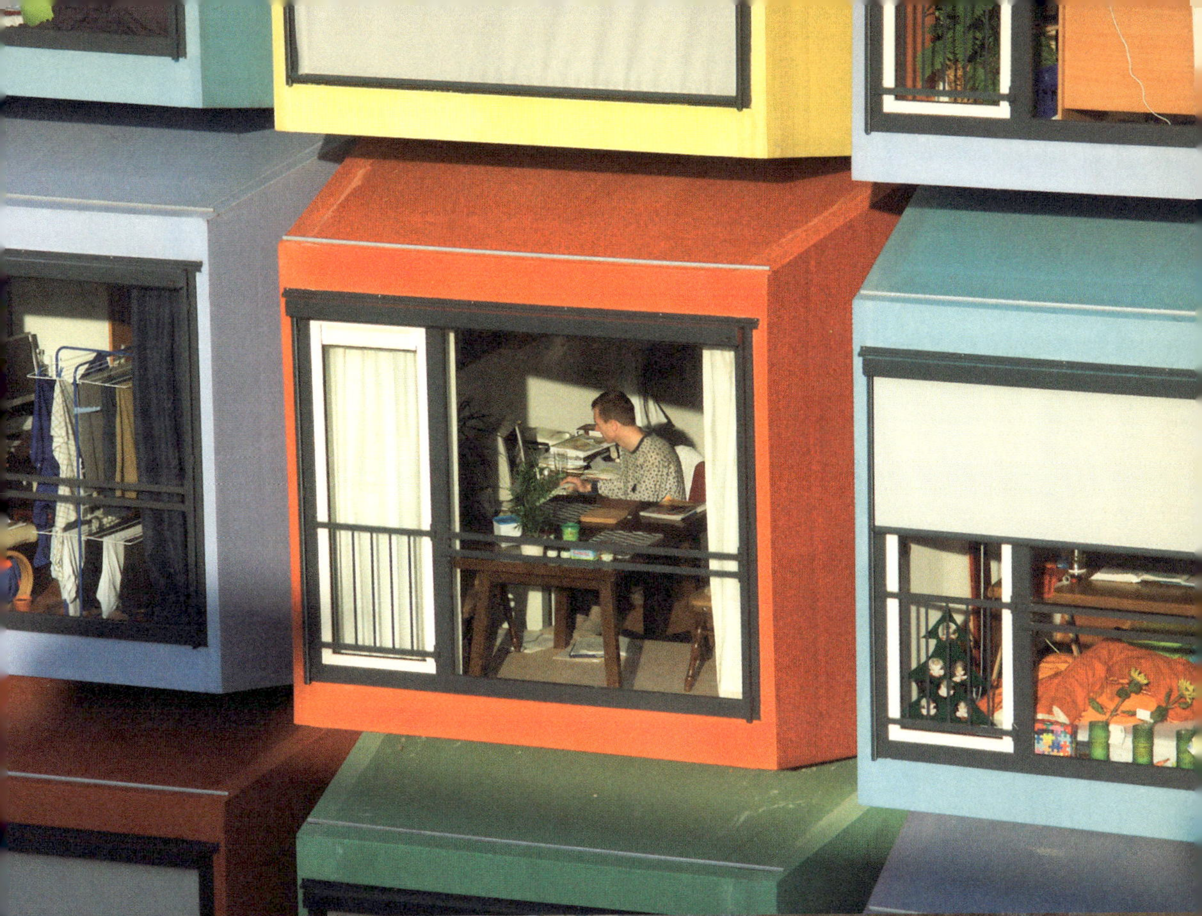

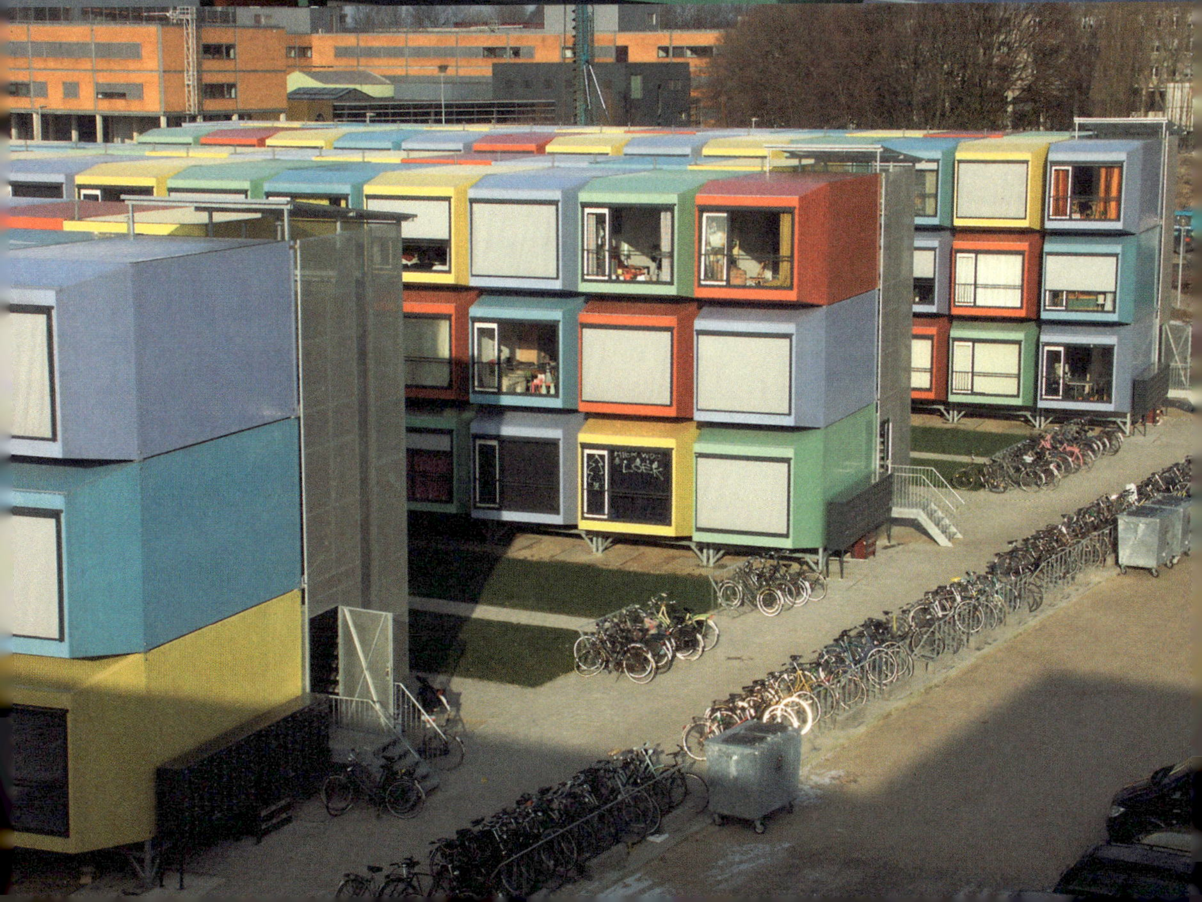

DEMOUNTABLE
Office of ABT/DAMEN, Delftech Park, Delft, Netherlands, Hubert-Jan Henket architecten, 2001

The mercurial attitude of businesses towards accommodation often means that buildings get demolished before their time. At Delftech Park, an industrial site in Delft, you can find two examples of buildings that tackle this problem each in their own way. The office shared by ABT consulting engineers and DAMEN consultants is a demountable building. Whenever it no longer serves its purpose it can be dismantled and reassembled elsewhere. This in contrast to the end-of-life strategy chosen by the designers of the XX office next door. As described earlier on page 19, this building was designed for a short lifespan of no more than two decades. This means that by that time, various parts of the building are past their prime and become recycled. The components that do still function can be individually reused in new buildings.
Symptomatic of the ABT-DAMEN building is its toned-down engineer's architecture. Architect Hubert-Jan Henket worked closely with the engineers at ABT to design a building whose ground floor is largely kept free for parking. The upper storeys sit behind a glass screen that acts as a buffer between inside and outside. All detailing is low-tech. One advantage in using simple standard building products is that it can be expected that these will always be obtainable. This in contrast to many high-tech proposals, where effective management and upkeep can suffer when special components disappear from the market.
Building practice is an intractable affair. Floors and foundations in particular are critical factors along the road to complete demountability. The piles under the ABT-DAMEN office are almost impossible to remove and the applied floor system of precast concrete floor slabs has a finishing layer that for constructional reasons has to be inextricably bound to the substrate. As for the remaining components, 100 per cent disassembly and reuse have proved easier to achieve. The inner leaf of the facade consists of elements that can be removed for maintenance. The parts are interchangeable so that the facades can be altered at any time.

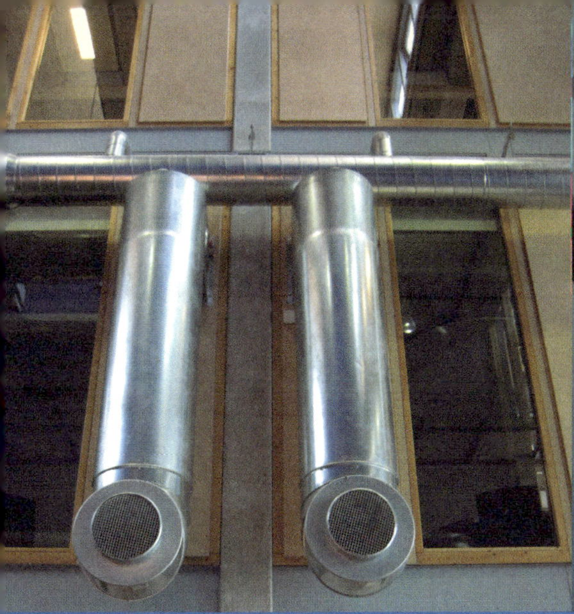
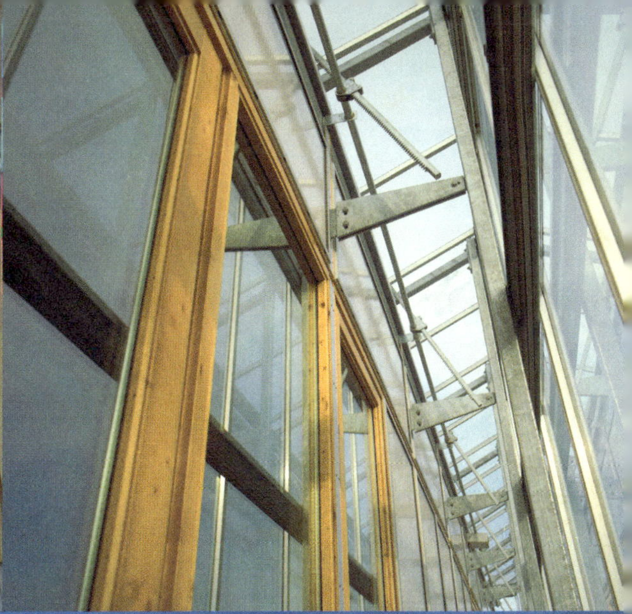
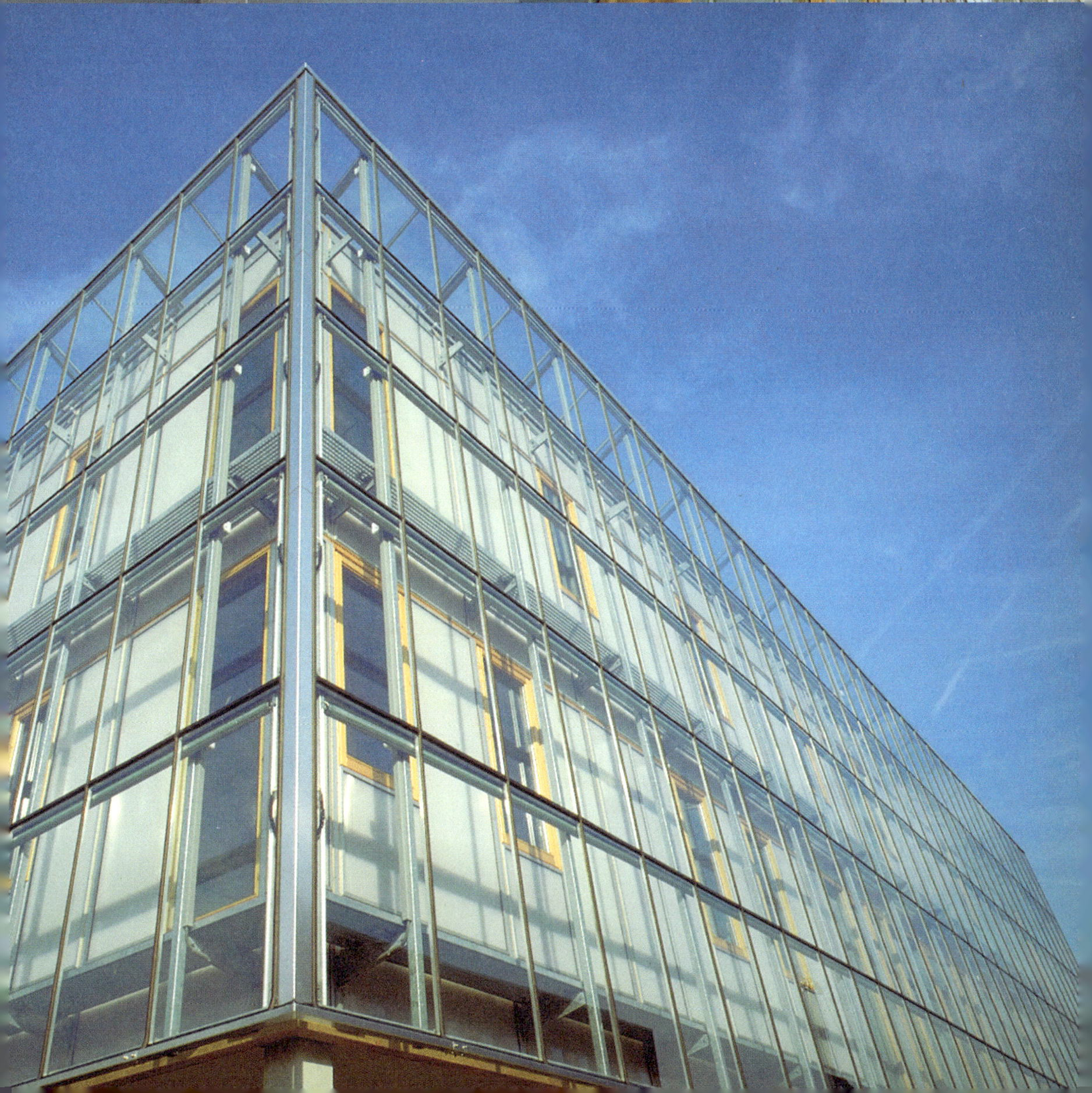

238

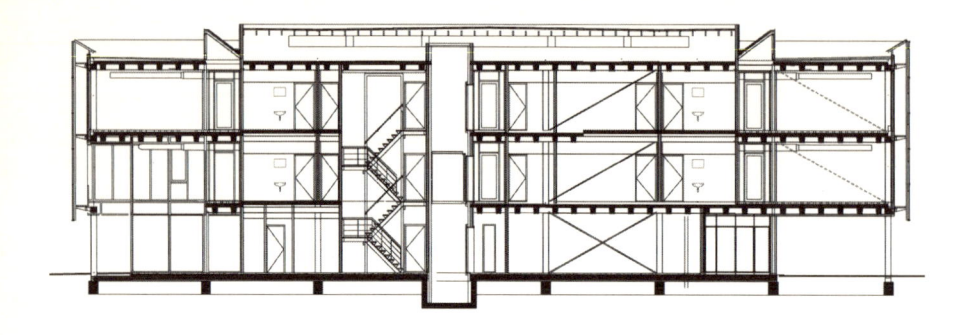

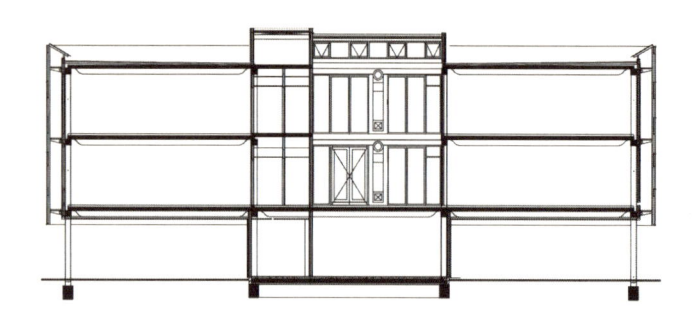

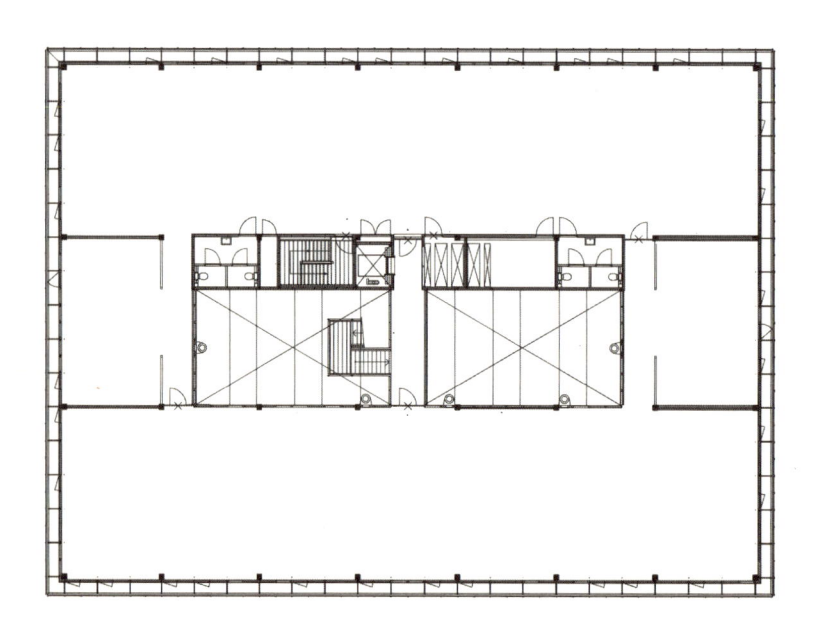

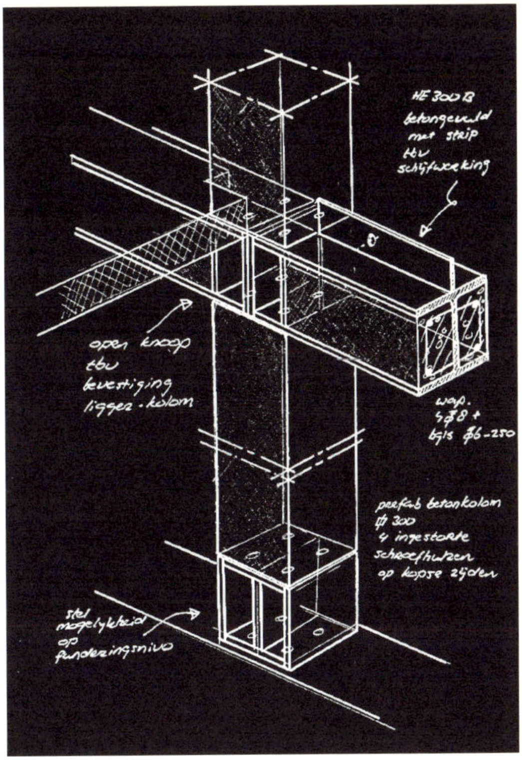
HE 300 B
betongevuld
met strip
tbv
schijfwerking
open knoop
tbv
bevestiging
ligger - kolom
wap.
4∅8 +
bgls ∅6-250
prefab betonkolom
∅ 300
4 ingestorte
schroefhulzen
op kopse zijden
stel
mogelykheid
op
funderingsnivo

MAXIMUM FREEDOM FOR THE OCCUPANTS

Hellmutstrasse, Zurich and Wuhr, Langenthal, ADP-architekten

For ADP-architekten adaptability is the pre-eminent means of giving residents greater freedom of use. The housing block in Hellmutstrasse, Zurich, and the live/work buildings in the Wuhr district of Langenthal consist of two parts, one permanent and the other changeable, with a clear dividing line between them to facilitate modification.

In the Wuhr project these principles have been worked up at the macro scale. The project comprises five volumes slotted into the former village core of Wuhr. The housing blocks have structural facades and a fixed core of amenities.

Non-bearing walls separate the units. Each unit has a loggia whose position is influential on how the floor plan is laid out. This aspect alone ensures a wide range of dwelling interiors.

The housing block in Hellmutstrasse in Zurich has a fixed structure of bearing walls and service cores. The space this creates can be variously divided by secondary elements such as cupboard units, additional doors and freestanding glass screens. The servant spaces stand in the centre of the dwelling flanked by functionally neutral areas where occupants can organize the rooms as they see fit. The Zurich housing block was designed in discussion with the future occupants and makes much of the relationship between public and private spaces. There is a gradual transition between public and private, with residents sharing the internal courtyard and galleries. Units are reached from a half-open court that acts as a transitional zone between them and the street. Three open gallery-style stairwells stand along the court side with a view of the street. Parts of this 'gallery' can be annexed as outdoor space by the open kitchens.

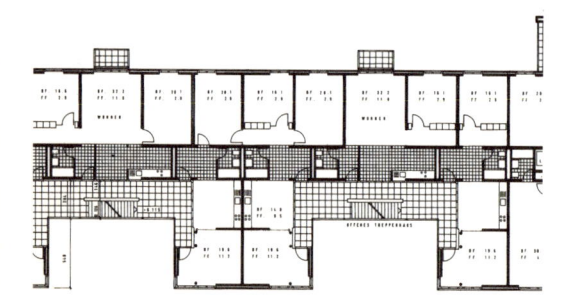

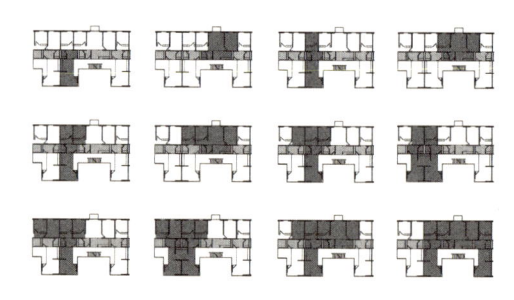

Housing on Hellmutstrasse, Zurich, ADP-architekten

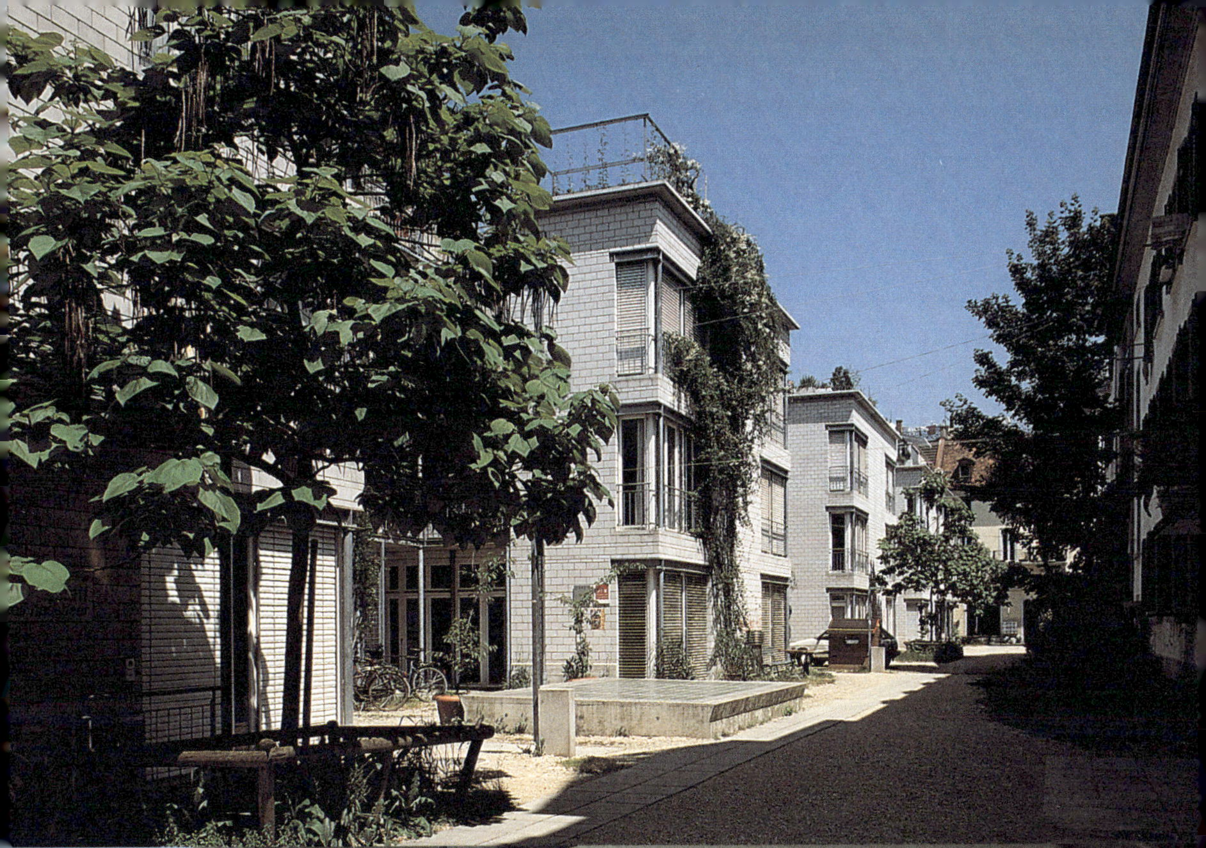
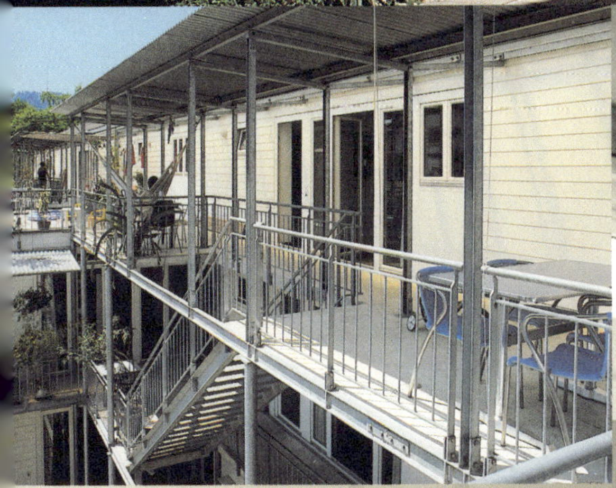
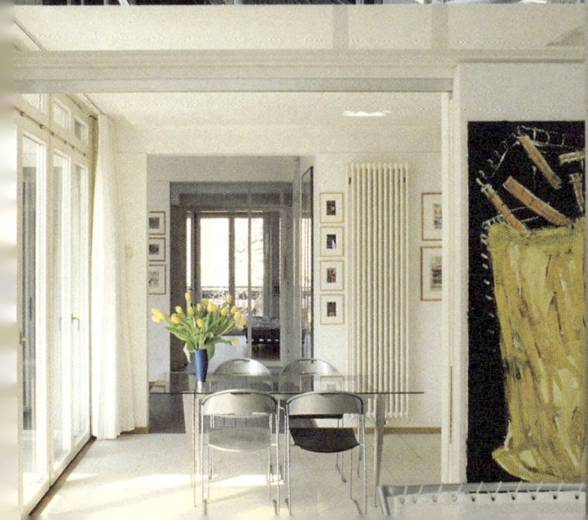
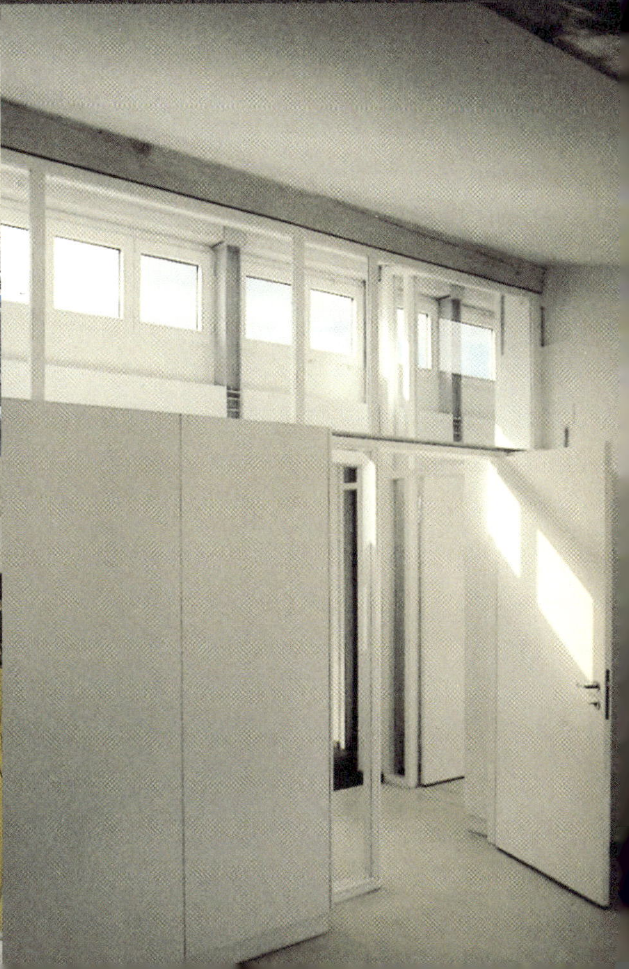

Housing in Wuhr, Langenthal, ADP-architekten

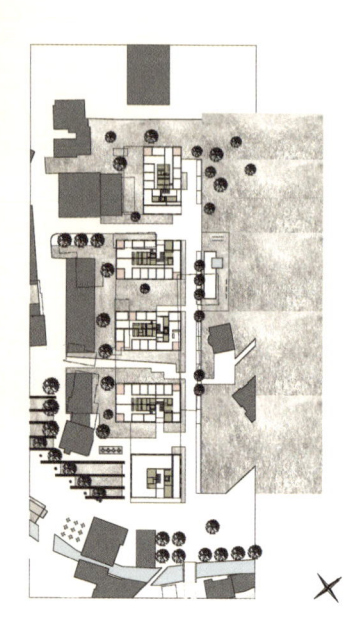

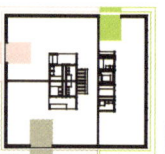

Wohnen und Arbeiten   **Wohnen**

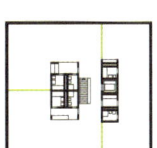

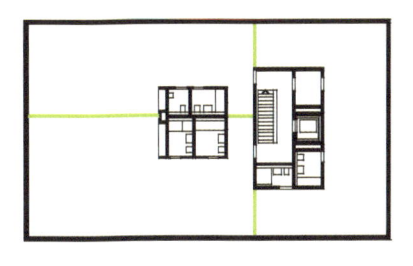

REFERENCES

Sources

Fortress on The Sound
Wingårdh Arkitektkontor AB
www.wingardhs.se

Wærn, R. 2001. *Gert Wingårdh, architect.*
Basel: Birkhäuser

Cathedral for a new millennium
Estudio Rafael Moneo
www.olacathedral.org/
www.arcspace.com/architects/moneo/cathedral_feat/
www.arcspace.com/architects/moneo/cathedral_feat/

Polyvalent houses in Vienna
ATS architekten
www.ats-architekten.at

Unconventional dimensions
Riegler Riewe Architekten
www.rieglerriewe.co.at

Flexible offices
Gaetano Pesce, New York, 1994
Duffy, F. 1997. *The New Office.* London: Coran Octopus

Estraden Houses
Büro popp.planungen
www.popp-planungen.de

Day and night arrangements
Aranguren & Gallegos Arquitectos S.L.
www.arangurengallegos.com
Mozas, J. 2003. A+T. Vitoria-Gasteiz: A+T ediciones.

A multifunctional entrance zone
Riken Yamamoto & Field Shop
www.riken-yamamoto.co.jp
www.codan.jp

Mon Oncle revisited
AllesWirdGut, Architektur ZT GmbH,
www.alleswirdgut.cc

Twenty-first century warehouse
De Architecten Cie
www.cie.nl

Bijdendijk, F.Ph. 1997. *Duurzaamheid loont; hoe sober en doelmatig bouwen de armen arm houdt.* Haarlem: Architext
www.hetoosten.nl

Structural facades
Rapp+Rapp
www.rappenrapp.nl

City garden
Atelier Kempe Thill
www.atelierkempethill.com

Base building and fit-out
www.osakagas.co.jp/rd/next21/
Habraken, N.J. 1961. *De dragers en de mensen.* Amsterdam: Scheltema & Holkema. Translated as *Supports: An Alternative to Mass Housing.* London: The Architectural Press, 1972/1999

Work building in a greenhouse
GDA bv
www.gda-bv.nl
www.architectenweb.nl/aweb/print/print_project.asp?PID=718

Housing on IJburg
Maccreanor Lavington
Maccreanorlavington
www.maccreanorlavington.com

Billboard facade
Groosman Partners
www.gp.nl

Renkens, J. 1996. *Gevels & Architectuur.* Nieuwegein: VMRG

Layered structure
Itten+Brechbühl AG
www.ittenbrechbuehl.ch
www.aia.org/nwsltr_print.cfm?pagename=aah_jrnl_openbuilding_102704

Living on a plug-in floor
DKV architecten
www.dkv.nl/projecten/inontwikkeling/oostelijkeHandelskade.htm

Leupen, B. 2002. *Kader en generieke ruimte.* Rotterdam: 010 Publishers

Better and cheaper in Boliger
Juul & Frost
www.juulfrost.dk

Predicting the future
Erick van Egeraat associated architects
www.eea-architects.com

246

Brand, S. 1994. *How buildings Learn: What Happens After They're Built*. New York: Viking Penguin.

Neutral expression
RUIMTELAB
www.ruimtelab.nl
Heijne, H.P., Vink, J.A. 2001. *Flexgebouwen*. Rotterdam: RGD

Developers' freedom
ANA architecten
www.ana.nl

Elemental Chile
asel.kuenzel architects
www.paselkuenzel.com

Growth homes
Architectuurstudio Herman Hertzberger
www.hertzberger.nl

A-Factory
Neutelings Riedijk Architects

TCN Property Projects
www.tcnpp.com

A chic makeshift classroom
Kempinga, W., et al. 2004. *Schoolparasites*. Amsterdam: Valiz
www.schoolparasites.nl

Student housing
De Vijf
www.devijf.com
www.spacebox.info

Demountable
Henket en partners architecten
www.henket.nl
www.zibb.nl/bouw/dossier.asp?dossier=714&hoofdstuk=5

Maximum freedom for the occupants
ADP Architekten AG
www.adp-architekten.ch

Picture credits

4D PLUS 192
ABT bv, consulting engineers Delft 77, 788, 236 top, bottom, 237 top left, top right
Ake E:son Lindman 128, 129 top left, top right, bottom
Architectuurstudio Herman Hertzberger 220
Aurofoto 133 top right
Bas Princen 141 bottom right, 142 bottom right
Beat Jordi 239 top, middle left, bottom
Christian Richters 204, 205 top, bottom
Courtesy of Morley Construction 132 bottom 133 bottom right
Duccio Malagamba 132 top, 133 top left, bottom left
Eduardo Sanchez 152 top, bottom, 153 top, middle, bottom
Ger van de Vlugt 83 fig 4 bottom
GDA 181 top
Gemeente Hoorn/RLB 209
Hans Juul / Torben Eskerod 200, 201top, middle, bottom
Herman van Doorn 88 fig. 14, 89 fig.16
Itten+Brechbuehl 193 bottom right
Jan de Vries fotografie 188,189
Jens Willebrand 87 fig 13 a en b
Jeroen Musch 225, 227
Kim Zwarts 169 top left, top right, bottom
Maarten Laupman 229 top, bottom
Maccreanor 99 fig. 2, 98 fig. 5
Maccreanor Lavington/Anne Bousema 184, 185 from top to bottom
Manfred Seidl 137 top left, top right, bottom
Mart de Jong 232 top, bottom, 233 top
Mischa Erben 138 top, middle, bottom, 139
Niels Donckers 111 fig. 3, 110 fig. 4 t/m 8
Paul Ott 141 top, middle, bottom left, bottom right,142 top, bottom left
Riegler Riewe 53 fig 1
Riken Yamamoto & FIELD SHOP 157 top, bottom left, bottom right
Techdata 193 top left, top right, middle, bottom left
Walter Rammler 162, 163 top, bottom

Credits

This study is part of the project 'Context and Modernity' at the Faculty of Architecture, Delft University of Technology.

The book was made possible by the generous support of the Netherlands Architecture Fund, Het Oosten housing corporation, TCN Property Projects, Stichting Experimentele Volkshuisvesting and the Faculty of Architecture, Delft University of Technology.

Academic referents
Prof. Dr. Hilde Heynen, Katholieke Universiteit Leuven
Prof. Jan Westra, Technische Universiteit Eindhoven
Dr. Helen Welling, Associate Professor, Institut for Planlægning, Kunstakademiets Architektskole, Copenhagen

Editors
Bernard Leupen and Jasper van Zwol (Faculty of Architecture, Delft University of Technology), René Heijne (Ruimtelab, Rotterdam)
Part one: Bernard Leupen and Birgit Jurgenhake (Faculty of Architecture, Delft University of Technology)
Part two: René Heijne and Jacques Vink (Ruimtelab, Rotterdam)

General text editing
John Kirkpatrick

Translations
John Kirkpatrick (Dutch-English), Vox et Lingua (German-English), Arturo Reyes and Sarah Tisdall (Spanish-English)

Graphic design
Piet Gerards with Ton van de Ven (bPG), Heerlen/Amsterdam

Printed by
Die Keure, Brugge

© 2005 The authors and 010 Publishers, Rotterdam www.010publishers.nl
ISBN 90 6450 536 5

Since designers of buildings – those people generally called architects – have to deal with aspects of time, the time-base could also become relevant to architects.
Leupen

The dynamics of time-based building are already a fact of life and come natural to the built environment, but as long as that reality is not fully embraced by the architectural profession as inspiring and challenging, a truly new time-based architecture will not take wings.
Habraken

An important design strategy for conditioning mixes of function and interchangeability of living and working is to provide more than one access system.
Van Zwol

A Solid is a sustainable building; sustainable in the economic, functional, technical and emotional senses of the word.
Bijdendijk

We enjoy thinking about the use of things as a process. Something that cannot be foreseen – that things happen that we cannot imagine, not even based on the boldest scenarios.
Riegler

A flex-building need not necessarily be able to take up every possible function. 'Functional bandwidth' is a current term: which functions are involved? You don't always need flexibility.
Heijne and Vink

The matter would be to access the **un**finished definition and the '**in**frastructural' character of the dynamic systems through the analysis of combinatory mechanisms, destined to bring about processes of spatial organization in which the final form manifests itself as the precise snapshot of an interrupted development (a form in a 'state of latency' – on 'standby' – able to be associated with incompleteness and infinitude, properties emblematic of all open systems).
Gausa

Time will tell whether there is a market for physically changing buildings, that is, buildings whose structures allow for a variable volume.
Spangenberg

So it's all about the architect being disposed to designing not for just one condition but always for so much more. Perhaps this covers the words polyvalency, competence and performance. You have to be constantly aware of the fact that everything you make should be open to new interpretations as time goes by.
Hertzberger

The biggest enemy is time; slowing down processes creates disasters, changes in concepts and unhappy customers. In following our method we have produced real estate that is less time-sensitive and because it is based on a general market understanding it will be easier to adapt to the certain and mostly predictable changes in its use.
Stroink

One conclusion is that the buildings that have proven to be the most adaptable were those not originally conceived to be flexible, and that in most cases a designed flexibility has failed to live up to the promise.
Maccreanor

Culturally durable projects presuppose an approach to the design process, the design method, that differs from the so-called 'functional programme of requirements' method, which is still the basis of architecture, both in education and in practice.
Van Reeth

More than ever, architecture will benefit from the opportunities offered by the non-standard only on condition that it progressively and patiently constructs a genuine culture of digital production.
Cache and Beaucé